Handbook of
Educational Administration

Handbook of
Educational Administration
A Guide for the Practitioner
SECOND EDITION

Emery Stoops

Max Rafferty

Russell E. Johnson

ALLYN AND BACON, INC.
Boston   London   Sydney   Toronto

Library of Congress Cataloging in Publication Data
Stoops, Emery.
  Handbook of educational administration.

  Includes bibliographies and index.
  1. School management and organization—United
States. I. Rafferty, Max Lewis, 1917–   joint
author. II. Johnson, Russell E., joint author.
III. Title.
LB2805.S759   1980   371.2   80–17118
ISBN 0–205–07133–3

Printed in the United States of America

Printing number and year (last digits):
10 9 8 7 6 5 4 3 2 1   85 84 83 82 81 80

Contents

Preface

As in the first edition, the emphasis in this book is upon school district operations, rendering the book indispensable reading for superintendents, assistant superintendents, principals, assistant principals, supervisors, board members, and all who would understand or succeed to administrative responsibilities in America's schools.

This book has been completely revised and updated, although it is recognized that important ideas do not necessarily age. The chapter bibliographies have also been updated.

The purpose of this book is to prepare today's administrator for informed and competent leadership, while at the same time pointing out the changing role of administration. The emerging power of teachers as they use their associations to negotiate the policies that affect their professional lives and influence is explained.

American schools need qualified leadership as never before. School systems seldom rise above the vision and competency of the superintendent, and individual schools seldom rise above the leadership qualities of the building principal. These administrators need practical knowledge and skills as they confront the challenges that face them.

Throughout the book, the authors have sought to maintain a balance between theory and practice. Elements of theory that can be tested in administrative practice have been extensively covered. Numerous adaptable forms, figures, and illustrations are provided, making the book a handy reference for the administrator's desk.

Twenty-one chapters cover educational responsibilities and relationships at the federal, state, intermediate-unit, and district levels. Education is considered a federal concern, a state responsibility, an intermediate-unit service, and a district operation. Each of these levels and its specialized role in achieving better instruction and reciprocal community relations are described in detail.

The importance of placing administrative procedures on a policy basis is stressed throughout the book. The formulation of policies that give direction to administration is possible only when the superintendent exerts creative team leadership and works cooperatively with the teacher association during the negotiation process. The building administrator or principal, who is at the grass-roots level of administration, is the key to implementing policies and working on a personal basis with the school staff so that all children receive the education they richly deserve. The book's emphasis upon leadership, policies, and teamwork is a contribution intended for both practicing administrators and for graduate students.

There are "in-basket" administrative problems at the end of each chapter, which set up simulated situations similar to those that will be confronted in real life. Graduate students of school administration will be able to clarify their thinking as they seek answers to the suggested questions.

The authors appreciate the help and encouragement of such educators as John Dunworth, C. C. Trillingham, Maynard Bemis, Calvin Grieder, Harlan L. Hagman, Steven Knezevich, John Stallings, and James R. Marks. Dr. David H. Paynter, Robert N. Rowe, and Dr. Edward W. Beaubier supplied numerous ideas and materials that were used in several of the chapters. Appreciation is also extended to Joyce King-Stoops for her technical assistance in the preparation of the manuscript and to M. L. Cushman, Dean Emeritus and Professor of Education at the University of North Dakota, who reviewed the manuscript.

The authors join in wishing success and satisfaction to all administrators, administrators-to-be, and lay persons who read this book.

Emery Stoops
Max Rafferty
Russell E. Johnson

PART ONE

Introduction

CHAPTER ONE

An Introduction to School Administration

Education is a local operation, an intermediate-unit service, a state responsibility, and a national concern. The education of children is primarily accomplished at the local level; other levels are supportive. Each level—local, county, state, and federal—must be effectively administered. The school administrative structure and process have been evolving since early colonial times.

Constitutional Origins of School Control

Public schools belong to the people. The people, through their legislators, have enacted constitutional provisions and statutes for the establishment and control of public and private education. Either by default or design, education has become chiefly the responsibility of state government.

The Tenth Amendment to the United States Constitution, passed in 1791, clearly states, "The powers not delegated to the United States by the Constitution, nor prohibited by it to the states, are reserved to the states respectively, or to the people." The amendment implies that where the United States Constitution is silent, such powers are automatically the responsibility of state government. Although responsibility for education is left to the states, the courts have consistently ruled that under the "general welfare" clause of the Constitution, Congress may enact laws to express its concern for public education. This concern generally is translated into the form of financial subsidy.

A long list of court decisions provides that state legislatures, elected by the people, have plenary control over the establishment and maintenance of schools within the state. To establish and maintain effective educational programs within the state, legislatures have found it necessary to provide a central educational agency, the state department of education. To express its concern for education, the Congress has established the United States Department of Education. This Department performs various functions, the chief of which is the distribution of funds to state and local educational agencies.

The people's legislators in each state, charged with the responsibility for education, have provided for intermediate units and local school districts. The intermediate unit is essentially a service arm of the state department of education. The local district has been delegated the function of operating schools through a board of education and a staff of administrators and teachers. Technically, each board of education and its administrators have only those powers that have been delineated by the state legislature. In this sense, the people, through their legislators, own and control the schools.

Although legislators have responsibility for schools, their power is not absolute; they must design legislation in harmony with state and federal constitutions. Enacted legislation is not the final word for local school administrators; before it has finality, it must be tested in the courts. The United States Supreme Court renders the final decision with respect to policies or procedures at the local, intermediate, state, or federal levels.

Court Decisions and the School Administrator

The modern school administrator—whether at the federal, state, intermediate, or local level—must function with the *Education Code* in one hand and a battery of court decisions in the other. Since our system of checks and balances gives the courts power to review legislative enactments, administrators must function in harmony with decisions handed down by the United States Supreme Court.

The support of public and nonpublic (private or parochial) schools has always been an issue in American education. Historically, and until fairly recently, all public funds have been withheld from nonpublic schools and from children who attended nonpublic schools. In 1930, the United States Supreme Court held that children attending nonpublic schools may receive free textbooks, thus establishing, in effect, a new doctrine that has since been termed the "child benefit theory." This decision, resulting from the Cochran case,[1] opened up many possibilities for taxpayer support to

---

[1] *Cochran et al.* v. *Louisiana State Board of Education et al.*, 281 U.S. 370 (1930).

nonpublic schools. Seventeen years after the Cochran case, the legislature of New Jersey provided that both public and private school pupils were entitled to free transportation. This legislation eventually was tested in the United States Supreme Court, and by a vote of 5 to 4 the theory of child benefit was upheld.[2] Many Supreme Court decisions have sustained the child benefit theory as established in the Cochran case and expanded by the Everson case, but have limited the extent to which nonpublic schools can secure free textbooks, transportation, and other aids under the child benefit theory. Recent years have witnessed continuing demands for the use of public funds in nonpublic schools.

The right to attend public schools has been tested in two landmark decisions. The right of pupils to attend public schools regardless of race was tested in the United States Supreme Court in the *Plessy* v. *Ferguson* case in 1896. Out of this decision came the "separate but equal" doctrine. In 1954, the Brown case[3] upset the "separate but equal" doctrine and declared that all pupils of whatever race, religion, or nationality are entitled to attend public schools. In the period between the Plessy and Brown cases, other decisions had direct bearing on the "separate but equal" doctrine: *Sweatt* v. *Painter, Sipuel* v. *Oklahoma Board of Regents, Alston* v. *School Board of the City of Norfolk*, and *Missouri ex rel. Gaines* v. *Canada.* Following the historic Brown case, various decisions have not only demanded equal rights of attendance for all races and for pupils of whatever backgrounds, but have gone one step further and insisted that schools not only avoid segregation but take positive means to integrate pupils on the basis of race. The courts demanded integration on the basis both of *de jure*, or legal, separation and of *de facto*, or circumstantial, segregation. This has led to the issue of "busing" to achieve racial balance.

Out of this discussion, it would seem reasonable to conclude that although legislators have plenary power to control education, legislative enactment does not constitute final authority until tested in the courts. The United States Supreme Court is the final authority in all school matters at all school levels.

Historical Development of School Administration

School administration predates school administrators. With the 1642 founding of schools in Massachusetts came such administrative problems as teacher selection, housing, curriculum, budgeting, student control and

---

[2] *Everson* v. *Board of Education of Ewing Township et al.*, 330 U.S. 1 (1947).
[3] *Brown* v. *Board of Education of Topeka*, 347 U.S. 483, 74 Sup. Ct. 686.

others. These administrative tasks were performed by a School Committee with the help of a selected teacher. The basic administrative functions of the early days were less complex, but essentially the same as ours today.

As schools expanded, a second teacher was employed. At this point, the semblance of a school administrator began to evolve. It has been an established concept that when two people ride a horse, one has to ride in front. Just so when two teachers were appointed to the same school, one was called the "head teacher"—or later, the "principal teacher." School records in Cincinnati referred to the "principal teachers" as early as 1838, but St. Louis made them full time executives, about 1859.

As the number of teachers increased in schools, so did the number of schools increase in the school systems of fast-growing cities. School Committees and boards of education found it to be increasingly difficult to coordinate the work of a growing number of principal teachers, so Buffalo, New York and Louisville, Kentucky got credit for appointing the first superintendents in 1837.

The pioneer principals and superintendents took administrative assignments without specified training, credentialing, or required experience. Their duties were ill defined, consisting mostly of records, reports, and the necessities of keeping teachers and students in classrooms.

The preparation and duties of school administrators awaited the scholarly designations of authors like Cubberly, Reeder, Strayer, and others. Now there are many authorities on theory and practice who recommend educational preparation as high as the doctorate and a multiplicity of prescribed duties.

The accelerating complexity of our society is expanding administrative duties at a perilous rate. In addition to the basics of organization, leadership, and administration of the four perennial segments of the school process (instruction, personnel management, finance, and public relations), the modern administrator is confronted with a host of new emergencies. These new and nagging emergencies are driving some school administrators toward early retirement.

Some of the new emergencies and problems for school administrators are: loss of credibility, proposals for federal grants, collective bargaining, parent pressures, loss of financial support at elections, political manipulations, drug abuse on campuses, student violence and vandalism, and falling achievement scores. These difficulties are balanced, however, with some pluses. Superintendents and principals are better trained than ever before and have increased career status. Vexing problems lead to greater opportunities for leadership. More administrative assistants and better trained teachers are available for help in constructive programs. Salaries and fringe benefits continue to rise. Strong administrators continue to rise above current impediments and fashion a better educational program for the youth and adults of America.

What Is School Administration?

Halpin characterized school administration as a social process involving both problem solving and decision making.[4] Others have described administration as management, leadership, organization, manipulation, and control. None of these terms, however, is comprehensive or restrictive enough to define properly the role of the school administrator in his various capacities. A definition of administration at the local, county, state, and federal levels would differ somewhat depending upon the legal and functional roles of the several levels. For purposes of a working definition, the authors have chosen to focus on educational administration in the operation of schools.

Stoops and Rafferty define public school administration as *"The organization and leadership of all community personnel concerned with public education in such a manner as will effectively make for sound education within the framework of policy set up by the board of education."*[5] The authors believe that this definition, widely used since its formulation, is basically sound. It is restricted, however, to *public* education. The authors would like to refine and shorten the definition to read:

Administration at the local level mobilizes personnel and resources to provide maximum learning opportunities in harmony with legal stipulations.

This definition stresses the mobilization of personnel and resources. It implies that teachers, classified workers, community supporters, and all others join in the improvement and maximizing of learning opportunities. Resources refer to finance, transportation, facilities, equipment, and supplies. Learning opportunities are not limited to children, but should be made available to adults as well. All learners should be given greater opportunity regardless of interest, ability, race, age, nationality, or other defining condition. In essence, the definition means that learning opportunities should be provided to all. The administration of learning opportunities provided for all must be handled in harmony with legislative enactment and court decisions. The board of education, the superintendent, principals, teachers, and classified workers must function in ways made possible, or not prohibited by, tested statutes. The details of such an administrative operation are the subject matter of this book.

Briefly defined, the purpose of school administration is to make possible better instruction. Administration is supportive. It provides the classrooms, instructional supplies, and teachers. Then schedules are designed to direct students into the classroom learning situation where disruptions and distractions are kept to a minimum. Administration under-

---

[4] Andrew W. Halpin (ed.) *Administrative Theory in Education.*
[5] Emery Stoops and M. L. Rafferty, Jr., *Practices and Trends in School Administration,* p. 5.

girds better learning. It has no inherent budgetary justification except to make learning conditions more favorable.

A few misguided teachers have cried out for big slashes in administration so that more money would be left for teachers' salaries. Yet these teachers are not ready to assume the avalanche of paper work demanded by federal and state departments of education, to say nothing of the countless hours spent in logistical classroom support. If tied to administrative routine, when would teachers have time to teach? That is why school administration evolved. Teachers demanded and got it. Now that teachers have the best administrative arsenals in history, including help from supervisors, coordinators, psychologists, and many other staff members, the enlightened teachers will not surrender such assistance.

Just as teachers treasure the help that frees them from routine, administrators should keep their jobs in perspective and never let their office become more important than the classroom. The office exists only to enhance learning in the classroom. Superintendents and principals are not *the educators* but educator-helpers. When administrators play this role well, they are indispensable.

Responsibilities of Administration

Administration has both legal and professional responsibilities. Fulfillment of such responsibilities is another way of easing the burden on teachers so they will have time to teach. As administration shoulders the school's responsibilities, it not only supports instruction, but clears the way for good teaching and learning.

LEGAL RESPONSIBILITIES. The superintendent is responsible for administering an educational program in harmony with constitutional and statutory provisions as handed down from federal and state governments. Superintendents must be cognizant of court decisions affecting each section of the code.

One of the major legal responsibilities of the superintendent is to keep the lay board members informed concerning requirements and prohibitions. Informed boards can then pass local regulations, which the superintendent is responsible for enforcing.

The successful superintendent, in addition to conforming to requirements and prohibitions, must be aware of opportunities such as available federal or foundation grants that will help the school system. The best way for a superintendent to keep a school system on the legal track is to formulate policies for board approval. These policies will lead to procedures that are legal and constructive. Naturally, the policies must be subject to continuous study and revision.

No superintendent can know cumbersome constitutions and codes by memory. The availability of legal counsel is a must. Even in small school systems, the superintendent must have a ready source of legal advice. This is often supplied by county counsels, intermediate units, and state departments.

In essence, the superintendent is responsible for steering all school personnel away from illegal acts or omissions, and for taking advantage of legal opportunities. The principal has such responsibility for personnel at the building level.

PROFESSIONAL RESPONSIBILITIES. The people who own the schools expect administrators to obey the laws, but not to stop there. Constitutions and codes are only the foundation for the educational structure that the people expect.

To fulfill professional responsibilities, the modern administrator must have a well-rounded general education, with intense study in the specialized field of educational administration and supervision. It should be understood that a large order of common sense is indispensable. With such equipment, the school administrator is ready to move the system toward the overall goal of improving student learning.

The capable administrator should imagine, dream, and hope. Far-reaching, well-defined goals must be established. Otherwise the school system wallows in mediocrity.

In setting goals, administrators need the help of students, teachers, parents, labor and management leaders, professionals from other disciplines, star gazers, and down-to-earth prophets. When a series of goals with broad intent and without a specific time consummation are established, they must be prioritized and implemented by attainable objectives.

All goals are not equally important. The goal of educating toward proper grooming is not as important as the goal of educating toward better physical and mental health. Goals, then, must be listed in priority order.

An objective differs from a goal in that it is more attainable in a given time span. The objective's attainment is one step toward a desired goal. *The professional responsibility of administrators is to advance the school system as far as possible toward accepted goals via the stepping stones of objectives.*

Objectives and goals are not achieved without administrative effort. No matter how good an objective may appear, it must be field tested on the learning line. Constant testing, evaluation, and revision are the task of administrators.

The superintendent at the district level and the principal at the building level are indentured to a professional lifetime of testing, evaluating, and improving the goals and objectives of education. In this way, the school administrator earns an enviable position of leadership.

Who Administers the Schools?

Large schools are administered by numerous administrative specialists in line with statutes and policies. Small schools have fewer administrators who perform a multiplicity of functions. As the size of the school system grows, specialization replaces generalization. If one considers a reasonably large school, one begins with the board of education. Since the board members are laymen and have other full-time jobs, they set policies and delegate the implementation of the policies to a superintendent. The superintendent is generally faced with four or five discernible areas of responsibility. First, according to the *Education Code* and usual board policy, he should provide a good instructional program. Second, provision of a good instructional program requires competent certificated and classified personnel. Third, when personnel are employed, salaries and other phases of finance are involved. Fourth, when finances are involved, the schools have a public relations problem. So the superintendent must appoint assistant superintendents in charge of instruction, personnel, and finance. Ordinarily, the superintendent handles the overall public relations tasks, although public relations is everyone's job. As school systems grow larger, they often appoint an assistant superintendent in charge of the remaining miscellaneous functions, grouped together as special services; this person's title is sometimes "administrative assistant." In larger school systems, an assistant superintendent for pupil personnel services is often appointed to handle the testing program, the multitude of special classes, the health services, counseling and guidance programs, and educational research. Other members of the administrative complex are staff supervisors, coordinators, and technicians with special skills in such areas as instructional technology, instruction of the handicapped, data processing, schoolhouse planning, art, and science.

At the school building level, there are principals, vice-principals, registrars, and coordinators. The administrative complex and the teaching faculty are supported by a classified staff of secretaries, custodians, cafeteria workers, and bus drivers.

Administrative personnel increases not only with the size of school enrollment, but as a means of keeping up with new and expanded administrative duties. Every time a state legislature meets, it enacts statutes that require more administrative study and time. Extensive federal programs that require proposals and complex administrative techniques create heavy workloads for the administration.

Evaluating Administration

The administration of every school system is continuously evaluated. Evaluation may be formal and planned, or it may be informal, spasmodic, and uncontrolled. The formal evaluation is characterized by objectivity and approved techniques, with assessment at regular intervals and for specified purposes. The evaluation of the administration, and of administrators, should be constructive and pointed toward a level of management that will maximize learning opportunities.

As suggested earlier, the administration mobilizes personnel and resources to enhance achievement in classrooms. This is done by clarifying philosophy and setting long-term goals supported by obtainable objectives. For the achievement of these, the administration should be held accountable. The administration should be considered successful to the extent that goals and objectives are attained.

When an unbiased and constructive evaluation of the administration is completed, teachers, classified personnel, and community patrons will have greater confidence in the effectiveness of the management of the school system. One of the greatest values of well-planned evaluation is that it helps administrators to strengthen needed and important elements of the program and to eliminate those that have become archaic. Such an evaluation is also an excellent means of inservice improvement for the administrators themselves. Pupils, custodians, and teachers feel more comfortable when they know that administrators are evaluated in the same manner that they are.

Administrative Problems

In Basket

At the end of each chapter, the reader will find "In-Basket (simulated) Administrative Problems." They are typical of the situations and problems that administrators may encounter in their schools or school district. Seminar leaders can assign the problems to individuals or committees for solution. The facts stated in the problem should not be changed, but any data may be assumed if no contrary information is provided. Solutions should answer the question, "What will you do when given the facts listed in the problem?" It is possible that there might be several solutions to a problem.

The problems encountered in this book may encourage seminar members to draw upon their personal experience to develop their own "in-basket administrative problems." The leader can help the group determine the facts and present possible solutions for discussion.

Problem 1

McKinley School District has an enrollment of 10,000 and consists of ten elementary schools, one junior high school, and one senior high school. The district administrative staff consists of a superintendent, a business manager, an assistant superintendent for educational services, a curriculum coordinator, a director of pupil personnel, a supervisor for music education, and a director of certificated personnel. The teacher's association believes that the central office is overloaded with high-salaried administrators and that this situation prevents them from receiving the salary increase that they are demanding. They have asked the Board of Education to eliminate some of these positions. On the other hand, the administrators believe that they are overworked and have asked for more administrative help, such as a psychometrist, a reading consultant, a psychologist, a research assistant, a federal project coordinator, and a director for classified personnel.

As superintendent, how would you proceed to handle this problem?
What would you tell the Board of Education?

Problem 2

You are the new superintendent of a school district in a rural area. There are four elementary principals, a junior–senior high school principal and assistant principal. All live in the area and are well-known and respected. As the year progresses, you find that one elementary principal and the secondary assistant principal are not performing up to your expectations. You decide to develop an administrative evaluation program since there is no evidence that administrators have been evaluated previously.

How would you proceed in the development of an administrative evaluation program?
Whom would you involve?
How would you handle the ineffective administrators?

Selected References

CAMPBELL, ROALD F., et al. *Organization and Control of American Schools.* 3rd ed. Columbus, Ohio: Charles E. Merrill Publishing Co., 1975.

CARLSON, RICHARD O. *School Superintendents: Careers and Performance.* Columbus, Ohio: Charles E. Merrill Publishing Co., 1972.

CHERNOW, FRED B., and CAROL CHERNOW. *School Administrator's Guide to Handling People.* Englewood Cliffs, N.J.: Prentice-Hall, Inc., 1976.

ELLIOT, DAVID L., and THOMAS J. SERGIOVANNI. *Education and Organizational Leadership in Elementary Schools.* Englewood Cliffs, N.J.: Prentice-Hall, Inc., 1975.

FREY, SHERMAN H., and KEITH R. GETSCHMAN. *School Administration: Selected Readings.* New York: Thomas Y. Crowell Co., 1968.

FRYMIER, JACK R. *School for Tomorrow.* Berkeley, Ca., McCutchan Publishing Co., 1973.

GARMS, WALTER I., et al. *School Finance: The Economics and Politics of Public Education.* Englewood Cliffs, N.J.: Prentice-Hall, Inc., 1978.

GORTON, RICHARD A. *School Administration: Challenge and Opportunity for Leadership.* Dubuque, Iowa: William C. Brown Co., 1976.

HACK, WALTER G., and LUVERNE L. CUNNINGHAM. *Educational Administration: The Developing Decades.* Berkeley, Ca.: McCutchan Publishing Co., 1977.

HALPIN, ANDREW W. (ed.). *Administrative Theory in Education.* Chicago: Midwest Administration Center, University of Chicago, 1958.

HANSON, MARK E. *Educational Administration and Organizational Behavior.* Boston: Allyn and Bacon, Inc., 1978.

HOY, WAYNE K., and CECIL G. MISKEL. *Educational Administration: Theory, Research, and Practice.* New York: Random House, Inc., 1978.

KARLITZ, H. "Educational Administrators and Teacher Unions: An Alliance of Convenience." *Clearing House* 52:125–8 (November 1978).

KINDRED, L. W., et al. *School and Community Relations.* 2nd ed. Englewood Cliffs, N.J.: Prentice-Hall, Inc., 1976.

KIRST, M. W. "New Politics of State Educational Finance." *Phi Delta Kappan* 60:427–32 (February 1979).

KNEZEVICH, STEPHEN J. *Administration of Public Education.* Scranton, Pa.: Harper and Row Publishers, Inc., 1975.

MARKS, JAMES R.; EMERY STOOPS; and JOYCE KING-STOOPS. *Handbook of Educational Supervision: A Guide for the Practitioner.* 2nd ed. Boston: Allyn and Bacon, Inc., 1978.

MORPHET, EDGAR L. *Educational Organization and Administration.* 3rd ed. Englewood Cliffs, N.J.: Prentice-Hall, Inc., 1974.

MURPHY, J. F. "Fiscal Problems of Big City School Systems: Changing Patterns of State and Federal Aid." *Urban Review* 10:251–65 (Winter 1978).

POUNDS, RALPH L., and JAMES R. BRYNER. *School in American Society.* New York: The Macmillan Company, 1973.

STOOPS, EMERY, and M. L. RAFFERTY, JR. *Practices and Trends in School Administration.* Boston: Ginn and Company, 1961.

PART TWO

Control and Organization

CHAPTER TWO

The Federal Government and Public Education

Although American schools belong to the people, the federal government has a national concern for public education. The many public education laws and the grants of federal money to state and local districts attest to an increasing interest. This has created problems, both real and imaginary. Many educators express a concern about how much control the federal government will exert at the local level. There is a need for better coordination between the federal government, state government, and local school districts in relation to educational issues, finances, and laws.

American Schools Belong to the People

The underlying principle of the American system of public education is its lack of a system. It is at once the despair of the logical French, the scientific Germans, and the traditional English. In other nations, the schools belong to the government and are administered by government bureaus and appointees. They are financed through national taxes and directed by a secretary of education. This enables the school systems in these countries to operate independently of local whims and upheavals and simultaneously ensures a maximum of uniformity in school procedures. Indeed, some ministers of education boast that at any moment of the school day they can state with confidence the subject, unit, and text chapter being studied in every classroom of the nation. Such uniformity of necessity involves the granting of huge powers to the national government in the field of education, and a corresponding loss of local control.

Americans have developed attitudes that stress local, rather than national, control of schools. Where other nations have set up monolithic educational structures, the United States has a separate school system for each state and territory, each of which is more or less independent and the master of its own fate, except as affected by court decisions. In finance, organization, and control, a national school system does not exist in this country.

SIMILARITIES AMONG AMERICAN SCHOOLS. Though differing in many details, state school systems are strikingly similar in their fundamental characteristics. Most children study similar subjects, and most American schools are governed by locally selected boards of trustees. Most rely on some variation of the real property tax for local financial support. More important, a common goal has been set before the varying districts by the people. This goal is the free and compulsory education of every individual through the secondary level. With this ideal in view, American public schools have tended to become increasingly similar.

Communities have had a tendency to watch what other communities were doing in the area of education, and to adopt policies that have proved successful. Experimentation has thus tended to produce constructive imitation; the result has been the essential standardization of the American system of education along certain broad, accepted lines. This is in no sense a "national" system as it is understood in foreign countries.

UNIQUE FEATURES OF AMERICAN EDUCATION. There are some features that are unique to American education: The control of education is relatively decentralized. The people at the local level, rather than educators or government officials, are ultimately responsible for all of the basic policies relating to education, as well as the educational program of the local schools. Although the primary emphasis is placed on public schools, provision is also made for the existence of private schools. As far as possible, the public schools are safeguarded from partisan political control or influence. Education in the public schools is nonsectarian. Education at public expense is made available for all students at least through the secondary grades.

THE CONSTITUTION DID NOT PROVIDE FOR "NATIONAL" EDUCATION. The framers of the Constitution pointedly did not make any mention of education. State and local control of education and federal involvement are by implication. The basis for federal involvement in education is implied in Section 8 of Article I of the Constitution, which provides that Congress shall have the power to provide, among other things, for the general welfare. From the power implied there, Congress has derived the authority to tax and spend for public education.

The Tenth Amendment reserves to the states or to the people all the powers not delegated to the United States by the Constitution. The power of each state to provide and maintain public schools is thus inherent in this amendment.

There are several reasons for silence on educational provisions in the Constitution. Schooling in the eighteenth century was not considered a government function in any sense of the word; it was conducted under the aegis of church and home. Thus, almost by default, public education in America fell into a state and local framework, where it has remained ever since. To change the situation at this date would probably require a constitutional amendment, although Supreme Court decisions during the 1970s have permitted federal intervention in several areas of local education.

Federal Interest in Education

Despite the silence of the Constitution, the federal government has always shown considerable interest in education. President John Adams was most forceful in his espousal of the cause of public education.

> The whole people must take upon themselves the education of the whole people and must be willing to bear the expense of it. There should not be a district of one mile square without a school in it at the expense of the people themselves.

Washington and Jefferson made similar statements, and the government traditionally has proved willing to give certain types of aid to the public schools.[1]

LAND GRANTS FOR PUBLIC SCHOOLS.   The colonies had definite policies involving the grant of public lands for local schools. Under the Articles of Confederation of 1781, one lot out of every township was reserved for the maintenance of public schools. Beginning with the admission of Ohio into the Union in 1802, the granting of school sections was part and parcel of the system of admission under which the new states entered the Union. These land grants reached the considerable total of 121,130 square miles, and, including the land set aside in Alaska for education, have achieved a value that is estimated to be worth more than a billion dollars.

MORRILL ACT.   In 1862 Congress provided for the erection of land grant colleges by awarding 30,000 acres of government land for each member of Congress to which a state was entitled. The law provided that the states, in order to qualify for the free land, must provide buildings and equipment with their own funds. There are now sixty-nine land grant institutions;

---

[1] "Expressions on Education by American Statesmen and Publicists," U.S. Bureau of Education Bulletin, no. 28 (1913).

one out of every five college students in America attends a land grant institution.

SECOND MORRILL ACT.   The amount of aid given such colleges has been increased greatly from time to time. In 1890, the second Morrill Act gave a flat continual grant of $25,000 to each state and territory; in 1907 and 1935 supplementary grants were made. They now total over five million dollars a year.

SMITH–HUGHES ACT.   The federal government in 1917 took a big step toward extending national influence in education with the Smith–Hughes Act. This act, together with supplementary statutes in 1929 and 1934, supported the teaching of agriculture and home economics, and the mechanical arts and trades at the high school level.

GEORGE–DEEN AND GEORGE–BARDEN ACTS.   Annual appropriations exceeding 75 million dollars were provided through the George–Deen and George–Barden Acts (1937 and 1946, respectively). The first act helped to subsidize education for distributive (buying and selling) occupations; the second greatly increased the sums previously allotted for agriculture, home economics, and trade and industrial education.

Direct Federal Involvement in Education

While the government aids education only through categorical financial means, as in the examples cited above, there are certain areas in which it works directly in conjunction with local districts, and, occasionally, educates directly.

PUBLIC LAWS 874 AND 815.   Following the Second World War, school districts in which federal defense projects or installations attracted multitudes of families were unable to solve financial problems arising from such a population impact without some sort of aid. In 1950 Public Law 874 reimbursed schools for the education of children who, without the presence of certain types of federal enterprises, could not have been accommodated in the local schools. Public Law 815 was intended to accomplish a similar function in the area of school building and capital outlay. Thus, the United States government found itself in the position of supplying the financial needs of a number of local school districts by paying out a definite sum each year for the instruction and educational housing of federally connected pupils.

INDIAN EDUCATION.   The federal government supports the education of more than 77,000 Indian children. Almost half of this number are enrolled in the 300 Indian schools operated by the government. The remainder attend public schools, with tuition paid by the government. Federal funds spent annually for Indian education total over $10,000,000.

TERRITORIES AND POSSESSIONS.   In Puerto Rico, the Virgin Islands, Samoa, and Guam, education is supported in part or largely by federal grants and appropriations.

ARMED FORCES SCHOOLS.   The United States operates various armed forces schools: West Point Military Academy, Annapolis Naval Academy, Air Force Academy, Army Medical School, Army War College, National War College, and the Air University. The government also establishes schools at posts, foreign garrisons, or camps for the benefit of the armed services personnel or for their dependents.

EMERGENCY FEDERAL EDUCATION PROJECTS.   During the Depression and World War II, certain short-lived educational projects were undertaken by the national government and subsequently terminated when the original need for them ceased. Among these were the Civilian Conservation Corps, the National Youth Administration, the Public Works Administration, the Works Progress Administration, and the Servicemen's Readjustment Act.

Types of Federal Grants to Public Schools

There are two basic types of federal grants-in-aid for public schools. The categorical grant is awarded for specific purposes. Critics have said it is divisive and fragments the overall educational program; proliferates programs that are difficult to change; reduces the choice of alternatives at the local level; requires an inordinate amount of time to prepare proposals and evaluate programs that are requested by those outside the system; oversimplifies programs and services in the "national interest;" and requires external controls, contrary to the American educational system.[2] Examples of such categorical aid are cited above. Others which the federal government believes contribute to important national goals are of a continuing nature.

The second type is the general purpose grant, intended to strengthen the total educational program by compensating for deficiencies in the public school tax base while continuing local control. The funds are provided with no strings attached and with minimum limitations on their use so that the local school districts can use them as they see fit. The Elementary and Secondary Education Act of 1965 is considered to be a

---

[2] William P. McLure, "Financing Education at the Federal Level," *The School Administrator*, p. 46.

historic breakthrough in federal funding since it comes close to being a general grant. Although there are some restrictions, school districts have the flexibility to use certain portions of the funds for salaries, construction, textbooks, and curriculum aids according to their needs.

An analysis of two "titles" under E.S.E.A. shows its divergence from the categorical-type grants:

Title IV.   Libraries, Learning Resources, Educational Innovation, and Support

Part A.   Appropriates $495 million for the year ending 1976 and other sums as may be necessary for succeeding years. These include appropriations for the states, various possessions of the U.S., schools for Indian children, and schools operated by the Department of Defense overseas. Amount given to any state is based upon the number of children five to seventeen years of age in the state.

The state Department of Education must submit a satisfactory plan to the Commissioner of Education for the state. Under some conditions, nonpublic schools may be aided. The local educational agency has complete discretion in how it will use funds received, but the state must provide proportionately greater funds for poor districts that tax themselves more than the state average, for those with many hardship cases such as poor families or sparsely populated regions, or for those with many non-English speaking families. Evaluations of the effectiveness of each program shall be conducted periodically.

Part B.   Provides for the acquisition of library materials, textbooks, and other printed and published instructional materials in public and private elementary and secondary schools. Includes the acquisition of laboratory and other instructional equipment for teaching academic subjects (with religious materials specifically ruled out) and for minor remodeling of space needed. Funds may also be used for testing, and the counseling and guidance of students.

Part C.   Funds may be used for the establishment of educational centers and services to stimulate the development of vitally needed educational services (including preschool, vocational, special, and dual-enrollment educational programs) not generally available. Exemplary programs may be set up and facilities modified or constructed for such.

Demonstration health and nutrition centers may be set up in areas of concentrations of low-income families. Training of needed professional and school personnel is approved.

Funds may also be used for strengthening the leadership resources of state and local educational agencies, and particularly for supporting schools in low-income areas or those which have large numbers of students who do not complete secondary education.

Generally programs shall involve participation of persons broadly representative of cultural and educational resources of areas to be served, including educational agencies, private schools, institutions of higher education, public and private nonprofit agencies such as libraries, museums, musical and artistic agencies, radio, and television.

Title IX.   Ethnic Heritage Program

The Commissioner of Education is authorized to make grants to and contract with public and private nonprofit educational agencies to assist them in planning, developing, establishing, and operating programs of ethnic-heritage studies. The sum of $15 million is appropriated for each fiscal year ending in 1978.

Each program assisted under this title shall develop curriculum materials for use in elementary, secondary and higher-education institutions relating to the history, geography, society, economy, literature, art, music, drama, language, and general culture of ethnic groups within the American heritage. Materials are to be disseminated or use is to be permitted in all schools in the country. Schools shall cooperate with persons and organizations having a special interest in ethnic studies to assist them in promoting and encouraging ethnic-related activities.

Private and public schools may develop programs. Institutions of higher education, related organizations, and foreign students in the United States should be utilized. Each local program shall have an advisory council. Funds may be used for the training of staff, and stipends may be provided trainees under regulations set up by the Commissioner.

Since 1968, Congress has been considering "block grants" as a type of general aid. In that year, it approved a block-grant approach to vocational education. Under a block grant, money would be distributed to the states for education with the federal government either prorating the funds between the blocks or leaving this decision to the state legislatures.

Present categorical and other federal grants-in-aid would be consolidated into four major blocks: (1) general elementary and secondary education, (2) higher education, (3) vocational education, and (4) education for the handicapped and disabled. Some propose that all federal assistance be divided into the first two blocks.

Block grants, it is argued, would provide general federal fiscal assistance without control. Channeled through the states and through local districts, they would permit flexibility in their use and help release creative potential to improve education in each school district. They would eliminate some of the time-consuming paperwork, the period of waiting to see what happens to applications, and late funding, all of which have been prevalent with categorical assistance programs.

Public Laws and Acts

Federal money for education that is administered by the U.S. Department of Education is allotted for programs, instruction, administration, teacher and professional training, student assistance, and research, as well as other programs when new public laws are passed. In 1969, federal money for education was authorized for 118 programs that were administered by the U.S. Department of Education. There were 10 programs for school construction; 62 programs for programs, instruction, and administration; 31 programs for teacher and other professional training and student assistance; and 15 programs for research. Several of these programs might be authorized by one public law. It would be impractical to list or explain all of these programs in this book. Those who want additional, up-to-date information concerning federal appropriations for education should write to the Budget and Manpower Division, Office of Administration, U.S. Department of Education. However, a few of the more important public laws are described here.

PUBLIC LAW 346. Commonly called the G.I. Bill, it provides liberal educational opportunities for veterans.

PUBLIC LAW 507. In 1950, it established the National Science Foundation that provides loans, grants, fellowships, and institutes to strengthen research in mathematics, science, and engineering for the purpose of securing the national defense.

PUBLIC LAW 85–864. The National Defense Education Act of 1958 (NDEA) authorizes a little more than one billion dollars in federal aid to schools. Its avowed intention is to find and encourage talent at all levels of education. The act was originally composed of ten titles, but was raised to eleven when it was amended in 1964.

PUBLIC LAW 88–452. The Economic Opportunity Act of 1964, also called the Anti-Poverty Bill, authorizes funds for programs from preschool to adult education. Its purpose is to eliminate deprivation and poverty and to give everyone an opportunity to work and to live in decency and dignity.

PUBLIC LAW 89–10. The Elementary and Secondary Education Act of 1965 (ESEA) has been considered one of the most significant educational achievements in the history of the nation. For the first time, federal law recognized the national responsibility for educating all of America's children. Under this law, federal control is prohibited.

Because of the problems in handling federal assistance, some districts have found it practical to employ an administrator for the sole purpose of handling federal funds. The duties of this position are to determine what funds are available; how to get them; to write the necessary projects to become eligible; to apply for the funds; to handle the extra paperwork; and to administer the funds at the local level.

The Issue of Federal Participation

A controversy that seems destined to agitate the country for many years centers around the degree to which federal participation in education shall be permitted. It should be noted that the argument focuses on the *degree* of participation, not the actual fact of participation. No one seriously proposes that our government withdraw from its myriad educational interests as they now exist. No longer can one overlook the role of the federal government in its influence on education. However, the role of federal, state, and local governments in education needs to be redefined. The question might be asked, "How far and to what extent should the federal government help the state and local school districts solve their own problems?" Or, "Are their problems the concern of the federal government?"

In answer to the question of whether the federal government should play a role in education, Campbell states that "education is too closely linked to the national well-being, particularly in terms of trained manpower and economic growth, for any answer other than federal participation."[3] Such legislative enactments as Public Law 874, the Smith–Hughes Act, and the various statutes designed to support vocational and distributive education have become part of America's educational pattern and receive the general support of most people. The purpose of the newer federal programs is to change educational institutions and to develop skills that are applicable to the new technology. This trend differs from the traditional mode of solely stabilizing and strengthening existing educational programs. National participation in education is, through the increasing speed and magnitude of federal grants-in-aid, approaching national federalism of education. The present volume of educational legislation indicates that a national educational policy may not be far off.

Education in the United States has traditionally been handled by local communities and generally controlled by the states. Nevertheless, the widely divergent standards of educational competence in different sections of the country, coupled with the equally contrasting abilities to finance adequate educational programs, have given rise to proposals for greater federal

---

[3] Roald F. Campbell, "Federal–State Educational Relations," *Phi Delta Kappan*, p. 17.

financial aid to general education. A so-called "federal equalization" program, designed to assist states and local districts to establish certain minimum standards for salaries, school plants, curriculum improvement, and equipment, is seriously proposed by many educators. Legislation to this effect has been introduced and hotly contested in Congress.

Of the several objections that have been raised to large-scale federal aid to education, the most potent is that which invokes the specter of federal control. The argument assumes that the gift of national funds to the states for educational use will inevitably result in the abdication of local and state control of the people's schools, and the immersion of public education in an unwieldy and insensitive federal bureaucracy. Protagonists of this theory also warn against the imminent danger of political propaganda emerging within the framework of federal control of the schools.

Menacker has pointed out some of the complexities of congressional behavior as they affect educational legislation. He states that "a review of federal activity reveals a piecemeal approach in which support is forthcoming only when improving education seems a necessary response to a real or imaginary national emergency. Corollary to this is the fact that federal aid is not primarily intended for the improvement of education per se, but rather for the achievement of certain specific objectives for which the educational structure provides the most suitable vehicle."[4] The use of the word "defense" in the National Defense Education Act of 1958 is an example. The war on poverty and civil rights have been other considerations. Race relations, the public-private school controversy, and the issue of federal control are the chief political issues relating to federal aid to education, according to Menacker.[5]

School districts have problems in predicting what federal assistance they will receive. Congress changes and cuts appropriations, making it difficult for a school district to plan ahead. Many children are deprived because the costs of education go up, but federal assistance either remains static or is cut. Many projects have been dropped when federal funds were decreased or withdrawn. Plans should be made for worthwhile programs to be continued. Perhaps the particular federal agency should require the local school district to commit itself to maintaining its new programs before the original funds are granted. Otherwise, state and local governments must take on the added burden of supplying funds to establish new programs. School districts cannot operate efficiently under this arrangement. There are those who believe that the federal government should raise the support of public education to a minimum of one-third of the total cost of education. At present it is considerably less.

Proponents of federal aid hasten to disassociate themselves from what they call the "straw man" of federal control. They point out that virtually

---

[4] Julius Menacker, "The Organizational Behavior of Congress in the Formulation of Educational Support Policy," *Phi Delta Kappan*, p. 78

[5] Menacker, "The Organizational Behavior," p. 80

no one advocates any form of federal control over education, and that the coupling of federal aid with federal control is a prime example of non sequitur reasoning. It is difficult to demonstrate that the granting of national monies to land grant colleges, or to vocational and distributive education, or directly to the schools through subsidies for federally connected pupils, has resulted in the supplanting of local by federal control to any perceptible degree. The friends of federal aid point to the low standards of schooling in certain states, analyze the correspondingly high tax rates and lowly assessed valuations in the same areas, and challenge the opposition to demonstrate any conceivable way to solve the problem on a purely local level.

Dr. James E. Allen, Jr., then Assistant Secretary for Education and U.S. Commissioner of Education, made this statement in 1970:

> The unique feature and obligation of Federal participation in education is that of perspective—perspective which allows for identification of those problems and needs that transcend State borders and thus require a broader approach; perspective which permits the overall appraisal of the needs and progress of education that can serve as a basis for the continuing improvement and renewal of the educational enterprise, and the marshaling of the resources to facilitate it.

He also stated that federal responsibility falls into two major areas of action:

1. Research and development, planning, demonstration, and dissemination . . . in order to provide practical answers and technical assistance for use of the State and local levels.
2. Finance that is more equitable, efficient, and adequate.[6]

Federal Interest in School Integration

The Fourteenth Amendment, by implication, guarantees all children equality of education. America's survival is dependent upon this; minorities are not excluded. They are entitled to all rights and privileges—including the education to which all others are entitled. In the 1954 Brown case, the Supreme Court ruled that segregation in the public school was unconstitutional because it deprived people of equal protection of the laws as guaranteed by the Fourteenth Amendment.[7] This reversed a Court ruling made in 1896 which had established the doctrine of "separate but equal."

Title VI of the Civil Rights Act of 1964 bans racial discrimination in programs and activities receiving federal financial assistance, and author-

---

[6] James E. Allen, Jr., "It Must Be a Three-way Partnership," *CTA Journal,* pp. 18–19.

[7] *Brown* v. *Board of Education,* 347 U.S. 483, 74 Sup. Ct. 686.

izes federal agencies to impose sanctions for noncompliance, including the withholding of federal funds.

School districts must take positive action. They should adopt policies that provide for racial balance among the professional and nonprofessional staff and widen promotional opportunities for minority personnel. Budgets should be adopted that provide for additional staff, educational programs, facilities, and equipment in the inner city and transitional areas. Concentrated effort must be made to attract highly qualified teachers to these areas; incentives need to be provided for them. These teachers should be provided with assistance so that they will have the competence, materials, and equipment to function effectively in disadvantaged areas. Classes should be kept small, and paraprofessional help should be provided. All of these measures have budget implications for the school board and administration to consider. The community, which provides some of the funds, must also be concerned. It, too, must have a voice in the policies and procedures of the school district. Minority members of the community are no longer willing to be dictated to by school boards or administrators.

For many years the national government has been moving slowly toward the abolition of racial segregation in all of its many agencies and projects. In pursuing this policy, it is encountering apparently immovable opposition in certain states. At almost the same time the movement for integration began, it received a massive boost from recent Supreme Court decisions that outlawed all forms of segregation.

The resulting conflict has posed the most serious threat to federal authority since the Civil War. At the present time, all government-operated schools are being integrated, with every indication that further federal extension into various areas of public education will carry with it unalterable opposition to the principle of racial segregation. In the area of state-supported education, complete integration may be a generation off. Such "inner city" school systems as Washington, D.C. are becoming increasingly —not decreasingly—segregated as a result of the so-called "white flight." The situation remains fluid.

The United States Office of Education

Established in 1867, the "Office of Education" (existing under various names) has now been established for over a century. During that time, its three chief functions have been research, publication, and the furnishing of educational leadership.

1867–1906.   The first period of the Office of Education's development saw the production of a large amount of biographical and historical research conducted and published under its auspices. The Indians of Alaska came under the jurisdiction of the Office at this time, providing for the education of their children. The administration of $5,000,000 annually in the form of federal subventions to the land grant colleges was also a responsibility of the Office.

1906–33. A considerable enlargement of the activities and personnel of the Office of Education took place during this period. The services of its experts for the purpose of surveying school districts were first made available in 1911, and the importance of that activity was underlined by numerous requests for similar surveys in succeeding years. New divisions were constantly being added to the Office, notably in the fields of rural education, higher education, and education for blacks. A monthly publication, *School Life*, was issued, and the Biennial Survey of Education was first issued in 1918. Concomitantly, a marked rise in the Office's annual appropriations occurred, from $300,000 to $1,600,000.

Since 1933. The administration of vocational education under the Smith–Hughes Act was added to the responsibilities of the Office of Education in 1933. The Great Depression and the war that followed brought many new duties and obligations to the Office, including a burgeoning of requests for technical assistance on many fronts. The modern period of the Office's history has seen three supplementary functions added to its traditional interests: the establishment and administration of experimental centers; cooperation with state and local school systems in the areas of vocational education and land grant colleges; and the handling of emergency education programs.

Since 1953 the Office of Education has been part of the Department of Health, Education, and Welfare. In 1972, Congress established the Education Division within HEW. The division has consisted of the Office of Education and a new agency, the National Institute of Education, devoted to the promotion of educational research.

Over the years, the responsibilities of the Office of Education have increased greatly with the enactment of federal laws authorizing it to make grants and loans and to administer programs designed to improve the quality of education at every level throughout the country. The Office has provided support to elementary and secondary education in broad areas of strong national interest, such as compensatory education for the disadvantaged, education of the handicapped, vocational education, and assistance in federally affected areas. It made grants to school districts to help them meet the special needs incident to the elimination or prevention of minority-group student segregation; bestowed grants to developing institutions of higher education; and administered several programs of financial assistance to college students.

In the field of services, however, the Office probably played its most important role. A city or district superintendent of schools owes much of his success as an educational planner and tactician to the research findings released at periodic intervals by the United States Office of Education. Statistics on almost every conceivable subject, however remotely related to education, have been painstakingly collected, correlated, and charted by the Office personnel, and made available without cost to educators in the field. Such services removed much of the guesswork from school administration and made possible scientific planning by administrators.

The Department of Education

For over ten years, various educational associations discussed the need for a Secretary of Education to head up a cabinet-level Department of Education. The movement gained strength in 1971 when the "Big Six," composed of the American Association of School Administrators, the Council of Chief State School Officers, the National Association of State Boards of Education, the National Congress of Parents and Teachers, the National Education Association, and the National School Boards Association, unanimously endorsed the establishment of a cabinet-level Department of Education. This idea was opposed by the American Federation of Teachers.

Upon the urging of President Jimmy Carter, Congress, in September 1979, passed a bill which created a new federal Department of Education, taking education from the Department of Health, Education, and Welfare. President Carter appointed Judge Shirley Hufstedler as the first cabinet-level Secretary of Education. The bill creating the department states that "The establishment of the department shall not increase the authority of the federal government over education or diminish the responsibility for education which is reserved to the states and the local school systems."

The new department will administer some 170 educational programs which had been scattered throughout numerous federal agencies. It proing the administration of federal programs, eliminating duplication of vides a means for coordinating the various educational activities, improveffort, and raising the status of education in America. The legislation which established the department cut in half the number of principal offices handling education and reduced the number of offices through which educational rules, regulations, budgets, and legislative proposals must be reviewed.

The "Big Six" also recommended the establishment of a national advisory commission on education, appointed by the President to encourage lay participation in education on the national level. It also proposed a legislative program that included the following items:

1. The amending of all applicable federal legislation to provide for a minimum of a three-year authorization with funds to be appropriated

one year in advance, on a level at least equal to the appropriation of the previous year.
2. Full funding of all federal education programs.
3. Increase of federal funding of education programs to at least one-third of total education expenditures within the next five years.
4. Support of comprehensive manpower-training legislation.
5. Increased federal funding to public schools for the encouragement of early childhood development programs.
6. Full funding of the federal share in the amended National School Lunch Program.
7. Recognition of the continuing need for federal financial aid in lieu of taxes impacted by federal activities and low-rent housing.
8. Support of the revision and extension of higher education legislation.[8]

Summary

American education has always been decentralized and essentially local in nature. Despite this fact, the common goals of citizenship, literacy, and productivity have led to a surprising similarity in educational structure, curriculum, and output.

One reason for this is the involvement of and the interest taken in education by the national government, dating back before the adoption of the Constitution in 1789. Though education is not mentioned in that document, the "general welfare" clause has prompted Congress to exert leadership over the years in such areas as land grants to schools, vocational education, and more recently in the broader sectors of curriculum, library science, and racial integration.

A great national debate is presently occurring over the degree of federal participation in education, especially concerning the need to equalize educational opportunities in different parts of the country. The question is an old one: How much federal control would and should accompany this kind of participation?

The U.S. Office of Education, which, since its inception more than a century ago, showed steady growth, especially in the post-Sputnik period when federal concern over the quality of American schools was spurred by the Cold War. Such growth led to an increasing demand for a Secretary of Education who would enjoy cabinet status. As a result, a new Department of Education was created in 1979 to be headed by a cabinet level Secretary of Education. Any federal controls would doubtless be administered by this new department.

---

[8] American Association of School Administrators, *Hot Line*, 3, 2 (February 1971).

Administrative Problem

Problem

Mr. Jones is superintendent of a school district in a disadvantaged area. There are many bilingual and learning problems. The superintendent and his staff want to apply for federal funds under Title I of the Elementary and Secondary Education Act to provide a better educational program. However, the Board of Education has always been violently opposed to all federal aid and has indicated that it will not approve such a request.

What can Mr. Jones do to convince the Board of Education of the need for federal assistance?

If the Board rejects the application for federal funds, what should the superintendent attempt to do to gain support for the needed program?

Selected References

ALLEN, JAMES E., JR. "It Must Be a Three-way Partnership." *CTA Journal* 66 (January 1970).

AMERICAN ASSOCIATION OF SCHOOL ADMINISTRATORS. *Hot Line* 4 (February 1971).

Brown, Rex v. *Research and the Credibility of Estimates.* Homewood, Ill.: Richard D. Irwin, 1971.

CAMPBELL, ROALD F. "Federal–State Educational Relations." *Phi Delta Kappan* 49 (September 1967).

———, et al. *Organization and Control of American Schools.* 3rd ed. Columbus, Ohio: Charles E. Merrill Publishing Co., 1975.

COMMITTEE FOR ECONOMIC DEVELOPMENT. *Education for the Urban Disadvantaged from Preschool to Employment.* Washington, D.C.: The Committee, 1971.

"Federal Programs Fail to Promote Change." *USA Today* 107 (December 1978): 11–13.

FLYGARE, THOMAS J. "Federal Desegregation Decrees and Compensatory Education." *Phi Delta Kappan* 59, No. 4 (December 1977): 265–66.

GALLUP, GEORGE H. "Ninth Annual Gallup Poll of the Public's Attitudes Toward the Public Schools." *Phi Delta Kappan* 59, No. 1 (September 1977): 2, 22.

HACK, WALTER G., and LUVERNE L. CUNNINGHAM. *Educational Administration: The Developing Decades.* Berkeley, Ca.: McCutchan Publishing Corporation, 1977.

HANSON, MARK E. *Educational Administration and Organizational Behavior.* Boston: Allyn and Bacon, Inc., 1978.

KIRST, M. W. "New Politics of State Educational Finance." *Phi Delta Kappan* 60 (February 1979): 427–32.

KLAUSMEIER, HERBERT J. "Proposals for Change in Federal Policy on Educational Research, Development, and Implementation." *Phi Delta Kappan* 59, No. 1 (September 1977): 31–32, 49–50.

KNEZEVICH, STEPHEN J. *Administration of Public Education.* Scranton, Pa.: Harper and Row Publishers, Inc., 1975.

MANN, DALE. "Education Policy in the Carter Administration." *Phi Delta Kappan* 59, No. 1 (September 1977): 27–30.

McCLURE, WILLIAM P. "Financing Education at the Federal Level." *The School Administrator* 24 (February 1967).

MENACKER, JULIUS. "The Organizational Behavior of Congress in the Formulation of Educational Support Policy." *Phi Delta Kappan* 48 (October 1966).

MORPHET, EDGAR L. *Educational Organization and Administration.* 3rd ed. Englewood Cliffs, N.J.: Prentice-Hall, Inc., 1974.

MOYNIHAN, DANIEL PATRICK. "The Carter Administration: Creative Proposals Will Come—Slowly." *Phi Delta Kappan* 59, No. 1 (September 1977): 2, 22.

MURPHY, J. F. "Fiscal Problems of Big City School Systems: Changing Patterns of State and Federal Aid." *Urban Review* 10 (Winter 1978): 251–65.

NEILL, SHIRLEY B. *School Energy Crisis: Problems and Solutions.* Arlington, Va.: American Association of School Administrators, 1977.

QUATTLEBAUM, CHARLES A. *Federal Education Policies, Programs, and Proposals.* Washington, D.C.: U.S. Government Printing Office, 1960.

STEVENS, JOHN M. "The Good News of *Bakke.*" *Phi Delta Kappan* 59, No. 1 (September 1977): 23–26.

ST. JOHN, NANCY H. *School Desegregation: Outcomes for Children.* New York: John Wiley & Sons, Inc., 1975.

TYRE, KENNETH A., and JERROLD M. NOVOTNEY. *School in Transition.* New York: McGraw-Hill Book Co., 1975.

CHAPTER THREE

The State's Relation
to Education

Each state has a responsibility for its educational program which it operates according to specific laws. All states have a definite organizational structure, consisting of an education department, a chief school officer, and numerous divisions headed by administrators. There is debate regarding the amount of control that the state should exert on local school districts. However, all districts look to the state for leadership and service.

Similarity of State Organization

The first state to establish a means for the supervision and control of education was New York, in 1784. Although called the University of the State of New York, it actually functioned as a state board of education and has continued to operate as such. Since that time, every state in the Union has set up an educational department with at least one board having responsibility for the supervision of schools.

Sections concerning education appear in all state constitutions. The legislature establishes the enabling acts for a state's system of public education, specifies laws for local boards of education, appropriates the money for financing education, and passes laws. Although it delegates power to local boards of education, it retains absolute authority over public schools. The amount of delegated power varies from state to state.[1]

---

[1] Robert E. Wilson, *Educational Administration* (Columbus, Ohio: Charles E. Merrill Books, 1966), p. 198.

QUALIFICATION FOR STATE BOARD MEMBERSHIP.   Several states have set up qualifications for membership on state boards of education. Some require all congressional districts to have equal representation; some require a certain percentage of members to be professional educators; and some prohibit membership of professional educators. No state requires any educational qualifications, but the vast majority of state board members throughout the country have attended college. It is the general consensus that board members be persons interested in public education, of high character, and without political axes to grind. Americans favor lay state boards of education, composed of laymen selected from various walks of life. The National Council of Chief State School Officers states that, "In each state there should be a non-partisan, lay state board of education composed of seven to twelve able citizens, broadly representative of the general public and unselfishly interested in public education, elected by the people in a manner prescribed by law."[2]

SIZE OF STATE BOARDS OF EDUCATION.   The number of members of state boards of education ranges from 3 in Mississippi to 27 in Indiana. Thirty states range from 6 to 10 members, with 9 being about the average.[3] An uneven number is desirable so that voting stalemates do not occur.

METHOD OF SELECTING STATE BOARD MEMBERS.   The method of selecting state board members varies from state to state. They may be appointed by the governor with or without legislative approval; elected by popular vote; selected by conventions of local school board members; appointed by the state superintendent (Wyoming); or selected by the legislature. Although consensus favors the elective method of selecting state board members, the governors of most states appoint all or most of the members. Educators favor the election of state board members over the appointive method. Whatever the method used, it is difficult to recruit competent people to serve.

TERMS OF OFFICE FOR STATE BOARD MEMBERS.   The terms of office for state board members vary considerably, ranging from two to fourteen years, with four to six years the most common.[4] If a member is to serve effectively, four years should be the minimum. In states where members are appointed by the governor, their tenure should be the same as that of

---

[2] National Council of Chief State School Officers, *Our System of Education* (Washington, D.C.: The Council, 1950), p. 20.

[3] Clayton D. Hutchins and Richard H. Barr, *Statistics of State School Systems,* DE-20020-66, U.S. Department of Health, Education, and Welfare (Washington, D.C.: U.S. Government Printing Office, 1968), p. 20.

[4] Wilson, *Educational Administration,* p. 199.

the governor. Terms of office should overlap in order to assure continuous operation.

FUNCTIONS OF STATE BOARDS OF EDUCATION.   State boards of education are not analogous to local school boards in terms of function. They have certain legislative and policymaking powers, but most of their activities fall into three classifications: (1) the direction of the state department of education; (2) the furnishing of expert advice to the state legislature; and (3) the constant study of state educational problems. Common policymaking responsibilities include direction of state-operated schools, adoption of textbooks and courses of study, and the execution of the provisions of legislative statutes. The distinction between separate duties is not always clear. In some states, the boards also have executive duties. It is recommended that boards do not take on administrative functions because these should be the responsibility of the chief state school officer.

The Chief State School Officer

New York pioneered the office of state superintendent of schools, appointing the first such officer in 1812. The duties of this position were largely financial, concerned with the management of funds used to furnish grants to local districts. Maryland provided for a similar officer in 1826. Although neither of these offices proved continuous (both were abolished and then re-established some years later), they mark the first attempt to provide a director for the ramifying operations of public education within individual states.[5]

All states today have some sort of officer whose special responsibility is to direct public education on a state level. Although the title of this officer is usually Superintendent of Public Instruction, there are local variations such as Commissioner of Education and Director of Education.

SELECTION AND TERM OF OFFICE.   The chief state school officer is selected in three ways:

1. Election by popular vote in eighteen states.
2. Appointed by the governor in five states.
3. Appointed by the state board of education in twenty-seven states.

Although each method may have its advantages, the National Council of Chief State School Officers recommends that the chief state school officer be selected by the state board of education on a nonpartisan basis.[6]

---

[5] H. R. Douglass and Calvin Grieder, *American Public Education* (New York: Ronald Press Co., 1948), pp. 148–49.

[6] National Council of Chief State School Officers, *Our System*, p. 20.

When the chief state school officer has to run for office, politics are usually involved—even when the position is considered to be nonpartisan. Competent people may not run because of the necessity of campaigning and the time and money it involves.

The advantage of having the state board select the chief state school officer is that the board is more aware of the office requirements and can select the most competent person to cooperate with it.

Regardless of how they are selected, it is often difficult to get qualified, professional educators to accept the position because of the low salaries. District superintendents, especially in large city districts, receive much higher salaries than many state superintendents.

All chief state school officers should have legally prescribed terms of office of not less than four years. This is necessary in order to exercise powers and carry out duties in an effective manner. Removal from office should only be for cause according to legally established policies, and not for political reasons or at the whim of the state board. The assurance of security in office and the payment of adequate salaries should attract competent people to administer a state's educational programs.

DUTIES AND RESPONSIBILITIES OF THE CHIEF STATE SCHOOL OFFICER. The powers and duties of state school heads vary from state to state. Most states spell out, not only the requirements for office, but the duties and responsibilities.

In general, the powers and duties of a chief state school officer may be described as follows:

1. Serves as executive officer of the state board of education.
2. Recommends policies and regulations for educational programs.
3. Recommends improvements in educational legislation.
4. Interprets educational laws and regulations.
5. Submits periodic reports and data regarding the educational system to the governor, the legislature, and other agencies.[7]
6. Serves in a leadership capacity in working with other state agencies.
7. Conducts research and collects and tabulates statistical information in the educational realm.
8. Keeps the public informed regarding educational programs of the state, the needs and accomplishments of the schools, and financial matters.
9. Advises the legislature about the financial needs of the state's school systems.
10. Distributes federal and state funds to local school districts.
11. Approves or accredits public schools and sometimes private schools.

[7] Edgar L. Morphet, Roe L. Johns, and Theodore L. Reller, *Educational Organization and Administration*, pp. 263–64.

The State Department of Education

The state department of education should consist of a state board of education, a chief state school officer, and the necessary staff to carry out its functions. It should be the legislative body of the state's educational system. Because education is a nonpolitical function, the state department should not be involved in politics.

It is difficult to compare programs of state departments of education because the duties of state school officers are not the same, resources vary, and programs delegated by state legislatures are different. The larger the state, the more complex the organization of the state education department becomes. Usually, several main divisions are established with their own directors or assistant superintendents, as illustrated in Figure 3–1. Some large states, like New York, may employ many hundreds of persons on the professional staff of the state department, whereas smaller ones, such as Alaska, may employ very few. In addition to the professional staff, there are secretarial and clerical assistants, regional and district supervisory staffs, administrative staffs for the chief state school officer, and operation and maintenance people.[8] Generally speaking, the stronger and more universal the public school program of a given state, the more complex and well-manned is its state department.

FUNCTIONS OF THE STATE DEPARTMENT OF EDUCATION.   State departments have four major functions: (1) leadership; (2) regulation; (3) operation; and (4) service.

Insofar as state departments provide strong leadership, they can help improve education at both the state and local level. They have the facilities and manpower to conduct research and collect information which can be made available to local school districts.

Regulation is concerned with minimum programs, personnel, school plants, child accounting, and finance, and provides a framework for instructional programs.

Operational responsibilities refer to the operation of various programs such as vocational rehabilitation, library services, adult education, and teacher-placement and retirement services. There is disagreement as to how much the state should be involved in operational functions. Fewer problems will arise, however, if there is effective state leadership.

Service functions may be performed for the state as a whole or for local school districts; this varies from state to state. Lane explains that:

> In some states, service to the state as a whole is rendered by the State Department of Education, acting as an educational information center for interpreting education in the state to the chief executive of the state,

---

[8] Hutchins and Barr, *Statistics of State School Systems*, p. 20.

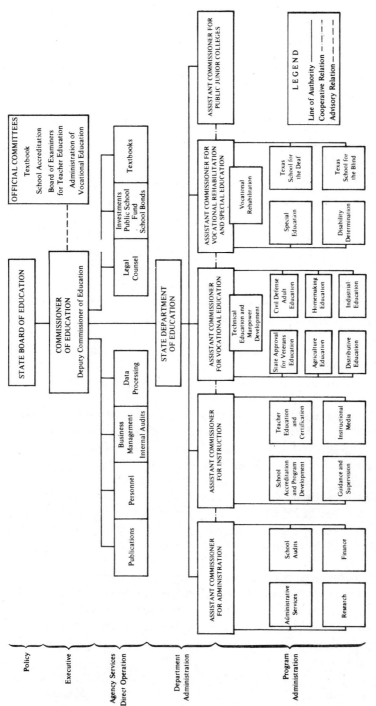

FIGURE 3–1. Organization of a State Education Department.

the state legislature, and the people through comparative studies, statistical information, advice, clarification of laws, statutes and regulations. In other states, the state department may be responsible for operating special schools (for the blind, deaf, and so on), archives, libraries, teacher-placement agencies, teacher-retirement funds, controlling interscholastic athletics, programs of rehabilitation for the handicapped, and many other activities.[9]

One practical example of how a local school administrator can utilize state services is in connection with a decision to initiate and implement a new program. A telephone call or letter requesting assistance in planning for the installation of pre-primary, special, or continuing education—to list three possibilities—will in most states be sufficient to bring to the local district one or more state department of education specialists who will, usually at no cost to the district, use their expertise and experience to set up a complete program on paper for later board approval.

If money is lacking, the state department representatives may put the district superintendent in touch with the person in the Department of Education in Washington, D.C. who is in charge of appropriate grants-in-aid. In the event that state legislation is required for the program desired, the state consultants are often able to set up conferences for the local administrators with key legislators and legislative committee leaders whose responsibility it would be to write, introduce, and steer the bill through the legislative process.

These are only a few examples of the importance of the state department's service functions. They are almost limitless.

The state has the responsibility of organizing the state educationally into districts or subdivisions of some sort; of determining the degree of authority to be exercised by these subdivisions; of supplying certain financial support to educational activities; of certifying teachers; and of determining the basic educational program for all schools.

The state department should have the ability to deal flexibly with the broad and rapidly changing array of opportunities and problems in education and administration. There must be collaboration and communication across all levels of educational administration.

PROBLEMS VEXING STATE DEPARTMENTS OF EDUCATION.   Although it is agreed that state departments of education should be in strong positions of educational leadership, this is not often the case. Organizational and financial inadequacies, over which the departments themselves exercise little control, operate to circumscribe their effectiveness. Laws made by state legislatures, sometimes without consulting the state department of

---

[9] Willard R. Lane, Ronald G. Corwin, and William G. Monahan, *Foundations of Educational Administration: A Behavioral Analysis*, p. 163.

education, become policy. Coordination and cooperation between the legislature and the state education department need to be promoted. Among the problems vexing state departments of education are the following:

> Political implications when the chief state school officer must run for election.
>
> Inadequate number of qualified personnel.
>
> Salaries too low to attract and hold outstanding educators, causing unnecessary turnover.
>
> Lack of coordination among the various departments within the state department of education.
>
> Divided responsibilities and duplication of effort among state agencies.
>
> Powers and responsibilities not clearly defined.
>
> Departmental organization cumbersome and archaic.
>
> Conflicts with the state legislature caused by legislative mandates and fiscal controls which affect long-range planning.
>
> Inadequate budget.

The Intermediate Unit: County School Administration

The intermediate, or county, unit stands between the state and the local school district. It can provide services for those districts that lack the organization, personnel, and facilities to produce quality education. Each intermediate unit has an organizational structure comprised of a governing board, chief administrative officer, and various departments headed by administrators. Because of its position—straddling the state and local levels—it has problems and is being subjected to reorganizational considerations.

Historical Role of the Intermediate Unit

Colonial settlers in the New World brought with them jurisdictional concepts of towns, districts, parishes, counties, and states. The town (or township) expression of a geographical unit was prevalent in New England; the parish, in French-dominated Louisiana; and the county, subdivided into townships, in the Midwest and Southwest. Public schools in the towns of Massachusetts received supervisory and inspectional service, provided by the state and, later, by subdivisions of the state. The earliest school inspectors were not educational officials, but existing governmental officials, such as the county clerk, the justice of the peace, a county judge, a land commissioner, or the chairman of the county board of school visitors.

This miscellaneous hodgepodge of county, district, or parish officials proved to be unsatisfactory as school visitors and supervisors. In 1829, legislation was enacted in Delaware providing for an official whose sole duties would be school supervision and visitation; it marked the beginning of the first intermediate unit, or county superintendency. Other states (New York in 1843) quickly followed Delaware's lead in setting up county or area superintendents.

As early as 1879, thirty-four of the existing thirty-eight states had established the office of county superintendent. Several states abandoned the office but after a short lapse re-established it. The states that allowed the office of the county superintendent of schools to lapse were Mississippi, California, Texas, Idaho, and Arizona. All of these states have since re-established some form of intermediate school administrative unit. Even states that now have a somewhat different system from the county administrative unit—Maine, New Hampshire, New York, and Vermont—at one time had the office of county superintendent. Connecticut, Massachusetts, Hawaii, and Rhode Island are the only states that have never had a county superintendent of schools and have retained the organization of the local district or group of districts, plus the state department of public instruction.

The county school administrative unit was especially well adapted to the new lands beyond the Mississippi. Many of the new states to the west had some type of county school supervisory service, even while they were still territories. The county superintendent was often an elected official and was as much an accepted part of each county's government as the county treasurer and the county clerk. The functions and personnel of the county office have changed considerably in recent years and should change even more.

Importance of County School Administration

It can be said that the United States does not have an educational system, but has fifty educational systems. The concept of education as a state function is universally accepted. However, the state department of education, from territorial and early statehood days, has proved to be geographically and psychologically too far removed from the local districts. The intermediate unit has evolved out of a need for closer supervisory help and coordination at the local level.

Early in its history the county office was called upon to keep official records, to select, to certify, and to place teachers, and to arbitrate district boundary problems. It has often been called the administrative right arm of the state department of education because it has performed the task of enforcing laws and upholding minimum standards. Such standards have applied to school finance, physical facilities, teacher preparation, pupil attendance, and the instructional program. Not only has the county office served in this capacity, but it has also functioned as a service and reporting agency to the state department. Some outstanding county superintendents with close experience at the local level have helped state departments of education to develop effective policies and procedures. The county superintendent has played an important role by maintaining two-way communication between local districts and the state office.

From an original responsibility involving semipolicing of local school districts (often dealing particularly with governing boards of one-room schools), the office has evolved into a service center for both small and large districts.

Teachers need to be trained in service. Educational supplies need to be selected and wisely used. Courses of study have to be written and interpreted. Teacher vacancies in rural areas have to be filled. Traveling libraries must be established. Audio-visual aids have to be procured, distributed, and interpreted. Pupils have to be transferred or adjusted, and district boundaries have to be adjudicated. Federal projects have to be written in order to request federal funds. Data processing equipment must be appraised, purchased, and used effectively. These educational needs have caused in recent years the intermediate unit to emerge more as a service and leadership organization than as a primary law enforcement arm of the state.

Variations in Intermediate Unit Organization

The organization of the intermediate unit occurs in three main types of categories: (1) a supervisory union, (2) a county superintendency, or (3) a combination of county–local district units. The supervisory union is most prevalent in New England, where two or more towns have been joined together to form a supervisory or intermediate district, with a superintendent. The supervisory unions often cover rural areas, while a large city may function as an independent unit and deal directly with the state department of education. States with a supervisory union type of organization are Connecticut, Maine, Massachusetts, New Hampshire, New York, Rhode Island, and Vermont. New York has 175 supervisory unions, whereas Rhode Island has only two.

The islands of Hawaii are controlled by the State Department of Public Instruction in Honolulu, but suboffices in centers like Hilo serve functions similar to those of mainland county offices.

States that operate with the county system are largely in the Midwest, West, and Southwest, where the county was early established as a governmental unit. These states are Arizona, Arkansas, California, Colorado,

Idaho, Missouri, Montana, Nebraska, North Dakota, Ohio, Texas, Washington, Wisconsin, and Wyoming. About 2,000 county superintendents serve the school administrative subdivisions of these states. It is estimated that about an equal number of other professional and highly trained personnel assist the county superintendent in these areas. California has by far the largest number of professional helpers, with a ratio of more than ten professional helpers for each county superintendent.

In some of these states an entire county has been organized as a school district, but the county–district unit is the exception rather than the rule. In the county–district unit type of organization, there is no intermediate or county office, because the county or parish jurisdictions are identical to the school district.

There are variations of the county–district organization, generally created to accommodate population concentrations. In Florida and West Virginia, for example, all school districts have been combined into districts that follow county or city boundaries. Louisiana has 3 city school parishes and Utah has 5 city school districts in addition to the larger units administered by a county–district superintendent. In Maryland all units follow county boundaries and are administered by a county superintendent, with the exception of the city of Baltimore. Virginia entitles its organizational units "divisions" that are administered similarly to the county units in other states. Ten of these divisions, however, include 2 counties each, and one contains 3 counties. Others contain city and county combined, and 22 are city school districts. Utah has a peculiar combination of county districts, city districts, and combined counties as single county unit districts. States that have the county unit system in various forms of organization are Alabama, Florida, Georgia, Kentucky, Louisiana, Maryland, Nevada, New Mexico, North Carolina, Tennessee, Utah, Virginia, and West Virginia.

The organization of the intermediate unit has developed chiefly along county lines, but with so many exceptions and variations that no single definition can include all types. The variety of organization does, however, represent a singleness of purpose—namely, the enforcement of state regulations, as adopted by the people through their legislators, and the furnishing of services, leadership, and research that the local districts cannot provide adequately for themselves. The organization of the intermediate unit has developed, not as a political expediency nor as a vestige of previous institutions, but has expanded to meet vital school needs where control is close to the people.

Basic Principles of School Organization

As a means of identifying the place and function of the intermediate unit in the American pattern, it is well to consider some basic principles that affect organization at the several levels. These principles deal chiefly with concern, responsibility, and operation. A discussion of them follows.

EDUCATION AS A NATIONAL CONCERN. A high level of education for all citizens has become a concern of the federal government and of all who exert nationwide influence. It is increasingly recognized to be essential for efficient production, wise consumption, good public health, free institutions, and national strength. In fact, without a high level of education, the survival of a people and their institutions of liberty and freedom are in jeopardy. Education must be a national concern with adequate financial support if it is to be a means of sustaining national survival and well-being.

EDUCATION AS A FUNCTION OF THE STATE. The several state constitutions, legislatures, and courts, as well as the Supreme Court of the United States, have repeatedly held that education is a function and a responsibility of the people in each state. The state has delegated that responsibility, in part, to the intermediate unit. In this sense, the intermediate unit is a partner of the state department of education, following the statutes and constitutional provisions as does any other subdivision of government. Because the intermediate unit is in fact a subdivision of state government, carrying out a state function, it should be financed by the people of the entire state, rather than by local political subdivisions. This is particularly important as counties merge into larger regions.

CHARACTERISTICS OF THE LOCAL, INTERMEDIATE, AND STATE LEVELS. The local school district is primarily operational; the intermediate unit is primarily for coordination and service; and the state department is primarily concerned with leadership, research, and enforcement.

The operation of schools should be kept close to the people, with a minimum of supervision from higher levels. Every function involved in the education of children should be performed at the lowest possible level. The intermediate unit should perform only those functions which, because of limited facilities or untrained personnel, the district level cannot carry out. Likewise, the state department should perform only those functions for which the intermediate unit lacks resources. It follows, then, that as districts grow or become consolidated or unified, they should assume more of the functions of operation. One of the chief purposes of the intermediate unit is *to help the district to help itself*. Furthermore, the state department should not bypass the intermediate unit and give direct district services, but should work through the intermediate unit.

COOPERATIVE POLICIES AND PROCEDURES. Although the state department bestows leadership and operates as a policymaking and enforcing unit, it should not formulate policies from a purely theoretical viewpoint, nor impose hampering rules and regulations. Policies should evolve out of operational practice at the lower level. Educational policies must be expressions of all the people. In this sense the people, through their legislators, determine school policies as they are observed through the experience of local school districts. It is then the function of the state department of education to define and enforce the policies that have been initiated at the local level and modified through cooperative participation in their development. All who are affected by the policies and procedures should have a voice in their formulation. The intermediate unit plays a dual role in gathering and interpreting information from the operational level, and in the legal analysis and interpretation of state legislation. In all cases, the growth and development of children should be the guide to policy formulation.

SERVICE ORIENTATION OF THE INTERMEDIATE UNIT.   The best way for the intermediate unit to strengthen operation in the local district is to furnish needed services, rather than to exert punitive force. Local districts need help in the interpretation of school law, review of local budgets, certification of attendance, inservice training for teachers and classified personnel, coordination with other schools and with government and business agencies. They need assistance with federal projects, help in selecting and using instructional materials, in recruiting and selecting teachers, and in providing a consulting service for local governing boards. The service concept in the role of the intermediate unit is growing and should grow more as local districts expand their operations. Coordination rather than domination is the best service.

Personnel and Functions of the Intermediate Unit

PERSONNEL IN THE INTERMEDIATE UNIT.   The superintendent, professional assistants, and clerical helpers constitute the personnel in the intermediate units, whether organized as supervisory unions, county superintendent's offices, county–district units, or regional areas. For the most part, the county superintendency began as a political unit and still often possesses a partisan character. Salaries for county superintendents have lagged behind those for similar positions in large city school systems. Adequate professional qualification requirements have lagged behind the needs of the expanding office, although in recent years there has been a trend toward higher professional status for the county superintendent, resulting in higher salaries. Regionalism is enhancing this trend. Alaska has fine Regional Resource Centers, which help the state department serve schools in the vast areas of that state.

The requirements or qualifications for the office of intermediate-unit superintendent vary considerably among 47 states. Three have no specified requirements, and others range all the way from requiring one year of college training to a requirement of six years of college training, with at least seven years of public school experience and possession of an administration certificate. The median requirement among the states is now four years of college, with experience in teaching or administration.

In too many counties, the intermediate unit is still headed by a superintendent and a clerk or a few clerical workers. There is a trend, however, for the superintendent to secure more budgetary help and to establish positions classified as assistant superintendent, director, supervisor, consultant, and coordinator. This practice strengthens the office of the intermediate-unit superintendent, and provides better and more specialized service to school districts. It is no longer possible for one person to be proficient in all areas. Local districts need expert consultant services in finance, legal interpretation, guidance, curriculum development, audiovisual aids, child welfare, health programs, and vocational education.

FUNCTIONS OF THE INTERMEDIATE UNIT. The county superintendent of schools initially was responsible for keeping a few records and inspecting the school area. These functions were routine and "housekeeping" in nature. From this small beginning, the county superintendent's functions have multiplied, but still consist of two general types: (1) records and reports and (2) professional services.

The required records and reports are necessary in the review of budgets, auditing of accounts, control of expenditures, verification of average daily attendance, determination of district boundaries, maintenance of certificate requirements, and enforcement of school code provisions. Other recording and housekeeping functions include accounting for retirement and Social Security approval of payrolls and warrants, calling and conducting school elections, enforcing compulsory education laws and issuing work permits, assisting with quantity purchasing, transportation and housing, dissemination of information concerning county counsel or attorney general opinions and court cases, and help with data processing. These activities are largely perfunctory and mechanical, but they are necessary for the legal operation of school districts. With the meeting of each legislature the list becomes larger and more complicated. Many of the functions can be handled by classified workers without teaching or administrative certificates. In addition to these routine functions, many of the county superintendents with vision and professional point of view have established helpful services for school districts.

These services are designed primarily to improve instruction for children and youth, but are varied and complex in nature. The application of the services tends to strengthen the operational level by reinforcing teachers, counselors, and administrators with needed instructional plans, materials, techniques, and consultant help.

Some of the services that the intermediate unit can offer to the local districts are:

1. Direct supervision of classroom teachers. (This diminishes as school districts grow larger.)
2. Coordination of area programs among districts.
3. Inservice education of certificated and classified personnel.
4. Preparation of communication and publication aids.
5. Adoption or preparation of courses of study.
6. Provision of audio-visual, library, educational TV, and other materials or programs.
7. Consultant help with pupil personnel services.
8. Operation of federal programs, such as Title III (ESEA), and assistance to districts that apply for federal programs under the several titles of ESEA.
9. Cooperation with business and industry to improve vocational education.
10. Scoring, interpreting, and summarizing standardized testing.
11. Furnishing leadership toward innovations such as flexible scheduling, programmed instruction, team teaching, Head Start and preschool education, collective bargaining or professional negotiation, continuing education in business and industry, citizenship, and skills in human relations.
12. Coordination and cooperation with problem departments, law enforcement agencies, legislative committees, character-building organizations, and community support groups.

HISTORICAL DEVELOPMENT OF THE COUNTY SUPERINTENDENT IN CALIFORNIA. Magee has traced the growth and development of the office of the County Superintendent of Schools for Los Angeles County. The development in this case study, although it only applies to California, somewhat parallels the evolution of other county offices in the United States and brings into focus the increasing emphasis upon the county superintendent as an instructional leader. The following is a chronology of the Los Angeles County superintendency.

1. The Office of the County Superintendent of Schools was created by the legislature in 1852; each county assessor acted in the capacity of county superintendent.
2. County superintendents were elected by the people in 1855 and are still elected in most counties.
3. Prior to 1870, the superintendent's primary duties were certifying teacher credentials and visiting schools.

4. The first Los Angeles County teachers' institute was held in 1870.
5. The County adopted all textbooks used in the schools up to 1885.
6. The Legislature increased the powers of the County Superintendent and in 1895 put the county high schools under the jurisdiction of his office.
7. In 1911, the County Superintendent was permitted to pay expenses for trustees' institutes, and county boards could pay for the transportation of students to county high schools.
8. In 1915, the County Superintendent was empowered to employ a county supervisor of attendance if a majority of districts so petitioned.
9. Supervision from the County Schools Office was authorized by the Legislature in 1921.
10. Los Angeles County was one of the first in the state to operate a county schools office.
11. The office of the County Superintendent of Schools serves as an intermediate unit between the state and local school districts. One of its primary functions is the receiving and disbursing of school money.
12. The Office of the Los Angeles County Superintendent of Schools was the first to inaugurate the following educational services:
   a. Secondary curriculum coordination.
   b. Screening devices for local district boards in their selection of chief administrators.
   c. Custodial training for maintenance and operation employees.
   d. Institute programs for noncertificated employees.
   e. Apprisal of school districts, through the Regional Planning Commission, of proposed construction in the area.
   f. Preschool orientation programs for new teachers.
   g. Summer workshops for elementary school administrators.
   h. Child study workshops.
   i. Classes for mentally retarded children in small districts.
   j. Consultant services to districts for bookkeeping and accounting problems.[10]

This historical study shows that the office of the Los Angeles County Superintendent of Schools is now acting as a service organization and has pioneered many educational services. It has thereby fulfilled its instructional leadership role by stimulating educational programs in local districts.

State Controls over Private Education

All early American schools were private. For many decades during the Colonial period, private school enrollment was greater than public school enrollment. In recent decades, and especially since universal compulsory

---

[10] Lawrence Thomas Magee: "Historical Developments Affecting the Administration of the Office of the Los Angeles County Superintendent of Schools" (unpublished doctoral dissertation, University of Southern California, 1955), pp. 205–8.

education laws were enacted, the percentage of the school-age population in attendance at private schools has been decreasing. The percent of student enrollment in private elementary schools varies from about 15 percent in the northeast to about 7 percent in the west; in secondary schools it varies from about 12 percent in the northeast to a little less than 5 percent in the west. Declines in private school enrollment have been due to population changes, the closing of some Catholic elementary schools in some sections of the country, and a drop in public school enrollment. White flight to avoid forced busing for integration is increasing private school enrollment in some areas. People have the right to send their children to either public or nonpublic schools, and the courts have upheld this right.

Two reasons are commonly given by parents for sending their children to private schools (where they must pay tuition simultaneously with support of the public school system with their tax dollars). One reason is the belief that the private school has higher standards and more efficient instructional methods, particularly in the academic and classical curriculum areas. A second motive is the desire to give religious instruction to one's children, in addition to the citizenship training that makes up an important part of public school training.

All schools are subject to state control, whether public or nonpublic. Laws establishing standards for private schools, and providing for state inspection of their facilities and educational offerings have long been common in some states; in others, private schools are subject to little regulation. Private school standards vary greatly throughout the country today. Some states require the same minimum standards that exist for public schools, while others do little except check pupil attendance in the private schools.

Competition between public and nonpublic schools is unavoidable. Lack of financial assistance handicaps many private schools; they often cannot provide the books, equipment, or supplies that public schools have. Teachers may be less qualified in nonpublic schools because they do not have to be licensed by the state. Most nonpublic schools do not pay salaries high enough to attract the best qualified teachers. On the other hand, some private schools require their teachers to meet the standards for public schools. Parochial schools are often thought to be traditional and conservative, but this is not always the case. Some of the newest and most innovative educational programs exist in nonpublic schools. Public schools tend to offer a more impartial educational program. Nonpublic schools approach education from their particular bias.

The issue of how much financial support the state is obligated to provide to nonpublic schools has not been resolved. Parents who send their children to nonpublic schools complain that they are doubly taxed.

Some believe that since the state does not pay for the education of their children in public schools, it would be equitable to give the private school the money (other nations do this). Others claim that because of the constitutional separation of state and church in America, this would constitute a gift of public funds to a sectarian enterprise. Because parents made the choice, it is argued, they should have no recourse. It should be noted, however, that some states provide financial assistance for textbooks and transportation. The National Defense Education Act and the Elementary and Secondary Education Act also have some sections that apply to private schools.

COOPERATION BETWEEN PUBLIC AND NONPUBLIC SCHOOLS.   Many public schools cooperate with nonpublic schools by lending materials, allowing nonpublic schools to use their facilities, enrolling nonpublic school students in some classes, and sending educational specialists to nonpublic schools. A large percentage of school systems with enrollments of 12,000 or more do not cooperate with nonpublic schools in any way. Of those that did cooperate, the most common practice was the lending or giving of materials. When public schools offer classes to nonpublic school students, enrollments are primarily in the following subject areas: driver training, industrial arts, home economics, vocational education, foreign languages, chemistry, physics, physical education, biology, and instrumental music. The largest enrollments are in vocational, technical, and scientific areas.[11]

Historical Function of the State in Education

As early as 1642, the colonies passed laws concerning education. It was apparently taken for granted, even in that early period, that state legislatures had the necessary power to enforce such regulations. In 1647, Massachusetts enacted a law compelling communities with a certain population to set up and maintain grammar schools, thus setting a precedent for state involvement in education.

Many settlements established local schools as the nation spread westward, but as soon as territorial or state governments became established, the larger unit assumed responsibility for the educational program. Many early schools were neither compulsory nor free. Massachusetts again led the nation in these progressive measures, establishing compulsory public education by law in 1852. Every present state constitution has a section

[11] National Education Association, Research Division, "Sharing of Resources by Public Schools with Nonpublic Schools," *NEA Research Bulletin* 45 (October 1967): 90–92.

clarifying the place of the state in education, and stressing the importance of schooling. By omission in the federal Constitution, the provision for public education is regarded as a matter for the state governments. Since 1876 Congress has required all states admitted to the Union to provide a system of public schools.

Although local school control is the result of a delegation of power from the state government and operates under authority granted to it by the laws of the state, in practice such local control has been jealously guarded from state interference. However, local operation is legally, if not in actual practice, the creature of the state, and may be modified or revoked at the pleasure of the state. State preeminence in the field of education has evolved because of the ever-growing conviction of the people that education is the most important single function of the state, and cannot be carried out solely on the basis of local peculiarities. Figure 3–2 depicts educational administration as a state function.

Public Education and State Laws

Legislation governing education is divided into two kinds: *mandatory* laws, which require the schools to conform to the exact specifications of the statutes; and *permissive* laws, which grant to the school district certain privileges under specified conditions. Examples of mandatory laws are those governing teacher certification, budgeting and finance procedures, the teaching of certain required subjects, and compulsory school attendance. Permissive laws enable districts to provide additions to the curriculum or basic program, such as health services, guidance programs, and adult education. Early state laws regarding education were permissive. Later, they became mandatory because local communities did not do enough. Modern thought generally holds that permissive legislation best expresses the principle of local freedom under state suzerainty. However, a dilemma is created for local school districts as they seek more state funds, while simultaneously desiring freedom of action. Certain controls inevitably accompany financial support.

Degree of State Control of Education

The amount of state control of education varies from state to state. Some have almost no controls or requirements, while others have a great deal. Every state, however, has established control over bond issues. Sometimes the state establishes requirements, but provides no financial support to implement them.

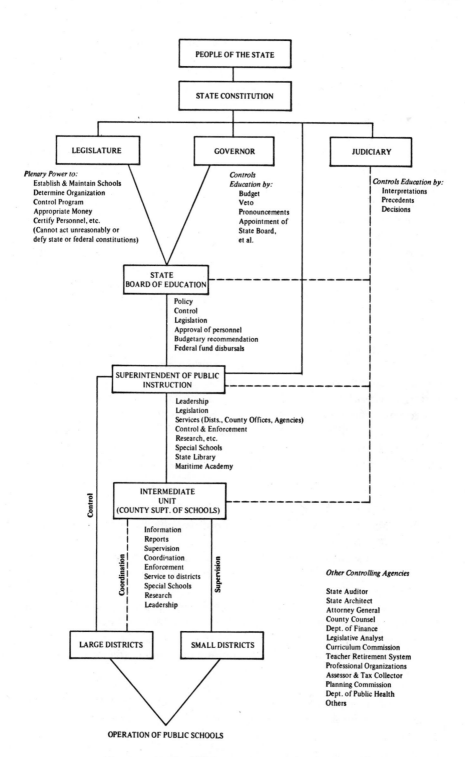

PEOPLE OF THE STATE

STATE CONSTITUTION

LEGISLATURE

GOVERNOR

JUDICIARY

Plenary Power to:
Establish & Maintain Schools
Determine Organization
Control Program
Appropriate Money
Certify Personnel, etc.
(Cannot act unreasonably or
defy state or federal constitutions)

*Controls
Education by:*
Budget
Veto
Pronouncements
Appointment of
State Board,
et al.

Controls Education by:
Interpretations
Precedents
Decisions

STATE
BOARD OF EDUCATION

Policy
Control
Legislation
Approval of personnel
Budgetary recommendation
Federal fund disbursals

SUPERINTENDENT OF PUBLIC
INSTRUCTION

Leadership
Legislation
Services (Dists., County Offices, Agencies)
Control & Enforcement
Research, etc.
Special Schools
State Library
Maritime Academy

INTERMEDIATE
UNIT
(COUNTY SUPT. OF SCHOOLS)

Control

Information
Reports
Supervision
Coordination
Enforcement
Service to districts
Special Schools
Research
Leadership

Coordination

Supervision

Other Controlling Agencies

State Auditor
State Architect
Attorney General
County Counsel
Dept. of Finance
Legislative Analyst
Curriculum Commission
Teacher Retirement System
Professional Organizations
Assessor & Tax Collector
Planning Commission
Dept. of Public Health
Others

LARGE DISTRICTS

SMALL DISTRICTS

OPERATION OF PUBLIC SCHOOLS

FIGURE 3–2. *Educational Administration as a State Function.*

Some persons feel that the state already exercises too much control over education. State officials, they claim, cannot possibly be cognizant of the needs of local communities; and state control may lead to indoctrination of citizens with a single point of view. These arguments are similar to those advanced in opposition to federal control of education. When the state takes over responsibilities affecting local school systems, it makes them dependent on the state and reduces their strength to make their own decisions.

Others believe that state control should be strengthened and made more inclusive. They point out that a community's neglect of its children's education is an actual offense against the state. They feel that such a situation can be avoided only by more stringent enactments by state legislatures in the field of educational standards and procedures.

It would seem that the most practical and desirable compromise that can be reached between these two conflicting philosophies would be a situation in which a maximum amount of financial aid would be given by the state, but very little control exercised on the operational level. A set of standards defining minimum educational offerings and facilities should be set up and enforced by the state and applied to all local districts, but individual communities should be permitted to exercise initiative in exceeding those minimums. Minimum standards give the assurance that all children have an equal opportunity to be educated.

The degree to which state departments of education are effective in helping local school districts is highly variable. Some do a great deal; others do very little. On the average, however, the following points can be made:

1. State adoption of minimum teacher salaries and number of days in the school year have a definite and positive effect on local educational programs.
2. Specific statewide curriculum requirements (such as United States history for certain grades) are important in shaping local classroom offerings.
3. In states that require specific textbooks to be used at various grade levels, the resultant local uniformity is usually significant.
4. By keeping teacher credentialing in the hands of the state, local districts are assured of at least certain minimum standards in the teachers they hire.

The state department should emphasize leadership, which is sorely needed in the improvement of instruction, rather than enforcement of regulations.

What the state department of education can accomplish through statewide planning and coordination, and through advice, assistance, and encouragement to local districts far outweighs the results obtained from mere enforcement of regulations.[12]

The major effect of all state legislation in the field of school control should be to ensure that no pupil be denied the right to a free public education because of race, creed, or economic condition. For this goal to be realized fully will require considerably more state control than is found in virtually any state today. In fact, states have done so little that federal legislation has been enacted to force achievement of this goal.

The State's Role in Educational Services

Resembling the federal function in education generally, but to a more localized and specific degree, the state's role in education will be increasingly that of service rather than domination. It should focus attention on functions that support constructive change. Today, the local school authorities in many parts of the nation are able to successfully call upon their state departments of education for expert aid in one or more of the following specialized areas:

1. Schoolhouse planning and site purchasing.
2. Financial accounting and bookkeeping.
3. Budgeting.
4. Providing for the needs of physically and mentally handicapped pupils.
5. Curriculum planning and development.
6. Adult education.
7. Guidance and counseling.
8. Community–school recreation.
9. Vocational education.
10. Agricultural education.
11. Business education.
12. Home economics.
13. School district reorganization.
14. School lunch programs.
15. Textbook and library services.
16. Special education program development.
17. Inservice education for teachers.
18. Technical advice in many areas.
19. Research data.

---

[12] Roald F. Campbell, John E. Corbally, Jr., and John A. Ramseyer, *Introduction to Educational Administration*, 3rd ed. (Boston: Allyn and Bacon, Inc., 1966), p. 38.

20. Teacher and administrator certification.
21. Interpretation of laws affecting education at the local level.

State consultants can help local school districts by working through the local authorities. It is increasingly important that the state decentralize its services and go out into the field, rather than remain in the state office building. In the future, local school administrators will be able to secure other and even more technical assistance from the state, especially in the fields of psychological and psychometric services, audio-visual techniques and materials, and scientific techniques and methods.

Summary

Education in the United States is a function of the state, which retains absolute authority over the public schools, although it may delegate its power to local boards of education.

Qualifications and terms of state boards of education and state school superintendents differ from state to state. In the main, however, state boards do not run local schools; rather, they concern themselves with directing their departments of education in research. State superintendents and commissioners usually act as administrators and executive officers of the state boards.

The state department of education is the legislative body of the state's educational system. It functions in leadership, regulatory, operational, and service capacities. It is typically organized into divisions, each dealing with a specialized sector of public education. Its problems center around inadequate financing and political involvement.

Traditionally, the intermediate or county educational unit has been supervisory. Most states have this unit today, although its functions have changed to enforcement of laws and upholding minimum standards. It appears that its future role will be as a coordination and service organization.

Essentially, the intermediate unit is a subdivision of state government, carrying out a state function. In this sense, it is not a local governmental unit, and should be financed by the entire state rather than by local political subdivisions. It should perform only those local functions that cannot be performed on the district level.

The county superintendent's functions fall into two general categories: (1) records and reports and (2) professional services. The first category includes budget approval, control of expenditures, and verification of average daily attendance. The second category includes such services as teacher supervision, inservice training, library and audio-visual aids, and operation of certain federal programs.

The historical development of the county superintendency in California is traced in order to show how it has developed into a service organization, pioneering many educational services.

Private schools are also subject to state control, although to a much lesser degree than public schools. Health and safety regulations must be adhered to, for example, and many states require regular inspection of their facilities and curricula. Some states, however, do little except check pupil attendance in the private schools.

While there is considerable disagreement over the amount of state control that should be exercised over local schools, the ideal situation would be that in which a maximum amount of financial aid would be given by the state with very little control exerted, at least on the operational level.

It seems fairly certain that the state's role in education will be increasingly in the field of service, furnishing expertise in specialized areas of education upon the request of local school districts.

Administrative Problems

In Basket

Problem 1

Mayfield School District consists of two elementary schools. It must send its secondary students to the adjoining North Forks Unified School District which has twelve elementary schools, two junior high schools, and a senior high school. Many of the parents in Mayfield want to join North Fork in the belief that their children will have a better educational program that is coordinated through all the grades. Their school board is not interested because it would like to keep its identity as a historic small district. The North Forks Board of Education and administrators are in favor of the reorganization that would bring Mayfield's two elementary schools into its own district.

What should the North Forks Unified School District do to help bring about this reorganization?
What can the Mayfield parents do?
What role should the State Department of Education play in working with the two school districts?

Problem 2

A number of minority organizations in your state have been complaining that the tests used as a basis for assigning children to special education classes discriminate against minority children. They believe that many of their children are unfairly assigned to classes for the mentally retarded because the tests do not evaluate their real intelligence.

The state administrators' association has invited you, as the State Director of Special Education, to speak at its annual state conference regarding this growing problem.

What research would you do to prepare your speech?
Whom would you consult?
What would you propose as an answer to the test criticisms?
What would you say your office plans to do to alleviate the problem?

Problem 3

You are the assistant county superintendent charged with the responsibility of helping school districts with educational planning. Several districts are investigating the possibility of developing alternative schools. The superintendents and boards of education have asked you to help them with their planning.

What research would you use to inform yourself?
How would you proceed in working with the superintendents and boards of education?
What would you recommend that the districts do to help them decide whether or not to develop alternative schools?

Selected References

BEEM, H. D., and J. A. THOMAS. *A Report of the Michigan Committee for the Study of the Intermediate Unit of Administration.* Chicago, Ill.: University of Chicago Press, 1956.

CAMPBELL, ROALD F., JOHN E. CORBALLY, JR., and JOHN S. RAMSEYER. *Introduction to Educational Administration.* Boston: Allyn and Bacon, Inc., 1966.

FISHER, THOMAS H. "Florida's Approach to Competency Testing." *Phi Delta Kappan* 59, No. 9 (May 1978): 599–602.

"From Rural to Specialized Services: Intermediate School Districts." *Michigan Education Journal* 44 (May 1967): 8–10.

GARMS, WALTER I., et al. *School Finance: The Economics and Politics of Public Education.* Englewood Cliffs, N.J.: Prentice-Hall, Inc., 1978.

GELLEN, MURRAY I., and DOROTHY S. LAIRD. "Florida Profs Develop Exit Exam for Teachers." *Phi Delta Kappan* 60, No. 8 (April 1979): 596.

GITTELL, MARILYN (ed.) *Educating an Urban Population.* New York: Sage Books, Inc., 1969.

GUTHRIE, JAMES W. "Proposition 13 and the Future of California's Schools." *Phi Delta Kappan* 60, No. 1 (September 1978): 12–15.

HART, GARY K. "The California Pupil Proficiency Law as Viewed by Its Author." *Phi Delta Kappan* 59, No. 9 (May 1978): 592–95.

HOY, WAYNE K., and CECIL G. MISKEL. *Educational Administration: Theory, Research, and Practice.* New York: Random House, Inc., 1978.

KIRST, M. W. "New Politics of State Educational Finance." *Phi Delta Kappan* 60 (February 1979): 427–32.

LANE, WILLARD R., RONALD G. CORWIN, and WILLIAM G. MONAHAN. *Foundations of Educational Administration: A Behavioral Analysis.* New York: The Macmillan Company, 1967.

MORPHET, EDGAR L. *Educational Organization and Administration.* 3rd ed. Englewood Cliffs, N.J.: Prentice-Hall, Inc., 1974.

MORRISETT, LLOYD N., SR. *Power Play for Control of Education.* Denver, Col.: Education Commission of the States, 1967..

PIPHO, CHRIS. "Minimum Competency Testing in 1978: A Look at State Standards." *Phi Delta Kappan* 59, No. 9 (May 1978): 585–88.

POUNDS, RALPH L., and JAMES R. BRYNER. *School in American Society.* New York: The Macmillan Company, 1973.

SHER, JONATHAN P. "A Proposal to End Federal Neglect of Rural Schools." *Phi Delta Kappan* 60, No. 4 (December 1978): 280–82.

SKENES, ROBERT E., and CAROLYN CARLYLE. "CAL Community School— Small, Rural, *and* Good!" *Phi Delta Kappan* 60, No. 8 (April 1979): 589–93.

STOOPS, EMERY. *Report of the Study, Title III, ESEA.* Sacramento, Ca.: State Department of Education, 1970.

WILSON, ROBERT E. *Educational Administration.* Columbus, Ohio: Charles E. Merrill Publishing Co., 1966.

CHAPTER FOUR

The School District's Role in Education

The local school district is the level at which the education of students takes place. It is influenced by state laws and the will of its electorate. Although districts vary in size and organization, they function under similar policies adopted by the local board of education. An administrative staff is necessary to administer each school district and to carry out the rules and regulations of the school board. Sound, board-adopted policies are needed to help with problems such as teacher militancy, community involvement, and integration.

School districts are defined as local, independent governments which administer a system of public education, within a prescribed geographical area. School districts are usually politically autonomous and fiscally independent. This independence was originally provided to free the schools from subservience to partisan governmental bureaus and agencies. It is still treasured by almost all educators for this reason.

The local district has certain advantages. It preserves the flavor of American frontier democracy and sturdy independence. It renders the schools quickly responsive to sudden changes in the manners and morals of the citizenry that supports them. By closely identifying the schools with the community, it compels educators to associate with the lay public more frequently and intimately. By placing control in the hands of lay boards, the local district system theoretically ensures immediate and lasting interest in school affairs by the general public from whose ranks board members are periodically selected. The solution to many problems posed by modern methods of district organization probably lies in the direction of synthesis and compromise between the demands for increasing efficiency and support, and the desire for local independence.

A Satisfactory Administrative Unit

It is impossible to classify rigidly the 150 types of legally authorized school districts found in the various states. No state has succeeded in abolishing the district system, although a good many have made considerable progress toward combining and streamlining their districts. In thirty-five states, so-called "basic" and "intermediate" units are involved in the total picture of district organization. The basic units are operated locally by elected boards, and usually constitute local taxing units as well. In Hawaii, the entire state is administered as a single district.

It is generally agreed by educators that the greatest single handicap to educational progress and efficiency is the small, rural administrative unit, a relic of America's past. In addition to being improperly staffed and financed, these units waste millions of dollars annually, largely through inadequate personnel-pupil ratios.

Some time ago the Council of State School Governments developed some criteria for the ideal school district that still remain applicable. The Council stated that a properly organized school district should be able to provide the resources to offer a comprehensive program of education from kindergarten through high school, and to make provision for post–high school and adult education at a reasonable unit cost. It should be able to procure capable educational leadership and to maintain a competent, well-balanced staff of teachers, supervisors, and specialists; and it should be able to finance its school program and develop competent instruction at a reasonable cost. School buildings should be located so that minimum time is spent in transportation. The size of the district should be such that the people therein can exercise a knowledgeable vote in choosing the school board, in developing educational programs for all age groups, and in expressing their ideas regarding planning and policymaking.[1]

With these standards in mind, and knowing that a considerable number of the states have a majority of school districts employing nine teachers or less, it is easy to conclude that such standards are far above those of the existing state organizations. Only through a long-range program of extensive district reorganization can modern school services be offered to the majority of American children with any degree of efficiency and economy.

School District Reorganization

The new interest in district reorganization is especially marked in rural areas. Most rural schools are unable to provide the educational program

---

[1] *The Forty-eight State School Systems* (Chicago: The Council of State Governments, 1949), pp. 51–2.

found in the more populated areas. Rural schools, on the average, pay their teachers a third less than do urban schools. The school year ranges from two to four weeks less than it does in the urban areas. It is difficult to avoid the conclusion that millions of children living in the great rural areas of our nation are being shortchanged educationally. Where pupil population is scattered and the tax base is low, equalization of educational opportunity is impossible without district reorganization. Such reorganization can be justified in two main areas: economy of operation and improved educational services.

ECONOMY OF OPERATION. With reorganization of school districts the taxpayer seldom gets the same education for less money; he usually gets better education for about the same price. On the basis of pupil-per-year costs, however, tremendous reductions in costs can be realized. The cost per pupil in small schools is very high compared with pupil costs in larger schools.

In many places, economies may be effected by reducing the number of unnecessary administrative positions, by better utilizing school buildings, by improving the use of teaching staffs, and by streamlining transportation and other auxiliary services.

IMPROVED EDUCATIONAL SERVICES. Unified or consolidated districts make possible a degree of teaching specialization unknown in the smaller districts. In high schools, especially, no one can be expected to teach in more than two subject fields competently. Some of the educational advantages found in the consolidation of unified districts include the following:

1. Every year of the child's learning experience in the public schools can be planned in a logical, sequential manner from kindergarten through twelfth grade.
2. Equality of basic educational opportunity may be more easily achieved in a unified district than in another type of organization.
3. A broader and more comprehensive educational program can be effected more easily and more economically. (This is not to say that school taxes will decrease, but rather that a complete program becomes more economically feasible.)
4. A more prudential use of funds is possible through the coordination that can be effected under a unified school district.
5. Community unity can be more easily attained when the citizens are concerned with one group of trustees, a single tax, a single bond issue, and one school system, than when they must be concerned with two or more school systems with separate issues. Community action to achieve the kind of school program desired by the people is also more practical.

6. There can be a much greater flexibility in developing a grade organization designed to meet the community's educational needs. For example, the potential for developing an effective junior high school organization for grades seven through nine is increased.
7. Better personnel policies and procedures are possible. For example, a single salary schedule is more practical in a unified district. Furthermore, teachers can more readily be assigned to the grade level in which they can work most effectively.

Criteria for Reorganization

STANDARDS FOR REORGANIZATION. It should be stressed that there is a vast difference between standards set up for administrative districts and those established for attendance areas. A modern city has only one administrative office, but operates many schools that are in effect attendance areas. While enlarging administrative districts may bring about some reduction in the number of schools, it will not affect the attendance areas of schools that are purposely large for the sake of efficiency.

Because conditions differ greatly throughout the country, each state should set up its own criteria for district reorganization. Such individual standards may well be judged by their conformity to the following general criteria:

1. The tax base of a district must be wide enough to carry whatever local educational load the state may decide is necessary, without unduly burdening local taxpayers.
2. District boundaries should be laid out to coincide wherever possible with natural community lines.
3. Districts should include enough population and pupil enrollment to allow for an adequate school program.
4. Long bus rides should be eliminated by proper reorganization. High school children should never have to ride more than one hour each way and elementary children not more than thirty minutes each way.
5. Districts should be as geographically homogeneous as possible.
6. Boundary locations should consider sociological aspects of the community wherever possible, especially when it is necessary to include within the district more than one community center.

The average size of the districts may range from a few square miles in some states to thousands of square miles in others. The number of districts per state ranges from fewer than twenty to thousands. There is such a variety of school organization that it is difficult to discern any pattern.

It is generally recommended that the ideal district, K–12 or K–14, include a minimum of 10,000 pupils. Exceptions to this size are made for smaller, relatively remote areas to provide for a potential of at least 2,000 K–12 students. The current size of the school district cannot be considered to remain static; every study should include an examination of the potential future enrollment for the area. This potential should include sufficient students for an adequate high school. Larger districts are also able to provide better facilities, administrators, educational specialists, and counselors. And they can provide more effectively an articulated educational program from kindergarten through high school or junior college.

When considering the size and boundaries of school districts, study groups should be urged to examine the curriculum requirements for a good high school, junior high school, and elementary school program. They should consider future changes and requirements that may affect the educational program. Education throughout the country must progress with the society in which it exists. Advances in energy, automation, and social progress should be included in the curriculum to provide the training necessary for modern society.

The Local School Board

Legislative groups exercising control over local school districts operate under various titles: board of education, board of trustees, board of school directors, or, simply, school board. These boards have a dual function. Primarily, they represent the people of the school district in the administration of the schools, but they also represent the people of the entire state, inasmuch as education is a delegated state function. The office of school board member differs nationally, but has certain common points. For example, the membership of such boards is composed of lay people who are representative of all classes of the population, rather than only business and professional groups. It was formerly thought that prominent businesspeople made the best school board members; indeed, such persons still make up a majority of the membership of school boards. Some people seek election to the school board as a stepping stone to a political career rather than for the more idealistic purpose of improving the education of children.[2] However, the tendency to select board members in accordance with their interest in the schools and their ability to serve intelligently is becoming well established. Wage earners and retired persons from all ranks of life are serving more frequently on America's school boards. Teachers and administrators can serve on school boards not in their own district.

School boards in most states are granted great authority by legislative action. Aside from ascertaining that school operation and personnel meet minimum state requirements, local boards exercise most of the details of

---

[2] Andrew W. Halpin (ed.), *Administrative Theory in Education* (New York: The Macmillan Company, 1967), p. 177.

management. These basic requirements usually deal with the teaching of certain subjects, the number of school days per year, standards of teacher certification, and minimum salaries. These are all "floor" requirements; there are no "ceilings" placed on local schools insofar as quality is concerned.

While a school board's legal powers may not be confined to legislative actions, in practice its judicial and executive powers are increasingly falling into disuse. The problem of executing board decisions, formerly tackled directly by the board itself, or, worse yet, by individual board members, is now placed in the hands of the superintendent and his staff. The growing complexity of school affairs makes it unwise and even impossible for the board to attempt to handle all the multitudinous details of administration, supervision, and finance. Most boards today confine the bulk of their activity to legislating, i.e., adopting policies and approving the means by which policies are executed. Examples of this legislative activity are providing for new buildings and equipment, employment of teachers, and adoption of textbooks.

There are still some school boards, however, that try to administer. As a group, or perhaps an individual or two, they may want a voice in every business or administrative procedure. This interference with the superintendent's functions should be discouraged.

Two other functions that closely accompany the legislative process are planning and appraisal. In the former, policies of the school system are carefully studied before being put into effect. This is usually done in close cooperation with the professional personnel employed by the district. Questions such as the legality, wisdom, and practicality of proposed board policies are examined during the planning phase of board legislation. Just as planning is a prelegislative phase of school board activity, so is appraisal a postlegislative one. Appraisal involves evaluation by the board of the work of the schools and the personnel employed to operate them. Because they are laypeople, they may not fully understand how to judge the effectiveness of the programs they have approved. "Under these circumstances, for the sake of the program and to protect his own hide, the educational administrator must become not only the executive but the teacher of the board of education."[3]

In the process of evaluation, the board must examine questions of whether or not the tax dollar is being well spent, whether the schools are turning out adequately educated persons, and whether any changes in any area are desirable. Both planning and appraisal are indispensable supplements to the school board's principal function—legislation.

School board members from all walks of life assume their duties with little conception of the complexity of their jobs, and with little pretraining. Continuing information and guidance are essential. In this connection,

---

[3] Halpin, *Administrative Theory*, pp. 177–78.

an excellent "creed" for school board members has been developed by Phi Delta Kappa, and may be obtained from that fraternity by a request directed to its national headquarters in Bloomington, Indiana.

STANDARDS FOR SCHOOL BOARD ORGANIZATION.   The school board should hold an annual organizational meeting between July 1 and July 15 of each school year. At this meeting it should:

1. Elect one member as president, one as vice-president, and one as clerk.
2. Designate the superintendent as its chief administrative officer.
3. Designate who should be the acting superintendent when the superintendent is out of the district.
4. Designate who shall sign all warrants.
5. Readopt all existing policies, publications, rules, and regulations.
6. Adopt the school calendar.
7. Adopt the schedule of regular board meetings.

The superintendent as secretary to the school board should be directed to:

1. Prepare and handle the board agenda.
2. Prepare and handle board minutes.
3. Handle all official district and board correspondence.
4. Attend all board meetings.[4]

The board should act as a united committee on all matters coming before it; i.e., no member is ever given authority to act as an individual on behalf of the board. All actions are taken only in legally called board meetings and board members serve as such only at board meetings. Meetings are presided over by the president, conducting them in accordance with generally accepted rules of order. Newly elected or appointed members should be oriented to board procedures prior to beginning their term of office.

Board members should be encouraged to attend annual conferences of their state and national school board associations. These conferences enable board members to share ideas, discuss mutual problems with board members from other districts, broaden their outlook, and keep up to date on educational problems and trends.

THE SCHOOL BOARD AND THE INSTRUCTIONAL PROGRAM.   Governing boards seldom give sufficient time to the instructional program, as discovered by many surveys and research studies.

---

[4] Irving R. Melbo et al., *Report of the Survey, South San Francisco Unified School District* (Los Angeles: University of Southern California, 1967), p. 94.

From these studies it is significant to note that only 7 percent of the time of the governing board was given to curriculum and instruction, contrasted with 11 percent for general functions, 25 percent for personnel, and 20 percent for school plant concerns. It is recommended that close to 50 percent of the board's attention be given to matters concerning better instruction and guidance for pupils. At least one board meeting a month should be devoted more or less exclusively to curriculum items.

Powers of the Local School District

With a few exceptions, the local school district is independent of all other branches of government that operate at stratums lower than the state level. It is answerable only to the people of the district and to the state department of education, in that order. In most states, local control is virtually absolute. The local district must rely, of course, on other governmental bodies to perform certain necessary functions (such as tax collection), but its control within its own area is indisputable. Indeed, because the school district is a creature of the state, it may actually take precedence over certain nonstate local governmental bodies whenever a conflict of authority occurs in an uncharted area of the law.

The state has given the local board of education powers necessary to do whatever is needed to conduct the schools, to secure land for school purposes, to enter into contractual obligations, to levy taxes, and to employ personnel. Teachers and administrators are actually exercising board authority in the areas of their assigned duties; this authority is legitimately delegated, unless specifically prohibited by statute. How much they share in the responsibility of operating the public schools is determined by the pleasure of the board.[5] In any proper field of educational activity, school district employees act with full state authority, because powers and duties delegated to them by the local board originally stemmed from the state.

In all but a few states, school districts are immune from suit, although they are liable for tort. The theory behind this immunity is twofold: first, the district, in sharing the authority and responsibility of the state, also shares the state's traditional immunity to suit; second, such immunity guarantees that school funds shall not be diverted to the paying of judgments which, regardless of their equity, would perforce be noneducational in nature. This immunity to suit does not, of course, extend to school employees, who are often proceeded against in court. Even in this case, the authority delegated to teachers stands up against most types of legal action. The teacher, under common law, may do anything with, for, or to a child that the child's own parents may do, including disciplinary

---

[5] Halpin, *Administrative Theory*, pp. 176–77.

action; the courts have ruled this is fair as long as the punishment is not excessive. The teacher stands, in fact, *in loco parentis*, and has such broad powers in this connection that it is permissible to exert authority during hours when school is not in session, and away from school property.

The federal government and state legislatures and boards of education are moving into areas traditionally reserved to local districts. This is due to the hesitancy of local boards in acting on programs that are of state and national interest, such as integration, vocational education, and programs for disadvantaged children. In an attempt to equalize the educational opportunities for all youth, federal and state governments are charting procedures that will accelerate the introduction or implementation of new programs.

The legal structure of the school district may be defined as a school board gifted with both permissive and mandatory authority by the state government, and subject to the state's authority within the framework of legislation setting forth its powers and limitations. The school board is also subject to local community control through the regular election of its members. Its authority is exercised largely through the professional employees of the district, but also by the board itself in legal session. The proper use of these great powers is dependent upon the election of upright and conscientious board members, and, in turn, upon their delegation of authority to able and alert teachers and administrators. When one or the other of these two factors is tampered with, the powers of the local district may quickly be perverted to evil or foolish uses, and may do as great harm as they are capable of doing good.

Written Rules and Regulations

School districts and boards that operate within the framework of a written policy handbook are less apt to be accused of abuses of power. Some city districts have written rules and regulations; few rural ones do. A policy handbook, adopted by the board on the basis of recommendations put forth by the superintendent, outlines administrative procedures and relationships in addition to codifying and systematizing previously adopted board policy. It enables each employee to know his or her functions, thus fixing responsibility. New employees benefit particularly, and the training of inexperienced personnel is facilitated.

Board rules and regulations should be formulated jointly by the board of education, school administration, and the teacher or noncertificated organizations. Those that affect personnel are arrived at by negotiation and collective bargaining. They should be in accord with state laws. When final agreement is reached, the board should officially adopt the rules and regulations as policy and distribute them to all employees. Periodic, perhaps annual, reviews should be made and changes incorporated as necessary. See chapter 19 for further discussion of the negotiation process.

BOARD MEETING AGENDAS.   Written agendas should be prepared by the superintendent's office, distributed to board members prior to the regular meeting date, and followed during the meeting. They should include all anticipated business, arranged in proper order under such headings as "Reports," "Old Business," or "New Business." They may also include pertinent enclosures, such as correspondence, financial reports, and lists of outstanding bills, duplicated and attached to the main body of the agenda. In general, there should be *action* items, *study* items, and *information* items. The distribution of an agenda several days prior to the meeting will afford ample time for consideration by board members, and will save valuable time at the meeting itself.

STANDARDS FOR SCHOOL BOARD MINUTES.   School board minutes are extremely important as the official record of all board proceedings and actions. They must be meticulously kept as no expenditure can be made unless shown as approved by the board. Many actions taken by school boards, even though not adopted as official policy, are expected to be followed as if they were policy.

Minutes become official after approval by the board, with corrections, if necessary. They should then be available to the public and all personnel.

Melbo has developed standards for school board minutes to serve as a guide to superintendents and school boards. These are shown in Table 4–1.

ADMINISTRATIVE RELATIONSHIPS.   Every school district of any considerable size should prepare an organizational chart showing administrative relationships, school positions, and interrelationships of various parts of the school organization. Such a chart makes it possible to see in outline the entire school organization, and to detect any weaknesses, such as overlapping authority.

A large district cannot operate effectively without such a chart; a smaller district may improve its efficiency by preparing one. The chart is a visual supplement to a policy handbook with the added advantage of being instantly intelligible to lay persons interested in the schools.

The illustrated organizational charts should serve only as models. The basic philosophy, size, and amount of money available to employ administrators and support personnel affect the organizational plan. Although only line relationships are shown, each division should have its own organizational pattern showing the breakdown of each position as well as staff relationships. Medium-to-large-size districts could be those with twelve or more schools. Figure 4–1 is an organizational chart for a

TABLE 4–1.   Standards for School Board Minutes

STANDARD	PERFECT SCORE
I. CONTENT: BOARD PROCEDURES (150 Points)	
The minutes should show:	
1. The date of each meeting	10
2. The place of each meeting	10
3. The type of each meeting: regular adjourned, or special	10
4. Members present, by name	10
5. Members absent, by name	10
6. The call to order	10
7. The arrival of tardy members, by name	10
8. The departure of members, by name, before adjournment	10
9. The date and place of the next meeting	10
10. The adjournment of the meeting	10
11. Record of written notice for special meetings	20
12. Record of all items of business to be considered shown in agenda	20
13. Post agenda as required by law for meetings	10
Subtotal	150
II. CONTENT—BOARD ACTIONS (700 points)	
The minutes should show:	
*1. The approval, or amendment and approval of the minutes of the preceding meeting	30
2. Complete information as to each subject of the Board's deliberations	40
3. Complete information as to the action taken on each subject	30
a. The maker and seconder of the motion	10
b. The vote on the motion	10
c. A roll-call record of the vote on a motion if not unanimous	10
4. All Board resolutions	XX
a. In complete text	30
b. Numbered serially for each fiscal year	10
5. A record of all contracts entered into	40
6. All employments and resignations or terminations of employment	50
7. A record, by number, of all purchase orders approved	50
8. A record of all bid procedures	XX
a. Calls for bids authorized	10
b. Bids received	10
c. Bids let, or other action taken	10
9. A record, by number, of all warrants issued	30
10. Adoption of the annual budget	30
11. Periodic financial reports, as required	20
a. Transfers of funds from one budgetary classification to another	10
b. Collections received and deposited	10
c. Sales of personal property	10

TABLE 4–1.   (Continued)

STANDARD	PERFECT SCORE
12. The salary schedule for the current year	30
13. A record of all important correspondence	30
14. A record of superintendent's reports to the board	30
15. Approval of all policy documents, such as a course of study, board policies, etc., prepared for district use	50
16. A record of all delegations appearing before the board	30
17. Adoption of the annual school calendar	30
18. Approval of duties of school employees	50
Subtotal	700

III.   FORMAT (100 points)

STANDARD	PERFECT SCORE
1. The minutes should be typewritten on single sheets of durable white paper	10
2. Pages should be numbered serially for each fiscal year	10
3. Pages should be entered in a heavy loose-leaf type binder	10
4. Each item of business in the minutes should have a brief topical heading, preferably in the left-hand margin	10
5. Each item of business should be entered as a separate paragraph, or a series of paragraphs	10
6. All motions should be numbered consecutively for each fiscal year; the number of the motions should appear at the left of the first line recording the motion or below the topical heading	10
7. An index of the minutes should be prepared for each fiscal year	10
8. All minutes should be signed by the proper officers of the board	10
9. A duplicate set of minutes should be kept	10
10. Documents which are made a part of the minutes by Board action should be included in the minute books or Board reports	10
Subtotal	100

IV.   HANDLING OF MINUTES (50 points)

STANDARD	PERFECT SCORE
1. The original minutes book should be secured in a fireproof file, safe or vault in the district offices	10
2. The duplicate set should be kept in the district office in a designated place where it is readily available for inspection	10
3. A copy of the minutes should be sent to each board member prior to the next meeting	15
4. The superintendent should be responsible for recording and preparation of the minutes	15
Subtotal	50
Grand total	1,000

Source: Irving R. Melbo et al., *Report of the Survey, South San Francisco Unified School District* (Los Angeles: University of Southern California, 1967), pp. 101–103.
* Not required at special meetings.

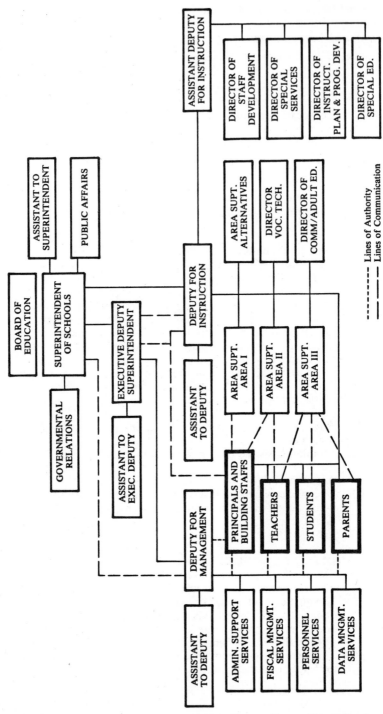

FIGURE 4–1. Organization of a Medium-to-Large-Size School District. Courtesy of St. Louis Public Schools.

medium-size school district. The organizational chart for a small district (with fewer than twelve schools) is shown in Figure 4–2. Because there are many districts with an enrollment of 1,000 or less, some of the positions shown in the figure may be combined.

Districts that plan to show organizational relationships should involve representatives from every school and department, certificated and noncertificated. Decisions must be made as to whether the chart should be developed on a "position" or a "function" basis or a combination of both. Positions require a title and a name connected with it. Functions are more nebulous and are difficult to chart; they also must have some designation of "who" is responsible for carrying out the function. Examples of categorized functions are: services, assessment and evaluation, research, staff development, curriculum planning, and management. "Lines of authority" are usually indicated by a solid line, and "lines of communication" or "staff relationships" are usually shown by dashed lines. Because there are many communication and staff relationships, it is usually impossible to show all of them without cluttering up a chart.

The organizational plan that is agreed upon should be operable and clearly understood by the personnel and the public. When adopted by the board of education, it should be adhered to until revised.

The Superintendent and Staff

The superintendent should be an instructional leader. Instruction is the only reason a school district has for existing. It follows, then, that all other school functions of whatever nature are simply supporting and facilitating activities. They are not independent, nor are they justified in their own right; they exist solely to maximize the instructional program. It is desirable that these functions be coordinated under a central administration in such a way that the efforts of the many individuals in the system will be exerted effectively toward a common goal.

Although there are many patterns of organization extant, the following criteria for good school organization can be applied against any or all of them.

1. The pattern of organization should be clear. It is essential that its structure be easily understood by those working within it.
2. It should be unobtrusive. Any organizational pattern that attracts attention is poor. It exists as an aid, never as a goal in itself.
3. It should facilitate instruction. Organization is subordinate to instruction, and should never restrict or impede it.
4. It should possess rapid and facile multiple-way communication.
5. It should be flexible. School district organization should be able to

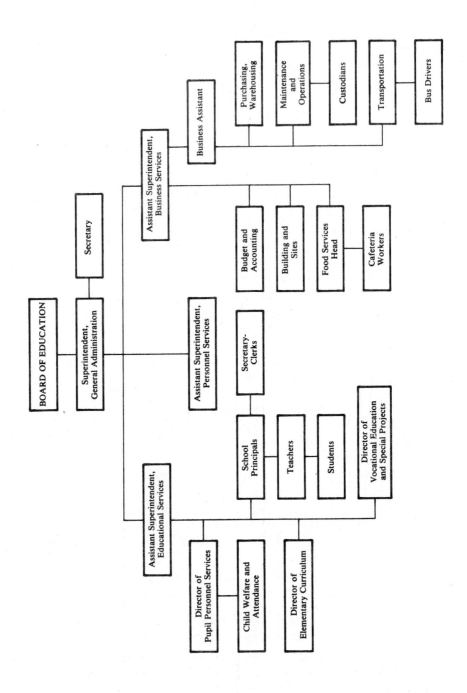

FIGURE 4–2. *Organization of a Small School District. Courtesy of Azusa Unified School District (Adapted).*

accommodate itself to the differing abilities and aptitudes of those who operate the schools.

6. It should be both integrated and composed of semiautonomous departments. Operating from a central headquarters, insofar as policy and philosophy are concerned, district organization should also feature self-sufficient divisions capable of acting independently if the need arises.

7. It should fix responsibility in terms of each person in the organization.

In most instances, school districts are small. In such districts, it may be expected that the organization will be composed of the superintendent and the clerical staff. The clerical staff, even in small districts, should be large enough to free superintendents from all office details and enable them to spend their time on policy-level matters. In this type of arrangement, it is necessary to organize the training and supervision of the clerical staff in such a way that the office work will be simple, efficient, and adequate.

In larger districts, the second officer of the administrative structure is an assistant for business affairs; the title of this person may be business manager, assistant superintendent, or director of business. This position should always be clearly subordinate to that of the superintendent of schools.

The employment of a director of curriculum is usually the next step in the creation of a district's administrative structure. This specialist is employed to direct supervisory activities, advise in the employment of teachers, and work generally toward the improvement of instruction. Large systems also may employ an assistant director or assistant superintendent of instruction. The superintendent, of course, retains basic responsibility for these phases of the school program; but with the addition of these assistants, it is possible to spend more time on supervision and overall coordination.

The third assistant should assume the management of employed personnel, both certificated and classified. Selection, retention, and separation, with all attendant functions, determine the duties and responsibilities of this staff person.

Districts of considerable size usually employ officers such as guidance director, health officer, library director, audio-visual coordinator, cafeteria supervisor, transportation officer, adult education director, pupil personnel director, and special services director. Research and special services have become so important that it is not unusual for large or medium-size districts to have an assistant superintendent or director in charge of these divisions. An administrator may also be placed in charge of communication and public relations. School districts participating in many federal programs have found it necessary to employ an administrator to handle them.

A good superintendent attempts to bring the organization together as tightly as possible, and to avoid the necessity of personally managing many varying facets of the educational program. The superintendent makes each director or supervisor responsible to one of the assistant superintendents. Coordination does not necessarily mean central control over multitudinous specific functions; rather, it should be a wise combination of all district activities in a common drive toward desired educational objectives. Regular conferences of key personnel and cooperative planning bring about coordination without rigid controls.

Organizational Adjustment to Local Conditions

The neighborhood in which a particular school is located should govern, at least partially, the educational activity of that school. Therefore, sufficient freedom under the organizational plan of the district should be made possible in order that each school may carry on educational activities suited to its individual environment. Such an organizational framework necessitates a building principal who knows how to make decisions and how to lead. Teachers willing to assist in a democratic organizational setup are also a necessity if such flexibility of control is to be a success. Supervision and administration emanating from the central office of each district should be aimed at improving the ability of the individual schools to exercise autonomy effectively.

Small elementary schools are characteristically staffed as follows: a teaching principal, a part-time school nurse, one teacher for each grade, and certain "shared" specialists, such as music teachers or art instructors. Clerical assistance is usually not provided; the principal, unfortunately, often spends much time doing routine paper work, and teachers are not assisted appreciably in clerical and recordkeeping tasks. Larger elementary schools may have sufficient office personnel to provide such assistance for teachers.

High schools are more often large, and consequently tend to be smaller editions of the district-wide organizational pattern. The high school principal is a nonteaching executive, often with a vice-principal or similar subordinate to assist, and with boys' and girls' counselors and an adequate clerical staff.

A school principal exists primarily to facilitate the education of children and should be freed as much as possible from routine tasks and the administration of clerical duties. Some of the many roles a principal must play are:

The manager of the school.

An agent of educational change.

The educational leader of the school community.

The evaluator, supervisor, and instructional leader of the school.

The school's innovator, expediter, morale builder, facilitator, and organizer.

The provider of specific information for long-range planning and development, implementation of programs, and evaluation.

The principal's instructional role requires refined technical, human, and organizational skills. The principal is in the center of communication activity among the school board, superintendent, teachers, students, parents, community, other school personnel and administrators, and the curriculum.

In order to accomplish these multiple demands, principals must establish priorities that enable them to give direction and emphasis to their activities. Principals and teachers must work cooperatively toward solving problems in all areas of the educational program. Teachers are qualified by professional training to help fashion the learning programs to meet the needs of all students. Those whose lives and work are affected by decisions must have a voice in arriving at those decisions. Along with the school staff, members of the community and students should be involved in developing educational goals and objectives for their schools. The assessment of success is based on the degree to which objectives are met.

In order to work cooperatively together, the principal must schedule meetings and conferences in which all members participate equally. However, the principal should act as the leader to keep discussions under control to achieve the desired ends of the meeting. The principal can also establish committees to work on specified projects or problems and to make recommendations regarding their implementation. Each committee should have a faculty member as a leader. In large schools, the principal may organize a faculty cabinet to serve as a type of executive board. As representatives of the teachers, the cabinet can help make decisions as to what should be brought to the attention of the entire staff and can save time by helping the principal make routine decisions. The cabinet also can act as a sounding board for the principal.

The autonomy of each school should be set forth in written policy statements developed by the board of education together with the staff and faculty. Certain rules and regulations should apply to all schools in the district, such as length of the school day, and the selection, assignment, and transfer of teachers. Separate schools should retain considerable freedom of action in areas such as instruction, scheduling, discipline, student government, staff professional growth and development, and faculty meetings.

In the field of finance, individual school autonomy does not apply. Central purchasing and deposit of all school monies is a highly efficient practice, and should be conducted on a district-wide basis. The position of each school as a neighborhood agency of education, organized and intended to meet local neighborhood needs as well as the broader district standards of education, should be safeguarded at all costs.

Patterns of School Organization

It is presumed that in each district individual schools will be organized so that the education of the children may be most fruitful and most economically managed. The presumption is somewhat optimistic; no one seems to have discovered the best scheme for school organization. It is unlikely that there is just one best way, for it is possible to have good schools and good schooling under different structures. What is best for one community may not be best for another; and within a single school system, schools with different internal organizations may have comparable achievements.

New organizational plans arise because of dissatisfaction with the concept of the self-contained classroom in which thirty to thirty-five students are taught by one teacher, with little attention given to individual differences. Any new organizational system should be planned carefully; it should have a goal of meeting educational needs of individuals more completely than the previous organizational structure. Poor planning usually results in the failure of the program. Schools may change the name of their organizational pattern, but make few changes in point of view, program, or structure. The success of any instructional organization will depend upon the extent to which the community, teachers, students, and administrators are involved in the planning, implementation, and evaluation of the program.

Vertical Organization

Vertical organization is based on the idea of promotion or movement upward either by grades or levels. School grade organization from very early times in this country has followed a traditional 8–4 pattern. The four-year high school originally was superimposed upon the existing eight-year grammar school; today, most small city districts and most town and village school systems are organized on this pattern. Kindergarten is often added at the lower end of the educational ladder to complete the organizational picture.

The introduction of the junior high school to American education prior to World War I served to break the universality of the 8–4 pattern.

Larger city school systems are more apt to follow a 6–3–3 plan (the middle number represents a three-year junior high school). The junior high school was originally developed to better serve the children of early adolescence. With this goal in mind, and also to bridge the social and psychological gap existing between elementary and senior high schools, the junior high was set up as an intermediate institution. In many instances, it has become a subject-matter-oriented, departmentalized small edition of a typical high school that has not always served the purpose for which it was developed.

To solve this problem, some districts have moved to a middle-school concept with a 5–3–4 structure. Middle-school advocates reason that because students are now maturing at an earlier age, sixth graders work better with seventh and eighth graders, and ninth graders perform better in a four-year high school. The middle school can be truly transitional.

There are many different plans in effect employing almost every conceivable combination of grades, although it is generally agreed that groups should not be too small. The most common examples of grade organization are: 6–3–3, 8–4, 6–6, and 6–2–4. There is less uniformity today than a few generations ago, when most school systems were of the 8–4 type. Kindergartens have been added and in many school districts there are nursery schools or preschools. At the upper end, junior colleges are being added at a rapid rate. In some cases, junior colleges are dropping the word "junior" as they attempt to become small colleges.

GRADED PLAN.   In the typical graded plan, each grade is grouped according to age in a self-contained classroom. The emphasis is on subject-matter achievement. Other types of vertical organization have been developed because differences in ability and accomplishment within any age group or grade have been recognized.

MULTIGRADING.   Multigrading provides for individual differences by grouping children from two or three sequential grades. Grade labels are kept, preventing a sharp break with tradition. Multigrading focuses on the learner's needs rather than on grade-level standards.

NONGRADING.   This is an organizational concept that received its impetus from John Goodlad.[6] It is based on the premise that every grade has a spread of academic achievement. It is similar to multigrading except that grade labels are removed and children are grouped for instruction according to their ability or achievement rather than by age. The nongraded class is usually in a self-contained classroom and is taught by one teacher. However, instruction is individualized and learner centered. Students

---

[6] John I. Goodlad and Robert H. Anderson, *The Nongraded American School.*

progress at their own rate. Nongrading requires changes in grouping practices, grading practices, curriculum content, methodology, and instructional materials. For nongrading to be successful, the teacher must diagnose and prescribe for individual students so that they receive instruction directed to their particular needs.[7]

Nongrading has been used in junior and senior high schools. Melbourne High School and Nova High School in Florida started nongrading early in the 1960s. Grade lines are eliminated, instruction is based on individual abilities, aptitudes, skills, and interests, and exploration is encouraged. Classes may be large or small. There has been some controversy, however, regarding the claims for success of nongrading at the secondary level.

CONTINUOUS PROGRESS.   Continuous progress is a variation of nongrading or multigrading. Children are neither promoted nor retained and there are no age levels. Bright pupils move ahead to more difficult tasks, while slower pupils are given more time to learn difficult concepts. Each pupil may work at different levels in various subjects, moving as rapidly or slowly as his ability permits. He may remain in a lower block an extra year after conferences with parents and the child.

EDUCATIONAL PARKS.   Educational parks are a total educational facility.[8] Their vertical organizational plan consists of an elementary school, a middle school or a junior high school, a high school, and in some cases, a college, all of which are grouped on a single site. An educational park can provide for better integration of children from different backgrounds, economy of operation, shared facilities, courses, and personnel, and improved community services. Shared educational facilities can include auditoriums, language labs, gymnasiums, and instructional materials centers that can be connected to a computerized teaching and information center. The problem of establishing an educational park is the size of the area needed, the number of buildings and facilities, additional busing, and the large original cost. Some fear a loss of student identity because of the size of the educational complex. And logistics can become an administrative headache.

STUDENT PROMOTION.   The vertical organization of a school district requires some method of moving students upward through the various grades. The promotion policy must explain the basis on which a student is promoted to the next higher level. Several principles concerning promotions

[7] Marian Pope Franklin, *School Organization: Theory and Practice*, p. 5.
[8] Frederick Shaw, "The Educational Park in New York: Archetype of the School of the Future?" *Phi Delta Kappan*, pp. 329–31.

that were proposed by the Department of Superintendence of the National Education Association are still pertinent today.[9]

1. Promotion should be decided on the basis of the individual pupil.
2. Promotion should be on the basis of many factors. The final decision as to whether a particular pupil should be promoted should rest not merely on academic accomplishments, but on what will result in the greatest good to the all-around development of the individual.
3. In order that promotion procedures may be more or less uniform throughout a particular school system, a definite set of factors should be agreed upon which each teacher will take into consideration in forming his judgment as to whether or not a particular pupil should be promoted.
4. Criteria for promotion must take into consideration the curriculum offerings of the next higher grade or unit and the flexibility of its organization, its courses of study, and its methods.
5. It is the duty of the next higher grade or unit to accept pupils who are properly promoted to it from the lower grade or unit and to adapt its work to fit the needs of those pupils.
6. Promotion procedures demand continuous analysis and study of cumulative pupil case history records in order that refinement of procedure may result and that guesswork and conjecture may be reduced to a minimum.

The school district must make decisions as to whether promotion is based on a grade average, number of subjects passed, chronological age, social maturity, or combinations of these or similar factors. Some of the common types of promotion policies that have been used are:

1. Continuous plan. All students are promoted regardless of achievement.
2. Double promotion. Especially bright or mature students are promoted two grades, skipping one.
3. Trial promotion. Students who have not achieved academically are promoted to the next level on a trial basis. If not successful, they are returned to their former grade.
4. Nonpromotion. Students who fail are not promoted. It is generally agreed that students should be retained only once, usually in the first grade.

Schools have used various plans to help students achieve educational success. Some of these plans are: parallel course of study, nongraded

---

[9] *Five Unifying Factors in American Education*, Ninth Yearbook of the National Education Association, Department of Superintendence (Washington, D.C., 1931), pp. 18–20.

classrooms, homogeneous grouping, ability grouping, cluster grouping, and combination grades. There are some educators who believe that a non-graded organization or an individualized approach offers the best alternative to the concept of retention and promotion because these plans prevent the stigma and discouragement that usually follow retention. However, research has not shown conclusively that any one method is better than another. It is known, however, that students who are retained seldom achieve more and sometimes achieve less in the year of retention. Good teachers will teach a child at his individual level and take him as far as possible, regardless of where he is in relation to the average of a given grade. Students who have been retained in a grade should be given every opportunity to make up their deficiencies and rejoin their normal grade or peer group. When grade adjustments are made, parents should have a conference with the teacher, the counselor, and the principal so that an understanding is reached. The parents' attitude in accepting a grade adjustment must be considered if the change is to be successful. The emotional and psychological attitude of the student is equally important.

Promotion is particularly important in the secondary schools. Colleges and universities are interested in the secondary-level academic achievement of students because they base their prediction of college success on high school success. Employers are more likely to employ those who have been regularly promoted and graduated. Nonpromotion and failure in secondary school is a major cause for dropping out and for delinquency. However, a student who fails to master a subject because of deliberate failure to apply himself leaves the teacher with little recourse.

Horizontal Organization

Horizontal organization divides students into groups and assigns them to classes, subjects, or teachers. The traditional form of horizontal organization is the elementary-level, self-contained classroom wherein about thirty pupils of about the same age are taught by a single teacher, responsible for teaching all subjects. Today, there are few, if any, such classrooms. Subjects such as art, music, physical education, and sometimes science are taught by specialists. Modifications may be made in several ways. Individuals, groups, or the entire class may use a wide variety of facilities, equipment, and materials such as the instructional materials center, a multipurpose room, shops, or visit community agencies as the classroom extends beyond its four walls.

OPEN CLASSROOM.   The open classroom is based on the philosophy that a child learns in a random way, at his own pace, and through self-motivation.[10] Children work independently or in small groups where they share knowledge and skills. They have the freedom to move to any one of numerous interest centers in the room, to study, to work on projects, or to read. Tables in various arrangements replace desks. There are many objects, games, displays, and learning materials. Teaching machines, programmed-learning kits, typewriters, and other technological instructional equipment may also be in the room. Open-classroom programs are not yet numerous, although they have been used in Philadelphia, North Dakota, New York City, and California. Some secondary schools have developed the open-classroom concept, notably the Philadelphia Parkway Program, the "school without walls" that commenced in February 1969. The school's program goes beyond the school walls and utilizes many community resources. Chicago and New York are among other cities that have started using a secondary open-classroom program.

DEPARTMENTALIZED ORGANIZATION. This type is subject matter centered. Teachers teach the subject in which they are most qualified; students go to the class for a class period in that subject. This is the usual pattern at high schools. Some junior high schools are completely departmentalized, while others are self-contained or partially self-contained in the seventh and eighth grades, and only departmentalized in the ninth grade. Many elementary schools use departmentalization or semidepartmentalization, usually in the upper grades.

Modifications can be made in both self-contained and departmentalized organizational plans when students are grouped heterogeneously or homogeneously in grades or in subjects. Homogeneous grouping is based on achievement or ability. Each type of grouping has its proponents, but research is inconclusive as to which method is best.

TEAM TEACHING. Team teaching is an organizational arrangement at either the elementary or secondary level in which two or more teachers work together and share their collective skills and expertise in planning the instructional program and in evaluating instruction. Teams can be of different sizes and be responsible for up to 150 students, depending upon the number of teachers involved. In some cases, all may receive instruction by a teacher with special skills, and then break into small groups for further exploration. Each faculty team has a leader and a noncertificated aide who relieves teachers of clerical duties. Auxiliary or assistant teachers may help the team, particularly at the elementary level. Team teaching requires a different arrangement of space, adaptable rooms, and

---

[10] Henry S. Resnik, "The Open Classroom," *Today's Education* 60 (December 1971): 16–17, 60–61.

workrooms. Scheduling is flexible and at the secondary level, varying modules of time may be used instead of class hours.

Modular or flexible scheduling creates a less formal organizational structure.[11] Modules are small periods of time that can be combined to provide various period lengths. Laboratory classes can consist of several modules. The schedule is less regimented, permitting unscheduled time for students to explore their interests, and to participate in mini-courses and seminar classes. The program can be tailored to each student's needs, interests, and abilities.

Vertical and horizontal types of organization may have overlapping characteristics. For example, a nongraded vertical organization may utilize a horizontal team-teaching plan.

SPECIAL TYPES OF SCHOOL ORGANIZATION.   Alternative schools are being developed in some areas to meet the needs of disenchanted students who are or have been school dropouts or failures.[12] These schools are non-graded and heterogeneous; instruction is personalized and individualized. The student–adult ratio is kept low. Course titles, curriculum content, and methodology are less traditional. The purpose of an alternative school is to maximize self-motivation and help students develop a desire to learn and to develop self-reliance, initiative, resourcefulness, and creativity. Alternative schools have received much criticism.

Continuation high schools and alternative schools are organized to meet the unique needs of problem students and to furnish adult education.[13] Eligible students are those with discipline problems, excessive suspensions, or constant failure, those who are married or pregnant, or those who must work part-time. Instruction is individualized and counseling is intensive. Goals are short-term. Students have their programs individually tailored to fit their needs and interests, and teachers encourage students to develop responsibility.

School Size

Differences in school size are caused by population density, land availability, location (rural or urban), and the philosophy of the district. Although opinions differ and research is inconclusive regarding the optimum size for schools, they should be large enough to offer a rich and varied program to meet the varied needs of youth and to be administered

---

[11] Gordon Cawelti, "Does Innovation Make Any Difference?" *Nation's Schools*, pp. 60–63.

[12] Frederick S. Bock and Wanda Gomula, "A Conservative Community Forms an Alternative High School," *Phi Delta Kappan*, pp. 471–72.

[13] Robert E. Botts, "Will J. Reid: Profile of a Continuation High School," *Phi Delta Kappan*, pp. 574–76.

effectively, efficiently, and economically. Other factors that are more important than mere size are: facilities, equipment, attitude and qualification of the staff, interrelationships, and the educational programs that are offered. However, schools that are over 2,000 in enrollment may become unwieldy, overcrowded, and difficult to administer while those under 500 may be uneconomical and less apt to offer a rich and varied educational program. Secondary schools tend to be larger, elementary schools smaller, and junior high schools fall somewhere in between.

Principles of School Organization

There are principles of organization and administration which, while they may not be set down with complete exactness and finality, seem to be logical and justified in business and personnel administration; they should be kept in mind as good general rules to guide in the organization of school administration and supervision.

Priority should be given to establishing objectives rather than to machinery and personal considerations. Administrative responsibility should be assigned to various personnel since one person cannot oversee every detail of the district's operation. When responsibility is delegated to others, the authority to carry it out must also be given, and too often this is not the case. Delegated responsibility and authority must be co-ordinated to avoid conflicts of interest, overlapping duties, and sometimes personality or psychological differences. Lines of communication between every school and every office should be clearly defined and always kept open.

The following general principles of internal organization can be used as a guide in establishing an educational organizational structure:

1. A sound philosophy should provide the foundation for the structure of organization.
2. Principles of the structure of organization should be established and used in connection with any coordinated group endeavor.
3. No detail of structural organization should be set forth in law.
4. A statement of major aims and objectives should be developed as the basis of the structure of organization.
5. The structure of organization should precede endeavor or operation.
6. Structural organization should be constantly improved.
7. When the number of members exceeds reasonable limits of control and supervision, a new and separate unit of organization should be established, resulting in a multiple organization.[14]

---

[14] Ray W. Johnson, "Principles of Internal Organization for Public School Administration" (unpublished doctoral dissertation, University of Southern California, 1952).

Summary

Almost all states delegate their powers over the schools to local districts which are largely independent and highly responsive to the wish of the electorate. Such districts, once extremely numerous, are decreasing in number due to consolidation. Yet there are still too many small rural districts, many of them impoverished and incapable of offering an adequate instructional program. Various criteria for a viable school district are cited.

The proper functions of a good school board are set forth, stressing its main job of legislating. A suggested time schedule and agenda for board meetings is also provided. The powers of the local board are described in detail, and the need for detailed written policies and rules is emphasized. Standards for board minutes are provided.

Organizational charts are supplied to illustrate how staffing can be worked out for various-size districts. They help to clarify lines of authority and lines of communication. The role of a principal is explained.

The need for sufficient flexibility to meet local needs is very real, including patterns of grade organization. Various types of vertical and horizontal organizational plans are described. Alternative schools and continuation high schools have been developed to meet the special needs of some students who need a more flexible program than is provided in more traditional grade structures. There are, however, differing opinions regarding the most desirable size for schools.

Districts should establish sound principles of internal organization, based on an agreed-upon philosophy. The structure of the organization should be based upon the established major aims and objectives. There should be clear lines of communication between all parts of the district organization.

Administrative Problems

In Basket

Problem 1

Dr. Dunbar has just become the superintendent of Jefferson Unified School District which has fifteen elementary schools, two junior high schools, and one senior high school. He discovers that there are numerous conflicts regarding staff responsibilities. For example, the personnel director believes that he has the authority to assign teachers to schools, but the principals think that they should have a voice in selecting their staff. The business manager has developed the budget with little help from others, despite the fact that administrators, department heads, and even teachers want a strong voice in budget preparation. Dr. Dunbar requests an organizational chart showing administrative and department relationships, but finds that the only one available is ten years old and bears little resemblance to the present district structure.

What steps should Dr. Dunbar take to develop an up-to-date, practical chart that shows organizational relationships as they exist today?
What role should the Board of Education play?
When the chart has been developed, how should the superintendent use it to solve the present conflicts?

Problem 2

The Central Springs Board of Education spends most of the time at its meetings on business and administrative affairs. The Board attempts to have the superintendent get its approval before he makes administrative decisions and gives the appearance of not trusting the judgment of school administrators. The superintendent has been unsuccessful in having the Board spend more time on reviewing and adopting policies and approving the means for executing them, thus leaving administrative details to the administrators. The superintendent would also like to see the Board become more interested in matters concerning the improvement of instruction.

If you were the superintendent, how would you go about changing the thinking of the Board of Education?

Problem 3

Three new members have been elected to the Central Springs Board of Education on a platform pledging to seek to overhaul the outdated and irrelevant educational program of the district. They outnumber the holdovers from the old Board three to two.

What procedure should the superintendent use in working with the new Board of Education majority?
How involved should the Board get in district educational reform? In what way?

Selected References

BLITCHINGTON, W. P. "Administrative Personality: Elementary School Principals." *Phi Delta Kappan* 60 (February 1979):457.

BOCK, FREDERICK S., and WANDA GOMULA. "A Conservative Community Forms an Alternative High School." *Phi Delta Kappan* 54 (March 1973).

BOTTS, ROBERT E. "Will J. Reid: Profile of a Continuation High School." *Phi Delta Kappan* (May 1972).

CAWELTI, GORDON. "Does Innovation Make Any Difference?" *Nation's Schools* 82 (November 1968).

CONANT, JAMES B. *Recommendations for Education in the Junior High School Years.* Princeton, N.J.: Educational Testing Service, 1960.

COX, A., and S. WILSON. "If I Ran the School." *Education Digest* 44 (December 1978):36–38.

CZECH, J. "Time for Leadership Is Now." *National Association of Secondary School Principals Bulletin* 63 (February 1979):117–18.

DOUGLASS, HARL R. *Modern Administration of Secondary Schools.* Boston: Ginn and Company, 1954.

FRANKLIN, MARIAN POPE. *School Organization: Theory and Practice.* Chicago: Rand McNally and Co., 1967.

GARBER, LEE D. *Law Governing School Board Members and School Board Meetings.* Danville, Ill.: Interstate Printers, 1963.

GOODLAD, JOHN I., and ROBERT H. ANDERSON. *The Nongraded American School,* rev. ed. New York: Harcourt, Brace, & World, 1963.

HALPIN, ANDREW W. (ed.) *Administrative Theory in Education.* New York: The Macmillan Company, 1967.

MCLOUGHLIN, WILLIAM P. "Individualization of Instruction vs. Nongrading." *Phi Delta Kappan* 53 (February 1972).

MELBO, IRVING R., et al. *Report of the Survey, South San Francisco Unified School District.* Los Angeles: University of Southern California, 1967.

NATIONAL EDUCATION ASSOCIATION, Research Division. "Departmentalization in Elementary Schools." *NEA Research Bulletin* 44 (February 1966).

————. "Public School Programs and Practices." *NEA Research Bulletin* 45 (December 1967).

RESNIK, HENRY S. "The Open Classroom." *Today's Education* 60 (December 1971).

SHAW, FREDERICK. "The Educational Park in New York: Archetype of the School of the Future?" *Phi Delta Kappan* 50 (February 1969).

THOMSON, SCOTT D. "Beyond Modular Scheduling." *Phi Delta Kappan* 52 (April 1971).

TRUMP, J. "Successful Principals Receive Accurate Feedback." *American Secondary Education* 8 (December 1978):38–42.

UNGER, R. A. "School Principal and the Management of Conflict." *American Secondary Education* 8 (December 1978):43–48.

WRIGHT, GRACE S. *Enrollment Size and Educational Effectiveness of the High School.* Circular No. 732. Washington, D.C.: U. S. Office of Education, 1964.

CHAPTER FIVE

Role of
the Local School

Classrooms in local schools are where education takes place. The educational organization of the school district, the intermediate unit, the state department, and the U.S. Office of Education exist only to serve programs administered in local schools. Schools vary in size, quality, teaching staff, student body, community support, and educational programs. Yet all schools are alike in setting one overriding goal—to better serve and educate students. This better education molds not only better individuals but a stronger nation.

The Administrative Staff

In small elementary schools, the administrative staff may be limited to a principal, even a teaching principal. In larger high schools, the administrative staff is comprised of the principal, assistant principals, and many department heads and specialists who deal with subject areas and services.

THE ROLE OF THE PRINCIPAL. The principal is the key to a better educational program. Seldom, if ever, does the quality of an educational program rise above the competency of the building principal. The principal's leadership role draws all staff members like a magnet toward an improved educational program. Or sometimes the lack of leadership is a wet blanket that stifles teacher creativity.

In selecting a principal, the superintendent's office should disregard such characteristics as sex, race, economic status, community popularity, and politics. The superintendent and governing board should select a man or woman with adequate training, rich experience, and a burning desire to improve the educational program. The selection of the principal should be upon the basis of merit and merit alone.

The same high qualities of educational competency and leadership should be kept in mind when the principal recommends for selection assistant principals, psychologists, directors of child welfare and attendance, counselors, and department heads. Not only attained competency, but prospects of further professional growth should be considered. Students deserve the highest caliber of employed personnel at the building level.

TRAINING OF THE PRINCIPAL.   The principal's training should be comprised of general academic education, courses for teachers and administrators, practical experience, and as many other supportive experiences as possible. With respect to college training, about one-fifth of the principals in the United States had top training of the bachelor's degree or less at the beginning of World War II. Currently, few principals have less than the master's degree, and an increasing percentage have completed the doctorate. The trend is toward more and better academic-professional training.

It is generally assumed that principals are selected because they are master teachers. It is important not only that principals should have excelled in teaching skills, but that their teaching should have covered a range of grades, preferably kindergarten through high school. Primary teachers, for example, are more apt to accept supervision from a principal who has taught in the primary grades. Then if the elementary school principal has taught at secondary levels, he/she certainly has a better concept as to where students are headed, and can improve vertical articulation. It is just as important that secondary school principals should have had elementary school teaching experience.

Since the principal must function as a leader, organizer, communicator, arbitrator, disciplinarian, supervisor, and the like, it is important that the principal in training should have experience in business and industry and be well acquainted with the problems of parents. Principal candidates cannot have too much varied experience but many have too little.

FUNCTIONS OF THE PRINCIPAL.   Breadth of training has been recommended because the principal's function is both extensive and intensive. In general the principal must serve both as a line and as a staff officer. Final responsibility rests upon the principal as a line officer at the local school. As a staff officer, the principal takes primary responsibility as helper, stimulator, expeditor, and supervisor. There is a large element of conflict between the principal's function as teacher-helper and teacher-evaluator. Only a skillfully trained person can step easily and cautiously from one role to the other. This the principal must do.

In addition to being a classroom helper or a central office enforcer, the principal has to be many things. As a practical psychologist, the principal must be able to inspire teachers, motivate students, placate parents, and increase the productivity of custodians, clerks, and cafeteria workers.

As a business manager, the principal must prepare the school budget, control expenditures, supervise food service, administer equipment and supplies, direct the maintenance and operation of the school plant, account for student and employed personnel, and keep accurate and adequate records. In performing this business function, the principal must act in harmony with all policies and regulations of the board of education, the state department, the *Education Code*, and the federal government. The community expects a little common business sense too.

As an educational leader, the principal stands in the position of having to know more about teaching and learning than anyone else at the school. The principal has to know what should be taught, how to make the teaching most effective, when to evaluate the results, and the best way to interpret them to students and parents. Late research, changes in law, and instructional innovations keep the principal in a continuous process of trying to improve the school program. As educational leader, the principal must continue as a master teacher and stay one jump ahead of the instructional staff. This means that the principal is a teacher of teachers, an accomplished professional trainer.

In recent years, the principal's function as a public relations person has become increasingly important. Schools became larger after World War II so that parents and other citizens were more remote and harder to contact. The principal has had to give more time and attention to public relations; specifically, two-way communication has become a must for the building principal.

In addition to skill in handling people, instruction, business, and public relations, the successful principal has functions about as extreme as joy and calamity. The hidden pleasure of having the poorest teacher in the school retire may be offset when a faithful student with 20–400 vision falls over a carelessly placed bench and breaks an arm. Surprises, emergencies, and unexpected problems upset well-planned priorities to round out the principal's busy day.

Always, the principal must keep in mind the long-term goals and shorter-term objectives. All functions must be focused toward the bullseye goals. The evaluation of teacher performance, for example, is accomplished by judging the extent to which the teaching objectives have been achieved. Written assignments for every employee help to define duties and pinpoint goals and objectives. A good school program is goal oriented, and the principal's job is to keep attention upon the goals.

As a summary statement, the principal's functions should be listed as follows:

Formulating goals and objectives

Recruiting teachers

Revising the curriculum

Scheduling classes and other activities

Supervising instruction

Assigning students to classes

Handling equipment and supplies

Inspecting the physical plant

Providing for food service and transportation

Improving school–community relations

Providing for exceptional children

Formulating policies for discipline and behavior

Presiding at staff and community meetings

Improving vertical and horizontal communications

Counseling students and teachers

THE PRINCIPAL AS A GENERALIST. Some of the principal's ancillary functions are playground inspector, plant supervisor, legal authority, public speaker, community leader, organizer, rules formulater, report maker, substitute teacher, safety expert, and good listener. Any unusual incident at school such as dead guinea pigs, burst pipes, illegal drugs, and fights between custodians and maintenance crowd their way into the principal's office.

Location of Schools—Rural and Urban

American schools range all the way from an isolated seven-pupil classroom for Eskimos in the far away Aleutians to crowded ghetto schools in Chicago. Children trudge through the snow at Grand Forks while others peel oranges on their way to school at Brownsville. Both rural and urban schools present special problems for the principal and staff.

ADMINISTERING RURAL SCHOOLS. Rural schools tend to have small and unpredictable enrollments. In the small school, it is more difficult for the principal to take a heterogeneous range of children and divide them up into meaningful grade levels. Some classrooms may be overcrowded, but ordinarily the numbers are small. This factor greatly increases costs.

Many small schools throughout sparsely settled areas have been consolidated or unified as a means of providing enough students for effective teaching and for being efficient with school costs. The consolidations have solved some problems, but have created others such as snow-bound buses, lack of individual attention for students, estrangement of parents, and eroded discipline.

The principal in a rural school usually has more difficulty recruiting a well-trained staff. Most teachers, especially young singles, prefer the bright lights. Or married teachers may have to follow spouses to big city jobs. It is more difficult for the principal to secure specialists to help in inservice training. The opportunities for further training at colleges and universities are more distant.

The principal is further handicapped because the school system often lacks an adequate financial base. This means fewer needed supplies and lower salaries for teachers. Most rural areas are lacking in factories, big utilities, and shopping centers which yield more tax returns.

In spite of the fact that rural school administrators face special problems, these schools have historically been the intellectual cradle for the great men and women of America. Rural students have some advantages such as more freedom and smaller classes that their urban cousins lack. Individualized instruction can be more of a rural reality than an urbanized paper objective.

Some rural administrators prefer the challenge and elbow room of the rural school. Education becomes more personal. It is freed from much of the staff militancy, community pressure, and racial tension that characterize large city schools. A more relaxed school gives administrators more time to be with their families and to follow avocations.

THE URBAN SCHOOL. Urban schools have always had problems, but those problems peaked with student activism in the sixties. Tensions have lessened, but have continued in various types and amounts to the present. Metropolitan areas have always contained sizable populations from the lower socioeconomic levels. Racial problems have been more dominant in city schools.

The local school in large city systems has increased problems of staff communication, community relations, and student control. Faculty members live in scattered areas of the city, parents are more remote, and students lack social control when they are anonymous.

The large urban school does, however, have advantages in more adequate supply and equipment budgets, more highly trained teachers and more varied courses of study. The larger high schools possess multitrack curriculums. Certainly vocational students have far greater opportunities in the large urban schools. Children usually live closer to the school, and many come from homes that strongly encourage a better education.

Children in big urban schools tend to get lost in the crowd and to have identity problems. Parents have no way of knowing members of the board of education and sink into apathy. As a result, there has been a growing credibility gap which has been about inversely proportional to the growth of urban school systems. Bigness is not always better.

One solution that has been tried in New York, Chicago, and Los Angeles is decentralization. Theoretically, this brings back school control to local communities. But actually the experiments have been less successful than desired. Decentralization has been at its best where the schools have had strong principals. These strong principals have improved school–community relations to the extent that parents look upon the local school as representing or *being* the school system.

The large school systems, centralized or decentralized, have received large federal grants, more money for supplies, and beyond-average budget allotments for schools in disadvantaged areas. This extra attention has helped, but has not solved some of the most nagging problems. In some of the cities, faculties have been "integrated" by scattering racial complexion and forcing long drives through peak traffic. Students have been bused by court order to more distant schools.

This judicial invasion of public schools may or may not have sufficient cause, but it has destroyed legislative local control. Boards of education have become more and more a rubber-stamping committee, particularly in the urban school districts. There is mounting evidence that this tampering with local control is weakening the basic educational opportunities for children. Student achievement as measured by standardized tests still drifts lower in the big urban school systems. In some places where forced busing has caused "white flight" the local schools have become more racially segregated, and discipline problems have risen.

School principals realize that the key factor in learning is the attitude which the student brings to class. Urban principals and faculties are making greater efforts to work with parents so they will send their children to school with more positive attitudes. But since the courts have scattered teachers into remote communities, it is very difficult for them to achieve much in the way of community relations. They are looked upon as outsiders.

The wise principal can oftentimes turn some of the urgent problems of the urban schools into vehicles for greater student learning. This has been done in some areas where larger schools actually graduate a higher percentage of student enrollees than do smaller schools in rural areas. Competition in larger classes stimulates students toward greater learning.

Hamilton and Lowe found that high school graduates from the largest-class-size category obtained more advanced degrees than graduates from the smallest-class-size category.[1]

Even though urban schools have special problems, principals with creative imagination have made some of these schools showcases for the entire school system. These principals have insisted that individual students must be recognized, their interests explored, and their needs met. This has led to revisions in the curriculum, oftentimes preparing students better for job entry or for post–high school training. The principal and staff have become closely related with community projects and have involved parents and community leaders in the concerns of the school. As a result, these few showcase schools from Harlem to Watts have graduated students who are superior in vocations, academia, athletics, science, and the arts. The opportunities are greater because the problems are greater. Capable administrators and capable faculties *can* solve the problems of the urban schools. It can be done because it *has been* done.

Discipline—Staff and Students

Disciplined schools, football teams, and military units succeed. Undisciplined organizations fail. With discipline, success is possible. Without discipline, chaos is certain. Discipline and order lead to better learning. Unorganized chaos leads to educational disaster. No game can be played without rules; neither can a school or school system succeed without them.

WHAT IS DISCIPLINE? Discipline at school is ordered behavior that leads to better learning. Webster's definition of discipline is: "To develop by instruction and exercise; to train in self-control or obedience to given standards."

The principal must take leadership in setting up needed standards for the school and in making those standards known to all concerned. The principal must also take responsibility for helping faculty and students grow and improve in self-control. This process is development by "instruction and exercise" as the means of achieving greater learning.

Discipline is not punishment. Punishment is used as a corrective to restore disciplined behavior. Discipline comprises the sum of the rule book. Penalties are assessed only to maintain the sanctity of the rules, but are not a substitute for the rules.

Discipline is not inactivity or lack of noise. Classroom discipline is that type of behavior that best promotes learning. The type of discipline

---

[1] DeForest Hamilton and Robert N. Rowe, "Academic Achievement of Students in Reorganized Districts," *Phi Delta Kappan,* p. 402.

called for in a silent reading class is quite different from the type needed in the auto body shop where trip hammers are pounding out fenders. The classroom teacher is responsible for formulating and maintaining standards that will best enhance learning, just as the principal is responsible for formulating and enforcing the kind of procedures that will maintain the best learning atmosphere at the school level.

FACULTY DISCIPLINE.   School principals must first discipline themselves. The disciplined principal can then require disciplined behavior on the part of certificated and classified employees.

All employees should be at work on time, and prepared to accomplish their assigned tasks with a maximum of effectiveness. Since the principal is held responsible for the total school program, he or she has the right to assign, supervise, and evaluate the performance of each employee. The central office should in turn evaluate the principal upon such performance.

The people own the public schools, and taxpayers support their operation. It is reasonable then to expect that every salaried employee serve efficiently and behave in a disciplined manner. When the school staff sets an example of disciplined behavior, it is much easier to expect, and to get, disciplined behavior from students.

STUDENT DISCIPLINE.   Discipline has deteriorated in schools. This partial breakdown of discipline in our schools has resulted in increased vandalism (crimes against property) and violence (crimes against persons). Two lists of student behaviors reflect the seriousness of this breakdown in discipline. One great American educator listed misbehaviors in 1941 as "running in halls, chewing gum, making noise, wearing improper clothes, and getting out of turn in lines." The January 1978 *Phi Delta Kappan* reported a list of offenses in 8,000 schools as: rape, robbery, assault, personal theft, burglary, disorderly conduct, drug abuse, arson, bombings, alcohol abuse, and carrying weapons.

Not only have student behaviors gone from classroom distractions to felonious conduct, but brutalized behavior is being carried out by younger and younger criminals. More than 40 percent of the serious felonies are now being committed by the group we used to call children—youths under eighteen years of age. An increasing number of girls are now guilty of such crimes as assault and arson.

Vandalism alone is now costing American taxpayers between $600,-000,000 and $1,000,000,000 annually. An absolute figure is impossible since the costs of security guards, fire prevention devices, and the like may be included or excluded by some reports. This approximate cost, however, is more than we spend for textbooks and soft supplies.

Violence has wreaked havoc upon both teachers and students. A recent issue of the *U.S. News and World Report* claimed that more than

5,000 teachers are attacked on campus each month. The head of security in one large school district reported an estimate of one student death per week from violent assault.

WHAT CAN THE PRINCIPAL DO?   The principal dare not take a *laissez faire* attitude toward discipline. Problems of vandalism and violence will not go away. Even with the best of efforts, the incidence of these behaviors will be too great. Criminal acts cannot be completely eliminated, but they can be lessened. The following list suggests approaches that the principal can use:

1. Define carefully the causes of, and cures for, misbehaviors at the local school level.
2. Establish and continuously revise discipline policies.
3. Help teachers to set classroom standards of behavior as their first priority when school begins. These standards should be studied, reviewed, and published in written form for both students and parents.
4. The principal should work with parents as a means of getting them to send better-behaved students to school.
5. The principal should give strong support to every teacher who enforces behavior standards. Not only should the principal give strong backing, but should hold teachers responsible for upholding standards with students.
6. Teacher unions and professional organizations place "good education" as their number-one goal. The principal should call upon these organizations to assume leadership in improving student behavior.
7. Since the discipline problem is the concern of students, teachers, parents, and principal, the principal should represent these groups in asking for strong support from the central office and the board of education.

Summary

The local school district has top priority in importance because that is where student learning takes place. Schools vary widely in many aspects but all have one common goal, improved education.

Staffing differs from school to school, but in all, the principal is the key to successful instruction. Those responsible for selection should winnow out the applicants with the best training, experience, and personal qualifications. The chief qualifying attribute of the principal is a burning desire to educate better all students.

Principals, in addition to being master teachers, must function in many capacities such as in human relations, business management, curriculum development, inservice training, public relations, supervision, and community leadership.

Some principals administer small schools in rural areas while others serve on large metropolitan campuses. Both rural and urban schools have advantages and disadvantages. Principals who serve in rural areas are often limited by financial support and by inadequate educational programs. But in spite of these limitations, rural principals enjoy closer contacts with school supporters and are better able to understand the desires of staff and students. Urban principals may have more money to work with but find greater degrees of student and parent estrangement. Students are more apt to misbehave. On the positive side, greater student competition in more adequate programs can lead to higher averages of success. Yet achievement scores in large cities go down along with standards of discipline. The judicial system has undermined the school and district prerogative of local control.

Every principal knows that a good school is a disciplined school. From K–12 and from principal to custodian, all who attend schools must honor codes of conduct. These codes have been challenged by younger offenders who commit felonious rather than disruptive offenses. The principal can never eliminate misbehaviors, but can lessen infractions by enlisting the support of all concerned in the formulation and enforcement of reasonable rules of conduct. As schoolwide conduct improves, so should the scores on examinations.

Administrative Problems   In Basket

Problem 1

The Maple Leaf elementary school has just lost its venerable principal by retirement. The faculty, students, and community have looked upon "Prof" McFadden as Mr. Education for many years. He has left an indelible imprint upon the Maple Leaf school because of his good humor, burly appearance, simplified-basic-no-nonsense curriculum, and a glad hand for all parents. Maple Leaf has been a "personality" school with an unrevised and static set of procedures. The older faculty members have settled comfortably into their academic nests of security.

You are the superintendent:

What qualifications will you look for in the new principal to be selected?
When selected, will you advise changes? What kind? How many? When?

Problem 2

You have just finished your master's degree at the university and obtained your administration credential. Time off from teaching and tuition has depleted your budget, so you must seek a position. Your last assignment was assistant principal, so the director of placement tells you that your papers are strong and that you should try for a principalship. The director believes that your best chance for a principalship will be either in a small rural school where applicants will be few, or at some inner-city school. The director made this latter recommendation because you had taught three years in the so-called ghetto area. But competition for positions would be too keen for an inexperienced principalship candidate in the middle-class suburban schools.

Choose a typical small rural and an inner-city school. Now take two sheets with a divider line in the middle of each page. Write down all of the ADVAN-TAGES and DISADVANTAGES for each school.

Problem 3

You are the principal of Riverbank High School with an enrollment of 2,600. Railways, airplanes, and city traffic disrupt classroom instruction. Student attendance at your school is next-to-the-lowest among seventeen schools in the city. Drug abuse, gang fights, incidents in the rest rooms, theft, threats and an occasional assault upon teachers, clandestine smoking and drinking of beer, and one case of arson have plagued your school. Taxpayers have put heat on the board because of the costs of vandalism. The superintendent has channeled this heat to you. It's Easter vacation for the teachers and students, but the superintendent's memo has spoiled yours. He wants an authenticated list of the procedures you have used thus far to protect lives and property at your school; then he wants an additional list of procedures that you will follow to improve discipline further.

Write the list of your new proposed procedures.

Selected References

BLITCHINGTON, W. P. "Administrative Personality: Elementary School Principals." *Phi Delta Kappan* 60 (February 1979):457.

COX, A., and S. WILSON. "If I Ran the School." *Education Digest* 44 (December 1978):36–38.

CZECH, J. "Time for Leadership Is Now." National Association of Secondary School Principals *Bulletin* 63 (February 1979):117–18.

Education for the Urban Disadvantaged from Preschool to Employment. Washington, D.C.: Committee for Economic Development, 1971.

EPSTEIN, BENJAMIN. "Principals: An Organized Force for Leadership." Reston, Va.: National Association of Secondary School Principals *Bulletin* 58 (January-August 1974).

FLIEGEL, SEYMOUR. "Practices that Improved Academic Performance in an Inner City School." *Phi Delta Kappan* 52 (February 1971).

HAMILTON, DEFOREST, and ROBERT N. ROWE. "Academic Achievement of Students in Reorganized Districts." *Phi Delta Kappan* 43 (June 1962).

HAVIGHURST, ROBERT J. "The Reorganization of Education in Metropolitan Areas." *Phi Delta Kappan* 52 (February 1971).

HOLT, JOHN. "Why We Need New Schooling." *Look* (January 13, 1970).

HUMMEL, RAYMOND C., and JOHN M. NAGLE. *Urban Education in America: Problems and Prospects.* New York: Oxford University Press, 1973.

JACOBSON, PAUL B. *Principalship: New Perspectives.* Englewood Cliffs, N.J.: Prentice-Hall, Inc. 1973.

LEVINE, DANIEL U. "Concepts of Bureaucracy in Urban School Reform." *Phi Delta Kappan* 52 (February 1971).

MARTIN, BETTY. *Principal's Handbook on the School Library Media Center.* Hamden, Conn.: Gaylord Professional Publications, 1978.

RELLER, THEODORE. *Educational Administration in Metropolitan Areas.* Bloomington, Ind.: Phi Delta Kappa, 1974.

SHER, JONATHAN P. *Education in Rural America: A Reassessment of Conventional Wisdom.* Boulder, Col.: Westview Press, 1977.

STOOPS, EMERY and RUSSELL E. JOHNSON. *Elementary School Administration.* New York: McGraw-Hill Book Company, 1967.

STRANG, RUTH. *Education in Rural Communities.* Chicago, Ill.: University of Chicago Press, 1952.

WATSON, BERNARD D. "Rebuilding the System: Practical Goal or Impossible Dream?" *Phi Delta Kappan* 52 (February 1971).

WAYSON, WILLIAM W. "Organizing Urban Schools for Responsible Education." *Phi Delta Kappan* 52 (February 1971).

PART THREE

School Finance and Business Administration

CHAPTER SIX

Financial Support
of Public Schools

It takes money to educate children, and the cost keeps going up. The problem of determining the best method of financing education is a major one; up to now no utopian method has been found. Local taxes are so much of a burden that further support must come from increased state or federal aid. Because the educational program is dependent upon available finances, the school budget must be based upon income estimates that are as accurate as possible.

The Increasing Need for Additional School Revenue

It would not be realistic to say that every shortcoming of which the public schools are accused can be corrected by simply providing more money; it would be realistic to say that few of them can be corrected without more money. Excessive class size, poorly qualified teachers, crowded school buildings, antiquated curriculum, insufficient and poorly written textbooks —all of these targets of criticism are casualties of insufficient revenue.

Yet not only do critics refuse to see the need for additional school funds, but they point to the rapid growth of school expenditures in this country as ample reason for retrenchment. In 1870, for example, we spent 63 million dollars on public schools; in 1950, this figure had reached 5 billion dollars,[1] and in 1978–79 the total estimated current expenditures

[1] *National Education Association Journal* 37, February 1948, pp. 86–7.

for public elementary and secondary schools had climbed to over 75.6 billion dollars.[2] Most of this increase was due to the depreciation of the dollar, inflation, and to the steady increase in the length of the school year. Improvement and expansion of school services have accounted for only about 15 percent of the total increase.

Teachers' salaries, which have more than tripled since the 1930s, actually have had difficulty keeping pace with the rising cost of living; considering the fact that the federal income tax was not deducted from their pay before 1940, the average teacher has experienced little financial improvement. When one considers that the level of school support before the growth of educational expenditures began was grossly inadequate, it becomes evident that school costs are probably still far below what they ought to be.

Even the most selfish opponents of sufficient money for education should be convinced by the statistics issued by the United States Chamber of Commerce and the National Association of Manufacturers. These reports demonstrate that the level of economic prosperity is in direct relation to the educational level of the population. States that have not supported their educational programs adequately are lagging behind the rest of the country economically. Public education invariably creates increasing demand on the part of consumers, and creates more efficient producers to keep up with the demand. Money spent on education is therefore money that comes back to private industry a hundredfold.[3]

One of the main problems currently found in the field of educational finance is the inequality in expenditures among the states. Some states spend approximately one-third less per pupil annually than others. In 1978–79, for example, New York spent $2,759 per pupil in average daily attendance, while Arkansas spent only $1,344.[4] The educational opportunities for students suffer when states do not support their educational programs with adequate finances.

Those who view with alarm the unevenness of public support of education, together with those who fear the increasing burden of local taxation posed by the deluge of children pouring into the school systems of the nation, unite in urging increased grants of federal funds to the schools. This attitude is sometimes coupled with a proposal for rigid curtailment of educational expenditures, and a concomitant criticism of school officials

---

[2] National Education Association, NEA Research, *Estimates of School Statistics, 1978–79*. Research Memo (Washington, D.C.: The Association, 1979). Copyright © 1979 by the National Education Association, p. 21.

[3] Emery Stoops and M. L. Rafferty, Jr., *About Our Schools*, pp. 26–8.

[4] National Education Association, NEA Research, *Estimates of School Statistics, 1978–79*, Research Memo (Washington, D.C.: The Association, 1979). Copyright © 1979 by the National Education Association, p. 36.

for indulging in unrestrained spending. Actually, as the National Education Association has pointed out, we have never spent, nor are we now spending, enough money on education.

America is spending less of its national income on education than it should. During the 1930s, for instance, annual public school expenditures averaged 3.7 percent of the national income. Figure 6–1 shows that the average annual percent of the federal budget spent on education in 1977 was only 5 percent. The amount that should be spent on education probably could be doubled without putting an excessive drain on the national income. Meanwhile, the amount spent on luxuries is usually considered to be double the amount expended to educate a space-age generation. The 1964–65 school year was historic because it was the first time that more money was spent on education than on alcohol and cosmetics.[5]

There are some, however, who believe it is useless to speculate upon the percent of money that should be spent on education. It is difficult to predict the gross national product as well as the percentages to be allotted to defense or other programs. The old American habit of allowing the state to set up numerous local districts, turning over virtually all school responsibility to these small and often impoverished units, and then withdrawing from any further interest in education (barring a few gestures on a state level toward "research" and "leadership"), is destined to become obsolete. It is clear today that improvement of the schools depends upon more money, and that more money must come from the state. The districts, straitjacketed by the antiquated property tax, have reached their financial limits. As has been shown previously, several states today are furnishing more than 50 percent of all district funds. The trend will continue, until within another generation or two, more of the school money will come directly from the state. The school district will be relieved of the necessity of providing a minimum program, but will be permitted to tax itself if it so wishes in order to exceed the minimum. The result will be increased educational opportunities for the nation's children, and relief for the real property owners who are now footing most of the schools' bills.

Main Sources of School Revenue

Approximately 95 percent of public school revenue comes from taxation, the remainder accruing from endowments, gifts, and rentals. The four

---

[5] *National Education Association* NEA Research Division, "Annual Report on Public-School Financing," *NEA Research Bulletin*, p. 90.

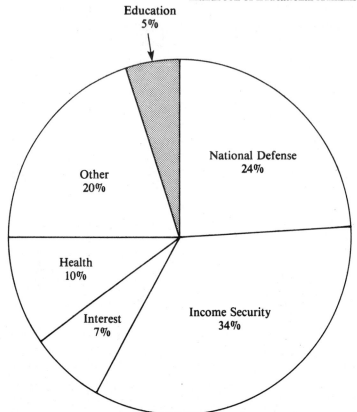

Education
5%

National Defense
24%

Other
20%

Health
10%

Interest
7%

Income Security
34%

FIGURE 6–1. Average Annual Percent Distribution By Func-
tion, of the Federal Budget: 1977. Source: U.S. Bureau of the
Census, Statistical Abstract of the United States, 1977, 98th ed.
(Washington, D.C.: U.S. Government Printing Office, 1977),
p. 246.

units of support for the schools are federal, state, county, and local.
Figure 6–2 shows the estimated percentages of income from these sources
as budgeted by a typical school district. These percentages vary from state
to state and from district to district.

Financial aid may be general or categorical. General aid is financial
assistance that is not specifically earmarked for a particular educational
program; the funds are available for expenditure at the discretion of the
local school district. The general state apportionment is a good example
of general aid. Categorical aid is financial assistance specifically earmarked for a particular educational program. The planned program and
the budgeted amounts are usually called a project and are subject to the
approval of the state or federal granting agency; examples are ESEA–Title
I and funds for teaching special education classes.

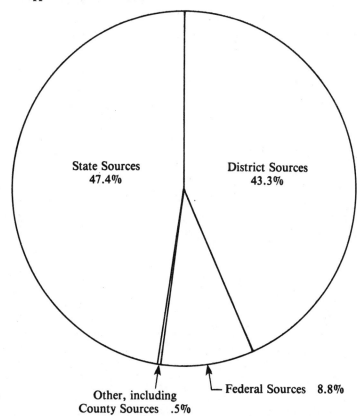

State Sources
47.4%

District Sources
43.3%

Other, including
County Sources .5%

Federal Sources 8.8%

*FIGURE 6–2. The School Dollar: Estimated Income Sources
for the School Year 1980–81 for a Typical School District.*

FEDERAL AID. Regular federal aid to education may be divided into approximately three categories: (1) aid to vocational education; (2) land and money grants to the states; and (3) federal aid under Public Laws 815, 874, and 864, and other educational support acts.

The Smith–Hughes Act of 1917 is the best example of the first, providing as it did federal funds for the teaching of agriculture, industrial education, and home economics. Each state receives funds on the basis of total population and must match the federal funds provided with equal amounts of their own money. The Morrill Act, the George–Deen legislation, and other examples of federal aid, discussed in more detail in chapter 2, represent related varieties of regular federal support for the nation's schools.

The Ordinance of 1787 contained the first example of government grant aid to the schools. One parcel in every township was to be reserved for the maintenance of public schools within the boundaries of the vast western territory, which comprised the present states of Illinois, Indiana, Michigan, Ohio, Wisconsin, and part of Minnesota. As other states came into the Union, the same principle was applied, although many of the later states received more than one parcel of each congressional township, under a liberalization of the original ordinance. A total of more than 98 million acres was thus set aside, an example of massive federal aid to education.

Land grants were not the only type of grant aid made by the government. Lesser money grants were made from time to time, among them the "Surplus Revenue Distribution" of 1837, and the "Five Percentum Fund" of 1803.

Since 1919 the National Education Association has supported bills introduced at almost every session of Congress to increase federal aid for education. After World War II, the federal government recognized that federal activities in certain areas had created increased enrollments without increasing valuations. In order to meet the increasing school cost and decreasing local tax income, Public Law 874 was passed to provide funds for the operation of the educational program. Public Law 815 provided funds for constructing school facilities in federally impacted areas, and Public Law 864 provided funds that strengthened national defense by supporting educational efforts. In the last few years, several educational acts have been passed to assist school districts.

Funds may be distributed as flat grants, special purpose appropriations, or general purpose funds. Some are available for private as well as public schools. The Elementary and Secondary Education Act of 1965 comes as close to being general support as any law yet passed. It is "the largest single commitment by the federal government to strengthen and improve educational quality and opportunities in elementary and secondary schools across the nation."[6]

Most federal aid up to this time has stressed emergency aid or long-range assistance in certain specialized areas. Some federal funds have been provided on a matching basis which in practice permits the rich districts to get richer and the poor to get relatively poorer. This is hardly an equalization. The majority of federal funds for operational expenses should be channeled into needy states and districts on some sort of rough equalization principle. At the present time, federal funds represent the least important source of public school revenue. Federal interest in education is discussed more fully in chapter 2.

STATE AID.   In 1929–30, the states furnished only 16.9 percent of public school support. In 1978–79, the amount ranged from a low of 9.4 percent

---

[6] U.S. Department of Health, Education, and Welfare, *Profile of ESEA, The Elementary and Secondary Education Act of 1965*, p. 1.

in New Hampshire to a high of 80.5 percent in Hawaii. Twenty-four states supplied more than 50 percent of school funds.[7] State taxes of various types produce this revenue—income taxes, property taxes, sales taxes, business taxes, and inheritance taxes.

Such state funds come largely from three sources: (1) appropriations made from the general fund of the state; (2) taxes especially earmarked for education; and (3) income from invested school funds. The first source is steadily gaining in favor as the ideal method of financing public education. The general property tax has been largely abandoned by the states as a reliable source of state school revenue. Income from invested funds supplies only a trivial amount, and earmarked taxes are falling into increasing disfavor.

State funds are distributed to schools on two bases: flat grant and equalization. Several states utilize a combination of both methods. The flat-grant aid is granted on a straight per-pupil basis, without regard to economic differences among the various school districts of the state. Either enrollment or average daily attendance may be used in figuring the amount to be paid. Equalization aid is distributed in proportion to financial ability, with the poorer districts receiving the larger amounts. Most states have a *foundation program* which is a form of equalization. It guarantees that the state and local district will jointly provide a minimum educational program for all children regardless of the amount of taxes raised in the district. The theoretical amount that the district is able to contribute is determined by multiplying a computational tax times the assessed valuation. In poor districts, the state makes up the difference between the cost of the foundation program and the available money raised by the mandatory tax rate.

The advantages of equalization are as follows:

1. All pupils are able to take advantage of relatively equal educational opportunities.
2. The real property tax rate in the local districts can be lowered or the program can be enriched.
3. The tax load in the different districts is made more equable.

State aid may be general or special, or both. The former may be used for all educational purposes not specifically prohibited by law. The latter is earmarked by the state for specific purposes or projects, such as transportation, supervision, libraries, and education of the handicapped. Too often, special aid is limited by the stipulation that the local district must match the state grant. This is a pernicious practice, rendering inevitable

---

[7] National Education Association, NEA Research, *Estimates of School Statistics, 1978–79*, Research Memo (Washington, D.C.: The Association, 1979). Copyright © 1979 by the National Education Association, p. 34.

the receipt of most money by the districts least in need. Such aid is not equalization in the accepted sense.

Two dangers have been traditionally cited as inherent in any system of state financial aid to local schools. The first danger is the potential stifling of local initiative and a growing tendency among citizens to lose interest in schools they no longer have the responsibility of supporting. The second danger is the possibility of encouraging the wasteful spending of state funds without appropriate controls.

Modifications of these two objections also form the cornerstone of the opposition to federal aid to education. It is safe to say that these dangers, while not entirely imaginary, are unrealistic. For example, if one were a resident of a community in which a state university, which derives its support from the state and federal governments alone, happens to be located, it does not necessarily follow that one will not be vitally interested in its functioning, nor that the community will lose interest in its work. In the case of the second danger, it should be stressed that nearly all public school officials and board members have had more experience with management of strict budgets than have governmental officials; local educators are not apt to change their thrifty habits and waste public funds simply because they are given an increase in state aid.

A certain amount of increased state control most likely will follow in the wake of increased state support. There is no reason, however, why such control should not be exercised in the name of higher standards. Smaller pupil–teacher ratios, cooperative purchasing of supplies, strengthened curriculum—these and other areas of current weakness are surely proper pretexts for state intervention. In addition, the state may properly demand the elimination of small and impoverished districts, amalgamation of all possible districts for the general improvement of administration, and the reorganization of transportation routes to make possible the elimination of unnecessary school busing. The local districts have wrestled unsuccessfully with these problems for generations; it is time they were assisted by higher authority.

The National Education Association some years ago produced a series of recommendations for the organization and objectives of state aid to education which may be summarized as follows:

1. The state should provide at least 60 percent of the total funds needed to support public education.
2. There should be one state fund for school aid, nearly all of which should be raised from sources other than the general property tax.
3. At least half of the state aid should be in the form of equalization.
4. The state should establish and guarantee a "foundation" program for all districts. Districts should be encouraged to supplement the foundation program from their own resources.

5. The state should aid in the construction of school buildings, also on an equalization basis.[8]

The old American habit of allowing the state to set up numerous local districts, turning over virtually all school responsibility to these small and often impoverished units, and then withdrawing from any further interest in education (barring a few gestures on a state level toward "research" and "leadership"), is destined to become obsolete. It is clear today that improvement of the schools depends upon more money, and that more money must come from the state. The districts, straitjacketed by the antiquated property tax, have reached their financial limits. As has been shown previously, several states today are furnishing more than 50 percent of all district funds. The trend will continue, until within another generation or two, more of the school money will come directly from the state. The school district will be relieved of the necessity of providing a minimum program, but will be permitted to tax itself if it so wishes in order to exceed the minimum. The result will be increased educational opportunities for the nation's children, and relief for the real property owners who are now footing most of the schools' bills.

The nation's schools should receive immediately a substantial increase in operational funds, from whatever source. When it is remembered that a larger proportion of the national income went for education during the depression, when schools were far below today's standards, it becomes apparent that massive amounts of additional revenue must be made available for education in this country.

No educator should be satisfied with the schools' share of the national wealth until education at least receives the equivalent of what is being spent in the United States each year on liquor, tobacco, and gambling. The trend is in this direction, and probably will bring in its train wholesale modification of present tax and assessment restrictions which now shackle the schools' spending. It is necessary that educators stop thinking in terms of pin money, and start thinking about educational financing in terms of between 5 and 10 percent of the gross national income.

COUNTY AID. The county educational unit is often used as an intermediate agency between the local district and the state. In some states, particularly in the South, the county and the local district are identical. These units raise money in the manner of local districts in other parts of the country—i.e., via the property tax. Other states use their county units primarily as an instrument for regulating and aiding local districts. County

---

[8] *National Education Association*, Research Division, "Attainment of Recommended Goals by Present School Finance Systems," *NEA Research Bulletin* 24, October 1946, pp. 93–6.

aid in such cases may be derived entirely from state sources, entirely from county taxation, or from a combination of both.

LOCAL SUPPORT.   The chief source of local school revenue has always been the property tax. While this tax at one time may have represented the true wealth of a school district, it is not now the case. The property tax is not suited to an era in which stocks, bonds, and commodities have replaced land and buildings as the main source of taxable wealth. Real estate owners today find themselves bearing the brunt of school support, and quite understandably object. Some states follow the policy of "separation of sources," and reserve almost all general property for local taxation, but in such cases the faults of the property tax outweigh whatever virtues it once may have had. It seems clear that one of the following alternatives must be chosen if a complete breakdown of local school taxation machinery is to be avoided: (1) The state must assume more and more of the financial support burden of the local school districts. (2) The state must make available to the local districts additional sources of tax revenue.

The mechanics of raising funds for the support of the schools are in the hands of local school authorities in nearly all states, and follow the procedure outlined below:

1. School authorities calculate the projected costs of the schools within their jurisdiction for the ensuing fiscal year.
2. They estimate the amount of state financial aid to be received.
3. They arrive at an estimate of monies to be received from all sources except state aid and local taxation.
4. The difference between estimated costs and income from sources listed above is then projected.
5. Finally, they levy the necessary tax on local real property in order to raise whatever additional funds are needed.

City school districts often depend upon the approval of municipal authorities for the levying of school taxes, as well as for their collection. Even school districts that are fiscally independent usually depend upon municipal or county tax officers for the assessing, levying, and collecting of taxes, although the districts themselves set their own rates, subject to statutory limitations. Only occasionally does the board of education, through its own agent, do its own assessing, levying, and collecting of taxes. Such practice is probably poor. Economy alone would seem to indicate the desirability of the district employing regular tax officers, available to carry out the actual mechanics of taxation, while the district remains independent of other civil authority in the determination of its tax needs.

RURAL AND SMALL TOWN SCHOOLS. In several states, refusal of voters to raise taxes has caused the closing of rural and small town schools as recently as 1979. During the 1980s, this trend may well continue, especially in the South. The pattern shows a concentration of population in the county seat, which has its own school district. The voters are willing to fund the city district, but refuse to assent to tax raises in the sparsely settled remainder of the county. Solution: a combination of increased state equalization aid and the legal raising of minimum tax rates.[9]

Dependence on Assessment Rates

All states fix maximum tax rates, but simultaneously defeat their own purpose by leaving to local option the rate at which property is assessed. Thus the assessment rate is often more important than the tax rate in determining the amount of school support. The local assessors are usually completely immune from school district control and may nullify the district's financial plans by lowering the assessment. Sometimes it is impossible for a school district to find out what the assessment rate will be, or the expected funds that it will provide, in time to prepare the district budget.

The district, pinned down by statutory tax ceilings, is then completely helpless, unless the state in which it is located permits the overriding of such ceilings by local election. Many states have set up agencies to equalize assessment rates, but they often do not operate very effectively.

Where such agencies do not exist, the variations in the assessment rates are even more glaringly apparent. The solution must be found in one of the following two alternatives: (1) All school assessment rates and valuations shall be arrived at by state action, with such activities taken out of local hands entirely. (2) Each school district through its voters shall adjust its own assessment and tax rates to suit itself, with the state's only concern being that each district shall contribute that portion of its taxable wealth that is fair in relation to its ability.

The problem of decreasing property–assessment rates and increasing district tax rates is strikingly similar in some of its manifestations to the inflationary spiral so notoriously apparent in the world's economy. The only way out of the dilemma now available to the school district is to ask its already heavily burdened taxpayers to vote to exceed the maximum tax rate; many districts have refused to do this. So many tax and bond elections have been defeated that some have described the situation as a "taxpayer's strike." School taxes are normally the only taxes on which voters have a direct voice. Other taxes are determined by city councils, county supervisors, or other governmental agencies.

---

[9] *Birmingham* (Alabama) *News,* September 15, 1979.

As the assessment rate slowly declines and the proportion of the district's true wealth, as represented by the property valuation, inexorably diminishes, the tax rate climbs upward. This is an intolerable situation that must be remedied as soon as possible. Not only must there be more rigid state control of the system of assessing property, but the base for school taxes must be broadened. Teacher strikes in various parts of the country are calling attention to the deplorable condition of school finance.

FINANCIAL EQUALIZATION. Financial equalization on both a state and local level must be achieved. The principle that all American children deserve the same minimum educational opportunities is basic to modern educational philosophy. However, at the present time children in various parts of the country, and even in adjoining districts of the same state, are being given schooling of sharply contrasting quality and quantity.

It is all very well to say in rebuttal that the solution lies, not in increased equalization aid from a higher source, but in an increased effort on the part of less favored communities. The truth is that some states, and some school districts, are already making truly staggering efforts to give their children adequate educations, but are failing simply because there is not enough money at their disposal to make their goal a possible one. Some states have approximately 35 percent more children per one hundred adults than others. When one considers that some of these prolific states, New Mexico, Utah, Mississippi, South Dakota, Louisiana, and North Dakota, for example, are for the most part those with the lowest per capita wealth, it is obvious that merely mouthing the word "effort" is not going to accomplish much. Local district taxpayers have been so overburdened by property taxes that many are rebelling.

In 1978, the rebellion surfaced in California, when the Proposition 13 initiative measure passed overwhelmingly. It cut that state's revenues from the ad valorem tax substantially.

Shortly before this happened, the winds of change were to be seen in the so-called "Serrano Decision," through which the California Supreme Court in effect mandated an end to exclusive local reliance on the real property tax. The Court said that the resulting division of the state's school districts into "rich" and "poor" categories made unequal educational opportunities inevitable, thus denying California's school children their constitutional rights.

Federal courts have since ruled that the terms of the Serrano Decision could not be applied nationally, but the California case has had a decided ripple effect in other states. Ohio and Michigan have passed tax proposals similar to Proposition 13.

Equalization operates in this manner: Assume three school systems, A, B, and C, each with the same number of children to educate. The state government guarantees every school district $150 per unit of average daily attendance, provided that each district levies a minimum school tax of $.75 per $100 in assessed valuation. In District A, which is wealthy, this tax yields ample funds to operate without additional state aid, so District A gets no additional state aid. District B is an average district; after levying its tax, it still needs approximately $20 per average daily attendance unit to function at the $150 level guaranteed by the state. Therefore, District B receives $20 per unit in state aid. District C, located in a so-called "bedroom" community, where there is no industry to tax but a large number of school-age children to educate, finds that even after levying the $.75 tax it is still $100 per pupil short of achieving the desirable $150 level. District C thus qualifies for and receives $100 from the state for each attendance unit annually.

All three districts are able in this way to guarantee to their pupils a satisfactory *minimum* educational program. Both District A and District B, of course, and especially A, will be able to tax themselves additionally if they so choose, and thus provide *maximum* programs. This ensures the preservation of local initiative and provides for a constantly rising standard of school support, while at the same time doing away with all educational standards below a certain level of excellence.

The same principle applied above to local districts holds when applied to states. Gross educational and financial inequalities exist *between* states in exactly the same way as they exist *within* the states. Approximately half of America's school-age children live in forty-one (82 percent) of the states and the District of Columbia.[10] Yet these states possess only 44.9 percent of the total personal income.[11] For many years bills have been regularly proposed to Congress that were designed to furnish federal funds on an equalization basis so that poor states would receive more than wealthy states.

There is no reason why the same equalization principle that has worked so well when applied to local districts cannot work equally well when applied to the states themselves. It seems certain that the near future will see this type of financial aid made available.

School money in the future will be raised where it exists and spent where it is needed. The wealthy district will receive purely nominal state aid above the basic per-pupil figure, but the poor district will receive massive aid. The goal for all districts will be a "floor" figure set up by the state and guaranteed to all districts, augmented by whatever additional enrichment the local district will feel itself financially able to provide. The equalization will thus extend to a minimum figure which represents an

---

[10] National Education Association, NEA Research, *Estimates of School Statistics, 1978–79*, Memo (Washington, D.C.: The Association, 1979). Copyright © 1979 by the National Education Association, p. 27.

[11] U.S. Department of Commerce, Bureau of Economics Analysis, *Survey of Current Business*, August 1977, p. 17.

adequate level of education; the districts will still be able to differentiate above this figure if they wish to make the necessary effort.

The School Budget

After the funds have been made available from their various sources, they are spent through the medium of the school budget. A good budget is actually a detailed financial program that outlines the educational program to be provided, the plan of spending, and the anticipated receipts. Virtually every policy adopted by the board of education in the course of the school year has some financial implication. Qualifications of teachers, length of school term, class size, capital outlays, upkeep of buildings—all must be planned for in terms of the budget.

Although the largest part of the budget is the plan for spending, income estimating and computation must be incorporated if the expenditure program is to be realistic. This is worked out in considerable detail and includes estimates based on past experience as well as needs for the coming year. A multitude of individual items usually appears, grouped under a number of major heads. School district budgeting is explained in more detail in chapter 7.

Concepts of School Support

Two outstanding changes have taken place in the past century in respect to the public's conception of proper school financing. First, the public has finally decided that education is a public function that must be supported through universal taxation, rather than a private concern of interest only to the parents of the individual child. The philosophical concept underlying this basic change in attitude holds that education, like military defense of one's country, is essential to the continued existence of the nation and the state. It benefits all the state's citizens, directly or indirectly; hence, it must be supported by all alike, whether or not all have children in attendance at the schools.

This concept has been blessed by the courts in hundreds of cases litigated in every state of the Union. The end result has been the establishment of a workable ideal at once simple and sublime: every pupil who is mentally competent shall be given without charge an education extending from the kindergarten through the twelfth grade.

The practice of universal taxation on such a massive scale to support such a wide range of education is unique among the nations of the world. Secondary schools are financed infrequently in foreign lands, and colleges and universities rarely. America embarked upon an experiment in mass education unique in history because it regarded equality of educational opportunity as the birthright of every citizen. Other countries go part way, financing elementary instruction, but weeding out by virtue of intense competition all save a select and brilliant few on the secondary level. Secondary education abroad is thus based on an entirely different principle from our own, and its curriculum and goals are understandably divergent from ours. The future will tell which method works better. Our striking force in World War II and our postwar industrial strength argue strongly for a high level of education for our populace.

The other great change in our conception of school financing—the increasing role of the state in providing educational funds—is still in the process of going on. Formerly, the entire burden of financing the schools was placed upon the local community. As our society changed from an agrarian to an urban one, local financing became an increasingly unequal burden. At a time when nearly all communities were agricultural, wealth was not concentrated in certain urban portions of each state, as it is today.

As this condition began to change, glaring inequalities in both educational opportunities and tax burdens in the various communities became more and more evident. The state did not volunteer its financial assistance; its influence was brought about by the trend of events. At any rate, the concept of the state's responsibility in setting up minimum educational standards and assisting all communities to comply with these standards has now become a universal one. All states now give financial aid to schools. The amount and degree of this aid is bound to increase.

Once thought of as local enterprises, school plants are now increasingly recognized as capital investments of the entire state. The acceptance of such a theory makes inevitable the growth of state aid for schoolhouse construction. Most states now offering such aid are doing so on a loan basis, with the money obtained from state bond issues, doled out to the local districts on a basis of need, and repayable over a twenty-year period from local tax revenues. The future doubtless will see the acceptance by the state of its responsibility of supplying such building funds without demanding eventual repayment. The need for more schools is preeminently the concern of the whole state, not merely of individual school districts.

Any discussion of apparent trends in school financial support would have to include such highly visible ones as combining districts—and even whole county school systems—into larger, more viable school districts, and the rapidly increasing use of data processing to make possible more intelligent financial decisions.

TOWARD COMPLETELY TAX-SUPPORTED SCHOOLS.   Further steps remain to be taken before all American public schools are totally tax-supported. Many states still do not furnish free textbooks to elementary school children; only half furnish them to secondary schools. Three-fourths of the states still require pupils to pay for their own school supplies. Some states still charge for tuition of rural pupils in high school, and some are still sending bills for transportation. All these hangovers from the past are negations of the worthy principle that the schools of America should be completely free to all. The trend, happily, is strongly toward completely free education in a free country.

Summary

The inflation of the late sixties and the early seventies, coupled with increasing voter resistance to school financial levies, points up the need for additional school revenue. While expenditures for public education have increased markedly during the past decade, with teacher salaries tripling in the last generation, most schools are still underfinanced.

This problem is accentuated by the inequality of expenditures, and hence the unequal educational opportunities for pupils in the fifty states. Increased federal funding is proposed to lessen such inequalities.

When public school revenue sources are examined, it is found that district, state, federal, and county taxes account for virtually all school money, in that order of importance.

Federal aid has a long history of categorical funding dating back to the Ordinance of 1787 and is divided into three main categories: vocational education, land grants, and recent strengthening acts such as Public Laws 815, 874, National Defense Education Act (NDEA), and Elementary and Secondary Education Act (ESEA). The latter comes close to being general aid rather than categorical aid.

State aid may be in the form of flat grants or equalization, or a combination of both; it may also be general or special, or both. State aid is sometimes objected to on the same basis as federal aid: it allegedly would lead to state control and to an end of local school independence.

Local support comes in the form of real property tax receipts, and traditionally has been in most states the mainstay of the schools. One of its weaknesses is the dependence of the school district upon other branches of government to assess, levy, and collect such taxes. County aid to local schools is primarily regulatory and supervisory rather than financial.

The most urgent need in school finance is for statewide equalization to ensure at least the same minimum educational opportunities for all children; this cannot be achieved by increased local effort alone.

Administrative Problems | In Basket |

Problem 1

The Modoc School District is situated in a rural community spread over a large area. There are four elementary schools and one small junior–senior high school.

Because of the long distances students must travel, transportation has always been necessary. School costs have risen continuously, yet the district is operating on a tax rate approved seven years ago. Tax elections were defeated overwhelmingly four years ago and again two years ago.

The district has diminished services, raised class loads, and eliminated some personnel. The breaking point has been reached; it appears impossible to balance the budget for the coming year. The Board of Education has decided to go to the people again and ask for a $.75 tax rate increase. This is the minimum that will be necessary over the next two or three years, even with tightened belts. It does not allow for the restoration of any of the reduced services or personnel but would permit the continuation of the bus services.

As the superintendent, how would you propose to gain community support?
In what capacity would you involve various school personnel?
What campaign strategy would you plan?

Problem 2

Assume the same situation exists as in Problem 1. The superintendent has asked each building principal to develop a plan for gaining support in his attendance area for the tax rate increase, an issue in the upcoming election.

If you were the junior–senior high school principal, how would you proceed?
What are the possible plans you would propose to the superintendent for your school?
As one of the elementary school principals, how would you proceed and what plans would you propose?
If you were the superintendent, how would you handle the problem if some principals drag their feet and do almost nothing?

Selected References

BARATZ, JOAN C., and JAY H. MOSKOWITZ. "Proposition 13: How and Why It Happened." *Phi Delta Kappan* 60, No. 1 (September 1978):9–11.

BENSON, CHARLES S. *The Economics of Public Education.* Boston, Mass.: Houghton Mifflin Co., 1968.

DERSTINE, R. "Accounting Income vs. Taxable Income." *Journal of Business Education* 53 (February 1978):197–9.

Education Vouchers. *A Report on Financing Education by Grants to Parents.* Cambridge, Mass.: Center for the Study of Public Policy, 1970.

GALLUP, GEORGE H. "The 10th Annual Gallup Poll of the Public's Attitudes Toward the Public Schools." *Phi Delta Kappan* 60, No. 1 (September 1978):33–45.

GARMS, WALTER I., et al. *School Finance: The Economics and Politics of Public Education.* Englewood Cliffs, N.J.: Prentice-Hall, Inc., 1978.

KIRST, M. W. "New Politics of State Educational Finance." *Phi Delta Kappan* 60 (February 1979):427–32.

MURPHY, J. F. "Fiscal Problems of Big City School Systems: Changing Patterns of State and Federal Aid." *Urban Review* 10 (Winter 1978):251–65.

NATIONAL EDUCATION ASSOCIATION, NEA Research Memo. *Estimates of School Statistics, 1978–79.* Washington, D.C.: The Association, 1979.

———, Research Division. "Rankings of the States, 1973." Research Report 1973–R1. Washington, D.C.: The Association, 1973.

———, Research Division. "Annual Report on Public-School Financing." *NEA Research Bulletin* 43 (October 1965).

NEILL, SHIRLEY B. *School Energy Crisis: Problems and Solutions.* Arlington, Va.: American Association of School Administrators, 1977.

NELSON, D. LLOYD, and WILLIAM M. PURDY. *School Business Administration.* Lexington, Mass.: D. C. Heath and Co., 1971.

Newsfront. "A First: States Spend Most for School Support." *Phi Delta Kappan* 60 (April 1979):555.

PINCUS, JOHN (ed.) *School Finance in Transition: The Courts and Educational Reform.* Cambridge, Mass.: Ballinger Publishing Co., 1974.

ROPER, DWIGHT, and SUSAN ROPER. "The Accountable School: Elective Courses, Competition, and Cost Effectiveness." *Phi Delta Kappan* 60 (March 1979):527–28.

STOOPS, EMERY, and M. L. RAFFERTY. *About Our Schools.* Los Angeles, Ca.: Education Press, 1955.

USA Today. "Federal Programs Fail to Promote Change." *USA Today* 107 (December 1978):11–13.

U. S. DEPARTMENT OF HEALTH, EDUCATION, AND WELFARE. *Profile of ESEA, The Elementary and Secondary Education Act of 1965.* OE 20088A. Washington, D.C.: U. S. Government Printing Office, 1967.

———, National Center for Educational Statistics. *Revenues and Expenditures for Public Elementary and Secondary Education.* Washington, D.C.: The Department, 1975–76.

CHAPTER SEVEN

School District Budgeting

A school district budget is an organized, written plan representing the financial picture of the district. It should be based on past experience but should look ahead to the future. Careful, continuous planning is necessary if the budget is to meet the needs of the district. In the last few years, some school districts have utilized the systems approach of planning-programming-budgeting (PPBS) in their approach to budget development.

The Budget and Overall School Planning

It is a mistake to think of a school budget in terms of a balance between revenue and expenditures only; more important, it is an educational forecast drawn up a year in advance that reduces school planning to a systematized form. The school budget is different from the budget in business or industry; it has as its goal the securing, not of financial profit, but of the greatest possible educational dividends from the investment of the taxpayers' money.

Educational benefit is the measure of good school business management, not monies saved or records accumulated. Effective management in the public interest will require the wise expenditure of money for educational purposes and the avoidance of any waste. The principle that must be kept in mind while working with a budget is that business administration is merely one of several facilitating services in the advancement of the educational program; it is subordinate to educational administration, but should be integrated with it. The business office should never dominate the school program. Sometimes it appears that the budget determines the educational program. Should this situation ever develop, the educational program may easily degenerate into a succession of inventories and tightened economies. There is little point in running a school system that is financially prosperous but educationally poor.

On the other hand, intelligent business management is absolutely necessary if the educational program is to prosper. Poor administration of the district's financial affairs can result in spending money in ineffective areas and in diverting administrators' attention from the educational problems of the district to tasks that could be carried on by clerical personnel under the proper direction. The channeling of business affairs into the appropriate areas of the district-wide educational picture can best be charted through the medium of a properly constructed budget.

The school budget states in dollars and cents the policies and philosophy of the school district. It "is one way of expressing a set of purposes translated into a plan of action for a stated period of time."[1] It exercises decisive control over the aspects of the school program that are to be emphasized or de-emphasized. The budget also serves the purposes of public relations by bringing the public into closer contact with the schools through published figures, public hearings, and joint committees. It enables the people to judge the cost of the educational program in terms of educational services provided. The budget should be the expression of the will of the people of the district. Finally, the budget must be married to the curriculum. The two go hand in hand. It is impossible rationally to consider the one without the other.

Proper Budgetary Procedures

School budgetary procedures may be divided into three main parts: preparation, consideration and adoption, and administration. A fourth step, often considered as part of the budget administration, is appraisal.

PREPARATION OF THE BUDGET.   Too much importance cannot be attached to the proper preparation of the school budget. Its advantages, summarized years ago but still pertinent, are as follows:

1.   It makes for better educational planning.
2.   It gives an overview of the school program.
3.   It aids in the analysis of details.
4.   It develops cooperation within the school.
5.   It stimulates confidence among the taxpayers.
6.   It contains a balanced estimate of receipts.

---

[1] Stephen J. Knezevich (ed.) *Administrative Technology and the School Executive*, p. 65.

7. It provides a legal basis for the proper authorities to levy the necessary local taxes.
8. It authorizes expenditures.
9. It aids in the economical administration of the school.
10. It improves financial accounting procedures.
11. It aids in administering extra-curricular activities.
12. It projects the school into the future and thus stimulates long-range planning and forecasting.[2]

Despite the lack of standardization in budgeting among the various states, there is a growing area of agreement centering about the classifications of expenditures. The United States Department of Health, Education, and Welfare has listed the headings commonly employed as follows:[3]

ADMINISTRATION
100 Series

110. Salaries
120. Contracted Services
130. Other Expenses

INSTRUCTION
200 Series

210. Salaries
220. Textbooks
230. School Libraries and Audio-visual Materials
240. Teaching Supplies
250. Other Expenses

ATTENDANCE AND HEALTH SERVICES
300–400 Series

300. Attendance Services
400. Health Services

PUPIL TRANSPORTATION SERVICES
500 Series

510. Salaries
520. Contracted Services and Public Carriers
530. Replacements of Vehicles

---

[2] C. A. DeYoung, *Budgeting in Public Schools,* pp. 9–14.
[3] U.S. Department of Health, Education, and Welfare, *Financial Accounting for Local and State School Systems,* pp. 27–35.

540. Pupil Transportation Insurance
550. Expenditures in Lieu of Transportation
560. Other Expenses for Operation and Maintenance

OPERATION OF PLANT
600 Series

610. Salaries
620. Contracted Services
630. Heat for Buildings
640. Utilities, Except Heat for Buildings
650. Supplies, Except Utilities
660. Other Expenses

MAINTENANCE OF PLANT
700 Series

710. Salaries
720. Contracted Services
730. Replacements of Equipment
740. Other Expenses

FIXED CHARGES
800 Series

810. School District Contributions to Employee Retirement
820. Insurance and Judgments
830. Rental of Land and Buildings
840. Interest on Current Loans
850. Other Fixed Charges

FOOD SERVICES AND STUDENT BODY ACTIVITIES
900–1000 Series

900. Food Services
1000. Student Body Activities

COMMUNITY SERVICES
1100 Series

1110. Recreation
1120. Civic Activities
1130. Public Libraries
1140. Custodial and Detention Care of Children
1150. Welfare Activities
1160. Nonpublic School Pupils

CAPITAL OUTLAY
1200 Series

1210. Sites
1220. Buildings
1230. Equipment

DEBT SERVICE FROM CURRENT FUNDS
1300 Series

1310. Principal of Debt
1320. Interest on Debt
1330. Amounts Paid into Sinking Funds
1340. Expenditures to Schoolhousing Authority or Similar Agency
1350. Other Debt Service

OUTGOING TRANSFER ACCOUNTS
1400 Series

1410. Expenditures to Other School Districts or Administrative Units in the State
1420. Expenditures to School Districts or Administrative Units in Another State
1430. Tuition to Other than Public Schools

In the three steps of budgetary development listed by DeYoung, the first is educational planning, and it centers in its financial aspect around the expenditure categories described and listed above.[4] Before figures are placed in the budget, important decisions must be made. Planning should not only be concerned with the coming year but look ahead for several years. It is not wise to start a program that cannot be supported financially for more than the year ahead. However, fragmentation occurs when planning is only short range. Continuity is essential if improvements are to be made.

Long-range policy decisions should be made regarding many factors. A determination should be made as to who should be educated; whether the program will include kindergarten, junior college, and adult education opportunities. Enrollments should be projected five to ten years. Additional sites, buildings, equipment, and personnel should be projected. The length of the school year must be established. Decisions must be made regarding teacher load, provisions for educating exceptional children, guidance services, transportation services, lunch programs, special teachers for special subjects, health services, the education of the culturally different, maintenance and operation services, summer school programs, salary

---

[4] DeYoung, *Budgeting*, p. 30.

schedules, and fringe benefits for personnel. Policies should be developed regarding the type of secondary schools to be provided and the grade organization: comprehensive or vocational high schools, junior high schools, or intermediate schools. There should be decisions regarding the curriculum to be offered at all levels including electives, vocational-technical and career education, and adult education.[5]

All school policies adopted by the school board contribute to the size and content of the budget in the sense that the material expression of these policies is found primarily in the budget. All problems of curriculum and personnel must be attacked first through budgetary provision.

The second step in budgetary development consists of planning the program of expenditures. When this step is allowed to come first, and to assume priority over educational planning, it may constitute the entire budget. It is a common mistake to start budget figuring from the stand-point of an assured income, and to compel the various expenditure categories to accommodate themselves to the fixed revenue. This second step in budgeting should be directly dependent upon the first step—educational planning—and should in turn govern the third step—income planning—instead of being determined by it.

The interpretation of plans into costs is one of the outstanding contributions that the business office performs.

Planning the income constitutes the third step. When the educational program for the coming year has been decided upon, and when the expenditures needed to finance that program have been determined, then the final step in budgeting is to determine whether the expected income will support the program, and if not, how to augment it. When a discrepancy between projected income and proposed expenditure is found, the productivity of each source of income should then be examined with an eye to a possible increase in revenue production. Other possible sources then should be sought out and scrutinized and eventually used in an attempt to finance the planned program.

The superintendent of schools is the chief executive officer of the district. He should therefore be given the primary responsibility for the performance of the task that is basic to the efficiency of the school system, the preparation of the budget.

In line with policies previously adopted by the board of education, the board approves and amends the budget as it is presented by the superintendent. Whereas the superintendent knows more about the educational needs of the system than anyone else, the board members, by virtue of their residence in the community for many years, know more about the financial

---

[5] Edgar L. Morphet, Roe L. Johns, and Theodore L. Reller, *Educational Organization and Administration*, pp. 395–411.

capabilities and desires of the community than do the school personnel. Cooperation between the board and its superintendent is therefore essential.

Such cooperation extends beyond board–superintendent relations; it involves other school employees as well. All school principals and department heads should be consulted as to needs and requirements, but democratic budgeting should go still further. It should attempt to secure the cooperation of teachers, custodians, and clerical employees in making the school budget an expression of the needs of the whole school system. Consulting the staff will not only assure the superintendent of the securing of much needed information but also contribute to employee morale and status.

Forms such as those illustrated in Tables 7–1 to 7–7 can be used to gather specific budget information and recommendations from schools and departments. These should be compiled after consultations with all members of the staff. The business office or administrative council can meet with those who completed the forms and analyze them. At this time priorities should also be established. If the total for the budget is not approved, items with highest priority would then be included.

Budget making should be considered a year-long activity. Definite deadlines should be adopted for the completion of the several phases of budgeting in order to avoid last-minute improvisation. The following Budget Calendar is an example of a schedule for planning and adopting a budget:

Oct. 20, 1980	Presentation of Classified Salary Proposals to the District Superintendent.
Nov. 1–28	Conferences of Classified Employees Negotiating Council with Superintendent and selected staff regarding salaries.
Dec. 1	District Superintendent presents Classified Salary recommendation to the Board of Education at the first meeting in December.
Dec. 13	Budget Request Forms for ensuing year's budget in the hands of Division Heads, Principals, and Department Heads.
Dec. 10–Jan. 14	Division Heads, Principals, and Department Heads meet with their staff to develop a division and school budget. Expenditure estimates due in Business Office by January 15.
Jan. 5, 1981	Enrollment projections for 1980–1981 from Principals to the Assistant Superintendent, Instructional Services, with copy to the District Superintendent.

Jan. 14–Feb. 4	Business Manager and Director of Maintenance and Operations will meet with School Principals and review major items of maintenance for buildings, grounds, and equipment.
Jan. 14–April 8	Planning meetings with the Board of Education, District Superintendent, Cabinet, Administrative Staff, and Negotiating Council.
Jan. 16	Principals and staff members to submit two copies of personnel needs for 1980–1981 (one to the Superintendent and one to Business Office). This would include both certificated and classified personnel.
Feb. 11	Principals and Department Heads will submit requests for major repairs to buildings, grounds, and equipment.
Feb. 16	School Principals and staff members submit estimate of needs for ensuing year for Capital Outlay items, replacement of equipment, maintenance needs.
Feb. 18–March 23	Preparation and assembly by Business Office of first draft of working budget by detailed classification.
March 2	Presentation of Certificated Salary Proposals to District Superintendent.
March 11–April 1	Conferences by Negotiating Council, District Superintendent, and selected staff regarding salaries.
March 18	Copy of Tentative Budget given to District Superintendent for study.
March 31–April 10	Tentative Budget referred to Division Heads, Principals, and staff for review. Conference scheduled with Superintendent and Business Manager for appropriate revision.
April 8–10	District Superintendent recommends salaries to Board of Education.
April 20–24	Adoption by Board of Education of Certificated Salary Schedules for the ensuing year (provided state apportionment needed and known).
May 4	Contracts issued.
May 4–8	Presentation to Board of Education by District Superintendent of Preliminary Budget.
May 4–30	Revision and readjustment as required. Meetings with the Board of Education, Principals, and Department Heads on budgetary questions as necessary.
June 1	Tentative Budget presented to the District Superintendent by the Business Manager.
June 8–12	Tentative Budget presented to Board of Education by the District Superintendent at the first regular meeting in June.
	Board adopts resolution permitting Board to increase annual salaries during school year for certificated and/or classified personnel.

June 22–26	Second regular meeting of the Board of Education in June to adopt the Tentative Budget to be filed with the County Superintendent of Schools.
July 1	Tentative Budget filed with County Superintendent of Schools or other higher authority if required.
July 15	Tentative Budget returned if it has been previously filed.
July 15	Meeting of Board of Education to adopt Publication Budget.
July 17	File Publication Budget with County Superintendent of Schools or higher authority as required.
July 24–31	Publication Budget in the local newspaper.
Aug. 3	Meeting of the Board of Education—Public Hearing and Adoption of Budget.
Aug. 10–14	Adopted Budget filed with County Superintendent of Schools.

The Budget Calendar should be adopted by the board of education, and regular reports should be made to the board showing the progress that is being made.

The final budget should present a complete picture of the school district's financial plans. Each proposed appropriation should be followed by supporting explanation and detail. There should be no "padding" and no money "hidden" in the various categories. If this occurs, people lose confidence in the administration and investigations may be requested. Because every expense cannot be predicted precisely, it is legitimate to budget contingency funds to provide for possible changes in enrollment, repairs, programs, or emergencies.

Many states prescribe rules governing the development of the budget and prescribe a standard budget form. In states that have no such requirement, the superintendent should prepare the budget according to the classifications recommended by the United States Department of Health, Education, and Welfare (see pages 123–5). Subheadings can be developed within the recommended categories to fit the needs of each district. For example:

213   Teachers
213.1   Salaries, Regular Teachers
213.2   Salaries, Special Training Teachers
213.3   Salaries, Speech Teachers
213.4   Salaries, Home Teachers
213.5   Salaries, Dental Health Teachers
213.6   Salaries, Guidance Teachers
213.7   Salaries, Substitute Teachers

TABLE 7-1. *Certificated Personnel Needs.*

School or
Department: Washington Elementary School
Note: Personnel needs are to be requested and set forth on the basis of *existing* facilities or known additions. Please explain fully in "justification" column the reason for any additional personnel requested.

JOB TITLE	GRADE OR CLASS	CURRENT STAFF	STAFF REQUESTED	INCREASE OR DECREASE	JUSTIFICATION
Principal		1	1	0	
Teacher	Primary	10	10	0	
Teacher	Upper Grade	7	8	+1	Expected increase in enrollment.
Teacher	Kindergarten	2	4	+2	To establish single-session kindergartens instead of double-session ones.
Teacher	Educationally Handicapped	0	1	+1	To establish program for educationally handicapped pupils.
Counselor	1–6	0	½	+½	To provide needed counseling services.
Speech Therapist	1–6	0	½	+½	Many children have speech problems that should be corrected.
Teacher	EMR	2	2	0	
Reading Specialist	1–3	2	3	+1	Reading scores show need for additional teacher.

TABLE 7-2. Classified Personnel Needs.

School or
Department: Washington Elementary School
Note: Personnel needs are to be requested and set forth on the basis of *existing* facilities or known additions. Please explain fully in "justification" column the reason for any additional personnel requested.

JOB TITLE	CURRENT STAFF	STAFF REQUESTED	INCREASE OR DECREASE	JUSTIFICATION
Secretary	1	1	0	
Clerk	0	½	+½	Increased enrollment entitles school to additional part-time clerk.
Noon Duty Assistants	3	4	+1	Due to increased enrollment.
Teacher Assistants	0	8	+8	To enhance the educational program by relieving teachers of "chores" to do their professional job.
Custodian	2	2½	+½	To return to previous year's custodial service which was cut this year.
Cafeteria Manager	1	1	0	
Cook-helpers	3	4	+1	Due to increased enrollment and cafeteria usage.

131

TABLE 7–3. Budgetary Requests for Conferences.

School or
Department: Washington Elementary School

NAME OF CONFERENCE	DATES	LOCATION OF CONFERENCE	JUSTIFICATION	NUMBER ATTENDING	ESTIMATED COST PER PERSON
CESAA	Mar. 22–25	Los Angeles	Professional growth.	1	$ 40.00
Claremont Reading Conference	Spring	Claremont	To update information on reading programs.	2	35.00 each
ASCD	Mar. 15–19	San Francisco	To gain information on new programs and curriculum trends.	1	150.00

TABLE 7-4. Budgetary Request for Printing and Forms.

School or
Department: Washington Elementary School
Note: Include report cards, diplomas, attendance forms or any other printing to be done at district expense. If allowance is made for unforeseen items, please indicate as such. Quantities of printed materials should be requested on the basis of a one-year supply.

DESCRIPTION	TYPE OF FORM	QUANTITY REQUIRED	ESTIMATED COST	LENGTH OF TIME QUANTITY WILL LAST	DATE NEEDED
Promotion Certificates	Standard form for 6th graders	120	?	1 year	5/1
Bulletin	Summer school announcements to send home	1,000	?	1 year	3/1
Cards	Summer school enrollment cards	500	?	1 year	5/1
Report cards	Standard summer school form	500	?	1 year	5/1

TABLE 7–5. *Budgetary Request for Replacement of Equipment.*

School or
Department: Washington Elementary School

QUANTITY	TYPE OF EQUIPMENT (BRAND, MODEL, YEAR PURCHASED)	PRESENT CONDITION	CAN ITEM BE REPAIRED?	COST OF REPAIR	ESTIMATED CURRENT VALUE	ESTIMATED COST OF REPLACEMENT
1	Primary electric typewriter (1970)	Fair	No		$50.00	$250.00
4	Basketball goals and poles (1965) Brush (1965)	Poor	No			250.00
2	Tape recorders: Webcor BP 7340-1 (1967)	Poor	Doubtful			230.00 ea.
1	16 mm Victor 65-10 Movie projector (1967)	Poor	No			650.00
1	Desk, secretary (1960)	Fair	Maybe	$25.00	20.00	200.00
1	Desk, principal (1960)	Fair	Maybe	25.00	20.00	200.00
3	Chairs, visitors (1960)	Fair	Yes	10.00 ea.	5.00 ea.	50.00 ea.
4	Record players	Poor	No		5.00 ea.	120.00 ea.

134

TABLE 7–6. Budgetary Request for Buildings, Needed Repairs and Rehabilitation.

School or
Department: Washington Elementary School

ROOM OR BUILDING	DESCRIPTION	ESTIMATED COST	JUSTIFICATION
Rooms 1–12	Replace classroom light fixtures	$1,500.00	Present lighting is below acceptable standard.
All rooms	Replace gas heaters	5,000.00	Present heaters are outdated and illegal.
All rooms	Paint interior of all classrooms	3,000.00	They have not been painted for ten years and are in poor condition.
Playground	Replace all playground equipment	1,000.00	Present equipment is worn out and dangerous.
All rooms	Add electric outlets	?	Rooms now have only one or two outlets which is not adequate for equipment in regular use.
A and B	Replace clocks	50.00	Present clocks do not work well and need constant adjustment.

TABLE 7-7. *Budgetary Requests for New Equipment.*

School or
Department: Washington Elementary School

QUANTITY	DESCRIPTION OF EQUIPMENT	ESTIMATED COST	JUSTIFICATION
18	Independent study carrels	$ 80.00 ea.	To allow pupils independent work space when using taped or filmed materials.
1	Controlled Reader—EDL	275.00	To develop reading skills in upper grades.
1 set	Controlled Reader programs	600.00	To use with Controlled Reader in upper grades.
1	Tachistoscope, EDL, Tach-X	350.00	To develop visual discrimination skills and visual memory—upper grades.
1	Tach-X program	375.00	For use with Tach-X in upper grades.
1	Planetarium, Ken-A-Vision	95.00	For teaching elementary astronomy.
10	Globes—Readiness, Beginner	45.00 ea.	None available. Needed to introduce geography concepts.
4	Maps, simplified political, U.S. and world	40.00 ea.	No usable maps for lower grades.
5	Projectors, film strip	150.00 ea.	These are compact, low-voltage projectors and are needed for individual or small-group instruction.

To keep various categories within reason, expenditure percentages should be allotted according to general practice. As an example, thirty-eight unified school districts in California allotted the following percentages to the main categories of their school budgets:

SERIES	CATEGORY	PERCENT OF CURRENT EXPENSE OF EDUCATION
100	Administration	3.28
200	Instruction	75.40
300	Attendance Services	.05
400	Health Services	1.36
500	Transportation Services	1.24
600	Operation	7.93
700	Maintenance	4.65
800	Fixed Charges	6.09
Total current expenses, classifications 100–800		100.00

New budgets are generally compared with previous budgets. To help with this comparative analysis, a budget should show the previous year's expenditures, the current budget, and the estimate of expenditures for the year ahead. To be realistic, every item should be justified.

Most budgets show only what the expenditure buys. The performance budget is coming into use and supplements the figures by explaining, after each item, what is to be achieved by the expenditures. Table 7–8 is an example of such a budget.

CONSIDERATION AND ADOPTION OF THE BUDGET. The duty of the superintendent of schools is to prepare as clear and concise a budget as possible, and to present it to the school board in a manner designed to secure its adoption with as few changes as possible. Reciprocally, it is the duty of the board to refuse to approve any elimination or decrease of a budgetary item without consulting the superintendent. In the presentation of the budget, two principles should be followed:

(1) The public should be informed. Ample publicity is a necessity in modern administration. Many states now require public budget hearings, on the sound grounds that the manner in which the budget is prepared and adopted has a direct relation to the public pocketbook. Despite its tax implications, however, the average budget hearing is not noted for its heavy attendance. It is necessary, therefore, to see that the public is informed about this vital feature of school planning by using all available media.

(2) All requests should be justified. The budget is not a mere statement of intent; whenever an increased appropriation is requested for a certain item, an explanation and justification for the increase should be

TABLE 7–8. *Example of a Performance Budget.*

CLASSI-FICATION NUMBER	ITEM	EXPLANATION		1980–81 ACTUAL PREVIOUS YEAR BUDGET	1981–82 CURRENT YEAR BUDGET	1982–83 PROPOSED YEAR BUDGET
230	*Textbooks*					
231	Elementary Supplementary Texts	2,982 Pupils @ $ 2.00		$4,150	$4,800	$5,964
232	Junior High Supplementary Texts	788 Pupils @ $ 3.00		982	1,027	2,364
233	High School Texts	1,340 Pupils @ $15.00 = $20,100				
233.1	English Department	Dictionaries	100 copies	1,694	2,134	3,500
		9 Grammar Basic	350			
		9 LMCL	40			
		10 LMCL	40			
		10 LBLA	30			
		Replacement	50			
233.2	Homemaking Department	Clothing	40 copies	729	40	840
		Home Management	40			
		Home Economics I	40			
		Replacement	20			
233.3	Foreign Language Department	Spanish I	85 copies	821	1,439	1,020
		Grammar I	55			
		Replacement	30			
233.4	Mathematics Department	Replacement		593	1,276	300
233.5	Science Department	Life Science	325 copies	1,837	—	2,250
		Replacement	50			

given. In order to do this successfully, detailed information should be provided by all departments and individuals working to formulate the budget, so that every request can be justified.

The budget as it is finally presented by the superintendent to the board of education should be either in typewritten or mimeographed form. Each board member should be presented with a copy, labeled and placed in individual loose-leaf folders. Although not necessarily in this order, the following subjects should be presented:

Title page.

Table of contents showing series numbers, budget categories, and page numbers.

List of charts, graphs, figures.

Letter of transmittal from the superintendent to the board of education.

A statement of the educational philosophy from which the budget is developed.

A statement regarding proposed programs.

A statement regarding population growth trends.

Budget summary.

Definitions of special terms.

Supporting data.

Index.

Usually, the use of pictorial and graphic representations in connection with the budget is for the benefit of the general lay public, rather than for school personnel or board members. The picture of the tax dollar, with wedges representing the proportionate expenditures in each of the budgetary categories, is a common device and is often reproduced in leaflets and brochures for public distribution. Figure 7–1 is an example of an expenditure dollar.

After the tentative budget has passed through the various departments and has been developed to the superintendent's satisfaction, the presentation is then made to the school board. Following preliminary discussions of various sections and incorporation of whatever changes may be deemed necessary, a public hearing should be held. The budget is then adopted by the board, and, under most state laws, presented to the necessary municipal, county, or state authorities for approval. After final adoption and approval, it then becomes the legal instrument governing the school district's finances for the next fiscal year. The entire budget should be open to all people because it is a public record; copies should be readily available.

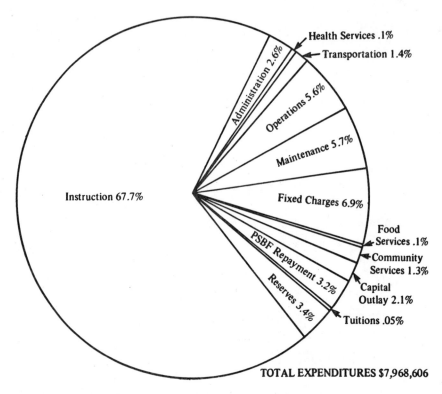

Health Services .1%
Transportation 1.4%
Administration 2.6%
Operations 5.6%
Maintenance 5.7%
Instruction 67.7%
Fixed Charges 6.9%
Food Services .1%
Community Services 1.3%
PSBF Repayment 3.2%
Reserves 3.4%
Capital Outlay 2.1%
Tuitions .05%

TOTAL EXPENDITURES $7,968,606

FIGURE 7–1.   Example of an Expenditure Dollar.

ADMINISTRATION OF THE BUDGET. Either the superintendent or the business manager, depending upon the internal organization of the school system, administers the budget as an executive function. Expenditures that remain within the amounts authorized by the budget are made as the need arises and without further action by the school board. Should the occasion arise when an emergency appears to necessitate the spending of sums over and above existing amounts in specific budgetary categories, board approval for the transfer of funds from the reserve will be necessary. Reserves usually should be maintained at a figure totaling not more than 10 percent of the entire budget. Some states require a "general reserve" for carry-over purposes during tax-scarce months; this normally cannot be touched for inter-budgetary transfer purposes. All states permit an "undistributed reserve" which can be tapped to meet unexpected expenditures or similar emergencies.

It should be remembered that, while a budget should be followed as closely as possible, it should not always be followed blindly and slavishly, regardless of school needs. A budget, even in its most efficient form, is only an estimate; it is never a perfect projection of the future. There is always an "x," an unknown quantity which necessitates a budgetary revision sometime within the subsequent year, however slight. The variance may be due to unexpectedly large school enrollment, requiring an unexpected expenditure of funds for a particular item. It may result from heightened expenditures due to a flood, fire, earthquake, or other natural calamity. An inflexible interpretation of the budget will result in scrimping and perhaps cutting back on priority categories in order to avoid a deficit. A more liberal interpretation will meet the emergency in one of two ways: either by borrowing money or by transferring funds from one budgetary category to another.

Every board of education should strive for a balanced budget. To say that a budget should not be interpreted inflexibly is not to say that it should be interpreted loosely. Every school district should operate within its income limits. It should be remembered that borrowing money to pay current operating expenses is as risky as an individual borrowing in order to pay for food and rent. However, deficit financing over a period much in excess of a year should be discouraged.

In connection with good budget administration, it goes without saying that a financial accounting system should be established that makes it possible for school officials to know from month to month how much money is available in any appropriation item. Such a system should be closely allied in form and structure to the budget forms themselves, and should show not only amounts actually expended from each appropriation item, but also all encumbrances upon each appropriation item. Obviously, regular semiannual reports should be made to the school board, which also should give final approval to any and all budgeting expenditures.

Planning-Programming-Budgeting Systems (PPBS)

Many districts are now moving to some form of a planning-programming-budgeting system, or a systems-analysis approach based on goal setting and long-term projections. It is output oriented, and divides its objectives into short-term and long-term categories. It can be administered either horizontally by autonomous administrators or vertically by one person. Usually a specially trained administrator must be employed when PPBS is installed. The specialized knowledge required by this system will come with that instructor.

ZERO-BASED BUDGETING AND OTHER SYSTEMS. For districts not wishing to employ additional specially trained administrators, it is possible to use various forms of zero-based budgeting. The underlying principle, as the name implies, is to build the budget each year in accordance with the indicated financial requirements of the district, without depending upon specific goals and objectives. It is short-term rather than long-term budgeting, and does not require the elaborate preplanning necessary under PPBS.

For more general and historical information, good sources are Stephen Knezevich's *Administrative Technology and the School Executive* (Washington, D.C.: American Association of School Administrators, 1969), and Sue Haggart's *Program Budgeting for School District Planning* (Englewood Cliffs, N.J.: Educational Technology Publications; Copyright 1972, The Rand Corporation).

Summary

A school budget is a planned forecast and a systematized form of educational planning. In addition, it states in dollars and cents the philosophy of the school district.

Proper budgeting procedures furnish a test of school administration; hence, the preparation of the budget is extremely important. The three steps of budgetary development are (1) educational planning; (2) expenditure program planning; and (3) income planning. This should be done under the supervision of the school superintendent, but should also involve other school employees and should be a continuing year-round activity during which a detailed budget calendar should be followed.

The final budget should be a complete picture of the district's financial plans, with each item accompanied by an explanation; this constitutes a "performance budget." Two basic principles to be observed in budget presentation are to inform the public and to justify all requests.

After its adoption, the budget should be administered as approved, with any changes due to unforeseen circumstances requiring action by the school board. To facilitate such administration, an encumbered bookkeeping system should be used.

Many districts are now moving to some form of a planning-programming-budgeting system, or a systems-analysis approach based on goal setting and long-term projections. It is output oriented, and divides its objectives into short-term and long-term categories. It can be administered either horizontally by autonomous administrators or vertically by one person. Usually a specially trained administrator must be employed when PPBS is installed.

Administrative Problems   In Basket

Problem 1

Mrs. Richards is the principal of John Adams High School which has an enrollment of 1,800 students. In December, the business manager sent all department heads and principals forms on which to list their budget requests for the following school year in the areas of personnel needs, conference attendance, equipment replacement or repair, new equipment, new books and supplies, printed forms of all types, and building and ground repairs and replacement.

It was explained that because department heads and principals would probably not be able to get everything they wanted, they should each list the requested items in priority order.

What procedure should Principal Richards use to determine her budget requests?
How should she go about setting her priorities?
If conflicts arise between departments (athletic, foreign language, business education, and vocational education) in establishing priorities, how might Mrs. Richards solve them?

Problem 2

The Big Valley School District consists of twenty elementary schools, four junior high schools, and two senior high schools, and has an enrollment of 25,000. After lengthy consideration, the Board of Education and the Superintendent have decided to institute a planning-programming-budgeting system (PPBS). Mr. Murdock, the business manager, has been given the task of developing the system and of bringing his tentative plans to the Board of Education for discussion.

How should Mr. Murdock start?
What information will he need?
How should he suggest that the plan be integrated into the present system?
What time schedule should he recommend?

Problem 3

The Paramount School District board wants its superintendent to develop a streamlined Budget Calendar to reduce the amount of administrative and board time spent annually on this process.

What portions of the schedule could be omitted without damage?
What portions of the schedule could be combined or synchronized?

Selected References

BURTON, WARREN C. *District School As It Was.* Lauderdale, Fla.: F. E. Peters Co., 1977.

CAMPBELL, ROALD F., et al. *Organization and Control of American Schools.* 3rd ed. Columbus, Ohio: Charles E. Merrill Publishing Co., 1975.

DERSTINE, R. "Accounting Income vs. Taxable Income." *Journal of Business Education* 53 (February 1978): 197–99.

DEYOUNG, C. A. *Budgeting in Public Schools.* New York: Doubleday and Co., 1936.

GORTON, RICHARD A. *School Administration: Challenge and Opportunity for Leadership.* Dubuque, Iowa: William C. Brown Co., 1976.

HAGGART, SUE A. (ed.) *Program Budgeting for School District Planning.* Englewood Cliffs, N.J: Educational Technology Publications. Copyright © 1972, The Rand Corporation.

HARTLEY, HARRY J. *Educational Planning–Programming–Budgeting: A Systems Approach.* Englewood Cliffs, N.J.: Prentice-Hall, Inc., 1968.

KNEZEVICH, STEPHEN J. (ed.) *Administrative Technology and the School Executive.* Washington, D.C.: American Association of School Administrators, 1969.

——. *Administration of Public Education.* Scranton, Pa.: Harper and Row Publishers, Inc., 1975.

MORPHET, EDGAR L., ROE L. JOHNS, and THEODORE L. RELLER. *Educational Organization and Administration.* 3rd ed. Englewood Cliffs, N.J.: Prentice-Hall, Inc., 1974.

MURPHY, J. F. "Fiscal Problems of Big City School Systems: Changing Patterns of State and Federal Aid." *Urban Review* 10 (Winter 1978):251–65.

NELSON, D. LLOYD, and WILLIAM M. PURDY. *School Business Administration.* Lexington, Mass.: D.C. Heath and Co., 1971.

PARKER, STEPHENSON. "PPBS." *CTA Journal* 65 (May 1969).

POSTER, CYRIL. *School Decision-Making.* Exeter, N. H.: Heinemann Educational Books, Inc., 1976.

"Program Budgeting Design for Schools Unveiled, with Much More Work Still to Go." *Nation's Schools* 84 (November 1969).

RATH, GUSTAVE J. "PPBS Is More Than a Budget: It's a Total Planning Process." *Nation's Schools* 82 (November 1968).

SENATE HEARING. "School Construction . . ." Washington, D.C., SB 2997, 95th Congress, May 16, 1978.

U. S. DEPARTMENT OF HEALTH, EDUCATION, AND WELFARE. *Financial Accounting for Local and State School Systems.* Washington, D. C.: U. S. Government Printing Office, 1960.

CHAPTER EIGHT

School Accounting Procedures

Accounting provides statistical information and data regarding the educational program, personnel, finances, and business procedures of a school district. It expresses the actual functioning of the budget throughout the school year. Good accounting practices furnish the means for appraisal and evaluation and help to build trust and confidence in the school district's programs and procedures. There are several essential parts to an accounting system and many records must be kept. The system should be kept as simple as possible, yet be adequate and well organized.

Accurate Organization of Data

An accurate supply of information is essential to any business or profession, and education is no exception. There should be no place in thoughtful policymaking for vague guesses and estimates. Statistics, accurate and ample, are the building blocks of school administration; they provide the underlying skeleton upon which the remainder of the school program must depend. Administrators must rely upon accounting to provide such data.

In policymaking, for example, the selection and implementation of guiding principles based upon any information other than the most complete and reliable will be apt to result in confusion and internal conflict. Assuming that sound policies have been arrived at, any attempt to execute them without using statistics as a guide will result in confusion. In the area of appraisal, the use of accurate and detailed data is absolutely essential, unless the many phases of the school system are to be allowed to run themselves. Records should never be accumulated for their own sake, but as a measure of the efficiency of every piece of material, every employee, and every process concerned with the running of the school system.

Good accounting practices accomplish a number of purposes. They provide an accurate historical record of all the business procedures of a school district and information for board of education decisions. Because of annual audits, they assure that legal prescriptions have been met and public funds are safeguarded properly. They form a sound basis for improved administrative decisions because data is available for budget preparation and revision. Accounting procedures provide a public record of the stewardship charged with handling public funds. They provide the financial records for administering the educational program.

Controlling the Administration of the Budget

A central system of financial accounting should always be associated with the central budget for the annual operation of a school district. Accounting practices have differed widely from district to district, and good procedures have been nonexistent in many. It was not until 1957 that the first acceptable plan for standardizing accounting practices was developed when the U.S. Office of Education published *Handbook II, Financial Accounting for Local and State School Systems.* Many states have adopted variations of this standard form and provide them for the use of local school districts. More emphasis has been given to developing good accounting practices during the last few years. This has been brought about in part by the public demand that school districts be held accountable and publicize and justify their financial needs.

Because all accounting depends upon the accumulation and preservation of adequate records, it should be kept in mind that red tape for its own sake should be stringently avoided. Record keeping should be made as easy and simple as possible for all employees; in particular, reports should be regularly used and examined, so that employees will not have the feeling that no use is being made of their work. The collection of statistical data from school employees should be conducted in line with the following principles:

1. Make certain that the employees who make the reports know what use is being made of the reports.
2. Set and maintain reasonable deadlines for filing reports.
3. Do not ask for superfluous or unnecessary information.
4. Impress upon all persons concerned the importance of the reports and the need for accuracy.
5. Avoid the use of ambiguous report blanks.
6. Design report blanks so that they can be filled out in as brief a time and with as little effort as possible.
7. Endeavor to delegate all purely clerical work to a clerk.
8. Design reports and forms so that they can be adapted to the existing business office machines or computers.

Adequacy, Simplicity, and Standardization in Accounting

Adequacy in accounting implies a survey of all the necessary elements of a good system, and the inclusion of all these elements in the actual system adopted by the school business office. Simplicity becomes necessary in school accounting because of the frequent lack of professional accountants among the personnel who work with the books, and also because of the chronic shortage of time available to perform such work. Standardization is effected when the classification of the accounts achieves a wide degree of uniformity throughout all school systems and a similar degree of continuity from year to year.

In the past, such uniformity has been theoretical with some practical application. In accounting forms, definitions, and nomenclature, school financial-accounting systems have been widely and justly criticized for their lack of standardization. Although school accounting is similar to the practices used by government and business, it is not identical to either. Following New York's adoption of a uniform accounting system in 1916, most states have adopted similar systems that prescribe regulations for record keeping, official reports, auditing, purchasing, and payment procedures. More recently, state accounting manuals for school district use have been based on the standards developed in the U.S. Office of Education Handbook. Such uniformity gives rise to the following advantages:

1. Easier auditing of accounts, because auditors have to contend with only one kind of financial-accounting system.
2. Easier reporting by school officials to federal, state, and county authorities.
3. Easier comparison of financial practices in one district with those in others.
4. Easier training of school clerks and business personnel in financial-accounting methods.

Melbo lists standards for financial accounting, bookkeeping procedures, and handling of cash. These standards can be adapted for use in any school district.[1]

RECOMMENDED STANDARDS FOR FINANCIAL ACCOUNTING

1. Financial statement regarding expenditures presented to board each month.

---

[1] Irving R. Melbo et al. *Report of the Survey, Paramount Unified School District,* published by authority of the Board of Trustees, Paramount Unified School District (Los Angeles: University of Southern California, 1970), pp. 80, 82, 84.

2. Unencumbered balance shown for each major account in financial statement.
3. Budgeted receipts, total receipts, receipts to date, and revised estimated receipts for year included in financial statement.
4. Annual financial report provided board.
5. Financial statements provided for each fund.
6. Financial statements posted on bulletin board of each school.
7. Monthly collection report made to board.
8. Bank accounts (student body and cafeteria) reconciled monthly.
9. District books balanced with county offices monthly.
10. Principals informed each month regarding status of supply budgets.
11. Head of food services and school board informed each month regarding status of cafeteria account.
12. Cost-analysis reports provided for major functions.

RECOMMENDED STANDARDS FOR BOOKKEEPING PROCEDURES

1. Machine bookkeeping should be used. Larger districts are moving toward the use of computers that will make "double entry" bookkeeping a must.
2. All contracts and purchase orders should be encumbered as issued.
3. Utilities should be encumbered for each month at beginning of the year.
4. Appropriation accounts should be correlated with budget classifications.
5. All warrants should be posted immediately after receipt from county offices.
6. A receipt ledger should be maintained for each source of revenue.
7. Prior years' expenses should be recorded on separate ledger form.
8. The bookkeeper should be allowed sufficient time to post books daily without frequent interruptions.
9. The bookkeeping machine should be operated in a separate, soundproof room adjacent to the other business offices.
10. Payment for materials should be charged to year in which they are received.
11. Double entry bookkeeping revealing cost of food, labor, etc., and showing exact financial condition each month should be used for the food service programs.
12. An appropriation ledger, a receipts ledger, and a general ledger should be maintained.

RECOMMENDED STANDARDS FOR HANDLING CASH

1. Printed prenumbered receipts supplied in triplicate should be provided.

2. One person in each school designated to make all collections for school.
3. Record maintained by business office of all receipt books issued.
4. Collections turned into business office daily with duplicate copies of receipts.
5. Master receipt given by business office to schools for collections.
6. Original receipt given to person from whom collection is made; duplicate sent to business office with money; and triplicate kept in receipt book to be checked in to business office at end of fiscal year.
7. All collections deposited with county treasurer at least once a month.
8. All deposits made with county treasurer noted in board minutes.
9. No illegal collections.
10. All persons bonded who handle money.
11. Procedure established to differentiate between revenue receipts and abatements.
12. Procedure established to make sure all money due district is collected.
13. All sales authorized by board.
14. Bids obtained for sales in excess of $200.
15. Money collected for lost or damaged state textbooks sent to state department of education.
16. Securities deposited with county treasurer.

Essential Parts of an Accounting System

ORIGINAL RECORDS. First, original records must be preserved of all financial transactions, embracing two major types of data: those showing assets and liabilities, and those showing income and expenditures. To allow these two sets of data to be available at all times, the original documents should be filed by category and should include receipts, requisitions, purchase orders, invoices, cancelled checks, payroll lists, and any other evidence that will support financial transactions. Receipts should be given and copies retained for all monies received just as records are kept for all expenditures. Auditors find such original records indispensable to the proper performance of their annual duties.

VOUCHER RECORD. Some schools still utilize the daybook or journal for the retention of records. A more modern practice is the use of the voucher record, in the form of a book or sometimes an envelope wherein are filed the records to be kept, and on which is recorded the distribution of expenditures for later copying into the ledger.

LEDGER. This is the classified record of expenditures. It should be itemized in exact correspondence with the budget, only in vertical columns where the budget items are listed on horizontal lines. This is the portion of the system most prominently in need of the uniformity in accounting procedures which previously has been stressed as of the utmost importance. The standardized system of accounting described earlier in this chapter centers about the ledger, and is usually called the "National System." Its classifications should be synchronized completely with those of the district budget. A separate ledger form should be provided for each of the major classifications of the National System: administration, instruction, attendance and health services, pupil transportation services, operation of plant, maintenance of plant, fixed charges, food service and student body activities, community services, capital outlay, and debt service from current funds. Figures 8–1 and 8–2 show examples of actual school revenue and appropriation ledger forms.

Studies of unit costs are facilitated by the use of code numbers or letters as follows: elementary school expenditures are coded "E" and expenditures for high schools are coded "H." Similarly, coded numbers or letters can be applied to each of the many services, departments, or buildings of the school district. A more detailed coding system is the system originally developed by Engelhardt and Engelhardt, which provides a four-digit system from 1,000–2,000 for all receipts and revenues. In addition, the character classes of expenditures are subdivided and coded on the ledger sheets. General control is subdivided into two categories—business administration and educational administration. Under the former come columns headed "school elections," "school census," "board of education," and the like. Educational administration subdivides into "superintendent's salary," "superintendent's clerical help," "superintendent's supplies," and other expenses.

CASH–RECEIPTS BOOK.   All revenues as they are made available to the district should be listed in a cash–receipts book. All entries should be made on a monthly basis, thus enabling the monthly financial statements to be at least partially based on the data contained in the cash–receipts book. Prenumbered receipts should be issued in triplicate: the original to the person from whom the collection was made, the second to the business office, and the third should remain in the receipt book. Figure 8–3 shows a sample page from a cash–receipts book.

Three Main Bases of an Accounting System

THE CASH–DISBURSEMENTS BASIS.   In a system organized upon this principle, only actual income and payments are considered and no account is taken of deferred payments, uncollected receipts, and short-term loans. Cost figures in this type of accounting include current costs plus cash

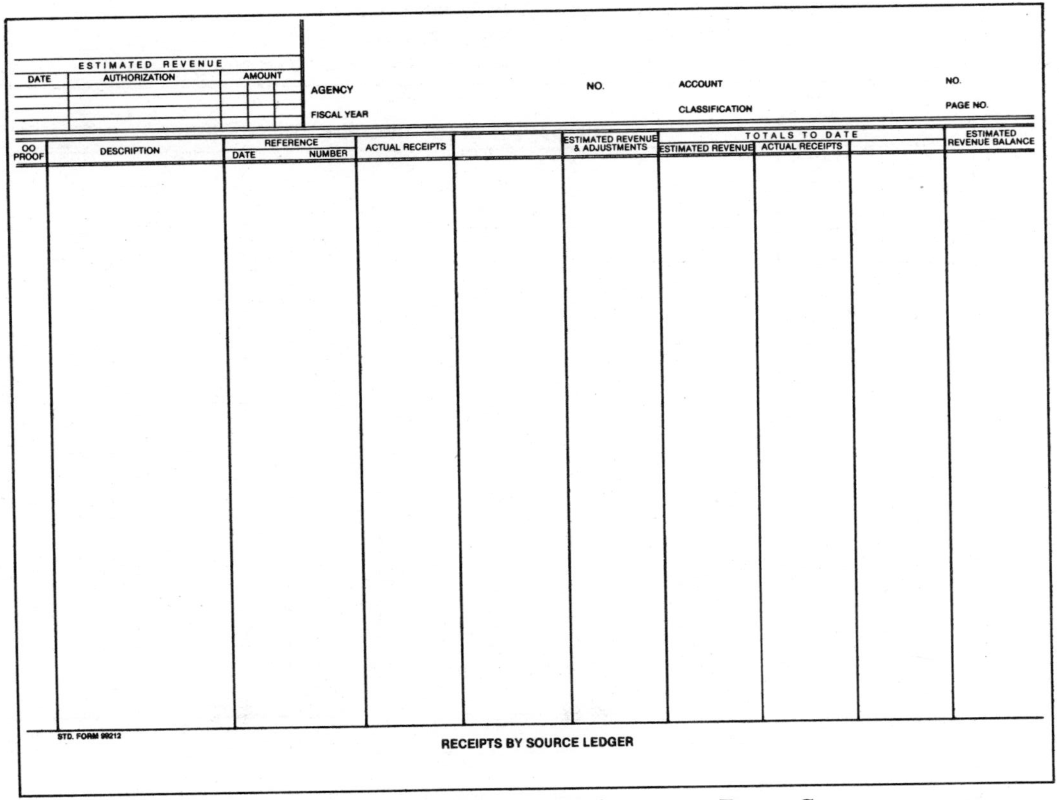

ESTIMATED REVENUE		
DATE	AUTHORIZATION	AMOUNT

AGENCY NO. ACCOUNT NO.
FISCAL YEAR CLASSIFICATION PAGE NO.

OO PROOF	DESCRIPTION	REFERENCE		ACTUAL RECEIPTS		ESTIMATED REVENUE & ADJUSTMENTS	TOTALS TO DATE			ESTIMATED REVENUE BALANCE
		DATE	NUMBER				ESTIMATED REVENUE	ACTUAL RECEIPTS		

STD. FORM 99212

RECEIPTS BY SOURCE LEDGER

FIGURE 8–1. Example of a School Revenue Form. Courtesy of the Paramount Unified School District, Paramount, California.

AGENCY: PARAMOUNT UNIFIED SCHOOL DISTRICT NO. APPROPRIATION NO.

FISCAL YEAR CLASSIFICATION CODE PAGE NO.

DESCRIPTION	ENCUMBRANCES						TOTALS TO DATE			
	REFERENCE									
	DATE	P. O. NUMBER	WARRANT NUMBER	RESERVED	CANCELLED	EXPENDITURES	APPROPRIATION	ENCUMBRANCES	EXPENDITURES	UNENCUMBERED BALANCE

NCR Systemedia Division 877046

APPROPRIATION AND EXPENDITURE LEDGER

FIGURE 8–2. Example of an Appropriation and Expenditure Ledger Form. Courtesy of the Paramount Unified School District, Paramount, California.

RECEIPT Date_____19____

Received From_____

Address_____

_____Dollars $____

For_____

ACCOUNT			HOW PAID				
AMT. OF ACCOUNT			CASH				
AMT. PAID			CHECK				
BALANCE DUE			MONEY ORDER			By____	

FIGURE 8–3. *Sample Page from a Cash–Receipts Book. Courtesy of the Paramount Unified School District, Paramount, California.*

payments for plant increase (such as site purchasing, equipment, and buildings, and the payment of interest on necessary loans). The cash basis is limited by many factors which combine to complicate obtaining a true picture of the district's financial condition. Wehn lists these unaccounted-for items as follows: state aid not yet received; tax collections still in arrears; collection of tuition from other school districts; payment of bills in a year subsequent to that in which they were incurred; underwriting costs of financing bonds; and others.[2]

THE ACCRUED–ECONOMIC–COST BASIS. This system takes into consideration everything that has worth or value, including all assets, accounts payable, and deferred payments. Cost reckoned on this basis includes current expense plus the interest on all capital invested and the annual depreciation on equipment and buildings.

THE INCOME–AND–EXPENDITURE BASIS. This is the principle adopted by most of the standard school accounting methods. It represents a compromise between the cash-disbursement and the accrued-economic-cost basis; and it accounts for all actual and potential assets and liabilities, but does not usually attempt to estimate depreciation as an accounting factor.

In any discussion of desirable school accounting principles, it should be kept in mind that school accounts differ widely from business accounts in that proprietary interest does not apply. A balance sheet should be replaced with a statement of assets and liabilities that presents a picture of the financial status of the school district.

---

[2] W. C. Wehn, "School Accounting on the Basis of Income and Expenditure," *American School Board Journal*, pp. 29–30.

Receipts

In addition to listing receipts by the sources from which money has been received, it has been found useful to group them under the threefold classification of revenue receipts, nonrevenue receipts, and revolving-fund receipts. Revenue receipts are those that do not result in increasing school indebtedness or in decreasing school assets; taxes are an example. Non-revenue receipts create an obligation which must be met at some future date. Insurance adjustment receipts and sale of property are examples of this kind of income. Revolving-fund receipts are so called because they include money received from services that the board renders as an agent. They may relate to cash that has already been obligated or expended for which an accounting must be made and for which a return is anticipated. Examples are the sale of textbooks or shop supplies by the district to pupils at cost.

Periodic Financial Statements

There are two types of financial statements that take stock periodically of the fiscal condition prevailing within the school district.

THE ANNUAL STATEMENT. A yearly financial statement, showing an itemization of the income and expenditures during the year just closed, is a legal requirement in most states. Usually published in a local newspaper or as a bulletin, this document interprets the financial condition of the school district to the general public. Accompanying it should be an auditor's statement to the effect that the accounts have been audited and that they are legally in order.

THE MONTHLY STATEMENT. This statement is a comparative device, showing appropriations compared with expenditures. It should be made either by the superintendent or the financial officer to the board of education, and should list the sources of income, the budget amount, and the budget available. Contractual and other planned expenditures should be handled on an encumbrance rather than on an actual disbursement basis. The encumbered column shows the amount expected to be paid when a contract or purchase order is made out. The expenditure column shows the amount actually expended after the bill is received. The unencumbered balance shows the amount that has no encumbrance against it. All existing liabilities are accounted for, thus serving to prevent the year's expenditures from exceeding appropriations. This type of statement enables school officials to keep informed of the status of school funds, and simultaneously to make comparisons of the finances with those of the preceding year or with earlier months of the current fiscal year.

It is recommended, in addition to the financial statements described above, that the school district should prepare an annual balance statement at the end of each year. This would be merely a statement of assets compared with liabilities, contrasting positive factors—such as school sites, buildings, permanent equipment, taxes, and appropriations receivable— with such liabilities as accounts payable, bonded indebtedness, short-term loans, and interest payable. This has the inestimable advantage of confronting the taxpayer with a simple balance sheet instead of a bewildering array of figures and peculiar bookkeeping techniques wherein operating expenses are confused with capital expenditures, and the like.

AUDITING. Auditing of school funds is essential because it inspires public confidence, renders an account of stewardship, and improves procedures.[3] The Association of School Business Officials has stated the following objectives for an audit program:

1. To safeguard money, property, and employees.
2. To determine the adequacy of the methods of internal check.
3. To maintain adherence to the established standards, policies, and procedures—financial, accounting, and operating.
4. To check condition and use of property and equipment, particularly from the standpoint of adequate return.
5. To maintain and coordinate internal auditing procedures with those of the public accountant.
6. To present accurate, complete, and unbiased statistics with respect to the operation of the educational system.[4]

There are two types of audits: continuous and annual. In the case of the former, usually the school's regular business and financial officers conduct the audit, which goes on constantly as monthly and other short-term financial statements are made ready and tentative balances are arrived at.

The annual, or periodic, audit is preferably conducted by an agency independent of the school business office. A special agency appointed by the state department of education to audit all school district accounts would be the best solution to the problem of periodic auditing. Failing this, the use of the services of a certified public accountant is to be preferred. This has the advantage of being a paid service, with a resulting drain of district funds better spent on educational needs, and also of involving an accountant in a highly specialized area, namely school finance, where he may not have had any previous experience. A wise school district will select an auditing firm that is experienced and competent in auditing school accounting records.

---

[3] Melbo, *Report of the Survey, Paramount,* p. 85.
[4] Thor W. Bruce, "The Why and Where of Auditing," *Proceedings, the Association of School Business Officials* (Chicago: Association of School Business Officials of United States and Canada, 1950), p. 236.

Occasionally audits are performed by committees of school board members or by committees of laymen appointed by the board for that specific purpose. This method is pregnant with potential blunders and scarcely better than no audit at all.

In dealing with an auditor it is important to convince him of the necessity of confining his attentions to the functions of an audit. He is being paid to discover errors in the accounts, if any, and to expose any misuse of funds from a legal standpoint. He is not to succumb to the urge to deplore the wisdom of the board's judgment in spending funds. An auditor may also be employed successfully as a consultant in business practices and methods. School funds that are kept in a county treasury are already subject to at least one and frequently two audits. However, school district accounts that are maintained in banks should be audited more frequently than the funds mentioned above.

Cost Accounting

A school system bears sufficient resemblance to a well-administered private industry to render advisable periodic studies of the cost of its product and of the several processes which go to make up its internal functioning. The practical value of such studies to the school administrator lies in judging the adequacy of the financial support enjoyed by his district and in evaluating the distribution of expenditures among the various budgetary items.

UNIT COSTS.   The basis of cost accounting is unit costs. Unit costs are determined by dividing the total cost of education, or any part of it, by the total units of school, classroom, child, etc.

Unit costs may be compared with corresponding costs for similar services at previous times and in different school districts. One of the most popularly compared cost units is cost per child. It may be compared, for instance, to similar cost units in other schools of the same general area, or, internally, cost per elementary child may be compared to cost per secondary child in the same system. Such information will often make it possible for a school district to lower its costs without decreasing the quality of the service provided. Costs, of course, should not be calculated for trivial items; only where the expenditure is large enough to make possible an economy that outweighs the expense of making the cost calculation should the operation be performed.

Several different types of unit-cost studies might be made. As an example, a study might be made comparing cost per pupil for a certain kind of service with that for another kind of service in the district—e.g., teacher cost per pupil v. educational supply cost per pupil. Studies of the cost of furnishing particular supplies on a per-classroom basis are also common. Proportion of expenditures going for maintenance and operation within individual schools of a given system may also be of value, and may often be studied through some type of unit-cost approach. Cost analysis provides information for the school board, school administrators, the staff, and the public to evaluate the efficiency of various types of programs and operations.

There are two main problems to be solved in making a unit-cost study: (1) securing comparable and accurate data, and (2) determining the best cost unit for computing the cost of the particular item upon which information is desired.

COMPARATIVE COSTS. The evaluation of local levels of financial support usually can be conducted objectively only with the aid of comparative data from other school systems with similar characteristics and problems. Only with such information can a school administrator decide whether the amount spent upon a school system is sufficient, compared with the amounts spent upon other systems, and whether the amounts spent on different areas of the instructional program are properly proportioned.

The reliability of intersystem studies is sometimes difficult to establish because several items are not always reported in exactly the same way. It is generally better to attach more significance to comparative costs of different subjects in the same system than to comparisons between systems.

It is never wise for an administrator to attach too much importance to comparative cost data. Allocation of expenditures to the several classes may differ from district to district; school accountants may be inexperienced and make mistakes. The conditions that determine the appropriateness of any school expenditure differ from one part of the country to another, and often from one part of the same state to another. A district cannot be allowed to straitjacket itself within cost table norms when, in relation to local needs, its action may be completely wrong. However, comparative costs do make it easy for an administrator to identify quickly and accurately expenditures that are conspicuously too high or too low. This is all comparative cost accounting can do; it can never say by itself which expenditures are justified and which are not.

Internal Accounting

In any large high school system, internal accounting should be decentralized insofar as is consistent with fiscal prudence and efficiency. The following are examples of how an otherwise monolithic and insensitive degree of centralization can be avoided.

SCHOOL LEVEL. Under the general supervision and direction of the district business manager, principals should each keep their own books, accounting in detail for such items as supplies received, repairs and alterations made by local school custodians, overtime work requested and performed, and nonbudgeted emergency expenditures. Forms used should be those approved by the district's business office. An annual audit of school-level accounting should be made by the main office.

DEPARTMENT LEVEL.   A large high school will in turn be well advised to set up an accounting system for each of its instructional departments. The several department chairmen will prepare their own budget requests. When approved by the principal and by the district business manager, these departmental budgets will then be used as the basis for departmental purchasing, part-time hiring and requisitioning, just as the school budget is used for the combined entity. The principal will be expected to check departmental accounts and figures regularly throughout the fiscal year.

EXTRACURRICULAR ACTIVITIES.   Certain extracurricular activities are conducted by most secondary schools; virtually all such activities, in addition to those nonclassroom services provided by the schools, are revenue-producing and revenue-spending. Activities and activity centers such as lunchrooms, bookstores, athletics, school clubs, and publications create a problem of the management of nonpublic funds within the framework of district accounting. The need for the governing board to establish rules and regulations controlling the finances of these activities is obvious. Although the funds involved are not strictly public in nature, they necessarily fall within the purview of public interest. Inexperienced administrators have experienced difficulties in accounting for such funds, probably because the monies expended for these purposes are not commonly considered to be in the same category as district funds. Difficulties can be avoided by having such funds audited annually by the district auditor. This is a legal requirement in some states. The auditor can be of invaluable assistance in helping to establish proper controls that will prevent inadvertent or intentional misuse of such funds. Several methods have been developed to account for internal revenues and expenditures.

The traditional way has been for boards of education to include such funds in the regular accounting systems by providing for a revolving-fund account; such an approach to the problem is not now recommended. It assumes that there is no distinction between these funds and those used by the school district for operational purposes and makes no provision for student participation in the handling of student money.

Many schools have elected to set up mechanisms to account for these funds separately. In many cases, they are placed under the supervision of the principal or a staff member who reports regularly to the board of education through the superintendent. Although this method distinguishes properly between "activity" and "general" funds, it does not encourage pupil participation.

A separate bank account is used by some schools. Receipts from all high school activities are deposited in the bank to the credit of the organizations raising the money. The student treasurer authorizes expenditures by means of vouchers signed by the faculty sponsor of the particular activity, and a complete accounting is required of all monies received; vouchers, issued by the treasurer and adviser of each organization and countersigned by the treasurer of the activity fund, are used to authorize expenditures. A central office clerk or school bookkeeper can serve as treasurer of all activities funds from each school in the system. These are kept in a single bank account. A special ledger designed to keep track of the various school activities should be used. Monthly financial statements showing the status of the schools' student-body funds should be made to the school board for their approval, since ultimately they should be responsible for the supervision of these funds. Each student-body organization should prepare a budget at the start of the fiscal year forecasting its expected receipts, needs, and expenditures.

Student-body funds, which come primarily from students, should be used for the benefit of those students and not be permitted to accumulate for an indefinite future, which is often the case. They should not be used to purchase materials or equipment that the school district legally should provide. Because these are student-body funds, students should have a strong voice in how they are collected, invested, banked, and dispersed. The principal or faculty sponsor serves as adviser, however, so that mismanagement does not occur.

PETTY CASH.   Abuses are more apt to occur in this area of decentralized accounting than in any other. Granted that small amounts of cash are often necessary to meet emergency needs, warrants signed by three school employees including the principal with carbons kept methodically and filed under a predetermined system should be required. The cash itself should be kept in a safe, preferably in the principal's office. The amount of petty cash kept on the school premises should be relatively small and its annual budget figure should not be exceeded.

Food Services Accounting

The school lunch program is monumental in size. Over three billion meals are served annually in the schools, providing over a billion dollar market for the nation's food industry.[5] Because of the scope of food services, more detailed accounting records usually are required than are necessary for

---

[5] Robert E. Wilson, *Educational Administration* (Columbus, Ohio: Charles E. Merrill Books, 1966), p. 676.

ordinary internal accounting systems. The business management of the program should be centralized in the district office. All purchasing, fiscal accounting, property accounting, construction, maintenance, and employment of cafeteria personnel should be handled centrally to effect savings.[6] Accounting records consist of kitchen and service records, purchase orders, cash-record vouchers, and requisitions. Records and purchases of federal allocations of money and purchases of surplus foods also should be kept. Although cost accounts should be kept for each school's lunch program, the total program should be financed as one district account. Food services accounting is based more on a profit-and-loss basis than on a revenue-and-expenditure basis (more frequently characteristic of school finances). The governing criterion is the ability of the food services program to be self-supporting.[7]

The board of education should receive monthly and annual reports showing income, expenses, profit, and loss of the food services program.

Accounting Technology

Accounting practice has progressed toward automation. Few, if any, business offices do all their work by hand. In order of sophistication, accounting is handled mechanically, electromechanically, or electronically. Most large school districts, in fact, now use computers extensively to assist in such things as accounting inventories. The more sophisticated office machines become, the more they cost. This, as well as the lack of electronic "know-how" on the part of business managers, is a deterrent to the improvement of accounting procedures.

Summary

Accounting provides and organizes the statistical data needed for the administration of any school district. In addition, it provides the only device for controlling the administration of the budget. Problems involve avoiding unnecessary red tape while still keeping adequate records and reporting regularly.

Adequacy, simplicity, and standardization are the keys to good accounting, which is composed of several essential parts: original records, voucher record, ledger, and cash–receipts books. The accounting system should be founded on any one of three bases: cash disbursement, accrued economic cost, or income and expenditure.

---

[6] Wilson, *Educational Administration*, p. 676.

[7] Melbo, *Report of the Survey, Paramount*, p. 104.

Receipts should be classified by revenue sources, and periodic financial statements made to the school board by the administration, either annually or monthly. In either case, such statements should be audited.

Whatever accounting system is used, it should lend itself both to the determination of unit costs and comparative costs. Internal accounting should be careful and well organized, with special attention paid to the so-called extracurricular programs that are so often poorly accounted for. The food service program, too, needs more detailed accounting records than are often kept.

Administrative Problem   In Basket

Problem

Two small districts have just merged, forming the Lincoln Unified School District with fourteen elementary schools, two junior high schools, and one senior high school. Previously, neither district had done any cost analysis, making it impossible for the new district to evaluate the distribution of expenditures among the various budgetary items.

Clifford Jacobson has been employed as the new accountant. The morning after one of the first Board of Education meetings, he found a note from the business manager on his desk. It stated that the Board wanted to commence a cost-analysis program to determine whether expenditures were being allotted wisely. The accountant was asked to develop a cost-analysis plan. As a first step, the note asked that he determine the unit cost of all instructional supplies and give the business manager a preliminary report in four weeks.

How should Clifford proceed?
What information will he need?
What new accounting machines and systems should Mr. Jacobson recommend for use in the merged district?

Selected References

ARNOLD, ROBERT R., HAROLD C. HILL, and AYLMER V. NICHOLS. *Introduction to Data Processing.* New York: John Wiley and Sons, 1966.

BRUCE, THOR W. "The Why and Where of Auditing." *Proceedings, The Association of School Business Officials.* Chicago, Ill.: Association of School Business Officials of United States and Canada, 1950.

BUSINESS EQUIPMENT MANUFACTURERS ASSOCIATION. *New Techniques in Office Operation: Machines, Forms, Systems.* Elmhurst, Ill.: The Business Press, 1968.

COUZINS, J. "Put Away Your Pencils and Maps Because Computers Route Buses Better." *American School Board Journal* 165 (November 1978): 48–49.

DERSTINE, R. "Accounting Income vs. Taxable Income." *Journal of Business Education* 53 (February 1978):197–99.

GARVUE, RONERT J. *Modern Public School Finance.* New York: Macmillan Company, 1969.

LEVY, JOSEPH. *Punched Card Equipment: Principles and Applications.* New York: McGraw-Hill Book Co., 1967.

MAGARELL, J. "Supply and Demand in Public Accounting." *Chronicle of Higher Education* 17 (November 27, 1978):11.

MELBO, IRVING R., et al. *Report of the Survey, Paramount Unified School District.* Los Angeles: University of Southern California, 1970.

NELSON, D. LLOYD, and WILLIAM M. PURDY. *School Business Administration.* Lexington, Mass.: D. C. Heath and Co., 1971.

WILSON, ROBERT E. *Educational Administration.* Columbus, Ohio: Charles E. Merrill Publishing Co., 1966.

CHAPTER NINE

School Supply and Equipment Administration

Due to the proliferation of software and hardware and the increasing demands of teachers and administrators, modern supply and equipment management is a complex task. Logical, simple procedures should be cooperatively developed for selecting, purchasing, and handling supplies and equipment. Purchasing should be centralized and handled according to school board–adopted policies.

Supply and Equipment Management

Formerly, the methods followed in purchasing supplies and equipment were few and simple. Today, hundreds of different supply items may be discovered in the warehouses of a modern city school system, proof that the increasing specialization and size of education is being reflected in the complexity of supply administration. A sizable percentage of the annual expenditure of school systems is being spent for supplies and equipment.

Supplies may be defined as those items that are consumed or that enjoy a relatively short life, usually less than a year. Supplies may be divided into two categories, consumable and nonconsumable. Examples of consumable supplies are paper, pencils, and paints. Nonconsumable supplies are those that cost less than $10 and are not used up. Examples are small tools, scissors, staplers, and the like.[1]

Equipment refers to nonexpendable items which are more or less permanent, have a long life, and qualify as a capital expenditure. There

---

[1] Emery Stoops and Russell E. Johnson, *Elementary School Administration*, p. 176.

are two categories of equipment, fixed and movable. Examples of fixed equipment are built-in clock systems, counters, cabinets, and communication systems. Movable equipment includes such items as large tools, office machines, furniture,[2] television sets, and projectors.

Supplies and equipment are utilized for the most part by teachers, and their proper procurement and use are essential to the schools' primary function. Constant attention and study are needed to determine the most effective and economical types and brands of supplies and equipment and to have them delivered on schedule. Repair services must be provided to take care of equipment breakdowns.

TYPES OF SUPPLIES AND EQUIPMENT.   There are numerous types of supplies and equipment which may be categorized as follows:

> General instructional, such as the various kinds and sizes of paper, paints, pencils, crayons, clips and fasteners, folders, and other similar items.
>
> Audio-visual, including all types of projectors, maps, globes, charts, films, tape recorders and tapes, and pictures.
>
> Science.
>
> Music, art, and dramatics.
>
> Books and periodicals.
>
> Specialized supplies and equipment for special classes for the mentally retarded, the educationally handicapped, and the orthopedically handicapped.
>
> Vocational education.
>
> Business education.
>
> Homemaking education.
>
> Physical education and playground.
>
> Health and nursing services.
>
> Cafeteria.
>
> Custodial.
>
> Maintenance.
>
> Gardening.
>
> Transportation.
>
> Lounges and faculty rooms.
>
> Gymnasiums, auditoriums, and multipurpose rooms.
>
> Libraries.

---

[2] Stoops and Johnson, *Elementary School*, p. 177.

District office.

Other offices.

Some schools are using or planning to use newer types of equipment in classrooms, such as cable TV, cassettes, computers, and micro-processor-baesd teaching devices. However, there is still a debate about the costs, effectiveness, and acceptance of technological equipment. Equipment committees and administrators must investigate thoroughly and use good judgment before going overboard in purchasing sophisticated equipment.

OPERATIONS FROM NEED TO RECEIPT OF AN ARTICLE. Except for emergencies, supplies and equipment are ordered at specified intervals, either weekly, monthly, or annually. This assists the principal, department head, and central office in combining the individual orders into one large, coordinated order. The specific steps involved in ordering are as follows:

1. The individual schools, departments, and offices compile their list of needs.
2. Requisitions are filled out and sent to the central business office.
3. Centralized purchase orders are prepared and sent to the various vendors. Budget control must be maintained. Board of education authorization is needed before purchase or ratification afterwards.
4. The articles are delivered to the district warehouse. Upon receipt, they should be inventoried and checked against the purchase order.
5. Distribution is made to the various schools and departments as requested.
6. Finally, distribution is made to the person ordering the article.

Melbo sets forth fifteen recommended standards for requisitioning and warehousing.[3] These standards apply to a district large enough to have a central warehouse:

1. District operates central warehouse.
2. Warehouse contains approximately one year's needs.
3. Perpetual inventory maintained in business office.
4. Requisitions issued by principals for all needs of each school.
5. One person responsible for warehouse receipts and deliveries.
6. Requisitioner informed of disposition of each requisition.
7. Separate requisition forms provided for warehouse items and "buy out" items.
8. Each school placed on budget basis for supplies.

---

[3] Irving R. Melbo et al. *Report of the Survey, Paramount Unified School District*, published by authority of the Board of Trustees, Paramount Unified School District (Los Angeles: University of Southern California, 1970), p. 69.

9. Proper budget control exercised by business office.
10. Requisitioner provides helpful descriptive data but does not contact vendors.
11. Requisition forms printed, prenumbered, and supplied in quadruplicate.
12. Priced requisitions used.
13. Standard school supply list provided.
14. Daily deliveries provided.
15. Adequate supplies on hand for opening of school.

Selection of Supplies and Equipment

Many school systems today use committees to study needs and to make specific recommendations for the purchase of particular items. Even a small district can use consulting methods as a means of determining the kind of materials best suited to the needs of the schools.

The selection of instructional materials and equipment should be the responsibility of the individual school under the leadership of the supervising principal.[4] They should be selected to meet the predetermined purposes of the instructional program and provide a rich environment in each classroom so that students are given desirable experiences. Community lay persons may provide input in the selection of books and audio-visual materials. Selection should be made with reference to the following criteria:

1. The curriculum offerings.
2. The methods used in presenting information.
3. Specialized usage.
4. Simplicity and practicality of usage.
5. Quality.
6. Economy.
7. Availability.

Such criteria should make possible a dual efficiency because they facilitate selections that can be used widely throughout the school system, and at the same time serve the purpose of the particular department that made the order. In order to ensure uniformity in the quality of equipment, it is necessary to define the standards of quality desired for the particular items. Specifications should be complete, specifying the construction, composition, and nature of the items to be ordered.

---

[4] Sir James R. Marks, Emery Stoops, and Joyce King-Stoops, *Handbook of Educational Supervision*, 2nd ed. (Boston: Allyn and Bacon, Inc., 1978), p. 341.

Committees should do the following[5]:

1. Review the curriculum.
2. Define the instructional program.
3. Evaluate the strengths and weaknesses of the instructional program.
4. Determine the money allocated.
5. Arrange for textbook publishers and vendors to display and demonstrate their materials and equipment.
6. Consider the variety of cultures and needs of minority students.
7. Determine freedom from sex stereotyping.
8. Consider the possibility of developing pilot programs for certain instructional materials.
9. Consider the effectiveness of the ordering and distributing system for new instructional materials.
10. Evaluate student progress with the selected materials and equipment.

It is important that selection committees meet and discuss their needs directly with the sales person rather than relying solely on impersonal phone calls, catalogs, and written communications.

The result of cooperative action should be the preparation of standard supply lists that contain specifications for all items commonly used in schools. A school system should use as few kinds of supplies for a particular need as possible. Vendors customarily quote prices on a basis of quantity rather than on an individual item basis; it follows that the adoption of any policy that enables a school district to purchase items in greater quantity will result in considerable savings. Buying in this manner also simplifies warehousing and record keeping. Standardization makes supply administration much easier, but carrying the process too far results in crippling needed educational services. For example, a supply item that may be suitable for a given subject or grade may be inappropriate for another.

The public relations aspects of purchasing should not be overlooked. The purchasing administrator should establish a cordial relationship with vendors. Their supply houses and offices can be visited. Lunches can be scheduled away from busy offices to discuss business in a relaxed atmosphere. The more personal the relationship, the better are the chances for achieving a good business deal.

Standard supply lists call for careful appraisal and periodic revision. The list should include the name of each supply item and the grades, subjects, or offices for which the item is being ordered. A valuable aspect of the standard supply list is its ability to function as a requisition form where it can become the basis for eventual reorders. It is helpful to have a supply

---

[5] David H. Cole, *Curriculum Action Paper* 4, No. 1, November 1977, pp. 1–3.

list for each elementary school grade, and other lists for such special departments as custodial, clerical, library, and so on.

Centralized Supply Purchasing

There is an advantage in giving one person the responsibility for purchasing all school district supplies and equipment: it provides for up-to-date budgetary accounting, economy, purchasing in accord with instructional needs, and maintenance of balance in supply provision to various school areas.

The purchasing administrator should organize in a systematic way so that he can compile many requisitions into one purchase order, handle the purchasing, place bids as needed, inventory upon delivery, store and distribute many kinds of articles, and keep accurate records. "The purchasing officer needs to understand commercial transportation facilities and regulations, freight rates, shipping hazards, and packaging."[6] The purchaser must also have a knowledge of state laws regarding purchasing, contracts, and bids and an understanding of how to purchase economically.[7]

School Board Purchasing Policies

Supply and equipment administration requires a well-planned purchasing program that has been approved by the board of education. The purchasing administrator should initiate or approve all policies before they are presented to the school board because the administrator will be responsible for carrying them out. Policies should spell out purchasing priorities in terms of educational objectives; the budgeting of supplies and equipment; the handling of local purchasing and vendors; how specifications are to be developed; and who is to make the final approval of requisitions before purchase. For example, should the assistant superintendent for instruction approve all educational requisitions before they are purchased? Procedures must be developed to carry out these policies. Finally, all policies and procedures must be communicated to all people so that there is no misunderstanding.

One of the problems often overlooked in the development of standard procedures is the need for additional supplies and equipment when new rooms, new programs, and new schools are added. These contingencies should be planned far enough ahead for allowance to be made in the budget. There should also be a clear understanding of why these additional costs are needed.

---

[6] Edwin A. Fensch and Robert E. Wilson, *The Superintendency Team*, p. 219.

[7] Fensch and Wilson, *The Superintendency Team*, p. 219.

Melbo recommends the following standards for purchasing which should be considered by boards of education and administrators:

1. All purchases approved or ratified by board and shown in minutes.
2. Printed, prenumbered purchase orders supplied in quadruplicate.
3. Preference to local merchants only when all factors are equal.
4. Purchasing centralized in business office.
5. Open charge accounts not used.
6. Blanket monthly purchase order used for frequent purchases with single vendor.
7. Purchasing needs consolidated.
8. Bids obtained when required by law.
9. Estimates obtained to justify minor purchasing when bids not necessary.
10. County purchasing used when advantageous.
11. Detailed specifications used when bids are taken.
12. Bids authorized by board, accepted by board, awarded by board, and shown in board minutes.
13. Cafeteria purchases meet spirit of legal requirements.
14. Standard school supply committee used.
15. Wise and efficient purchasing effected.
16. No improper interest in purchasing by board or employees.
17. Proper ethics observed.
18. Purchase orders should be issued for all purchases.
19. With only rare exception, purchase orders should be issued for known amounts.
20. Board policies established for purchasing.
21. Purchasing calendar used.
22. Purchasing accomplished in time to meet educational needs.
23. Purchase order forms should be designed to permit use of window envelopes.[8]

DETERMINATION OF QUANTITY. The best way to determine the amount of supplies to be purchased for a given year is to base the order on accurate information supplied by the various schools and departments. This information should be gathered annually on the basis of a broad policy adopted by the board of education and administered by the superintendent or business manager. Policy should set forth who shall purchase; what amount of money shall be spent in any single transaction; what kind of supplies and equipment shall be purchased by the purchasing officer; what kind of reports shall be filed on purchases; and what the basis shall be for opening purchasing to bids. Board policy should remove board members from any active purchasing, delegating such duties to the superintendent, who usually delegates these duties to a purchasing administrator.

---

[8] Melbo, *Report of the Survey, Paramount*, p. 71.

An inventory is necessary in order to know what and when to purchase. A continuous inventory of all supplies on hand in the district warehouse may take too much time and money to be worthwhile. An annual inventory is a more practical method and can be kept in the warehouse or business office.

School districts having access to electronic or electromechanical data processing equipment can use it for equipment-, material-, and supply-accounting procedures such as:

1. Maintaining an inventory of equipment and furniture, including records of maintenance.
2. Maintaining textbook and instructional inventories and projecting annual needs in relation to enrollments and proposed programs.
3. Scheduling the use of equipment, instructional media, and materials.
4. Adjusting warehouse supply inventory continuously to show ordered, received, distributed, and on-hand material.
5. Reporting the requisition and distribution of supplies, materials, and equipment according to schools, classrooms, departments.
6. Drawing warrants, recording payments, verifying claims, providing cost data.

In addition, computers are able to provide daily and weekly activity and status reports as desired by the district. Districts that cannot afford computer systems should investigate opportunities for tying into a centralized computer system using teletype equipment for transmitting data.

If the proper supply inventory form has been used throughout the district, assuming that computers are not available, the supplies and equipment needed for the next fiscal year will be made known at the time of the annual inventory, usually in the spring. The form should list the date, quantities delivered on requisitions, supplies currently on hand, and a column indicating supplies that will be needed for the coming year. In estimating needs, the quantity used in preceding years should be kept in mind, together with such pertinent factors as projected enrollment and curriculum changes that may be contemplated. Such a form makes possible the correct appraisal of both current needs and available supplies, without the necessity of resorting to diverse reports or stapling inventories to estimate blanks.

The purchasing officer should always enter the amount of money anticipated to be involved in the purchase in the encumbrance column of the account ledger. This should be done immediately after the expenditure has been authorized via the purchase order. As a result of this anticipatory procedure, sufficient funds will always remain in the budget allocation to pay the bill when it has been presented subsequent to the delivery of the purchase. It is difficult if not impossible to overdraw an account during the period between filling out the purchase order and paying the presented bill, if proper encumbrance procedures have been followed. The amount of the encumbrance involved in an uncompleted transaction is always deducted from the last entry in the balance column, thus enabling the state of the account to be seen at a glance.

Bidding

Transactions involving large amounts of one kind of item are commonly arranged on the basis of bids submitted by the supply dealers to the school district. After lists of supplies and equipment have been drawn up and after quality and quantity standards have been set up, the district business manager submits the lists to supply houses and dealers for bids. Contacts are selected from a file of suppliers previously compiled and carefully screened for reliability and prompt service. The cooperation of vendors will be assumed if the purchasing administrator has established cordial relationships with them. Bids are called for to ensure competitive figures for exactly comparable items, thus gaining the advantage of the lowest possible cost for the district. Steps in calling for and receiving bids include:

1. Development of explicit specifications describing item and quality desired.
2. Sending of specifications to vendors and publishing of notice that bids may be made.
3. Publication of time and place at which bids will be opened.
4. Examination of bids.
5. Awarding of contract by the school board to the lowest bidder meeting the specifications.
6. Notification of all bidders regarding the school board's actions.

COOPERATIVE PLANNING. Neighboring school districts may legally cooperate in the purchasing of supplies. It is especially practical for small districts that have no occasion to order for themselves great amounts of supplies at any one time to join together in such purchasing in order to take advantage of the large savings to be effected by volume purchasing. Some states actually compel the rural schools of a county to purchase their supplies cooperatively through the office of the county superintendent of schools or through the county purchasing agent. Districts that are contiguous to one another can cooperate not only with each other but with municipal and county governments in purchasing certain supplies, thus saving money for each of them.

PURCHASING AT PROPER TIMES. School systems should follow the example of industrial concerns in studying the supply market and placing orders during months when prices in certain areas are lowest.

It is unwise to purchase for more than a year ahead of current need, and uneconomical to purchase for less than that period. Should purchasing involve overly long time spans, deterioration of stored supplies may occur; an inability to take advantage of innovations and improvements in a supply category would also result. On the other hand, larger orders secure' cheaper prices. A prudent solution to this dilemma would be to order all standard supplies one year in advance of current needs. This is especially advisable when, in addition to the price savings made possible by mass ordering, the saving of school officials' time in ordering, receiving, and checking is taken into consideration. Large districts often can order semiannually and still effect considerable savings owing to the mass nature of such orders.

The following time schedule for the purchasing of supplies is applicable:

January. Prepare for annual requisition of supplies. Involve principals and their staffs as well as department heads.

February. Return requisition forms to business office for preparation of bid forms.

March. Business office sends bid forms to bidders.

April. Suppliers submit bids by predetermined date.

May. Bids are tabulated, samples examined, and purchase recommendations made to the board of education.

June. Mail purchase orders to successful bidders.

School districts should allow for delays in delivery after purchase if factors such as the energy and fuel crisis or paper shortages continue or return.

TAX EXEMPTIONS. Although not all states provide for the same type of sales tax exemption, most school districts in the United States enjoy certain exemptions. Since the payment of unnecessary taxes by school districts is not only illegal, but also a useless dilution of school wealth, it is very important that school administrators be aware of and exercise their districts' rightful exemptions.

Receiving Supplies

One of the most important areas of supply administration is the establishment of proper machinery to ensure that the items received are those that were ordered originally, and that the amounts received match amounts ordered. Large districts handling hundreds of thousands of dollars worth of supplies usually employ special checking clerks. In smaller districts, the superintendent or business manager must perform this task. There should be central receiving facilities available to ensure prompt delivery, inspection, and verification of the orders. The best procedure to follow is to check the supplies received against the accompanying invoice to be sure of agreement, then to check the invoice against the copy of the purchase order retained by the school district, and finally against the requisitions that were combined to form the order. Delivery of the items ordered to the appropriate classroom or storeroom is made after these checking procedures. When satisfied with the delivery, a copy of the purchase order should be signed by the warehouseman or clerk and returned to the district business office.

Payment for supplies after delivery should be conducted as follows:

1. After billing is received on a given order, the total order is broken down by account categories in the distribution ledger, and each expenditure recorded in the proper category.
2. The exact expenditure is entered next to the amount of the encumbrance in each affected budgetary category, and a new balance is then arrived at.
3. A warrant is then made out to the supply house for the correct amount and submitted to the school board for approval before mailing. The warrant number also should be indicated on the purchase order.
4. At least two signatures should be required on each warrant to help guard against double payment of a bill and incorrect disbursements.

Supply Storage

There are two storage practices generally in use: the central warehouse system, wherein the supplies for the entire school system are stored; and the system of storing the supplies in the school where they are to be used. Supply stockrooms in the various schools are kept replenished by trucks operating out of the warehouse, and several weeks' supply of each standard item is customarily kept on hand in the smaller stockrooms of the individual schools. The records of a central warehouse should be set up in such a manner as to account both for the receipt of supplies and the issuance of them.

Supply Requisitioning

A carefully formulated supply requisitioning system is needed in every school district. A few districts have utilized so-called automatic issuance of supplies to all teachers, custodians, and other employees at stated intervals, and the employee is expected to gauge his usage accordingly. This is a somewhat inflexible method, however; most districts utilize some sort of requisitioning plan.

The old philosophy of supply requisitioning held that material should never be allowed to leave either the general storehouse or the school supply room unless a properly signed and approved document had been exchanged for the item in question. Such a regulation is properly applied to a central warehousing situation, where supplies are issued in bulk to different schools in the district. However, the tendency in individual school stockrooms is toward the use of the "open" stockroom. In the latter case, teachers are relied upon to behave in a cooperative and professional manner, and to check out only supplies that they need for the proper functioning of their classes. In schools with open stockrooms, teachers are free to enter the supply headquarters of the school at any time and remove the items that they need, without being obliged to fill out any requisitions or reports of any kind. Whatever method is used, materials should be available at the time needed and usable in terms of the appropriateness to the particular group or individual.[9]

Requisition forms should be provided by the district so that employees can file requests for individual items of equipment or supplies. The following information should be included on all requisition forms:

1. Date of request.
2. Name of person making request.
3. School, room, or department where request originates.
4. Quantity requested.
5. Stock number.
6. Description of requested item.
7. Appropriate approval signatures.
8. Listed unit price if available.

There should be spaces to show the quantities issued, the issuance and receipt dates, and the account number. An example of a requisition form is shown in Figure 9–1.

Summary

The increasing specialization in education is reflected in the complexity of supply administration. Since supplies and equipment are essential to the teacher and to the school's instruction program, the principle of democratic participation especially should apply to this field.

---

[9] Marks, Stoops, and King-Stoops, *Handbook of Educational Supervision*, p. 356.

Stockroom Requisition

Business Office No.
....
School No.
....
Date

School..Dept. Head or Teacher..........................
Signature

Department... (Whenever possible use separate request for each account)

| Quantity Requested | | Quantity Issued | Stock Number | DESCRIPTION |
Number	Unit of Issue			

K17 PF-6202540

Material Issued: APPROVED:

....

Rec'd ....
                                                  Principal or Supervisor

Date ....
                                                  Department Director or Supervisor

ACCOUNT NUMBER

FIGURE 9–1. *Standard Stock Requisition. Courtesy of the Santa Monica Unified School District, Santa Monica, California.*

Efficient supply administration decreases the frequency of individual "emergency" orders and favors large, coordinated orders, thus achieving economy through volume purchasing. Any sizable school district can save money by establishing and maintaining its own central warehouse.

The selection of supplies and equipment should be a cooperative process, with maximum standardization of commonly used items being one of the main goals. Committees of both certificated and noncertificated employees should participate in this process of selecting and evaluating.

Unlike selection, purchasing should be centralized, with one person delegated the responsibility. The purchaser should operate within the scope of a well-planned purchasing program which has been approved by the local board of education, and should follow definite standards of purchasing.

Determination of the quantity of supplies to be purchased for a given year should be based on information supplied by the individual schools and departments. For any large purchases, competitive bids should be sought.

Neighboring school districts should cooperate in supply purchasing, and should place orders during months when prices in certain areas are lowest. In addition, setting up proper machinery to receive supplies and to match them with the original purchase orders is essential. In districts of any size, supplies should be stored in a central warehouse where a continuous inventory can be kept. Finally, an efficient supply requisitioning system should be established and adhered to.

Administrative Problems

Problem 1

Assume that you are a junior high school principal in a small unified school district that has never used standard supply lists. Your new superintendent believes that such lists have many benefits and will lead to quality control. At a weekly administrative council meeting, he has asked you to form a committee and develop standard supply lists for educational supplies, secretarial and clerical supplies, and custodial supplies.

How would you organize your committee?
Which personnel would you select?
How would you proceed?
What criteria would you develop?
What problems do you foresee?

Problem 2

As the new principal of Truman Elementary School, you find that your school has always had a "closed" stockroom for supplies. Every other Friday, teachers fill out a supply requisition and turn it in to the school office. Henry Robinson, a sixth grade teacher, has charge of filling the requisitions and seeing that they are delivered to each classroom. He uses students to help him and to deliver the supplies. Sometimes, he is so busy that he has another teacher, the school secretary, or a custodian help.

In case of emergency, a teacher can place a special order for Henry to fill. Since he never complains, teachers take advantage of him; nearly every day he has one or more "emergency" orders to fill. This takes time after school hours and interferes with pupil conferences, lesson planning, and grading papers. Sometimes he gives his class an assignment and takes one or two of his best pupils to the stockroom during school hours to fill requisitions.

As the new principal, you see many problems in the present system and decide to have an open stockroom.

What procedure will you use in setting up an open stockroom?
What information would you give your teachers?
What problems might arise when you change from a "closed" to an "open" stockroom? How would you solve them?
How would you keep an up-to-date inventory?

Selected References   In Basket

ANNUAL PURCHASING DIRECTORY. "Equipment, Supplies, Furnishings." *American School and University* 50 (May 1978):70.

BURR, D. "Conserving Energy at School." *Vocational Education* 54 (January 1979):22.

CAMPBELL, ROALD F., et al. *Organization and Control of American Schools.* 2nd ed. Columbus, Ohio: Charles E. Merrill Publishing Co., 1975.

FENSCH, EDWIN A., and ROBERT E. WILSON. *The Superintendency Team.* Columbus, Ohio: Charles E. Merrill Publishing Co., 1964.

HARRISON, B. "Purchasing: Procedures, Policies and Programs." *American School and University* 50 (August 1978):30–31.

HARTMAN, ALLAN S. "Saving Money Through Better Business Practices." *School Management* 14 (December 1970).

HULBERT, L. A. and D. S. CURRY. "Evolution of an Approval (Book Selection) Plan." *College and Reference Libraries* 39 (November 1978):485–91.

LILLICROP, L. O. *Food and Beverage Service.* Boston: Herman Publishing Co., 1975.

MARKS, SIR JAMES R., EMERY STOOPS, and JOYCE KING-STOOPS. *Handbook of Educational Supervision.* 2nd ed. Boston: Allyn and Bacon, Inc., 1978.

McCAFFREY, M. "Let's Make the Billions Spent on Education Pay Off." *USA Today* 107 (November 1978):43–44.

MELBO, IRVING R., et al. *Report of the Survey, Paramount Unified School District.* Los Angeles: University of Southern California, 1970.

MULHOLLAND, R. E. "Television, Books, and Teachers." *English Education* 10 (October 1978):3–8.

MULVANITY, D. C. "Get Your Inventory Under Control." *American School and University* 50 (August 1978):21–23.

NEILL, SHIRLEY B. *School Energy Crises: Problems and Solutions.* Arlington, Va.: American Association of School Administrators, 1977.

NELSON, D. LLOYD, and WILLIAM M. PURDY. *School Business Administration.* Lexington, Mass.: D. C. Heath and Co., 1971.

PASNIK, MARION. "Survey Evaluation of Purchasing Procedures." *School Management* 14 (December 1970).

STOOPS, EMERY, and RUSSELL E. JOHNSON. *Elementary School Administration.* New York: McGraw-Hill Book Co., 1967.

WALLACE, J. "Evaluation of a Child's Chair." *Journal of Home Economics* 70 (Fall 1978):29–30.

ZACKRISON, H. B. "Uncle Sam Might Help You Pay for Improvements in Lighting." *American School Board Journal* 166 (January 1979):33–4.

CHAPTER TEN

School Insurance

Insurance has become a major financial burden of school districts, and its cost is continuously rising. Employees are demanding more and more insurance protection of all types. Vandalism and arson have become more prevalent, causing a rise in insurance rates and needs.

The Need for School Insurance

There are two main types of school insurance: (1) policies having to do with casualty, property, or liability insurance and (2) policies dealing with the wide spectrum of the health and welfare of school employees. The purchase of insurance by school districts is taken as a matter of course today, but in the past, particularly in the property, casualty, and liability fields, it was considered by many to be a dubious expenditure of public funds. A liberalization of court opinion and public sentiment has brought about a general desire to soften the blow occasioned by accidents involving innocent people. And a prudent desire to safeguard the tremendous capital investment represented by school plants has completed the acceptance of the insurance principle, particularly in the field of liability insurance. Likewise, the universal practice of inviting insurance companies and underwriters to participate in plant safety programs and in plans for new construction has resulted in the lowering of fire insurance premiums; better construction has similarly decreased the number of serious school fires and other calamities.

Material for this chapter was prepared in collaboration with Lewis Weldon, President of Employee Security Plans, Inc., Encino, California.

Policies of insurance involving the protection of school plants and equipment have become an integral part of the budgeting and financing of school districts. While the need for this type of insurance is readily discernible, there is dispute over the legitimacy of a need for policy coverage of the health and welfare needs of school employees, the premiums of which are paid by the school district. Nevertheless, policies of insurance covering employees have become a major part of the school insurance portfolio. The expansion of health and welfare insurance programs has been brought about by employee negotiation.

The only alternative to insuring school property is the creation and maintenance of a cash reserve fund by the district. Formerly, some large city districts avoided heavy insurance commitments on the grounds that their replacement program was a continuous one, and that it was actually cheaper to replace buildings damaged or destroyed than to pay many thousands of dollars in annual insurance premiums. Such an argument is seldom heard today except in the largest districts of the nation.

Protection of School Property

The various kinds of insurance that may be carried by school districts are dependent primarily upon the laws of the state. Assuming that permissive legislation exists, it is wise to carry certain types of insurance whenever the risk of loss is too large for the district to assume. A logical corollary to this rule is that small districts are in much greater need of insurance than are their larger neighbors.

NECESSARY INSURANCE. The following types of insurance should be carried by most school districts:

1. Fire insurance and extended coverage on buildings and contents. Replacement insurance should be considered.
2. Comprehensive liability and property damage insurance.
3. Workmen's compensation insurance.
4. Broad-form monies and securities.
5. Vehicle insurance.

OPTIONAL INSURANCE. Under certain circumstances, it is advisable for school districts to carry one or more of the following types of insurance:

1. All risk coverage, on specified items.
2. All risk coverage, such as musical instrument floater policy.
3. Plate glass policy.
4. Open stock burglary with theft endorsement.
5. Vandalism coverage as a part of the fire insurance program.

6. Boiler insurance.
7. Fidelity bond.

Fire Insurance Program

Every school district needs fire insurance. In order to secure proper and economical coverage, the following steps should be taken in the order listed:

1. Place responsibility for handling the school district's insurance.
2. Secure a reliable appraisal of property to determine insurable values.
3. Determine the method to be used in insuring the building and contents.
4. Develop a school form.
5. Obtain all possible rate deductions.
6. Maintain adequate records.
7. Establish an equitable plan for distributing insurance to companies and agents.
8. Obtain maximum adjustments on fire losses.[1]

Types of Fire Insurance

In deciding what type of fire insurance to procure for a given school district, the administrator should consider the following varieties.

FULL-VALUE, OR FLAT, INSURANCE. Before deciding whether or not to obtain full-value insurance, it is necessary to clarify what is meant by "full value" in the particular district. Factors such as the distribution of school property, the peculiar hazards involved, and the size and wealth of the district affect the amount of insurance that should prudently be carried. "Full value" would be the ideal goal, but for several reasons it may be difficult to achieve. The formula often used is that obtained by subtracting from a carefully determined estimate of the costs of replacement an equally carefully determined estimate of actual depreciation. A simpler method is to base real value upon an appraisal of the probable cost of replacement only. In most cases, considerable savings in premiums can be effected by insuring property for somewhat less than the "full value."

COINSURANCE. There is a common misunderstanding about coinsurance, to the effect that, in any loss, the insured must automatically pay a certain percent, with the remainder shouldered by the insurance company. As Linn and Joyner point out, this concept is erroneous; insurance companies

---

[1] H. H. Linn and S. C. Joyner, *Insurance Practices in School Administration*, p. 76.

will meet the loss up to the amount of the policy, if the insured has followed the requirement that the amount of insurance actually carried corresponds with the amount required to be carried.[2] Actually, coinsurance simply provides that the greater the amount of insurance carried on a risk relative to its full insurable value, the lower the insurance rate per unit of value. Except in the rare event of a 100 percent loss, coinsurance is by far the best bargain. The following formula[3] shows how coinsurance operates in case of a loss:

$$\frac{\text{Amount of insurance carried}}{\text{Amount required by form}} \times \text{Loss} = \text{Recovery up to face of policy}$$

"PROBABLE LOSS" INSURANCE.   A relatively small number of school districts insure without reference to full value. Some insure only their most hazardous risks, while others try to estimate "probable loss" and carry a small amount on each property. This is, of course, an imprudent method of insuring. Small premium savings may be effected, but the danger of a major loss that would be inadequately covered by insurance is so preponderant, it renders this course of action unwise.

Local Conditions and Fire Insurance Policy

The particular situation in which a school district finds itself often determines the kind of insurance that should be purchased. For example, nonfireproof buildings need to be insured at a higher percentage of full value than do steel and concrete structures. The more buildings owned by the school district, the more justified would be the purchase of some type of coinsurance policy. The nature of the community enters into the picture, also. A city with ultra-modern fire equipment and safety devices lends itself to coinsurance; a rural school, isolated and remote from firefighting apparatus, requires coverage by a flat policy.

Steps to Reduce Fire Insurance Costs

Although insurance rates are tending more and more to become standardized and fixed by statute, it is possible for well-managed school districts to keep their insurance costs at a reasonable level.

REGULAR APPRAISALS.   Insurance values should be determined by a reputable appraisal firm and kept up-to-date on an annual basis. A good

---

[2] Linn and Joyner, *Insurance Practices*, pp. 88–89.
[3] Linn and Joyner, *Insurance Practices*, p. 90.

plan provides for a complete appraisal once every five years, with annual appraisal checks on a revolving basis. School boards often pay insurance premiums on amounts greater than those that could be collected in case the property were destroyed. Frequent and accurate appraisals on the school property would assist in eliminating this source of waste.

The first step in appraisal is to fix the replacement cost of the property. Unit costs must be determined by establishing values for the different materials used in the building under consideration; from such costs, values for such portions of the structure as roof, floors, walls, and stairs are established. The cost of labor in the community in question enters into the final figure arrived at. After figuring the replacement value of the different building parts, it is then necessary to establish similar figures for fixtures and equipment in much the same manner. After these replacement values have been established, the depreciation is then deducted from the amounts decided upon. Serviceability as foreseen in the future may be as important a factor in such calculations as are age and obsolescence.

The figure reached by subtracting depreciation from the replacement value is termed the *sound value* of the property. To arrive at the *insurable value*, the cost of excavations and foundation work must then be deducted from the sound value.

REMOVAL OF FIRE HAZARDS. While it is true that school buildings are relatively free from fire hazards compared with other structures, school fires do continue to occur, illustrating the need for active and increasing fire prevention techniques. Virtually all fires are preventable; even those caused by lightning may be avoided by correctly installed and maintained lightning rods. The first step in any campaign to reduce insurance costs by eliminating fires must be diagnosis. Since electrical wiring and the heating system are leaders in causing school fires, the installation of these items should be carefully inspected, and their later maintenance scrupulously conducted. Arson is also suspected as being the cause of school fires. District employees can take an active part in the following additional fire precautions:

1. Eliminate the accumulation of rubbish in any area of the school plant.
2. Provide fireproof receptacles for all matches, paper, and other combustible materials.
3. Provide safe storage facilities for materials used in laboratories, shops, and home economics classrooms.
4. Provide each department and corridor with chemical extinguishers.
5. Sponsor regular "cleanup weeks," when all above precautions are especially stressed.
6. Strictly enforce fire prevention regulations applying to both the adult and pupil personnel of a school.

PERIODIC INSPECTIONS. The Engineering and Safety Service Department, American Insurance Association has prepared a form to be used for self-inspection by school districts to check on elimination of fire hazards (see Figure 10–1). While such inspections are often made by the director of maintenance and operations, or someone in a similar capacity from the district's business office, it is better from every standpoint that the inspector be an employee of the local fire department.

TRAINING IN USE OF FIREFIGHTING EQUIPMENT. The first three minutes of a fire are by far the most important from a control standpoint. It is important that all school employees are trained in the use of whatever firefighting apparatus may be at hand. No longer can the maintenance and custodial employees be relied upon to be in the proper spot when a fire occurs. It is far more likely that the employee nearest to a nascent blaze will be a teacher, a secretary, or a cafeteria cook. Once this is acknowledged, it becomes obvious that all district employees should be properly instructed in firefighting techniques.

FIRE DRILLS. Fires occurring in school buildings that result in loss of life fortunately have been rare. Nevertheless, they have happened, usually as the result of gas or boiler explosions. It is essential, therefore, that pupils and school employees be properly instructed in a routine to be followed in case of fire. Most states now require such drills in all schools on an average of once a month. Fire drills should be completely standardized throughout the district, and should be as parallel as possible to the standard procedure followed elsewhere in the state.

Each teacher should be held responsible for imparting fire drill instructions to all children in his charge. Fire drill instructions in brief form should be posted permanently in each room. They should be called to the children's attention frequently and mastered by them. Drills should be arranged so that they will ensure orderly, rapid evacuation of the building under any condition of the school day. It is advisable for the principal to keep a record of the date and time of every drill as well as a comment regarding its effectiveness. The following is an example of an evacuation order which can be used, not only for fire drills, but also for bomb threats.[4]

Example of an Evacuation Order

EVACUATION ORDER FOR ROBERT E. LEE HIGH SCHOOL

A. Explanation of Evacuation Signals
   1. A rapid ringing of bell is the signal to evacuate the building.
   2. *One* long ring of the bell is the signal to stop.

---

[4] Clinton Carter, *Evacuation Order* (Montgomery, Ala.: Robert E. Lee High School, 1971).

3. *Two* long rings of the bell is the signal to move forward.
4. *Three* long rings of the bell is the signal to return to classrooms.

B. Evacuation Procedure
  1. Close all outside windows.
  2. Close transom windows.
  3. Close door after room has been emptied.
  4. Maintain order during drill. No talking, shoving, or horseplay of any kind.
  5. Stay in line.
  6. If exit route is blocked it is the teacher's responsibility to find an alternate route.
  7. *Every person must leave the building during a drill.*

C. Routes (Circle your room number in red)
  Rooms 2–4–6–8–10–14–16 are to use the door at the extreme south end of the building to the playground.
  Do not cross the track.

  Room 12 exit at the outside door of 12 and move to the playground. Do not cross the track.

  Rooms 116–118 (Home Ec Dept.) and gym are to use the south end stairs to the basement on to the playground. Do not cross the track.

  Rooms 100–101–102–103–104–105–106–110 are to use the steps to the lobby and out the front door. Library and Guidance use the front door. Move to grass plot between parking lot and Ann Street. Even numbers right. Odd numbers left.

  Rooms 200–201–202–203–204–205–206 use the north stairs and out north door.

  . . . .

  . . . .

  . . . .

  Band rooms exit rear of auditorium into parking lot. Do not block driveway.

  Choral room exit rear of auditorium into parking lot. Do not block driveway.

THIS ORDER IS TO BE *POSTED PERMANENTLY* AND IN A CONSPICUOUS PLACE IN EACH CLASSROOM. TEACHERS KNOW EVACUATION ROUTE FOR EACH ROOM YOU USE.

Individual differences in drill patterns will of course exist even within a school district. Characteristics of the school plant, such as number of pupils, single-level or multi-level construction, width of corridors, and location of exits will largely determine the particular routine for conducting a fire drill. However, the main principles of a standard list of instructions should be observed on as broad a basis as possible in order

INSPECTION BLANK FOR SCHOOLS

Prepared by
AMERICAN INSURANCE ASSOCIATION
Engineering and Safety Service
85 John Street, New York, N. Y. 10038

INSTRUCTIONS

Inspection to be made each month by the custodian and a member of the faculty at which inspection only Items 1 to 23 need be reported. At the quarterly inspection, a member of the fire department should accompany the above inspectors, and the complete blank should be filled out. The report of each inspection (monthly and quarterly) is to be filed with the Board of Education or School Commissioners.

Questions are so worded that a negative answer will indicate an unsatisfactory condition.

Date . . . .

Name of School . . . . Address . . . .

Class: Elementary . . . . Junior High . . . . Senior High . . . .

Capacity of School . . . . Number now enrolled . . . .

1. Are all exterior exit doors equipped with approved panic hardware when serving 100 or more persons? . . . .
   Is the hardware tested each week? . . . . Is it readily operable? . . . .
2. Are all outside fire escapes free from obstructions and in good working order? . . . . Are they used for fire drills?
   . . . .
3. Are all doors in smoke control partitions in operable condition? . . . . Free from obstruction? . . . .
4. Is all heating equipment, including flues, pipes, ducts and steam lines:-
   (a) in good servicable condition and well maintained? . . . .
   (b) properly insulated and separated from all combustible material by a safe distance? . . . .
5. Is the coal pile inspected periodically for evidence of heating? . . . .
6. Are ashes placed in metal containers used for that purpose only? . . . .
7. Is remote control provided whereby oil supply line may be shut off in emergency and is it readily accessible? . . . . . .
8. Is an outside shut-off valve on the gas supply line provided? . . . . Is it readily accessible and marked? . . . .
9. Has automatic heating and air-conditioning equipment been serviced by a qualified service man within the past year?
   . . . .
10. Are the following locations free of accumulations of waste paper, rubbish, old furniture, stage scenery, etc?
    attic? . . . . basement? . . . . furnace room? . . . . stage? . . . . dressing rooms in connection with
    stage? . . . . other locations? . . . . (explain "No" answers under Remarks.)
11. Are spaces beneath stairs free from accumulation or storage of any materials? . . . .
12. If hazardous material or preparation is used for cleaning or polishing floors: Is the quantity limited as much as practicable? . . . . Is it safely stored? . . . .
13. Are approved metal cans, with self-closing covers or lids, used for the storage of all oily waste, polishing cloths, etc? . . . .
14. Are approved safety cans with vapor-tight covers used for all kerosene, gasoline, etc., on the premises and are they stored away from sources of heat or ignition? . . . .
    Is it essential that such materials be kept on the premises? . . . .
15. Are premises free from electrial wiring or equipment which is defective? . . . .
    (If answer is No, explain under Remarks.)
16. Are only labeled extension or portable cords used? . . . .
17. Is the correct size fuse being used in each electrical circuit? . . . .
18. Are electric pressing irons equipped with automatic heat control or signal and provided with metal stand? . . . .
    . . . .

(Continued on reverse side)

FP-131 (8-76)

FIGURE 10–1. Inspection Blank for Schools. Courtesy of the American Insurance Association.

19. Are sufficient proper type fire extinguishers provided on each floor so that not over 75 feet travel is required to reach the nearest unit? . . . .
    In manual training shops and on stage, 30 feet or 50 feet depending on extinguisher rating? . . . .
20. Is date of inspection or recharge shown on tag attached to extinguisher? . . . .
    Have fire extinguishers been inspected or recharged within a year? . . . .
21. Is the building equipped with standpipe and hose with nozzle attached? . . . .
    Is the hose in good serviceable condition? . . . .
22. Where sprinklers are installed: Are all sprinklers clean and unobstructed? . . . .
    Are all sprinkler valves open? . . . . Has the system been thoroughly inspected within the past year? . . . .
23. Are large woolen blankets readily available in kitchens and science laboratories for use in case clothing is ignited? . . . .

    Remarks (Note any changes since last inspection)
    The following items to be included in each quarterly inspection:-
24. Are there at least two means of egress from each story of the building? . . . .
    Are these so located that the distance to any single exit measured along the line of travel, does not exceed:-
        From any point in any classroom, 150 feet? . . . .
        From any point in an auditorium, assembly hall or gymnasium, 150 feet? . . . .
25. Are all windows free from heavy screens or bars? . . . .
26. Do all exit doors open in direction of exit travel? . . . .
27. Are all interior stairways enclosed? . . . .
    Are doors to these enclosures of automatic or self-closing type? . . . . Are they unobstructed . . . . and in operable condition? . . . .
    If automatic closing type, are they closed as routine part of fire exit drill? . . . .
28. Are windows within 10 feet above, 35 feet below and 15 feet horizontally of fire escapes glazed with wire glass? . . . .
29. Are manual training, domestic science, other laboratories and the cafeteria so located that a fire in one will not make the means of agress from other nearby rooms or spaces unusable? . . . .
30. Are heating plant and fuel supply rooms separated from other parts of the building by fire-resistant walls or partitions, and fire doors? . . . .
31. Do all ventilating ducts terminate outside of the building? . . . .
32. State type of construction of any temporary buildings in the school yard . . . .
33. Is nearest temporary building at least 50 feet from the main building? . . . .
34. State frequency of fire drills . . . . State average time of exit . . . .
35. Are provisions made for sounding alarm of fire from any floor of building? . . . .
    Is sounding device accessible? . . . . Plainly marked? . . . .
36. Signs giving location of nearest city fire alarm box posted? . . . .
    Give distance from the premises to box . . . .

            Inspector . . . . Title . . . .
            Inspector . . . . Title . . . .
            Fire Chief and/or Building Inspector . . . .

ATTACH COPY OF ANY "REMARKS" DEALING WITH INSPECTION FINDINGS

FIGURE 10–1.   (Continued)

that children transferring from one school to another in a given district, county, or state may be familiar with procedure.

INSTRUCTION IN FIRE PREVENTION. The average city or village fire department will willingly cooperate with a school system that requests special assistance in setting up some type of instruction in fire prevention for its students. Most local fire authorities will detach equipment and personnel to dramatize Fire Prevention Week, and will supply speakers to demonstrate fire hazards at school assemblies. Many states now require a certain amount of such instruction.

Comprehensive Liability and Property Damage Insurance

Under these headings are found two main types: property damage and bodily injury. Legal liability for property damage and bodily injury must be established by court action. Accidents that do not result from negligence are not legally actionable. But when negligence contributes to property damage or bodily injury, the school district (in certain states) or the individual becomes liable, and the insurance company is obligated to pay damages specified in the policy coverage. In order to assist the insurance company, a property damage report should be made out. An example is shown in Figure 10–2.

Although liability must be established by court action, companies that write property damage and bodily injury policies often seek out-of-court settlements and hold the insured free from suit or damages to the extent of policy coverage. In recent years, courts have awarded increasingly higher claims to successful plaintiffs. For this reason, school districts periodically should re-examine their property damage and bodily injury coverage.

The use of comprehensive liability insurance as required by the laws of the state should cover the liability of the district, the board of education, and district members, officers, and employees when acting within the scope of their employment. The amount of coverage should depend upon the number of employees and the value of the school district's property.

Workmen's Compensation Insurance

Many states require that district employees be protected by workmen's compensation insurance. In most cases, however, coverage is not provided for all classifications of employment. Wherever compensation insurance is compulsory, a required form is issued by the state and the rates are set by a central agency. In states where compensation statutes are either

FLOWING WELLS PUBLIC SCHOOLS
Tucson, Arizona

PROPERTY DAMAGE REPORT

School _____

Date of this Report _____ Report by _____

Type of Damage: ☐ Vandalism ☐ Burglary ☐ Other _____

Nature of Damage: _____

_____

_____

Specific Location: _____

_____

Estimated Time/Date of Damage: _____

PROPERTY STOLEN OR MISSING:

Item	Serial No.	Cost
Item	Serial No.	Cost
Item	Serial No.	Cost

Repair/Replacement Needs:

Item	Estimated Cost
Item	Estimated Cost

Damage Discovered by: _____ Date/time _____

Reported to ☐ Police ☐ Sheriff by _____ Date/time _____

Possible Suspects: _____

Other Information:

Principal's Signature: _____

Original: Superintendent   **1st Copy:** Director of Maintenance   **2nd Copy:** Principal

FIGURE 10–2.   Example of a Property Damage Report.
Courtesy of Flowing Wells Public Schools, Tucson, Arizona.

nonexistent or optional, school employees must then depend upon some liability system for reimbursement. Since compensation insurance favors employees by doing away with the need to prove or disprove negligence, and by furnishing definite reimbursement for industrial or occupational injuries, it is strongly to be preferred to ordinary employer liability insurance.

Fidelity Bond Coverage

Whether or not state law requires school districts to bond all employees who handle school funds, the coverage is of such self-evident importance that every district should acquire this protection as a matter of course. For the average school district, the best and most economical way to accomplish this is to use the blanket commercial fidelity bond. Individual bonds tend to be too specific and to result in possible heavy losses as a result of embezzlement on the part of employees not included in the categories covered by the bonds.

Optional Insurance

It is impossible to specify the need of any particular district for the several types of special insurance which may be required under certain individual circumstances. Insurance should be provided only after a careful analysis of the district's needs.

BROAD-FORM MONEY AND SECURITIES POLICIES. A policy of this type insures not only money and securities, but also other merchandise. It may be written to cover loss both inside and outside the premises. Money and securities are covered against risks of any kind, including fire, but other property is usually insured only against burglary. The amount of coverage, of course, is dependent upon the district's individual needs.

ALL-RISK COVERAGE. Many districts carry all-risk insurance, such as a floater policy on musical instruments and audio-visual equipment. Articles thus insured are protected both on and off the premises against various types of loss, such as theft, burglary, fire, and accidental damage.

PLATE GLASS POLICY. Modern schools with large areas of plate glass are well advised to insure this highly expensive feature by means of a policy that will replace all glass damaged in any way.

OPEN STOCK BURGLARY WITH THEFT ENDORSEMENT. Such insurance should be maintained as a matter of course by all districts that have valuables or expensive equipment that are kept in the school plant and that are not covered by one of the policies previously described.

VANDALISM COVERAGE.   Vandalism damage should be taken care of as a part of the extended coverage–comprehensive portion of the district's fire insurance program.

WIND AND STORM COVERAGE.   Protection against windstorms and other natural calamities should also be a part of the fire insurance coverage of the district.

BOILER INSURANCE.   In many districts the chief value of a boiler insurance policy may be the inspection service furnished by the insuring company, rather than payment for possible loss. All districts that use high pressure boilers should by all means carry adequate boiler insurance. Those that have only low pressure plants will find such insurance highly desirable but not essential.

Liability of School Districts

In states where school districts are not legally liable for accidents and damage caused by their negligence, they share such immunity with other governmental agencies. The theory behind school district immunity from liability relates to the historical concept of the common law rule of non-liability, based, in turn, upon the ancient concept that "the king can do no wrong." In this country, it has been assumed that the state is sovereign and cannot be sued without its consent. A further justification exists in the legal concept which holds that a school district, in performing a purely public and nonprofit function imposed upon it by law and for the benefit of society, is not subject to liability.

A number of states have recently modified and in some cases eliminated this immunity by enacting legislation. Legislation has been enacted in Alaska, California, Connecticut, Maryland, Minnesota, New Jersey, New York, North Carolina, Oregon, Washington, and Wisconsin that materially modifies the immunity of a school district from liability. Illinois has completely abolished the immunity of the school district. Even in those states where school immunity still exists, the courts have recognized certain exceptions such as: summer recreational programs and renting school facilities to other organizations; active or positive wrong; injuries arising as a result of the creation or maintenance of a nuisance; and taking or damaging private property for public use without offering adequate compensation.

A great variety exists among the states with respect to the liability of school districts for injuries arising out of its negligence; hence, each district should be aware of the extent to which it might be held liable. Generally, school board members, trustees, and similar persons are not held personally liable for negligence for their official actions. However, teachers and other school personnel may be sued for negligent supervision and other causes. Negligence, however, must be proven.

Once the exposure to liability has been determined in the school district, appropriate insurance should be carried as a matter of course.

Insuring Public Property in a Common Fund

South Carolina and Wisconsin were two of the first states to enact laws specifying that public property, including school buildings, shall be insured in a common fund by the state. North Carolina and Alabama later authorized such insurance. Insurance rates in these states vary from one-half to three-fourths of those charged by private companies, and losses are apparently made good with promptness and efficiency. Transportation insurance is provided to all North Carolina schoolchildren by the state; in most other states the local districts purchase such insurance. Apparently the opposition by private companies to such state or community insurance has been the main reason for the failure of such practices to spread widely.

Insuring Employee Welfare

INSURANCE FRINGE BENEFITS.   The rapid increase in benefits for school employees in the late 1960s and early 1970s is a carbon copy of the development of these benefits for industry during and following World War II. When prices and wages were frozen during that time, employers utilized fringe benefits to attract workers from a sparse labor market. Following World War II, unions bargained for and won broader and more comprehensive benefits. Once established, such benefits became a permanent part of the employment package.

As the population expanded, the need for more teachers and other employees also expanded and created an "employees' market." Again, fringe benefits were used to attract qualified employees into the school systems. These benefits then became a permanent part of the employment package. In many cases, salary increases were bypassed in order to provide broader and more comprehensive benefits. It was easier for many districts to raise revenue for such benefits than to increase salaries. Competition for employees became more intense as wages increased in industry and schools found themselves in a spiral of increasing salaries and fringe benefits. The evolution of these benefits for school employees followed the same pattern as industry, although it lagged behind by some fifteen to twenty years.

Fringe benefits are those forms of insurance for which premiums are paid by, or which are made available to the employee by, the school system. These benefits include:

1. Life Insurance.
2. Health Insurance.
3 Income Protection.
4. Dental Insurance.
5. Retirement Plans.
6. Tax Sheltered Plans.

TYPES OF COVERAGE AFFORDED BY FRINGE BENEFITS. Most fringe benefits are provided under group insurance policies, with the school district as the policyowner and its employees considered as the insureds. It is important to note that the employee is not a party to the contract. The policyowner is responsible for the timely payment of the premium and for the collection of any premium paid for by its employees. The employee receives a certificate of insurance which contains the important details of coverage but is not a contract in and of itself.

Group life insurance provides that in the event of the death of the insured employee, the amount for which he was insured will be paid to his designated beneficiary. These designations are made upon enrollment into the plan and can be changed by the employee by proper notification to the insurance company. Most group life policies also contain benefits for accidental death and dismemberment; these provide an additional amount usually equal to the amount payable under the life insurance (which would be paid in the event that the death were due to an accident).

Group health insurance provides for the payment of charges incurred as a result of the disability of the insured. While this is the intent of this type of coverage, it is a gross oversimplification to stop at this point. Charges that a disabled person can incur are varied and in some cases abstruse. In general, charges may be incurred as a result of hospitalization, surgery, physician's visits, medications, nursing, and medical supplies and appliances such as wheelchairs. Group health policies can be written to provide coverage for each source of charges or can be all-inclusive. The latter is generally referred to as Major Medical or Comprehensive Medical coverage.

The amounts that will be paid by the policy for charges incurred also vary and have a major impact on the premium that will be charged. For example, a policy that provides full coverage for charges made by a hospital would obviously cost more than one that limits the amount payable for room and board and ancillary services. Likewise, a policy with a smaller deductible would be more expensive than one with a larger deductible. Major Medical and Comprehensive Medical plans are typified by three features—a deductible, coinsurance, and high maximum benefits. The deductible is used to reduce the impact of the higher frequency of smaller claims which can be budgeted by the insured. Coinsurance causes the claimant to participate in the overall cost of the disability and, theoretically, reduces the overuse and abuse of medical facilities. The high maximum provides the coverage necessary for the serious disability which could lead to financial chaos.

Service-type plans such as Blue Cross and Blue Shield provide full benefits for charges incurred when their approved hospitals or physicians are used. In the case of Blue Cross, those charges for which benefits are paid would be incurred in a hospital that is a member of the Blue Cross organization. It is not necessarily true that full benefits would be paid for charges incurred in a nonmember hospital. Similarly, Blue Shield arranges for service-type benefits through its member–physicians.

The basic approach to rating varies between service-type organizations and private insurance companies. Service-type organizations tend to gear their rates to the experience which they sustain on a community-wide basis, while insurance companies tend to base their rates on the experience of the group itself. Competition has been very keen in the group health field; hence, the district should obtain a good cross section of bids prior to selecting their insurer. Staff members should participate in such a survey.

Income protection is a form of coverage that reimburses the insured employee for a portion of his lost income due to a disability. There are two categories of plans based on the length of time for which benefits may be payable. Short-term disability benefits usually will afford payments to the claimant up to twenty-six weeks and some up to fifty-two weeks. Long-term disability benefits can run up to lifetime benefits for disabilities due to an accident and up to age 65 for disabilities due to sickness. In either case, the plan generally will contain a waiting period before benefits commence. As in the use of a deductible, the longer the waiting period, the lower the rates.

Four states (Rhode Island, New York, New Jersey, and California) have compulsory disability benefits laws. These short-term disability benefits may be obtained from either the state fund or private insurers in each of these states, with the exception of Rhode Island, where benefits must be purchased from the state fund. A typical short-term plan might provide that benefits shall begin on the eighth day of covered disability and would be payable up to twenty-six weeks of continuous total disability. Long-term disability plans usually vary their definition of disability. They require that the insured be unable to perform the duties of his regular occupation for the first two years of disability, and thereafter be unable to perform the duties of any occupation for wage or profit for which he is suited by virtue of his education, training, and experience. Such a plan can be abused by employees and result in increased rates; the school system may find that it cannot bear the cost or, in some cases, find a suitable carrier for their plan. Plans are designed to avoid malingering and consequently should not afford more in the way of benefits to the disabled employee than he would have received had he not been disabled. Most long-term disability plans will limit benefits payable to 66⅔ percent of the employee's weekly or monthly salary and will integrate this maximum amount with benefits payable from other plans, such as state compulsory disability benefits; benefits payable under the disability provisions in retirement plans; benefits payable under Social Security; and other similar benefits payable under plans afforded by the employer. When an employee becomes disabled for an extended period of time, the idea of disability in itself is disabling, and if an adequate income is not guaranteed, recovery tends to be delayed. Premium rates will reflect loss experience under any group program, and increased costs for these plans could very well be transferred to the taxpayer. Selection of the plan and the insurer is an essential responsibility of school administration.

Dental insurance is a form of insurance that reimburses the insured employee for charges he might incur as a result of dental services performed by a qualified dentist. This is a more recently developed form of insurance, having become popular during the 1960s. Many school administrators have questioned its importance in the fringe benefit portfolio since it involves an expense that is more budgetable than severe illness and disability. Since most people need some dental work, and since premium rates tend to reflect the loss experience sustained by the insurer, some experts have raised the question of whether the future rates for this coverage might not be so high as to negate the value of insuring these charges. Administrators should evaluate their portfolios of fringe benefits carefully and set priorities for coverage. The highest priorities should be placed on coverages for which the school employee is least able to budget. Dental costs are more readily budgeted than the cost of a severe heart attack or a disabling injury.

There are a number of other insurance plans (vision care, accident coverages, nursing home coverage, etc.) which could be classified as a fringe benefit if adopted by the school system. These have not been adopted by many systems and are merely mentioned to point out the potential complexities faced by school administrators in the age of fringe benefits.

FINANCING THE COST OF FRINGE BENEFITS. Raising funds through taxation to provide fringe benefits for school employees traditionally has received little publicity since it is usually included as a part of a salary package. However, some systems find themselves affording fringe benefits amounting to 10 percent or more of the average employee's salary. The question then arises: should the school system pay the entire cost of these fringe benefits or should the employee share in some of the cost? Should the school system pay the cost of providing health insurance for dependents of its employees? Systems that have decided to provide dependent coverage then face the problem of equal benefits for single employees. Who pays the increased cost for existing plans when sizable rate increases are requested by the insurer? Can benefits be reduced or eliminated if taxes cannot be raised to pay for them? How much will it cost to expand an existing plan? What will it cost next year? School administrators are faced with these questions, the answers to which are often difficult to resolve.

SELECTION OF A PLAN OF BENEFITS.   Every insurance plan is based upon some need, but all needs are not insurable. Some needs lend themselves to the solution of insurance while others are best solved in other ways. The uncertainty of death and the financial loss created generates a need which can best be solved by insurance. The financial loss associated with lack of good health is not as clearly solved by insurance as in the event of death. For example, the medical profession has some difficulty in distinguishing between superannuation and disability. The aging process itself fosters lack of good health for which medical attention usually is required.

Insurance is based on events that are fortuitous in nature; it is not operating efficiently when selection of insured events can be controlled by those who would benefit by it. If maternity coverage were to be written only on the lives of pregnant women, then the cost of such coverage would tend to negate its value because the premiums needed by the insurer to cover all expenses would exceed the actual cost of maternity services.

Selection of a life insurance program can be based upon the lowest premium rate obtainable. Very little service is required of the insurer, and the event which precipitates the payment of benefits is quite definite and final.

Selection of a health insurance program is contingent upon the ability of the school system to pay the premiums. If only a nominal amount of money is available, then the most efficient use of it would be in the purchase of a benefit plan covering the more catastrophic types of disabilities, thus taking advantage of the reduced premiums afforded for higher deductibles and coinsurance. Certainly, a smaller number of employees would be able to collect benefits under such a plan, but those that really needed financial assistance for a severe health situation would be the benefactors. As larger sums of money are made available for health coverage, deductibles can be reduced and even eliminated for hospitalization and surgery; coinsurance can be eliminated for hospitalization and surgery; maximums can be increased; and limitations and exclusions can be reduced and, in some cases, eliminated. The plan should be designed to fit the pocketbook of the school system, rather than to fit the pocketbook to the plan.

Selection of a dental insurance plan may depend upon who will pay the premiums and how much they are willing to pay. In most instances, such plans involve the "trading" of premium dollars into claims dollars. If the school system is paying the entire premium, then employees would feel cheated if the plan had a deductible, coinsurance, and limitations for cleanings and x-rays. On the other hand, if the plan were to provide broad, full, first-dollar coverage, the cost of it could well exceed the actual cost of the dental services rendered; this would soon be recognized by employees if they were required to pay the premium. Again, by starting with a plan weighted in favor of the unexpected and serious dental conditions and then expanding toward more full coverage as funds become available, serious financial and personnel problems could be avoided.

SELECTION OF THE INSURER.   Differences in rates as well as service exist among insurance companies. It is to the advantage of the school system to select the insurer with the best plan of benefits at the best rates, who can also provide the most efficient and effective service. Several approaches to the selection of an insurer are available. Specifications of benefits can be put out under sealed bid. The hazard in this approach is that the carrier presenting the lowest bid might not have the most efficient and effective service, particularly important in the handling of claims. The advantage to this approach is that it relieves the school system of lengthy interviews with insurance company sales representatives. The specifications can be sent to a selected list of insurers who then come in individually to present their quotation. This approach allows the school system to look into the service qualifications of the insurers, although it can take considerable time. Both approaches require that the person or persons reviewing the bids be knowledgeable about insurance.

The broker-of-record approach has been quite popular throughout the country and has the advantage of placing an insurance expert between the insurance companies and the school system as a buffer; as a broker, his interests should lie with the school system. A disadvantage arising from this method can occur in the selection of the broker. If a broker is selected on a subjective basis (because he is popular in the area or for some other personal reason), then the hazard of lack of competence might arise. Some agents and brokers represent only one or a few insurers; this might not provide the school system with the exposure to the best insurer for the particular plan desired. An alternative might be to select an expert consultant for a fee or on salary to act in the best interests of the school system in designing plans and selecting the insurer. This could add cost on the one hand, but it could save premiums on the other. Whatever system is used will require some expertise in the field of insurance in order to produce the best results. If that expertise does not exist within the system, then it should be sought from outside.

Summary

One kind of school insurance covers district property; the other deals with employee health and welfare. Only the very largest school districts can avoid insuring property by maintaining a cash reserve fund; the others must insure.

Given the assumption that insurance should be carried whenever the risk is too large for the district to assume, it follows that small districts need insurance the most. Necessary insurance includes fire, liability, and workmen's compensation. Optional insurance is typified by all-risk coverage, plate glass, and vandalism policies.

Fire insurance is offered in various forms: full value, coinsurance, and "probable loss." The appropriate type is often determined by local conditions. A district can reduce fire insurance costs by regular appraisals, removal of fire hazards, periodic inspections, training in use of firefighting equipment, fire drills, and instruction in fire prevention.

Liability and property damage insurance is of two kinds: property damage and bodily injury. Negligence in many states is actionable, thus making such insurance necessary, while in others, school districts enjoy relative immunity from suit.

A blanket commercial fidelity bond should always be taken out on employees who handle school funds. Other optional insurance includes monies and security policy, all-risk coverage, open-stock burglary, and boiler insurance.

Tomorrow's employee contracts will increasingly include fringe benefits through insurance such as life and health insurance, retirement plans, and tax-sheltered annuities. Most fringe benefits are provided under group insurance policies with the school district as the policyholder and the employees as the insureds. Income protection is a recent addition to employee fringe-benefit packages, and may be either short-term or long-term.

Administrators are cautioned that such fringe benefit plans can constitute either a decided asset for the district or a perennial headache. Financing the cost is a continuing challenge, involving complicated questions such as maternity coverage, the difference between superannuation and disability, and the rapidly rising costs in any health insurance plan.

Since selection of the insurer is important, districts are advised to hire an expert consultant to act in the best interests of the district in designing plans and selecting the insurer.

Administrative Problems

Problem 1

There are 350 teachers in the Palomba Unified School District. The local teacher's association has become increasingly strong and demanding. Its newly elected president, Jim Brower, is a forceful and vocal young teacher. A membership drive has resulted in over 90 percent of the teachers joining the association.

Jim has appointed an insurance committee to look into increasing fringe benefits. Up to now, the school district has paid only part of the health and medical insurance which is handled through Blue Cross. The committee's objective is to have the district pay all the Blue Cross insurance premiums for teachers and part of the premium for dependents. It is also planning to request fully paid dental insurance and is looking into the possibility of the district paying income protection, life insurance, and tax-sheltered plans.

The superintendent has not been consulted by the teacher's association or the insurance committee, but has heard reports that they are planning to ask the Board of Education to authorize the payment of many additional insurance premiums. He does not believe that the district can afford to do this, especially because of the high salaries paid to teachers.

If you were the superintendent, what would you do when you heard about the teacher's association proposals?
What would you tell the Board of Education?
What stand would you take? Why?

Problem 2

Assume the same situation as in Problem 1. At this point, insurance committee has met with you and asked for your advice.

What kind of unified insurance package would you recommend to them?

Selected References

CAMPBELL, ROALD F., et al. *Organization and Control of American Schools.* 3rd ed. Columbus, Ohio: Charles E. Merrill Publishing Co., 1975.

CARTER, CLINTON. *Evacuation Order.* Montgomery, Ala.: Robert E. Lee High School, 1971.

CRESSWELL, ANTHONY M., and MICHAEL J. MURPHY. *Education and Collective Bargaining: Readings in Policy and Research.* Bloomington, Ind.: Phi Delta Kappa, 1976.

DOHERTY, NEIL. *Insurance and Loss Prevention.* Lexington, Mass.: Lexington Books, 1977.

EILENS, ROBERT D., and ROBERT M. CROW. *Group Insurance Handbook.* Homewood, Ill.: Richard D. Irwin, Inc., 1965.

HOY, WAYNE K., and CECIL G. MISKEL. *Educational Administration: Theory, Research, and Practice.* New York: Random House, Inc., 1978.

HUEBNER, S. S., and KENNETH BLACK, JR. *Life Insurance.* New York: Appleton–Century–Crofts, 1969.

KING, FRANCIS P. *Benefit Plans in Junior Colleges.* Washington, D.C.: American Association of Junior Colleges, 1971.

LINN, H. H., and S. C. JOYNER. *Insurance Practices in School Administration.* New York: The Ronald Press, 1952.

LONG, JOHN D., and DAVIS W. GREGG. *Property and Liability Insurance Handbook.* Homewood, Ill.: Richard D. Irwin, Inc., 1965.

MAGEE, JOHN H., and OSCAR N. SERBEIN. *Property and Liability Insurance.* Homewood, Ill.: Richard D. Irwin, Inc., 1967.

MELBO, IRVING R., et al. *Report of the Survey, Paramount Unified School District.* Published by the authority of the Board of Trustees, Paramount Unified School District. Los Angeles, Ca.: University of Southern California, 1970.

NATIONAL EDUCATION ASSOCIATION. *Guidelines to Fringe Benefits for Members of the Teaching Profession.* Washington, D.C.: The Association, 1969.

NELSON, D. LLOYD, and WILLIAM M. PURDY. *School Business Administration.* Lexington, Mass.: D. C. Heath and Co., 1971.

PICKRELL, JESSE F. *Group Health Insurance.* Homewood, Ill.: Richard D. Irwin, Inc., 1965.

PART FOUR

Administration of the School Plant

CHAPTER ELEVEN

Financing, Planning, and Constructing Educational Facilities

School buildings represent the culmination of carefully coordinated planning by personnel in education, architecture, governmental agencies, and, in varying degrees, the lay public. Because good planning takes time and financing and the construction of school buildings throughout the United States costs millions of dollars annually, expert management is required. Since this is only one chapter on a topic about which volumes have been written, it cannot go into minute detail on how to achieve various objectives that are part of the total plan.

Financing School Construction Programs

Construction costs have to be met if school building programs are to be accommodated. Situations vary from district to district and from state to state. The annual school construction costs in the United States have been estimated at over five billion dollars. The systems of financing construction that are most frequently applied are:

TAXES OR PAY-AS-YOU-GO. Current financing is generally reserved for school districts that are able to secure voter approval to provide enough

---

This chapter was prepared in collaboration with Dr. Robert E. Hummel, Superintendent of Hemet Unified School District, Hemet, California.

revenue to meet the building needs of the school district. The success of the pay-as-you-go method is dependent upon comprehensive public information campaigns.

BONDS.   Most school construction is financed by voter-approved bonds. There are four types of bonds:

1.   Serial bonds.
2.   Straight-term bonds.
3.   The sinking-fund type of bond.
4.   A callable bond.

Whatever type of bond is used, a competent counsel should be employed and the type of loan to be requested should be determined. When the type of bond has been determined, the amount and the date of sale should be advertised and should include the deadline date for bids.[1]

Generally, bonds are voted for a specific project or series of projects, depending upon the laws of the state in which the school district is located. Bonds are paid off from taxes levied over a period of time ranging as long as twenty-five to thirty years.

FEDERAL FUNDS.   Congress has made possible, in specific situations, the appropriation of funds to school districts.

PRIVATE GRANTS OR REQUESTS.   Parochial and private schools are more often the recipients of private grants or bequests that may be used to provide much needed facilities. Such funds generally are made available for a specific building project.

LEGAL ELEMENTS TO BE CONSIDERED.   Because school finance is a complex program, and because the laws differ in each state, the administrator must work closely with the legal adviser for the school district. Legal deadlines must be maintained. Sufficient time should be scheduled into the plan to allow for contingencies. The key to success is knowing legal requirements and planning accordingly.

IDENTIFYING THE NEED.   If any plan to obtain financing for school construction is to achieve success, it must be based upon a demonstrated need for the facilities. How the need is developed and justified to the voters is dependent upon local conditions. Nationwide reports of voter

---

[1] Clyde Bunnell, "Fiscal Planning," *Guidelines for School Planning and Construction, A Handbook for School Business Officials,* Research Bulletin No. 8 (Chicago: Research Corporation of the Association of School Business Officials, 1968), pp. 10–11.

rejection of bond proposals portends that any proposal that does not adequately justify the need in the minds of the voters is doomed to failure. Some techniques for identifying and assessing the needs for school construction are explained as master plan saturation studies for school district construction, pupil population studies, and a systematic examination of existing facilities related to building safety and projected pupil populations.

SATURATION STUDY.   The saturation study is a projection of maximum land use in the district based upon present zoning requirements and geographical conditions. This study develops the ultimate pupil and adult population for the particular school district, and may also project future school sites. It may be prepared by the school district, an architectural firm, a planning consultant, or a governmental agency. The district should choose and employ its own consultant wherever possible. It must be predicated upon the district's determination of class size, grade level organization, and school size. The saturation study becomes a valuable tool for planning building needs; thus, it is frequently known as a District Master Plan.

PUPIL POPULATION PROJECTIONS.   Projecting pupil population may be useful in projecting future building needs. Many variables can influence the data. People in the United States today are highly mobile. Industrial cutbacks, governmental spending, international crises, modern technology, the "pill," and other factors influence population projections.

Pupil population projections should be developed after a careful examination of data drawn from pupil enrollments of the past five years. Samples drawn from data covering fewer years can be subject to greater error.

Demographic studies are sometimes available from banking institutions, chambers of commerce, planning commissions, or other governmental agencies. A study of births recorded at local hospitals may reveal trends in pupil population at the preschool level. A review of permits for new construction, the record of water and gas meters set, or telephones installed may provide information useful in projecting pupil populations. Declines in the birth-rate level have had their effect on the number of pupils entering kindergarten and the lower grades in some school districts. School enrollment has been dropping nationwide from a high of 51,309,000 in 1970 to a predicted low of 43 to 44 million in 1984. Elementary school enrollment is then expected to start rising as children of those born in the postwar baby boom enter school. Secondary school increases will follow later.[2]

[2] U.S. Department of Health, Education, and Welfare, National Center for Education Statistics, *Projections of Education Statistics to 1986–87*.

To handle shrinkage, there must be a plan with agreed-upon goals and objectives. Projections must be made and the factual data analyzed to determine possible solutions and alternatives, such as:

1. Closing rooms or schools.
2. Converting vacant rooms to enrichment programs, libraries, or laboratories.
3. Converting to adult education centers.
4. "Mothballing" for a wait-and-see period.

Mothballing is a waste of investment. It would be better for the school and the community to work together in order to see what creative use might be made of surplus school property. By cooperative action, suggestions might include ideas such as: a senior center, a museum, an art and theater complex, a physical fitness center, or some other type of community school project.

When pupil populations are projected against available classroom spaces, they provide valuable data for assessing present space as related to future needs. Caution should be exercised in any straight-line projection of data, and pupil population figures should be reviewed annually.

SCHOOL PLANT ASSESSMENT.   Physically obsolete school buildings should be studied to determine whether cost of modernization is greater than the cost of building a completely new structure. Several variables influence the decision. Cities have changed due to zoning requirements. Schools that were in a neighborhood setting fifty years ago may now be surrounded by industry. Changes in the birth rate and in life expectancy also affect school populations.

Geological conditions affect schools. School districts in quake, tornado, or flood areas have employed licensed structural engineers or architects to make studies and recommendations. These recommendations become need assessments for planning future buildings.

New construction should be modifiable so that rooms can be altered easily as educational programs are changed. Movable structures may prove useful because they can be relocated on other sites as student population changes. Seven-year maintenance plans should be given consideration. In various suburban districts, community changes and drops in enrollment have caused school buildings to become vacant; long-range planning should take into account the possibility of converting them into community spaces or factories.

SCHOOL BOARD APPROVAL.   The proposed building program must be approved by action of the governing board of the school district. The school board must authorize the calling of the election to provide the building funds, generally approve the plan for public information on the proposal, and may participate with either the administrative team or citizens committee developed to carry the campaign to the people.

COMMUNITY.   The success or failure of any tax levy or bond election lies with the electorate. The people decide the issues. Therefore, strategy should be designed to create a positive impression of the building project in the mind of the voter. Each building project has to be justified as reasonable, necessary, and proper from the voter's point of view. A study of the people who influence voter opinions is vital. Who are the people who believe in the merits of the building project and can win voter support? This question becomes the key to the information campaign of the election. Planning the election program requires time and personnel skilled in communicating with people.

THE CAMPAIGN.   The organization of successful elections is hard work. It requires hours of preparation, organization, and management of the systems of information and action to get out the "yes" votes. The plan should be organized to permit feedback as it develops so that corrections or modifications may be made. A program planning chart with detailed subcharts is helpful in keeping all phases of the total campaign in mind. Informed and dedicated workers are indispensable in executing a well-designed election campaign plan. Success is based upon a people-to-people kind of contact. Victories in tax and bond elections do not just happen; they are the result of careful planning and hard work by a variety of people, all dedicated to the task of getting the voters' approval on the issue.

Planning for School Construction

In planning educational specifications for buildings, the school district should use the services of educational specialists. The Council of Educational Facility Planners in Columbus, Ohio, for example, has evaluated and abstracted school plant research; planning information of national relevance has been released to Council membership. It has also supplied the Educational Research Information Center (ERIC–USDE) with planning resumes and documents.

Other excellent sources of school building information are the School Planning Laboratory at Stanford University, The American Institute of Architects in Washington, D.C., the National Academy of Science in Washington, D.C., the Educational Facilities Laboratories, Inc., in New York, the Association of School Business Officials of the United States and Canada in Chicago, and the National Council on Schoolhouse Construction at Michigan State University.

SELECTING AN ARCHITECT. The responsibility for the actual design of the building lies most frequently with licensed architects who are responsible for the preparation of the working drawings, the written specifications, and the supervision of building construction. The architectual firm is employed by the school district to provide this technical service in the development of a building design that will meet the educational space requirements of the school district.

Research varies on when it is best to select the architect. However, it is generally best to select the most qualified architectural firm early and to utilize their services during the educational planning phase of the design as well as to enlist their aid in site selection, if this has not already been accomplished. Some architectural firms are available to provide service during the campaigns for securing voter approval of the building tax or bond issues.

Several criteria are helpful in considering architectural firms:

1. Is the firm familiar with the legal elements of the particular state and county in which the building is to be constructed?
2. Is the firm near enough to the school district to provide the necessary personnel as needed both for design as well as for construction?
3. Have they had previous experience in school construction of the grade level and quantity of pupils to be housed?
4. Do they have a staff of professionals large enough to successfully accomplish the design tasks?
5. Are former clients satisfied with the work of the architectural firm?
6. Does inspection of school plants designed by the architectural firm reveal that the buildings function properly for the educational program utilizing them?
7. How do those who use the buildings feel about the design qualities which the architect has put into the building?
8. Did the architect stay within the project budget?
9. Does the firm design a high quality, low maintenance building for the lowest dollar cost?
10. Does the architect employ capable, consulting professional engineers to provide the necessary electrical, structural, mechanical, and other design support staff personnel?
11. Does the architect provide the services required of the district at a fee suitable for the services rendered?
12. Does the architect employ fresh designs that add to the educational needs without becoming purely architectural monuments?
13. Is the architectural firm able to provide imaginative and creative solutions for the space requirements of the educational problems presented?
14. Does the firm employ the necessary consultant personnel for special-

ized needs, i.e., color, acoustics, landscape, and similar specialized needs?

15. Does the firm have personnel who will be easy to work with in the design and construction stage?
16. Does the firm have a selection of competent personnel at all levels of responsibility?
17. Can the firm deliver what it proposes to do for the agreed price and on schedule?
18. What is the firm's philosophy concerning change orders?

Current practice among school districts includes visitation to the offices of a selected group of architects who are considered as finalists in the selection process. Sometimes several finalists may be asked to interview the board of education and display some of their designs. School board members may wish to visit some of the buildings designed by various architectural firms. The final decision or selection lies with the board of education, which hopefully follows valid criteria.

ARCHITECT'S TEAM.   The architect may employ specialized personnel as a part of the office staff or contract with firms who provide specialized services to many different architectural firms. The architect should have access to design specialists, color consultants, draftsmen, field inspectors, specification writers, and related clerical and support personnel. The office may include or contract for the services of civil engineers, acoustical engineers, landscape architects, and other specialized personnel.

ARCHITECT'S CONTRACT.   The architect's contract is a legal document that should clearly answer the following questions:

1. Which buildings are to be designed (specific project or projects)?
2. What are the limitations on cost of project—i.e., if project bid exceeds architect's estimate by 10 percent, does he redesign at no cost to the district?
3. What fee is the architect to charge for services rendered? (An 8 percent fee has been the AIA standard.)
4. What fee will be charged for small special jobs which normally do not fall within the standard percent fee?
5. What added services will the architect provide beside normal preliminary and finished drawings and specifications? Will the firm also provide a landscape plan, a master plan for the school project? What about a sequential schedule of the building plan, time lines, and educational planning responsibility? What are the architect's responsibilities in the educational planning phase?
6. Is the architect liable for errors in design that cost money in change orders?

7. What responsibility does the architect have for inspection during construction?
8. What will be the fee for extras, i.e., copies of blueprints and specifications?
9. Who owns the design drawings and specifications when the job is completed?
10. How may the contract be terminated?

DEVELOPING EDUCATIONAL SPECIFICATIONS. Educational specifications have been defined as "the direct product of educational planning activity by the school district or an educational consultant. They incorporate an explanation of educational methodology or teaching techniques employed and an explanation of space requirements in terms of educational activities, materials, areas, and affinities. They form a list of specifics or directives to enable the architect to design the needed facilities. Educational specifications serve the architect as the building plans and specifications serve the contractor. Educational specifications are best presented in the form of written statements of the educational requirements of the school district."[3]

PLANNING TAKES TIME. The single factor most often mentioned by personnel engaged in planning for school construction is time. Good planning for finance, educational needs, design, bidding, and construction all takes time. A minimum of from two to three years will be required for the educational planning, design, and construction of good schools. The larger and more complex the facility, the greater the time necessary to complete the task.

THE PLANNING COMMITTEE. Research findings indicate that planning committees function best if limited to six or eight persons. Larger committees may be used, but it is desirable to establish a smaller executive steering committee to synthesize reports and translate the work of the larger committee into written directives to the architect.

The educational planning committee is generally composed of the following people: principal, superintendent of schools, teachers, assistant superintendent in charge of educational services, and business manager. Frequently, department chairmen or grade level teachers are selected to work on the larger committee under the direction of the superintendent or building planning specialist. All elements of the community, including parents and community leaders, should be involved in the decision-making process, since the school is a community institution.

---

[3] Robert E. Hummel, "Educational Planning Procedures for School Building Construction" (unpublished doctoral dissertation, University of Southern California, 1961), p. 11.

CONTENT OF EDUCATIONAL SPECIFICATIONS. The actual educational specification document, which should be written by specialists, may be structured in several ways: (1) a narrative document that follows the general content outlined below or an outline with paragraphs filled in as needed (to convey to the architect what particular requirements are desired in a specific learning space or area in the school).

The following outline includes educational specifications for a typical secondary school plant.

I. Introduction.
   A. Description of grade levels to be served.
   B. Statement of the philosophy of the school district regarding this age group of pupils or the district's philosophy for all grades.
   C. Description of courses offered and grade levels to be served.
   D. Number of pupils who will participate in each of the various courses offered.

II. General architectural requirements.
   A. Basic design considerations.
   B. Lighting requirements.
   C. Heating, air conditioning, ventilation, and acoustics.
   D. Treatment of inside wall surfaces (e.g., chalk and tackboards).
   E. Intercommunication and electronic equipment, closed circuit television or cable TV capabilities.
   F. Community service (park concept).
   G. Building orientation.
   H. Cabinet work.
   I. Furniture.
   J. Carpet or other type of floor finish.

III. Recommendations for general instructional spaces.
   A. General classrooms.
      1. Total number of rooms required.
      2. Approximate room size.
      3. Number of students to be accommodated.
      4. Activities to take place in these rooms.
      5. Location requirement in relation to other parts of the plant and other departments.
      6. Cabinet and storage requirements.
      7. Furniture and equipment.
      8. Other requirements and recommendations.
   B. Arts and Crafts. See details in this outline as under "A."
   C. Business Education.
   D. Foreign Language.
   E. Homemaking.
   F. Industrial Arts.
   G. Instrumental Music.
   H. Physical Education facilities.

        1. Interior.
        2. Exterior.
   I. Science.
   J. Special classrooms.
   K. Vocational Education.

IV. Recommendations for auxiliary spaces.
   A. Multipurpose.
   B. Curriculum materials area.
        1. Library.
        2. Textbook room.
        3. Audio-visual and multimedia space.
        4. Curriculum materials laboratory.
   C. Office area.
   D. Student health services.
   E. Faculty lounge.
   F. Other building areas including restrooms and storage area.
   G. Community services.
        1. Access to grounds and buildings.
        2. Storage.
        3. Restrooms.
   H. Maintenance and operation considerations.
        1. Landscaping.
        2. Mechanical systems.
        3. Hardware.
        4. Power and lighting.
        5. Site development.

After the specifications have been developed, they should be reviewed and agreed upon by a planning committee composed of administrators, teachers, and interested community people.

SITE SELECTION. Determining the best location for a future school is a complex process. Final determination of the most suitable location should be based upon careful research by authorities responsible for preparing the recommendation to the board of education. An architect may be helpful in the selection of a suitable site. Factors to be considered in site selection are presented below.

EDUCATIONAL CRITERIA. The educational criteria determine to a great degree the location, size, soil conditions, and topography of the school site. A given parcel that is of sufficient size and shape for an elementary school would be totally inadequate for a high school that requires a larger area. The educational philosophy of the school district regarding grade-level organization, educational program, and desired recreational and physical education facilities must be considered.[4] What grade levels will be assigned to the particular site? How many pupils will expect to be housed according to the master plan on this site?

LOCATION. The location of the school plant must be carefully planned. It land is not available, condemnation proceedings must be instituted; this takes time and is costly. Factors such as initial cost, size, access, and attorney's fees need to be considered. Questions such as the following must be answered:

1. How does the site relate to the proposed pupil population—i.e., will most pupils walk to the school or ride a bus?
2. How is the site oriented in relation to the prevailing winds?
3. Will the extremes of winter and summer weather adversely affect the building on the site?
4. What is the location of the site in relation to industrial noise, odors, traffic, and related distracting elements?
5. What zoning surrounds the proposed site, and will the school be compatible with the zoning in this area?
6. What utilities serve the proposed location?
7. Will the necessary service be provided without excessive cost to the school district?
8. What other factors should be considered in locating the school on the site?

SOIL CONDITIONS AND TOPOGRAPHY.

1. Does the location contain any geological qualities that would make it unsuitable for the school, e.g., earthquake fault lines?
2. What drainage qualities does the soil contain?
3. Does the soil provide adequate strength to support the proposed structure?
4. Will the topography permit development without extensive site development costs, e.g., grading, expense of trenching in rocky soil, problems of recompacting soil which is unstable, requires excessive fill, or is extremely sandy?
5. What other factors should be considered?

A SITE SELECTION CHECKLIST. To provide some means of evaluating the relative merits of several sites, it is well to identify various criteria that are

---

[4] Lester E. Andrews, "Site," *Guidelines for School Planning and Construction, A Handbook for School Business Officials*, Research Bulletin No. 8 (Chicago: Research Corporation of the Association of School Business Officials, 1968), p. 14.

TABLE 11–1. Site Selection Checklist.

CONSIDERATIONS

Location
A. Proximity to pupils
B. Zoning in area
C. Kind of neighborhood
D. Accessibility to pedestrians
E. Available utilities
F. Width and condition of streets
G. Weather factors
H. Freedom from industrial smoke and noise
I. Relationship to existing and future freeways
J. Available highways
K. Public transportation
L. Hazards
M. Police and fire protection
N. Community recreation value

Size
A. Size of parcel
B. Shape of parcel
C. Expansion features

Topography and Soil
A. Drainage
B. Terrain
C. Soil conditions
D. Special natural features
E. Special geological conditions

Cost
A. Availability
B. Initial cost of site
C. Development
D. Available utilities
E. Available streets
F. Other factors that could increase costs

to be used to measure the relative merits of several sites. Suggested criteria for evaluating proposed school sites are presented in Table 11–1.

Through the use of such a site evaluation device, a comparison of the relative strengths and weaknesses of several sites can be made.

PLANNING FOR CONSTRUCTION. Preliminary plans may need to be re-viewed and approved by designated officials at the county and/or state level. It is well to know in advance who should be involved and make certain that the planning and design program includes the necessary review and approvals required according to state or local practice.

A district-hired architectural consultant is almost a necessity if the district's long-range interests are to be protected.

The design of the school should be carefully monitored by various elements of the administrative staff to determine that the educational requirements have been met in the most efficient manner and that the design does not exceed the budget.

BIDDING.   The announced building project is advertised in trade papers as well as in local newspapers. The announcement advises bidders of the nature of the project, where plans and specifications may be obtained, and other details of the building project. It may also list a schedule of wage rates.

Competitive bidding by qualified contractors on the building plans and specifications is the most common method used to determine which firm will be assigned the job of constructing the building. Sealed bids submitted at a designated time and place are then opened by authorized personnel. The bids submitted by the various builders are analyzed. Some states require that a bond be submitted to assure the owner that the contractor will faithfully complete the project; these are called faithful performance bonds. The lowest qualified bidder is generally awarded the contract by action of the board of education.

PLANNING AND INSPECTION.   A pre-construction conference may be held involving the architect, school district officials, all principals from the construction firm, and consulting engineers. The meeting should clarify procedures of communication and working relationships for the duration of the project.

The law may require the school district to employ a qualified building inspector to assure that the building is built in accordance with the designed building plans and specifications. Consulting engineers, architect's representatives, and state representatives from the Office of Architecture and Construction may also, from time to time, visit the site and inspect the progress of the construction.

The school district will have various other personnel, other than the inspector, who will visit the construction site to monitor the progress. The district building inspector generally works through the architect to effect any changes or to resolve any problems.

The completion of the new physical structure is only part of the solution. Orders for the necessary furniture and equipment must be placed far enough in advance to allow for availability of the items upon the completion of the plant.

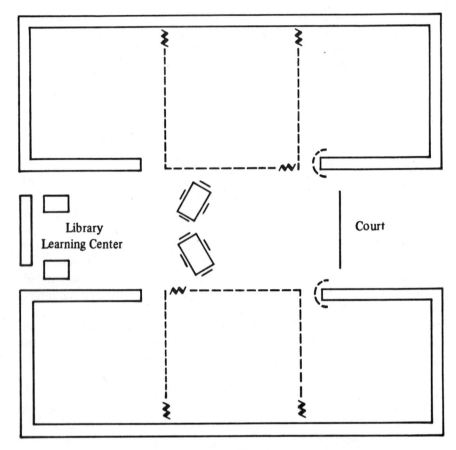

*FIGURE 11–1.   Example of a Building Using Modular Shell
Construction with Flexible and Open Spaces.*

New Concepts in School Construction

In the continuing effort to improve teaching, there have been many changes
in basic classroom concepts. Trends in design and construction have produced classrooms with movable walls, artificial lighting, air conditioning,
carpeted floors, heat-efficient buildings, and highly controlled environ-
ments. Figure 11–1 is an example of modular shell construction that offers
degrees of flexibility never before equalled; ability to vary interior spaces
is the most common illustration of flexibility. Construction techniques
using modular construction provide buildings with long-span shells and
few permanent interior walls. The mechanical and electronical systems are
integrated with the structure (i.e., they are fairly easy to move).

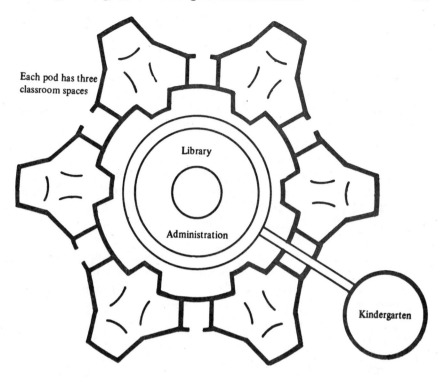

FIGURE 11–2. Example of a Building Using Cluster Plan Construction with Flexible and Open Spaces.

The latest concept in designing instructional spaces is to provide variously shaped classrooms. These include hexagonal, wedged, circular, squared, and triangular shapes, all in a clustered arrangement (see Figure 11–2). These rooms have all the latest components in modular-shell designs; the spaces are purported to stimulate innovative and experimental teaching methods, including team teaching, large- or small-group instruction, use of audio-visual and electronic equipment, and independent or exploratory study. These more imaginative designs are found in school districts experimenting with newer approaches, stressing cooperative teaching programs and various sizes of learning groups.

Some of the new educational techniques and media that must be planned for are: science, reading, and language laboratories, overhead and opaque projectors, microfilm readers, tape recorders, teaching machines, videotape equipment, closed-circuit television, multi-use rooms, and teacher–pupil planning centers. These are in addition to the usual movie projectors, film-strip projectors, and record players. New planning may include the installation of computers for data processing, class scheduling, and information retrieval. New schools must be constructed with sufficient wiring, electrical panels, breakers, and electric outlets to handle the extra load imposed by the use of newer instructional media. Older schools will need to be completely rewired.

Improvements are continuously being made in sound proofing, lighting, heating, flooring materials, and construction materials. Air conditioning is no longer a luxury; in some sections of the country it is almost mandatory. Experiments are being made in constructing schools without windows so that lighting is controlled better, outside distractions are minimized, and vandalism is reduced. All of these improvements help to create a better environment for learning which ultimately benefits the students.

Several factors are influencing new school construction: (1) rising fuel costs, (2) the energy crisis, and (3) decreasing free space. A solution is to build multi-level buildings to save both energy and space. Much construction is reconstruction, since many old schools are neither built nor equipped to handle innovations and changing educational programs. Remodeling and modernizing can be accomplished, but this is a costly process. However, if a school district is concerned with improvements in its educational program, any cost should be considered worthwhile.

Critical Path Method

Since its initiation in 1957, the Critical Path Method (CPM) has been used for planning and scheduling building programs by private industry and some forward-looking school systems. It is adaptable for computers where they are available but is also effective where they are not. CPM is:

> based entirely on the detailed logical analysis of a project into the component separate activities which make up the total project, and the arrangement of each activity in its proper sequence with respect to the other activities . . . The basic working tools of C.P.M. are the arrow diagram, sometimes called the network, and the printout or listing of tasks in their sequential order.[5]

When this method is used, construction can be speeded up, unnecessary steps removed, staffs adjusted for the work needed, activities run concurrently, inconsistencies eliminated, and performance improved.[6]

School districts planning to use CPM should contact its consulting service, discuss the possibilities of utilizing this type of service, and determine the fees.

---

[5] Henry F. Daum, "The Use of the Critical Path Method in Schoolhouse Construction," *Guidelines for School Planning and Construction, A Handbook for School Business Officials*, Research Bulletin No. 8 (Chicago: Research Corporation of the Association of School Business Officials, 1968), pp. 34–35.

[6] Daum, "The Use of the Critical Path Method," p. 35.

The success of CPM depends upon the administrator's understanding of its use. Many people should be involved: the school board, the superintendent, the business manager, principals, teachers, citizens, and contractors. The forward-looking school administrator should look into CPM or some similar program before commencing a building program.

Summary

The most common sources of revenue for financing school construction are current taxation, long-term bonding, or federal funds. Planning should include legal research, identifying the need, projection of maximum land use in the district, pupil population projections, and school plant assessment. After approval by the school board, the funding proposal must be presented to the electorate in such a way as to secure the maximum turnout of favorable voters.

In planning for construction, the first step is to select an architect in accordance with predetermined criteria. The architect will then choose a team of specialized consultants and in due course will present a contract for board approval. The next step is to develop educational specifications to guide the architect in planning, a process that will be aided by the appointment of a planning committee. The specifications should include the general architectural requirements, recommendations for instructional spaces, and suggestions for auxiliary spaces.

Site selection is a major consideration, embracing educational criteria and locating the new plant by using a site selection checklist.

In addition to seeking assistance from designated officials at the county and state levels, the district should employ its own consultant to protect its interests and monitor such problems as elimination of fire hazards, competitive bidding, planning, and inspection of actual construction.

New concepts of movable walls, modular-shell construction, and cluster plans should be considered in the light of foreseeable needs. The Critical Path Method (CPM) analyzes the component activities making up the total project and arranges each activity in its proper sequence with respect to the other activities.

Administrative Problems   In Basket

Problem 1

The Lancaster Unified School District is located in a rapidly growing area. Because several elementary schools need to be built, the Board of Education has voted to call a bond election to provide the funds for capital outlay. The superintendent also foresees the need for additions to the secondary schools.

As superintendent, how would you organize the bond election campaign?
Whom would you involve?
What information would you need, and how would you disseminate it to the public?

Problem 2

Assume that the bond election in Lancaster was successful. The superintendent has asked Mr. Hertel, the business manager, to select an architect to recommend to the Board of Education.

What criteria should Mr. Hertel use in selecting the architect?
If employed, what conditions should be explained in the architect's contract?
At what stage should the architect be employed? Why?

Problem 3

Assume the same situation as in Problem 2. Bill Bixby, an elementary principal, has been asked by the superintendent to select a committee to make recommendations regarding the type of buildings and educational facilities they would like.

Whom should Bill select for his committee?
What research should they do?
What are some of the educational specifications they might recommend?
What furniture and equipment should be recommended?

Selected References

AMERICAN ASSOCIATION OF SCHOOL ADMINISTRATORS. *Planning America's School Buildings.* Washington, D.C.: The Association, 1960.

EDUCATIONAL FACILITIES LABORATORIES. *Educational Change and Architectural Consequences.* New York: Educational Facilities Laboratories, Inc., 1968.

———. *Relocatable School Facilities.* New York: Educational Facilities Laboratories, Inc., 1964.

FROST, FREDRICK G. "The New Secondary School Environment." *American School & University* 41 (June 1969).

HACK, WALTER G., and LUVERNE L. CUNNINGHAM. *Educational Administration: The Developing Decades.* Berkeley, Ca.: McCutchan Publishing Corporation, 1977.

HANSON, CARROLL B. "How to Pass a Bond Issue." *School Management* 13 (July 1969).

"How 16 Award-Winning Schools Compare." *Nation's Schools* 85 (January 1970).

"How 18 Award-Winning Schools Compare." *Nation's Schools* 85 (January 1970).

HOY, WAYNE K., and CECIL G. MISKEL. *Educational Administration: Theory, Research and Practice.* New York: Random House, Inc., 1978.

KOERNER, THOMAS F., and CLYDE PARKER. "Happiness Isn't Necessarily When a Board Gets the Kind of a School It Deserves." *American School Board Journal* 157 (January 1970).

LEGGETT, S. "Research on School Building Problems." *American School and University* 51 (1978):45–50.

LEVIN, D. "Asbestos in Schools: Walls and Halls of Trouble." *American School Board Journal* 165 (November 1978):29–33.

MINTZBERG, HENRY. *The Nature of Managerial Work.* New York: Harper and Row Publishers, Inc., 1973.

MORPHET, EDGAR L. *Educational Organization and Administration.* 3rd ed. Englewood Cliffs, N.J.: Prentice-Hall, Inc., 1974.

MURPHY, J. F. "Fiscal Problems of Big City School Systems: Changing Patterns of State and Federal Aid." *Urban Review* 10 (Winter 1978):251–65.

NATIONAL COUNCIL ON SCHOOLHOUSE CONSTRUCTION. *Guide for Planning School Plants.* East Lansing, Mich.: The Council, 1964.

NEILL, SHIRLEY B. *School Energy Crisis: Problems and Solutions.* Arlington, Va.: American Association of School Administrators, 1977.

NORTH CAROLINA STATE DEPARTMENT OF PUBLIC INSTRUCTION. *Schools of Interest; Selection of Building Projects.* Raleigh, N.C.: Division of School Planning, July 1978.

SCHOOL PLANNING LABORATORY. *Shaping Schools to Change.* Palo Alto, Ca.: School of Education, Stanford University, 1967.

SHER, JONATHAN P. *Education in Rural America: A Reassessment of Conventional Wisdom.* Boulder, Colo.: Westview Press, 1977.

ZELIP, FRANK F. *Guidelines for School Planning and Construction, A Handbook for School Business Officials.* Research Bulletin No. 8. Chicago: Research Corporation of the Association of School Business Officials, 1968.

CHAPTER TWELVE

Administering the Operation of School Buildings

The primary purpose of a school building is the maintenance of a good educational program. The building in itself may be an architectural masterpiece, it may represent the largest capital investment of the entire community, and it may be the only cultural and recreational facility in the surrounding area. Meetings, operettas, dramatic clubs, and civic gatherings may depend upon the availability of the school building's auditorium and classrooms. However, it is the educational program that should determine the utilization of the building and its administration.

Maximum Use of a School Building

The efficiency of school plant utilization depends largely upon the degree to which the various rooms can be used during all hours of the day. In most schools, ordinary classrooms can be scheduled with an eye toward maximum utilization, but special areas such as cafeterias, auditoriums, and gymnasiums pose difficult and sometimes insoluble problems.

CIRCULAR USE OF THE SCHOOL BUILDING. It is customary in most large school districts to study the problems involved in maximum utilization of the school plant by means of "room-use" charts which show at a glance the rooms that are in use and empty rooms for each period of the school day. They may also include the number of pupil stations occupied or unoccupied during the several periods. A room-use chart should demonstrate maximum utilization potentialities such as multi-purpose rooms, furnishing of classrooms for dual use, and use of specialized areas for more than one purpose. There is no reason, for example, why a lunchroom or library connot double as a student lounge or organizational meeting room. Similarly, a chemistry laboratory may, with a minimum expenditure, be equipped to qualify as a physics classroom or even a natural science room.

By industrial standards, school building utilization is grossly inadequate. As an example, a typical factory will use its plant six or seven days a week, twelve months of the year, and twenty-four hours a day. Even the most streamlined school programs will not permit the use of their buildings anywhere near this potential. Elementary schools are usually able to utilize their space to more complete advantage during the school hours; high schools, handicapped by scheduling problems during the day, make up for this by a more complete utilization program during post-school hours. If there is circular use of school buildings, custodial cleaning cannot start when students are dismissed. It may have to be scheduled between 11:00 P.M. and 7:00 A.M.

The problem is twofold: first, the avoidance of waste in utilization of building space, and, second, the avoidance of setting up maximum utilization as an end in itself.

In determining the degree of utilization of a school building, a "building use" chart should be resorted to. Such a chart, or tabular representation of existing capacity as compared with actual use, should list the rooms by number and kind, and give the following information:

1. Number of pupil stations in each room.
2. Daily and weekly pupil-station capacity of each room.
3. Daily and weekly utilization of each room.
4. Percentage of utilization determined by dividing item 3 by item 2 (above) for each room.
5. Total percentage of utilization for entire building, determined by dividing room percentages.

The combination of a building-use chart with a room-use chart will provide the type of information needed to assure maximum utilization.

The largest nonutilization factor is found to exist in such special rooms as gymnasiums and cafeterias. Most special areas, but not all, are found in high school plants.

Auditoriums may be used for drama, speech, and debating classes, as well as for assemblies; cafeterias may be combined with libraries and used as reading and study halls by judicious use of movable partitions; and laboratories may be used for classes in subjects other than science.

NONCURRICULAR USE OF THE SCHOOL BUILDING.   No trend is more clearcut than that which indicates an ever-increasing community use of the school plant. With the exception of certain restrictions involving subversive and religious use of school facilities, most states now permit and even encourage the use of the school as a community center. All sorts of meetings, fraternal gatherings, public forums, youth groups, and social get-togethers are making use of school rooms, cafeterias, gymnasiums, and auditoriums. This is far from a new development in American education; rather, it is a rebirth of the bygone pioneer use of the schoolhouse as a public gathering-place.

Nonschool utilization of buildings and rooms will greatly increase the percentage of use of such facilities; therefore, it is to be desired, if only from the standpoint of the taxpayer. Adult education falls into a somewhat different category of community use, but is essentially an example of it. Most high school buildings are now being used for some sort of adult classes almost every evening of the week. Industrial concerns in large cities are utilizing school facilities for vocational and apprentice training. Some colleges are decentralizing their graduate courses for teachers and are scheduling them, if the enrollment warrants, at a district school. Community recreation commissions and directors usually work closely with the schools, and multiply their available playgrounds, gymnasiums, and auditoriums by entering into agreements with the local school districts for the after-school and evening use of their facilities. The bettering of school-use ratios, however, is only one advantage to be gained by encouraging such community–school cooperation. The use of the school buildings for civic and community activities will bring many into the schools who would not otherwise come; to that extent, it should be warmly supported by intelligent administrators.

Another type of noncurricular use of school plant facilities is to be found in the field of student co-curricular activities. Gymnasiums can be used for junior proms, student dances, and intramural sports. Cafeterias can be used in the evenings for athletic team banquets or class dinners.

Four main types of community use of school buildings may be cited:

1. Use by local groups upon application.
2. Use for school-sponsored activities.
3. Use for extracurricular and related activities.
4. Use by self-supported organizations.

Desirable as such community use of school property may be, it must not in any way conflict with the use of the same areas by the regular pupils of the school.

Certain other problems remain to be resolved. The supervision of school property during periods of community use poses several problems, such as, who is to pay for cleaning and heating, lighting, and other utilities. The presence of adults in large numbers at evening activities poses additional problems of policing and sanitation. There is little question that operational budgets go up proportionately with community utilization of school facilities. Despite these considerations, the school district, from a standpoint of public relations, will be well advised to assume all reasonable expenses in order to ensure maximum utilization of school buildings, and to induce lay citizens to come freely into the schools. As long as the instructional program is not interfered with, it is entirely to the schools' advantage to make their facilities available to the public on as broad a basis as required.

A prudent school policy dealing with community use of the school plant will always include a mimeographed or printed set of rules governing such use. This should set forth the legal obligations of the user, and should embody the local school district regulations insofar as they affect both parties.

Every applicant for permission to use portions of the school building or grounds for community or related purposes should be handed a set of these rules at the time of application. In addition, the applicant should fill out an application form, setting forth the reasons for seeking permission for use and making certain guarantees as to conduct of participants, care of building facilities, and type of activity to be carried on. Should the board of education have a policy on rental charges for profit performances in the school auditorium or multi-purpose room, for example, rates should be clearly set forth in the application form, and the applicant, in signing the form, agrees to pay such charges. The form will usually oblige the applicant to take whatever steps may be necessary to prevent the use of liquor or tobacco on the school premises during the time an outside organization is using them. It should also include a written affirmation that the use of the school building will not involve dissemination of sectarian religious precepts. Such an affidavit is necessary for the school district to ensure legal use of school property. An example of a school-use application is reproduced in Figure 12–1.

Proper Care of School Buildings

In any district employing a trained and experienced director of maintenance and operations, the chief administrator will be freed from personal supervision of school building care. Since most school districts, however, do not yet boast such an officer, the typical superintendent must take whatever steps may be necessary to ensure that buildings and grounds are kept neat and clean, and that natural deterioration does not exceed the bounds of normalcy. The chief administrator should set up a system that will include two main types of maintenance.

Santa Monica Unified School District
1723 Fourth Street
Santa Monica, California 90401

APPLICATION AND AGREEMENT FOR USE OF SCHOOL PROPERTY

Date of Application...

School...

Facility Desired

Purpose of the meeting...

☐ Auditorium

Expected attendance...

☐ Multipurpose room only

Is meeting open to the public?..............................

☐ Multipurpose room with kitchen

Will admission, solicitation or collection be made?...............

☐ Cafeteria

If yes, for what purpose will net proceeds be used?...............

☐ Cafeteria with kitchen

....

☐ Gymnasium with showers

....

☐ Gymnasium without showers

Indicate day, date and time of use below:

DAY	DATE	HOUR
		.........M to..........M
		.........M to..........M
		.........M to..........M
		.........M to..........M
		.........M to..........M
		.........M to..........M
		.........M to..........M

☐ Swim pool

☐ Class room

☐ Football field

☐ Football field with lights

☐ Baseball field

☐ Tennis courts

☐ Track

☐ Other...............................

Equipment Needed

We hereby certify that we shall be personally responsible, on behalf of our organization for any damage or unnecessary abuse of school buildings, grounds or equipment growing out of the occupancy of said premises by our organization. We agree to abide by and enforce the rules and regulations of the Santa Monica Unified School District governing the non school use of buildings, grounds and equipment and hereby acknowledge receipt of a copy of said rules and regulations.

☐ Piano

☐ Folding chairs

☐ Sound System

☐ Stage lighting with district electrician

Name of organization...

☐ Other...............................

☐ Other...............................

Name and Title of Authorized Agent

☐ Other...............................

Address...

Type of Food Service

Business Phone.....................Residence Phone.....................

☐ Banquet

☐ Potluck

Fee Charged $...............................

☐ Coffee and cookies

Payment $............... Receipt No............... Date...............

Contact must be made with the
Supervisor of Cafeterias for kitchen use.

Payment $............... Receipt No............... Date...............

Payment $............... Receipt No............... Date...............

Facilities are available ☐

Facilities are unavailable ☐

Application granted this...............day of...............19.......

On the date and time requested

SANTA MONICA UNIFIED SCHOOL DISTRICT

By...

....
Principal

OFFICE COPY

FIGURE 12–1. Example of an Application for
Use of School Facilities.
Courtesy of the Santa Monica Unified School District,
Santa Monica, California.

INDIVIDUAL BUILDING MAINTENANCE.   The maintenance of the individual school plant should properly be the administrative province of the building principal. Here, the primary factor will be the relationship between the principal and the school custodians. The former will necessarily chart the latter's work assignment and regular daily routine, supervise the work, and evaluate the results. The principal should meet with the custodial staff at the beginning of each school year, and cooperatively set up the master plan for building maintenance at that time. Since misunderstanding and friction between classroom teachers and custodians are unfortunately so common that they often interfere with the proper performance of maintenance duties, the principal should take whatever steps may be necessary to see that the views of the faculty are taken into account in planning the year's maintenance schedule.

Once the work schedule has been decided upon, the principal should plan on regular inspections of the physical plant. An inspection checklist should be prepared by the principal and the custodians, or a standard form supplied by the district business office. Such a form, even when it originates on a level higher than the individual school, should be the product of group thinking, and various component factors should be agreed upon in advance by all concerned. The checklist should be used whenever inspections are made, and should be marked by both the principal and the custodian whose work is being checked. It should never be used as a rating scale, but rather as a guide to improvement. A checklist of this type is shown in Figure 12–2.

The principal should be particularly alert to detect internal building flaws such as broken windows, inadequate lighting fixtures, defective wiring, and roof or wall leaks. Teachers should be asked to help identify similar maintenance needs and report them promptly to the office. Because these needs tend to be of a classroom nature, such as broken desks, burned-out light fixtures, or damaged blackboards, they should be reported to the principal by means of a form asking for special maintenance service. A form of this type is shown in Figure 12–3.

DISTRICT-WIDE MAINTENANCE.   Maintenance is defined as "those activities designed to repair or restore the plant and equipment to their original condition."[1] Modern schools with new facilities and a great variety of technical teaching equipment such as television, teaching machines, language laboratories, electronic installations, and vocational equipment increase the demands for maintenance.[2]

Each district possessing more than two school plants should organize some system of district-wide maintenance. An annual inspection of all

[1] Irving R. Melbo et al. *Report of the Survey, Laguna Beach Unified School District* (Los Angeles: University of Southern California, 1961), p. 329.
[2] Robert E. Wilson, *Educational Administration*, p. 671.

	Condition	Remarks
School _____ Date _____		
Building _____		
Custodians _____		

Roofs
  Roofing
  Flushing and Coping
  Skylights
  Gutters
  Vents

Exterior Wood Trim
  Rakes and Facia
  Soffits
  Window Frames, Sash
  Louvres and Vents
  Ceilings
  Doors

Exterior Plaster and Concrete
  Walls
  Ceilings
  Arcade Slabs
  Platforms
  Splash Blocks

Exterior Plumbing and Electrical Fixtures
  Hose Bibbs
  Fire Hose Cabinet
  Fire Extinguishers
  Break Glass Alarms
  Water S O Valves
  Gas S O Valves
  Switches and Plates
  Exterior Lights
  Yard Horns and Bells
  Electrical Panels
  Drinking Fountains

Exterior Metal
  Down Spouts and S Blocks
  Columns
  Louvres
  Grease Traps
  Doors
  Screens
  Sumps, Gratings

FIGURE 12–2. Checklist for Regular Inspections of Individual Maintenance.

Exterior Concrete, Brickwork, A.C. and D.G.

Curbs and Gutters	
Drive-ins	
Sidewalks	
Incinerators	
Water-Meter Boxes	
Gas-Meter Boxes	
Electrical Vaults	
Asphalt-Concrete Areas	
Decomposed Granite Areas	
Fences and Gates	
Bicycle Stands	
Flag Pole	
Parking Lots	
Splash Blocks	
Playground Equipment	

Exterior Areas

Turf	
Lawns	
Sprinkler Systems	
Trees	
Shrubs	

	Condition	Remarks		Condition	Remarks
Room No. ____			Room No. ____		
Floor			Intercom Amplifier System		
Walls					
Ceiling			Metal Partitions		
Wood Trim, Venetian Blinds			Tile		
Cabinets			Plumbin & Fixtures		
Drain Boards & Splashes			Kitchen Equipment		
Furniture			Stage Equipment		
Heating & Controls					
Hardware			Towel & Toilet Tissue Cab.		
Electrical Fixtures			Mirrors		
Educational Equipment					

FIGURE 12–2. (Continued)

PARAMOUNT UNIFIED SCHOOL DISTRICT

MAINTENANCE WORK REQUEST

Via Business Office—Retain Last Copy for Your Files

School or Department_____ _Building No._____ Room No._ Date _ _ _ 19__

WORK REQUESTED: List single item or group of like items (Type—Single Space)

For unusual or non-budgeted requests add justification statement. (Use separate sheet if necessary.)

Requested By:_____ Approved By:_____ _____
                                                         Principal or Department Head

Accounting Classification_____

Do Not Write Below This Line

MAINTENANCE DEPARTMENT INFORMATION

Assigned To: _____ Section

New Construction ☐   Maintenance ☐   Vandalism ☐   Crew: _____ _____

Estimated Man Hours _____   Signature of Workman: _____

Scheduled Completion Date _____   Remarks: _____

Actual Completion Date _____

Approved _____   Ass't Supt. Business Services

MATERIAL AND LABOR COST DATA (Attach extra sheet if required)

UNIT	MATERIAL USED	COST	DATE	LABOR USED	HRS.	RATE	COST

TOTAL MATERIAL   TOTAL LABOR

Remarks or Instructions of Maintenance Manager   TOTAL MATERIAL

TOTAL COST OF
COMPLETED REQUEST

FIGURE 12–3.   Maintenance Work Request.
Courtesy of the Paramount Unified School District,
Paramount, California.

school property should be a part of this system. School districts that are not large enough to have qualified experts on their staff should employ them from their own or nearby communities to conduct inspections, preferably at some time immediately prior to the consideration and adoption of the budget for the following fiscal year. The annual inspection should produce recommendations for district-wide maintenance measures to be reflected in budgetary items. Particular attention should be given to the following needs:

1. Roof and chimney repairs.
2. Window and door trim.
3. Guttering and drainage systems.
4. Plumbing and electrical service.
5. Heating systems.
6. Condition of stairways.
7. Condition of flooring.

A school district with more than three or four separate school plants should consider establishing a separate maintenance department, with a crew of trained workers who move from school to school in accordance with a definite schedule. Such a mobile force, under the direction of an expert maintenance crew chief, can follow up regular inspections with a comprehensive program of repairs and replacement that will closely follow the recommendations of the inspector. A maintenance center should be established at one of the centrally located school plants, or at a separate maintenance facility, with the maintenance crew operating out of that headquarters. This center should include office space, storage facilities, and a well-equipped repair shop. Except for unexpected emergencies, maintenance should be scheduled for individual schools approximately one month in advance. Building principals should be informed of impending visits of the maintenance crew and of the areas in which they plan to operate.

Small districts may not be able to afford the luxury of employing their own skilled tradesmen. They may find it more advantageous to contract for specialized services. Larger districts, on the other hand, usually employ their own plumbers, electricians, carpenters, painters, audio-visual repairmen, and other special technicians. Some districts find it more economical to contract for larger services, while allowing their own maintenance staff to perform smaller services.

The principal goal of school maintenance should be the maximum retardation of depreciation. Priority listings should be made to include all areas of school maintenance in the order of their probable deterioration; items of top priority should receive proportionately more frequent attention.

The essential element in all maintenance is speed, both in reporting and identifying deterioration, and in effecting prompt repairs. There is an almost perfect corollary between delay in making repairs in cases of minor damage, and the multiplication of such cases. Effective building administration, then, will establish a routine especially designed to identify, report, and repair promptly all instances of damage or deterioration.

Regular Operation of the School Plant

Plant operation has been defined as "those activities necessary to keep the plant in condition for use, such as cleaning, disinfecting, heating, care of lawns and shrubs and other similar work."[3] It includes the following activities:

1. Regular cleaning of building and grounds.
2. Regulation and operation of heating, lighting, plumbing, and ventilating facilities.
3. Selection, purchase, use, and care of operational equipment.

ORGANIZATION OF CUSTODIAL SERVICES. Perhaps the greatest single factor militating against operational efficiency is the lack of liaison between the custodial staff and the faculty of the school. Because the primary purpose of the former is to facilitate the work of the latter, a breakdown in common understanding must be avoided at all cost. The best way to accomplish this is to establish an operational pattern based on the following principles:

1. Each building principal shall be directly in charge of the duties and scheduling of the custodial staff working in the school building.
2. The district director of operations and maintenance shall serve as expert adviser to the principal on matters of technique and materials, and shall instruct the individual custodians as to the best and most economical ways of performing their duties.
3. During the weeks or months when school is not in session, the building operational personnel shall be under the supervision and control of the director of maintenance and operation, and may be used to augment the maintenance force of the district.

Such an organizational design helps to solve the problem of dual control. The operational services remain subordinate and responsive to

---

[3] Melbo, *Report of the Survey, Laguna Beach*, p. 329.

educational needs; and the temptation of individual custodial workers to "pass the buck" by playing off one "boss" against the other is greatly minimized. The perennial complaint of the custodian, that too many people give the orders, is eliminated; during the school year, only the building principal issues orders, and in the summer, only the director of maintenance and operations.

Evaluation of every operational program should be the function of the building principal, but this duty should be performed in close cooperation with the district director of operations. Regular meetings should be scheduled with the operations personnel by the principal, in the same manner that regular faculty meetings are held and for much the same reason. A job analysis that examines custodial duties and responsibilities should be used as a basis for developing a comprehensive description of each custodian's duties. During the custodian–principal conference, mutually agreed-upon decisions should be made about the custodian's duties and hourly working schedule.

Although building custodians are to have their duties assigned and their time scheduled by the principals, the technical details of their work are to be supervised by the chief maintenance and operations officer of the school district, who will decide on the precise nature of the supplies and equipment that are needed for the rapid and efficient performance of the custodian's duties.

The administrator must solve the difficult problem of keeping the teacher sympathetically aware of the custodian's duties and problems, and vice versa. If this is successfully accomplished, the school plant will operate harmoniously, and by combining utility and aesthetic appeal, will be a public relations asset.

IMPORTANCE OF THE SCHOOL CUSTODIAN. Custodians are important members of a school staff. Too often they are considered second-rate people who are expected to jump at the beck and call of teachers, and this attitude can cause them to neglect their assigned tasks. Building administrators should never permit this situation to happen.

Custodians should be chosen carefully and standards for their selection should be devised and adhered to. Physical examinations may be desirable, because physical ability to do the work is a necessity. Custodians who have the ability and personality to relate to students can gain their cooperation in maintaining and improving the safety and cleanliness of the school plant and grounds.

The custodian has the responsibility for keeping the building, grounds, and equipment clean and sanitary, properly storing materials and supplies, making minor repairs and reporting major ones, following operational schedules, and making reports as required. Women as well as men should be considered for custodial positions. Custodians may be deputized by the civil authorities to enable them to preserve the peace at public functions held on the school grounds.

EQUIPMENT AND SUPPLIES.   Great strides have been made in the field of operational supplies and equipment. Most items today are purchased on the open market from legitimate supply houses and qualify for most standards of efficiency and safety. The director of maintenance and operation should become acquainted with the vendors of operational supplies and equipment in order to keep up with improvements that are being made and to determine the best quality needed in the district. School districts that fail to provide the proper tools and supplies are not receiving their money's worth from their custodial employees.

Custodial Time Schedules

The custodian's work schedule should be supplemented by a daily time schedule, allotting certain duties to each hour of the custodian's work day. This schedule should be adhered to as strictly as possible, barring emergencies. A short example of a custodial schedule combining both work and time factors is shown in Table 12–1.

It is economical to stagger the working time schedule for custodians. Since the custodian's chief task is sweeping and cleaning, it is more efficient for most work to follow the dismissal of pupils.

If there is enough overlapping of duties, all custodians can meet together for a short time to discuss mutual problems. They can also help each other if some major task needs to be done. It is also a good idea to allow time for the head custodian at each facility to supervise or inspect the work of other custodians.

Many districts have had to reduce custodial services due to budgetary problems. Because of this, custodial schedules may be different from day to day. For example, classrooms may be swept only on alternate days. Needless to say, lavatories and drinking fountains should be cleaned every day.

Custodial Workloads

Many formulas have been developed for the measurement of reasonable custodial workloads. The chief ingredients of these formulas are square footage, rooms, students, or teachers. The type of construction, texture of surfaces, adjacency to dust or fumes, building usage, nature of cleaning

TABLE 12–1. Custodial Schedule Combining Both Work and Time Factors.

10:00 AM–6:30 PM (8-hour worker—30 min. for lunch)	
10:00–10:30 AM	Report to office at 10:00 AM. Dust administration unit. Inspect women's and men's toilets for paper, soap, towels, and other supplies.
10:30–11:00 AM	Set up cafetorium for lunch—morning custodian helping.
11:00–11:30 AM	Spot, wash windows, weed flowers, and do any small cleaning jobs needed.
11:30–12:00 AM	Eat lunch.
12:00–1:00 PM	Spot, wash windows, weed flowers, and do any small cleaning jobs needed.
1:00–3:00 PM	Work in cafetorium. This includes teachers' dining room and setting up for any afternoon or evening cafetorium use.
3:00–4:00 PM	Sweep, dust, clean toilets, clean drinking fountains, empty wastebaskets in rooms 21 and 22. Sweeping takes 20 to 30 minutes per room, depending upon the primary furniture in the rooms and including cleaning toilets and drinking fountains.
4:00–6:00 PM	Sweep, dust, clean toilets, clean drinking fountains, empty wastebaskets in rooms 1, 2, 3, 4, and 5.
6:00–6:30 PM	Clean administration unit.

equipment, and other factors must be considered as a supplement to any formula that is adopted. Local conditions cause many variables.

Whatever method of assigning custodial work loads is decided upon, it should be economical, impartial, and fair so that custodians maintain a high level of morale.

Summary

Maximum utilization of the school plant is the goal; it may be approached by circular use of the buildings and use for noncurricular purposes. In order to achieve this goal, proper care of the buildings is necessary, requiring the cooperation of all school personnel. A trained director of maintenance and operation can do much in this connection, but in the absence of such a person, the superintendent should establish a system which provides both for individual building maintenance and district-wide maintenance.

Regular operation of the school plant should combine efficiency and economy. Custodial services should be under the direction of the building principal, with the director of operation and maintenance serving as expert adviser to the principal except during the summer, when the director should assume control.

Operational charts and custodial checklists occupy much of this chapter, which is intended to be a very practical guide to school plant operation.

Administrative Problems   In Basket

Problem 1

As principal of an elementary school, you have instructed your teachers to have their pupils put away books, clear their desks, pick up papers, crayons, and pencils from the floor, and leave the room neat at the end of the school day. Windows are to be closed and latched and doors locked. The purpose is to make it easier for the custodian to clean and dust each room in the allotted time.

Mr. Perkins, a new fifth grade teacher, has paid little attention to your instructions and usually leaves the classroom in a mess. You have talked to him several times about this problem; after each conference, the room is left in better condition for several days but gradually returns to its former slovenliness.

Mr. Jones, the custodian, has complained to you numerous times about the difficulty of cleaning Mr. Perkins' room. This afternoon, he storms into your office and states that he is refusing to clean the room whenever he finds it too messy.

What will you tell Mr. Jones?
What action will you take with Mr. Perkins?

Problem 2

The Toyon Junior High School of which you are principal has many civic center activities scheduled. Cub Scout Pack 83 uses the multi-purpose room the third Wednesday of each month for its Pack meeting. Refreshments are served at the end of each meeting—coffee for adults and punch and cookies for the boys. Adults are permitted to smoke and ash trays are furnished. After each meeting, however, punch is left spilled on the floor, crumbs are everywhere, and cigarette stubs have been ground into the floor.

How should the principal handle this situation?

Problem 3

At a recent district administrative council meeting, several principals complained about their maintenance service. A summary of their complaints showed:

1. Two custodians are sometimes sent to do a one-person job.
2. Maintenance workers spend too much time drinking coffee and chatting with the school custodian.
3. Requests for repairs are not taken care of promptly, and unsafe conditions exist for days.
4. Repairs are often slipshod.
5. Phone calls to the maintenance and operations manager have resulted in promises to remedy the problems; but the problems remain, according to the principals.

The superintendent asks the business manager to investigate the complaints and to try to remedy the situation.

How should the business manager proceed?

Selected References

BARON, GEORGE, and D. A. HOWELL. *The Government and Management of Schools.* Atlantic Highlands, N.J.: Humanities Press, Inc., 1974.

FELDMAN, EDWIN B. *Housekeeping Handbook for Institution , Business & Industry.* New York: Frederick Fell, 1969.

GEORGE, N. L. *Effective School Maintenance.* West Nyack, N.Y.: Parker Publishing Co., 1969.

HILL, FREDERICH W., and JAMES W. COLMEY. *School Custodial Services.* Minneapolis, Minn.: T. S. Denison & Co., 1968.

KNEZEVICH, STEPHEN J. *Administration of Public Education.* Scranton, Pa.: Harper and Row Publishers, Inc., 1975.

KOCH, HARRY W. *Janitorial and Maintenance Examinations.* San Francisco Ken-Books, 1975.

LEGGETT, S. "Research on School Building Problems." *American School and University* 51 (October 1978):45–50.

LEVIN, D. "Asbestos in Schools: Walls and Halls of Trouble." *American School Board Journal* 165 (November 1978):29–33.

MELBO, IRVING R., et al. *Report of the Survey, Laguna Beach Unified School District.* Los Angeles, Ca.: University of Southern California, 1961.

OREGON STATE DEPARTMENT OF EDUCATION. *Oregon Custodial Training Program.* Salem, Ore.: State Department of Education, 1978.

ROBBIN, JERRY H., and STIRLING B. WILLIAMS, JR. *School Custodian's Handbook.* Danville, Ill.: Interstate, 1970.

RUDMAN, JACK. *District Supervision of School Custodians.* Syosset, N.Y.: Learning Corporation, 1979.

SACK, THOMAS F. *A Complete Guide to Building and Plant Maintenance.* 2nd ed. Englewood Cliffs, N.J.: Prentice-Hall, 1971.

SEXTON, J. J., and K. D. D. SWITZER, "Time Management Ladder." *Educational Digest* 44 (November 1978):34–35.

WATERS, JAMES E., and EMERY STOOPS. *Administration of Maintenance and Operations in California School Districts: A Handbook for Administrators and Governing Boards.* Sacramento: California State Department of Education, 1969.

WILSON, ROBERT E. *Educational Administration.* Columbus, Ohio: Charles E. Merrill Publishing Co., 1966.

PART FIVE

Administration of Special Services

CHAPTER THIRTEEN

Transportation Services

Transportation services have greatly expanded over the years. Today transportation is costly and creates financial problems for many districts, forcing some of them to eliminate or curtail their bus services. Rigid controls are necessary, requiring rules and regulations for the safety of the students and for the maintenance and efficient operation of the equipment. Because of their great responsibility, bus drivers should be selected carefully and trained to maintain the district's standards. Field trips by school bus are an important supplement to the educational program.

Growth of Pupil Transportation

The earliest record of transporting students to school was in 1840 at private expense. In 1869, schoolchildren in Massachusetts were brought to school in horsedrawn carts and carriages paid for by school funds. This represented the first form of subsidized pupil transportation, but such subsidies did not become either popular or prevalent until about 1920. The first motorized bus, called a "school truck," came on the scene in Pennsylvania in 1909. Laws were enacted in 1925 to regulate the speed at twenty-five miles per hour and to establish the rights of students on the highway. Today, millions of school pupils are driven to and from school each day at a cost of millions of dollars, and the cost is increasing because of busing for integration. Another factor in the growth of pupil transportation services has been the unification or consolidation of school districts.

Purposes of School Transportation

The major purposes of transportation services are to transport children to and from school; to provide the means for educational field trips; to transport students for co-curricular activities such as athletics, music, and dramatics; to bus for the purpose of integration; to transport the physically handicapped or mentally retarded students; and to bus for vocational work experience.

Each time students ride a school bus they have an opportunity to add to their social and educational growth, provided time and effort are used to promote these values. The teaching of safety and courtesy has direct application to bus riders.

Busing for Racial Balance

The concept of the neighborhood school has created problems in many parts of the country. American neighborhoods and communities are composed of black, Mexican-American, white, and Oriental children who may never have the opportunity to go to school with someone of a different ethnic background and culture. Many schools in lower economic areas, usually attended by minority children, are not as well built, maintained, equipped, or supplied as other more fortunate schools; and teachers are often not as well prepared or qualified. The opposite should be the case. Minority children need the best-trained teachers and the most up-to-date equipment and supplies.

One of the proposed methods for solving the problem of racial balance is to transport students from a minority area to a school in a predominately white community. In turn, white students would be transported to a minority neighborhood school.

The American Association of School Administrators and the National Education Association have resolved to support busing of students to implement desegregation plans. In 1973, a federal district court ordered the Department of Health, Education, and Welfare to enforce desegregation in seventeen states and directed the department to cut off federal funds to districts that failed to comply. The department is expected to appeal the decision. In 1973, the Massachusetts Supreme Court ruled that a state law that would have prohibited busing students without their parents' written permission was unconstitutional.

Numerous school districts have appealed to the courts about busing to achieve racial balance. State court rulings have differed, others are pending, and still others are on appeal to higher courts.

There are pros and cons regarding compulsory versus voluntary busing to achieve integration. A survey made in 1977 by the National Opinion Research Center showed that 85.3 percent of whites and 50.3 percent of blacks opposed the busing of black and white students from one school district to another to achieve integration. However, 84.8 percent of whites and 91.4 percent of blacks thought that black and white students should go to the same schools.[1] The implication is clear that most people favor the racial balance of schools but oppose busing to achieve this goal.

Forced busing to any extent and the legal situation have been confused and undecided. Also, there is no assurance that students will learn as much or more if they are forced to be transported to another school. In general, students accept busing with a better attitude than their parents.

Administrators must develop realistic guidelines and policies so that integration pressures can be met on a practical, moral, fair, and educationally sound basis. The cost to a school district for adding this type of busing can be enormous, whether it is compulsory or voluntary. It may mean the purchase of more buses, the hiring of more drivers, and the extension of bus routes. Budget considerations become important. Whether or not busing for racial balance is a solution has not yet been determined. What has been determined is that forced busing adds enormously to the problems inherent in administering a school district.

School principals have problems when busing for integration is effected. Schedules have to be changed, classes uprooted, teachers reassigned, school records rearranged, and extra personnel assigned to supervise loading and unloading the buses. Secondary schools have the problem of integrating students into the athletic teams and co-curricular activities, often causing extra bus runs.

BUSING FOR DIFFERENT TYPES OF PROGRAMS.   In addition to busing for racial integration, additional busing may be required for special types of schools. The alternative school, with an open, free type of curriculum and attended on a voluntary basis, may exist within a school system, requiring an interchange of students between it and other schools. A continuation high school for students who cannot adjust to the regular curriculum for various reasons may require extra busing. Special classes for atypical children in selected schools may also require extra busing.

PL 94–142 states explicitly that federal policy is that the states should assure access to free, appropriate, public education for all handicapped children in the least restrictive environment consistent with their needs and abilities. Under this law, the handicapped are to attend regular classes in the public schools. This means that transportation must be provided for these students, whether by bus or taxi.

Under the Vocational Education Act of 1963 as amended, Part B, federal grants are made to the states to assist them in maintaining, extending, and improving existing vocational–technical high school programs. The objective is to help prepare students for immediate employment upon graduation. This program includes part-time work in the community. To

---

[1] National Opinion Research Center, *General Social Survey*, 1977.

carry out this objective, the students need transportation to and from their working schedule.

District Policies for Pupil Transportation

In order to provide the best transportation service for pupils and to keep the service fair and impartial for all patrons, the governing board of the school district should set forth policies in writing.

Many problems will arise regarding the bus services, and parental and community pressures may become exasperating. Decisions should be made only according to established policies. School boards or administrators who make decisions without regard to policy expose themselves to increasing demands from others, and they cannot justify their actions. Transportation policies should be developed by the cooperative action of administrators, parents, teachers, bus drivers, and students. They should be made available, not only to school personnel, but also to the citizens of the community. School policies can be developed from the checklist shown in Table 13–1.

Administration of Transportation Services

The administration of school district transportation must be in conformity with "Highway Safety Program Standard No. 17," issued by the National Highway Traffic Safety Administration in 1972.[2] It says, "Each state, in cooperation with its school districts and its political subdivisions, shall have a comprehensive pupil transportation safety program to assure that school vehicles are operated and maintained so as to achieve the highest possible level of safety." The standard "established minimum requirements for a state highway safety program for pupil transportation safety, including the identification, operation, and maintenance of school buses; training of personnel; and administration." The standard's purpose "is to reduce, to the greatest extent possible, the danger of death or injury to school children while they are being transported to and from school." There will be a number of references to Standard No. 17 in the remainder of this chapter.

In larger school districts, transportation services are usually handled by a transportation manager working under the direct supervision of the administrator in charge of business services. In small school districts, the

---

[2] "Highway Safety Program Standard No. 17" was issued on May 2, 1972 by Douglas W. Toms, Administrator, U.S. Department of Transportation, National Highway Traffic Safety Administration. Published in the *Federal Register* 37, No. 89, May 6, 1972, it became effective thirty days after the publishing date.

TABLE 13–1. Checklist for the Evaluation of Transportation Services.[a]

ITEM	SUPERIOR	AVERAGE	POOR
1. The district should operate its own transportation system rather than contract for major services.			
2. The transportation program should be directed by an employee who has the ability, and who is allowed sufficient time to supervise adequately all operations.			
3. Only modern equipment in excellent mechanical condition should be used.			
4. Inspections by the State Highway Patrol should be welcomed and all recommendations should be followed.			
5. Under no conditions should anyone other than a properly licensed bus driver operate the vehicle while transporting children.			
6. Classified employees rather than teachers should be used as bus drivers.			
7. Classified employees not regularly used as bus drivers should be licensed as substitutes when necessary.			
8. A utility bus or buses should be available for use in case of emergency and for special field trips.			
9. An adequate plan for doing the repair work and servicing the buses should be followed.			
10. The district should try to standardize its transportation equipment. This simplifies repair work and other procedures. It is then possible to carry a minimum stock of needed parts.			
11. The district should provide safe and adequate storage facilities for gasoline and oil, and should purchase these items according to specifications on open bid.			
12. Adequate insurance protection should be carried.			
13. Controls regarding the dispensing of gasoline should be exercised the same as if cash were involved.			
14. Adequate cost records should be maintained.			
15. Definite regulations regarding pupil transportation should be adopted by the board and			

TABLE 13–1.   *(Continued)*

ITEM	SUPERIOR	AVERAGE	POOR

made available in writing to certificated and classified employees.

16.   Bus drivers should wear uniforms. The district should provide caps equipped with bus drivers' badges. The use of uniforms increases the dignity and authority of the bus driver in dealing with pupils as well as with the general public.

17.   No person other than public school pupils or adults assigned for supervision, should be permitted to ride on school buses.

18.   The bus capacity should never be exceeded by even one pupil.

19.   Loading of buses at school should be done at established safety zones under proper supervision.

20.   Buses should not be backed up on school grounds.

21.   Cost of transportation should compare favorably with transportation costs in other similar districts.

22.   All state regulations and all laws enacted by the state legislature should be adhered to rigidly.

23.   All bus routes should be approved by board action.

24.   Constant study should be given to bus routes to make sure that changes are made as needed, and routes laid out in the most efficient manner possible.

25.   Each bus driver should make daily written reports and weekly or monthly reports showing the condition of his bus and recommending any necessary repairs.

26.   Each bus driver should possess a valid first aid certificate issued by the American Red Cross or United States Bureau of Mines.

27.   No bus driver should require any pupil to leave the bus before the pupil has reached his destination as a disciplinary measure.

28.   No person should be permitted to serve as a bus driver for more than ten hours in any twenty-four hour period. Neither should bus

TABLE 13–1. (Continued)

ITEM	SUPERIOR	AVERAGE	POOR
drivers be permitted to do more than fifteen total hours of work in a twenty-four hour period when driving a bus with children is included.			
29. Each school bus should be kept clean at all times and should be thoroughly cleaned after each day's use.			
30. No smoking in a school bus should be permitted when pupils are aboard.			
31. No animals should be transported in a school bus.			
32. The bus driver should escort school pupils across the street or highway at any dangerous point.			
33. No school bus stop along the highway should be approved unless a clear view, when the bus is stopped, is available from a distance of 400 feet in each direction.			
34. The driver should bring the bus to a full stop at all railway crossings not closer than 10 feet and not more than 40 feet from the nearest rail. He should not proceed until he has opened and closed the entrance door of the bus and has, by hearing and by sight, ascertained that the tracks are clear in both directions.			
35. No bus stop should be approved that is closer than 200 feet from the nearest railroad grade crossing except at regular railroad stations or on highways which parallel the railroad.			
36. In general, large and heavy transportation equipment should be used rather than small, light equipment. This is recommended in the interest of efficiency and economy.			
37. Unless unusual traffic hazards exist, school districts should transport only those pupils for whom state-aid reimbursements will be received. On the other hand, all pupils who qualify for state-aid reimbursement should be transported.			
Total overall rating			

ᵃ Source: Irving R. Melbo, et al., *Report of the Survey, Taft City School District* (Los Angeles, Ca.: University of Southern California, 1960), pp. 270–72.

principal mày manage these services. The principal, regardless of district size, should have administrative and supervisory responsibility for bus service at the school level.

Featherston and Culp describe three criteria that should be applied in evaluating transportation services:[3] (1) Safety. This involves an understanding of the number of accidents and injuries; bus miles per accident; responsibility; safety training for drivers and students; and the maintenance of buses. (2) Economy. This pertains to the cost per pupil per bus mile; cost comparison with other districts and state averages; informing drivers and maintenance personnel of costs; the selection and purchase of equipment; a survey of instances where savings can be made; and the adjustment of schedules to eliminate unnecessary driving. (3) Adequacy. This relates to the written transportation policies; the difference between state and district regulations regarding eligibility to ride and walking distances; load limits that are prescribed; service to isolated areas; and the provision for sufficient seating.

The principal of each school and district administration has the immediate administrative responsibility for determining:

1. The number of children who need to be transported.
2. Where children live in relation to bus routes.
3. The location of the bus stops or stations for pickup and delivery.
4. The method of loading and unloading the bus at school or at the bus stations.
5. Transportation safety.
6. The control of discipline.
7. The extent of supervision on the part of teachers.
8. The compiling of records and reports that are required by law and by school district policy.

EVALUATION OF TRANSPORTATION SERVICES. Melbo has developed a checklist for the evaluation of school transportation services (see Table 13–1). It can be used to help in the development of transportation policies and in the administration of the services. Standard No. 17 requires each state to evaluate the pupil transportation program at least annually and to report to the National Highway Traffic Safety Administration.

Cooperative Determination of Bus Routes

Administrators, drivers, and business office representatives should meet early in the summer to map out the bus routes for the coming school year. Normally, the first step in this process is to list all eligible pupils by place

---

[3] E. Glenn Featherston and D. P. Culp, *Pupil Transportation: State and Local Programs*, pp. 139–41.

of residence. In most states, eligibility for free transportation to and from school is determined by law. Distance from school is usually the governing factor; students living less than one to two miles from school are expected to walk in most cases. Despite statutory provisions, most states allow wide latitude to the local districts in determining bus runs and stops. Hazardous traffic conditions, especially in large cities, may require the transportation of students over much shorter distances than would be the case in smaller communities or rural areas. Standard No. 17 requires states to minimize highway hazards by an annual review of routes for safety hazards.

MAPPING THE ROUTES. Any shift in pupil population or minor adjustment of school boundary lines may make a vast difference in a given bus route. Alterations may become necessary during a school year, and should be considered annually, preferably before the start of school in the fall. The best single tool for planning is a transportation map of the district, prepared and kept up to date by the school administration; the map will be based upon the data on eligible students. The data should include the name, age, grade, and house number of each student living within the area to be served, and should be collected for preschool children as well as for those already enrolled in school, so that plans may be made several years in advance.

Colored tacks can be placed on the map to show where students who are to be transported live. As an alternative, the number of students to be transported can be written on the map where their homes are indicated. If erasable colors are used, the numbers can be identified easily and changed as conditions change.

A string-and-colored-tack route map can be used in conjunction with or superimposed on the pupil residence map. An overlay route-and-stop designation map drawn on clear plastic may also be used, superimposing it on the school attendance area map. It should show the route covered and the direction traveled by each bus.

Once the map has been developed, the principal, the district transportation department, and the bus drivers should develop a time schedule for pickup and delivery of the pupils. Parents, too, may be invited to offer their suggestions since they are personally interested in the transportation of their children.

Schools having access to computers can use them to design school bus routes. The following variables must be considered when preparing the input data for the computer:

Adequacy.	Bus time.
Backtracking.	Economy.
Boarding location.	Efficiency.
Bus miles.	Grade level of students.

Location of driver's residence.	Safety.
Location of garage.	School starting time.
Railroad crossings.	Size of buses.
Road conditions.	Student miles.
Road gradient.	Student time.
Salary of driver.	Turnarounds.

Using this data, the school system is partitioned into individual bus routes. The computer then generates all feasible routes for each partition. The computer printout gives information on the best route for each bus. A breakdown on cost analysis can also be determined by using the computer.[4]

Pupils should never be picked up earlier than one hour before the opening of school; no student should ride longer than one hour at a time. The scheduling of more buses or larger buses will eliminate the necessity of pupils riding too long. However, in rural areas where students live far from school or are widely scattered, scheduling can create a problem.

TYPES OF ROUTES.   The use of one bus to travel more than one route is called "multiple routing" and is cheaper than a "single" one, because it enables one bus to perform the functions of several. In practice, the multiple route is much less desirable than the single one. For example, groups of students arrive at the school several minutes in advance of others. In addition, dismissal times have to be staggered, or supervision provided during lengthy intervals of waiting for pickups. Both daily programs and pupil discipline tend to break down under such conditions. Wherever the financial condition of the district will permit, the use of one bus per route is always to be preferred. Where the need for financial economy is too great to permit the single route policy, it is sometimes possible, where two schools are located relatively close to one another, to arrange opening and closing hours in such a way as to permit the same buses to serve both schools without the disadvantages mentioned here.

SCHEDULING BUS STOPS.   Buses at each school should be loaded at an established safe-loading zone, off main highways; this is required by Standard No. 17. The neighborhood loading zones should be located away from hazards and busy corners; children should not cross a busy street or highway, and no child should have to walk too far. The bus should not make so many stops that it delays covering the route within a reasonable time. Students should not have to wait so long at their loading zone that they cause discipline problems.

Parents should be instructed to have their children at the bus stop from five to ten minutes ahead of time. They should also be told that

---

[4] R. A. Boyer, *The Use of a Computer to Design School Bus Routes*, pp. 8–10.

sometimes the return to the stop may be delayed, since weather and traffic conditions, as well as the number of students who may be absent and not riding, may speed up or delay the time listed in the printed schedule. If parents understand this, they are less likely to worry or to call the school to find out where their children are.

DISTRIBUTION OF SCHEDULES. When the bus schedule has been developed, it should be duplicated and distributed to the teachers, the homes where students are to be transported, and the local newspapers. The printed schedule should include:

1. The location of the bus stops.
2. The bus number.
3. The name of the driver.
4. The time the bus will pick up the students at each stop.
5. The time at which students will arrive back at the stop after school is dismissed.

State Financing and Regulation of Pupil Transportation

There is no sphere of school financing in which the state has taken a more active interest than in pupil transportation. More than three-fourths of the states now provide some form of aid, and all states authorize the expenditure of local funds by the districts for this purpose. Many states that do not provide specific aid for transportation nevertheless include transportation costs in the formulas for basic and equalization aid to local districts. Transportation cost in 1973–74, according to the U.S. Bureau of the Census, was nearly two million dollars. The average cost per pupil was $87.04 and varied from a high of $210.05 in Alaska to a low of $43.47 in South Carolina.[5] No doubt, costs have gone up radically since the latest figures available.

TRANSPORTATION COST ACCOUNTING. The main purpose of cost accounting is usually the establishment of standard unit cost. In administering pupil transportation, accurate information on both total and unit costs is needed. Although innumerable studies of pupil transportation cost have been made, unit costs have proved impossible to determine because of the large number of variable factors involved. The following cost units are usually used: (1) cost per pupil, (2) cost per mile, and (3) cost per bus.

---

[5] U. S. Bureau of the Census, *Statistical Abstract of the United States*, 98th ed. (Washington, D.C.: U.S. Government Printing Office, 1977), p. 150.

Cost estimates are usually made shortly before the beginning of each fiscal year, and are designed to assist in making out the transportation budget. They are based upon the following factors:

1. Number of passengers involved.
2. Aggregate home–school distances.
3. Number of buses.
4. Length of routes.
5. Road conditions.
6. Price of bus supplies.
7. Wages of drivers.
8. Costs of maintenance and repairs.

Except when a new district transportation program is inaugurated, cost estimates are arrived at on the basis of previous experience. Where a new program is involved, it is advisable to secure comparable data from the state office or from nearby school districts that have been operating buses for some time and that have accumulated sufficient cost data to be of help. Cost accounting should compare the figures for five previous years to predict the trend for the following items:

1. Miles traveled.
2. Students carried.
3. Bus days.
4. Average miles per bus day.
5. Average students per bus day.
6. Average cost per bus mile.
7. Average cost per bus trip.
8. Average cost per bus day.

BUS DRIVER'S MONTHLY REPORT. In any state that gives financial aid to transportation on any direct basis, the bus driver's monthly report is of paramount importance. It is customarily kept up to date every day, or at least every week, and is turned into the business office once a month. From it are derived all data on costs, as well as data required by the state as a basis for financial reimbursement. It must be signed by the driver, and should be as complete as possible. Table 13–2 shows a sample Daily Bus Report form from which weekly and monthly reports can be compiled.

VARIABLE FACTORS IN TRANSPORTATION COSTS. The most important factors in determining transportation costs are density of population, number of stops, and condition of roads. Other factors combine to produce marked variability in transportation costs from state to state, and even from district to district: legal speed limits, traffic conditions, capacity

TABLE 13–2.   Daily Bus Report.

| Bus No. | Signature of Driver |
| Report No. | Date |

| | COMPLY WITH SAFETY STANDARDS | | |
EQUIPMENT	YES	NO	REMARKS
Steps			
Entrance and Exit Doors			
Speedometer			
Capacity Card			
Driver's View: Front, Side, and Rear			
Windshield			
Windshield Wipers			
Steering Device			
Driver's Seat			
Rear Vision Mirrors			
Signal Systems			
Horn			
Brakes			
Flares			
First Aid Kit			
Fire Extinguisher			
Heating System			
Defroster			
Lights			
Interior Lighting			
Fog Lamps			
Reflectors			
Windows, Glass			
Ventilation System			
Skid Chains			
Gasoline Gauge			
Tires			
Engine: Mechanical			

Costs	*Dollars*	*Cents*
Gasoline		
Oil		
Repairs (itemize)		
Servicing and Cleaning		
Other Costs		
Totals		

of buses, and weather. Topography can be very important in determining bus expenses. In comparing district costs to state averages, allowances must be made for varying local conditions.

Selection and Training of Bus Drivers

In one essential respect, the bus driver is the most important employee of the school district. Drivers must be skilled in safety and public relations; possess an understanding of students and be able to discipline them; and be skilled in mechanical ability.[6] Previous experience and training should be considered when drivers are employed. The ability to drive an automobile does not mean necessarily that a man or a woman can drive a school bus. To ensure the competency of school bus drivers, Standard No. 17 requires each state to "develop a plan for selecting, training, and supervising persons whose primary duties involve transporting school pupils, in order to assure that such persons will attain a high degree of competence in, and knowledge of, their duties."

CRITERIA FOR SELECTION.   All bus drivers must be certified by the state and of legal age, preferably twenty-one. A doctor's examination should be required, certifying physical fitness. Bus drivers should have a knowledge of state and local laws and regulations pertaining to school bus transportation; this should be determined by written and oral tests and an actual driving test. In addition to driving skills, bus drivers should be emotionally stable and have the ability to control students so that they can ride safely.

Drivers should refrain from the use of alcohol or narcotics before or while driving. They must possess a valid state driver's license to operate a school bus, a good safety record, and no prior convictions for a felony. The certificate or license should be valid for one year only, renewable on the basis of an annual physical examination and recommendation by the employing district.

METHODS OF SELECTION.   The business administrator or the director of the transportation services (assuming the school district employs such an officer) should recommend candidates for bus driver positions through the superintendent's office to the board of education for final appointment. Candidates should make out application forms, submit personal histories and qualifications, supply references and recommendations, and in general undergo the same rigid screening as an applicant for a teaching, secretarial, or administrative position. Sex should not be a factor since women as well

---

[6] Lester C. Winder, "Qualifications for Pupil Transportation Personnel," *47th Annual Volume of Proceedings*, 1961, pp. 191–93.

as men make good drivers and the law does not permit discrimination on the basis of sex.

DUTIES AND RESPONSIBILITIES OF BUS DRIVERS. The chief duties of bus drivers are to transport students safely and efficiently, to keep their buses clean and in good running condition, and to make minor bus repairs according to district policy. They should also maintain respect and order on the bus, assign seats to pupils, and escort pupils across the street where dangerous situations exist. Behavior that is out of the ordinary should be reported to the principal. After receiving the approval of the principal, the driver may refuse transportation to pupils when their conduct is detrimental to other passengers. Students should never be put off the bus for disciplinary reasons except at their own bus stop. Drivers who pass the school bus when red lights are blinking should be cited by the bus driver.

In addition to driving the bus, which usually takes only three or four hours a day, full-time drivers may be assigned to other duties such as bus maintenance, transportation of supplies, custodial or gardening work, or school-yard and cafeteria supervision. In no case should such activities interfere with scheduled driving duties; promptness in picking up and delivering students at the scheduled time is extremely important.

INSERVICE TRAINING. Upon employment, drivers should be properly inducted and oriented to their jobs. They should be given a copy of district policies pertaining to the transportation services, and the district "transportation manual." Uniforms, if required, should be purchased before actually commencing regular driving. It is good policy to have the new driver accompany a regular bus driver on a route to become familiar with district bus procedures.

With increasing traffic problems, mounting horsepower, and multiplying statutes and traffic laws, the need for comphehensive inservice training for bus personnel should be obvious. Students pose more disciplinary problems than in the past, and special understanding of how to cope with them is necessary. Drivers need instruction in how to recognize students who may be under the influence of drugs when they board the bus and what to do if such is the case.

Preservice and inservice training programs and workshops should be established. Standard No. 17 requires each state to develop a training program for school bus drivers. The goal of the training program is to promote safety, economy, and efficiency in the total transportation effort. The following list illustrates topics for discussion in a school bus driver workshop:[7]

---

[7] Furnished through the courtesy of Independent School District No. 624, White Bear Lake, Minnesota.

1. Driving Skills.
2. Human Relations.
3. Accident and Emergency Preparedness.
4. Vehicle Maintenance.
5. Laws and Regulations.

Bus Identification and Equipment

As a result of the requirements of Standard No. 17, states have adopted standardized regulations for bus identification and equipment. The main purpose of standardization is to provide safe equipment that is easily identifiable. Clear identification of school buses provides a safety alert for other drivers.

There are two classes of school vehicles: Type I refers to any motor vehicle used to carry more than sixteen pupils to and from school exclusively. Type II refers to any motor vehicle used to carry sixteen or fewer pupils to or from school; it does not include private motor vehicles. Type II vehicles must either comply with *all* of the requirements for Type I vehicles or be of a different color and have *none* of the identification or equipment required for Type I vehicles. States shall determine which of the specifications apply to Type II vehicles.

The following identification requirements and equipment are specified in Standard No. 17 for Type I school vehicles:

1. Identification lettering.
2. Color: national school bus glossy yellow.
3. Bumper color: glossy black.
4. Signal lamps.
5. Mirrors.
6. Stop arms: according to state option.
7. Seating: no auxiliary seating is to be used.
8. Lap belts—required to be worn if so equipped.

Individual states may also prescribe equipment regulations regarding the type of body, width of aisle, window guards, heaters, fire extinguishers, and other special equipment.

District Transportation Director

Whenever possible, a school district should employ a full-time transportation director or supervisor whose major duties should be supervisory and administrative. If the district is small, the director may also serve as a mechanic or part-time driver. The director should be the key person in selecting bus drivers and training them. Other responsibilities include: scheduling of buses, inservice training, recordkeeping, making reports, bus maintenance, and ordering supplies and equipment. A close working relationship must be maintained with the business office, since purchases and reports must be made through that office.

Large districts employ a dispatcher whose responsibilities are:

1. To see that the required number of buses is serviced and ready to roll each day.
2. To have stand-by buses available.
3. To call substitutes as needed.
4. To see that buses leave on time and follow their prescribed schedules.
5. To handle problems and complaints.

School districts will find it advantageous to install two-way radios in all school buses. They allow for more efficient scheduling and reduction of route mileage, and can advise of delays, problems, and road conditions. Two-way radios permit the driver to keep in constant communication with the dispatcher. Radios also permit drivers to talk to each other about road conditions and blockages, lights that are not working, or problems where a nearby driver can assist.

Care and Maintenance of Transportation Equipment

Each state should set up specific standards of bus construction based upon the following general standards in conformity with Standard No. 17: safety, comfort, economy, durability, and possibility of repair. Good quality lessens the need for constant repairs. Some school districts maintain their own repair shops while others contract out this work. When the district does its own work, major repairs are usually made at the transportation shops. Minor repairs may be made by the driver who should have some skill as a mechanic.

The bus maintenance facility should be large enough to house a bus being repaired and to provide enough working space for the mechanic. There should be equipment on hand to make any needed repairs. A well-supplied stockroom should be readily accessible and a checkout system set up to keep track of the items used. An office should be provided for the transportation supervisor.

Standard No. 17 requires that school vehicles "shall be maintained in safe operating condition through a systematic preventive maintenance program." Each bus should be thoroughly checked, greased, and oiled at monthly intervals or more often if trouble is suspected. Buses, according to the standard, must be inspected at least semiannually. If properly serviced and maintained, they should last at least ten years and costly repairs should be minimized.

Each driver should see that the bus is swept, washed, and kept clean. Students deserve to ride on clean buses, especially since cleanliness is one of the habits taught at school and at home.

Bus Behavior

Discipline is often a serious problem on the school bus. Students sometimes seem to feel that they can do as they please as soon as they leave home or school; it may tax the ingenuity of the driver to handle the situation. Problems should be reported to the principal. The driver may give a student a citation and a copy to the principal if the problem is a serious one. Pupils should be impressed with the fact that they are in school while they are on the bus or at the bus stop. Bus problems are actually school problems and must be dealt with as such.

TYPICAL BUS RULES.   Typical bus rules are:

1.   All students must obey the driver.
2.   There should be no loud talking.
3.   Students must stay seated at all times when the bus is moving.
4.   There must be no talking to the driver while the bus is in motion.
5.   Students are not to eat on the bus.
6.   All parts of the body must be kept inside the bus.
7.   Pets and animals are not to be transported on the school bus.
8.   There is to be no playing, pushing, poking, or doing other things that bother others or the driver.
9.   Students are not to scratch, write on, or mar the seats of the paint.

Although some of these rules may appear self-evident, children need many reminders about good conduct and safety. Standard No. 17 requires that "twice during each school year, each pupil who is transported in a school vehicle shall be instructed in safe riding practices, and participate in emergency evacuation drills."

Bus Safety

The transporting of up to seventy-five or more children on a bus is a tremendous responsibility; the bus driver must do everything in his power to provide for their safety. One of the driver's most important concerns is to keep the bus in perfect operating condition, particularly the brakes, lights, door mechanism, and tires. Standard No. 17 requires bus drivers to make daily pretrip inspections of the vital functions of the school bus and to make a prompt, written report regarding any defect, which should be repaired immediately. Each bus should carry a fresh and well-supplied first aid kit and the driver must know how to administer first aid.

MAXIMUM LOAD. All school buses are built for maximum loads; the maximum number of students permitted to be carried is listed inside the bus. At no time should a driver exceed the maximum number of passengers by even one child.

TRAFFIC PRECAUTIONS. Traffic laws, and particularly those that apply to school buses, should be obeyed at all times. Students should always be let out on the curb side of the bus, never on the traffic side. Route stops should be established so that few students need to cross a street; careful scheduling may eliminate all such crossings. At no time should a bus be backed up on the school grounds because of the danger of running over someone. Doors should never be left open, even in hot weather.

A SCHOOL PRINCIPAL'S RESPONSIBILITY. Principals have the overall responsibility for the bus service at their schools, particularly seeing that students meet the bus schedule on time, and behave in an orderly manner while riding. A bus safety program should be a regular part of classroom instruction. Occasional bulletins from the principal will help to call continuing attention to bus safety.

MOTORISTS. One hazard to bus transportation is the public motorist. Too many do not follow safety rules or obey traffic laws. Many do not know the rules for passing buses that are loading or unloading students and do not realize what the blinking red lights mean. Although the school can do little about this, school administrators and the PTA may have some influence on the driving habits of the school community by holding public meetings and securing newspaper publicity on the responsibility of motorists for the safety of schoolchildren.

CONSISTENT RIDING. Students who ride the bus should do so every time. If they ride part of the time and walk part of the time, drivers will never know whether or not a pupil has been left. Each student should get on and off at the regular bus stop, unless the parent has signed a note requesting otherwise. Some school districts require student riders to carry a bus pass, issued by the principal and shown to the driver when boarding the bus.

Field Trips

School districts have a rare opportunity to supplement the classroom educational program without too much added cost by utilizing their own buses and drivers for field trips. With careful planning, most field trips can be scheduled between the regular bus runs.

EDUCATIONAL VALUES OF FIELD TRIPS.   Field trips for instruction should be carefully planned, fit logically into the instructional program, and grow out of a need to supplement available textbooks. Firsthand information always leaves a more indelible impression than secondary sources. Follow-up activities enhance the value of a field trip.

SCHEDULING FIELD TRIPS.   Arrangements for field trips should be made at least one week in advance of the desired date. Parents should be informed and supply a signed permission slip indicating that their child has approval to take the trip. Requests for field trips, whether for educational or co-curricular purposes, should be forwarded by the principal to the transportation department through the district business office.

Accidents

If accidents do occur, the bus driver must make out an accident report giving the date, the name of the injured persons, the cause of the accident, the names of at least two witnesses, the first aid rendered, and the disposition of the case. This form should be forwarded to the central business office within twenty-four hours. If a child is involved, the principal, who may wish to make a personal contact with the parents, should also be informed. See Figure 13–1 for an example of a school bus accident report form.

Summary

Several different types of pupil transportation exist, among them school ownership and operation, private ownership with school operation, and school ownership with private operation.

The public generally opposes forced busing to achieve ethnic balance, although a few systems have bused voluntarily. In either case, busing to achieve integration has budget implications, as the cost can be enormous.

District busing policies should be established by cooperative action on the part of administrators, parents, teachers, bus drivers, and pupils. Busing should be administered whenever possible by a trained transportation

SCHOOL BUS ACCIDENT REPORT

INSTRUCTIONS: *File one copy with local Board of Education and one with the Department of Elementary and Secondary Education at the above address immediately following an accident. A school bus accident may occur on or off a school bus.*

I. GENERAL INFORMATION

Name of School District

County

Owner of Bus: *(check one)*

☐ District-owned Bus   or   ☐ Contractor (Name) _____

Day and Date of Accident

Location

Time: _____ A.M.
_____ P.M.

Estimated Damage to Bus .... $ _____
Estimated Damage to Other Vehicle .... $ _____

II. ACCIDENT CONDITIONS

Characteristics of Road/Street:

☐ Straight ☐ Curve ☐ Hill ☐ Bridge ☐ Intersection ☐ Driveway ☐ Parking Lot ☐ Loading/Unloading Area
Other: _____

Conditions of Road/Street:

☐ Dry ☐ Wet ☐ Snow ☐ Ice ☐ Fog ☐ Mud ☐ Other: _____

III. TYPE OF ACCIDENT *(check one)*

☐ Bus Collision with Other Vehicle(s): *(check one)*
  ☐ Bus front end   ☐ Bus side   ☐ Bus rear end
☐ Bus Collision with Train at Crossing
☐ Single Vehicle Accident Causes: *(check one)*
  ☐ Poor road conditions   ☐ Faulty bus equipment   ☐ Bus ran into fixed object
☐ Pupil Accident: *(check one)*
  ☐ Crossing road to board bus   ☐ Crossing road, leaving bus   ☐ Within bus (not associated with bus accident)
  ☐ Other: _____

IV. LIST OF INJURED (Including bus driver and the occupants in the other vehicle)

NAME	AGE	INJURED (x)		NATURE AND SEVERITY OF INJURY
		Pupil	Other	

(Use Blank Sheet, if Necessary)

V. SUPPORTING INFORMATION REGARDING BUS DRIVER

Name of Driver	Age	Sex	Was driver wearing seat belt?
		☐ Male ☐ Female	☐ Yes ☐ No

Number of State-sponsored School Bus Driver Training Workshops the bus driver has attended . . . . _____

VI. DESCRIBE HOW ACCIDENT OCCURRED AND DRAW A BRIEF DIAGRAM ON BACK SIDE OF THIS PAGE.

VII. SIGNATURE

Superintendent/Supervisor _____   Date _____

(Complete Reverse Side of Form)

FIGURE 13–1. School Bus Accident Report.
Courtesy of St. Louis Public Schools.

DESCRIPTION OF THE ACCIDENT

Please check any circumstances that apply.

BUS	CIRCUMSTANCES	OTHER VEHICLE
	Speed ☒ Exceeded Limit	
	Speed ☒ Too Fast for Conditions	
	Moving Violation Assessed	

EXPLANATION: _____

_____

_____

_____

_____

_____

_____

(Use Blank Sheet, if Necessary)

DIAGRAM:

USE ARROW
TO SHOW
NORTH

FIGURE 13–1. (Continued)

manager who should stress safety, economy, adequacy, and efficiency. Similarly, bus routes should be determined cooperatively and mapped extensively, with "multiple routes" favored over "single" ones, bus stops carefully scheduled, and bus schedules distributed publicly.

Financing pupil transportation increasingly is becoming a state function, although in both district and state financing, cost accounting and bus drivers' monthly reports are customarily required.

School buses rightly are subject to strict regulations because of the serious safety implications. A federal law, Highway Safety Program Standard No. 17 (June 1972), requires states to implement many controls over school district transportation systems. The selection and training of bus drivers should be two of the school administration's most important concerns. Transportation employees should be screened carefully, and should have their duties and responsibilities fully delineated, with inservice training required at regular intervals.

All states must have bus equipment that meets the requirements of Standard No. 17. Most districts have some person in charge of transportation who maintains a regular program of bus care and maintenance. Bus behavior and safety are rightly under the supervisor's direction, with maximum loads and traffic precautions carefully supervised. Drivers must understand exactly what to do in case of accidents.

The principal has the responsibility at the school level to see that students who ride the bus are given instruction in safety and bus behavior. Buses can be used for field trips to expand education beyond the confines of a school.

Administrative Problems

> **In Basket**

Problem 1

The Bellwood Unified School District maintains a fleet of fifteen buses to transport students to its two high schools, three junior high schools, and eighteen elementary schools. It has used buses to achieve integration on a voluntary basis because of community pressure. Over the years students have also been bused shorter distances than required by the state law. Parents have insisted on this because of the lack of sidewalks and unsafe walking conditions, and the Board of Education has authorized this extra busing.

Because of increased expenses, the district has cut back many services. Bus service has not been reduced because of the emotional impact it was expected to have on community feeling. However, in preparing the budget for the next year, it appears that bus service must be curtailed if the budget is to be balanced. The superintendent has asked the business manager to prepare a plan for reducing or even eliminating bus service.

If you were the business manager, what would you propose?
What type of information would you include in your report?

Problem 2

Assume the same situation as in Problem 1. The decision was made to drastically reduce bus services, especially the "extra" busing which is more than the law requires.

As superintendent, how would you explain it to the public?
How would you handle the reduction of transportation personnel?
What would you do with the buses that are no longer needed?

Problem 3

Assume the same situation as in Problem 2. The parents rise up in arms and pack the next Board of Education meeting demanding to be heard. During the day, the district administrative office has been picketed by angry parents.

What should the superintendent do about the pickets?
If you were the superintendent, how would you handle the Board meeting?
What would you do about the transportation services in the months ahead?

Selected References

"Bold New Proposal for School Buses." *American School and University* 47 (February 1975):46–47.

BOYER, R. A. *The Use of a Computer to Design School Bus Routes.* Project No. 1605. Washington, D.C.: U. S. Department of Health, Education, and Welfare, Office of Education, 1964.

COTTLE, THOMAS J. *Busing.* Boston: Beacon Press, Inc., 1976.

"Computer Router: Program for School Bus Routes." *Saturday Review of Education* 1 (May 1973).

COUZINS, J. "Put Away Your Pencils and Maps Because Computers Route Buses Better." *American School Board Journal* 165 (November 1978):48–49.

DEMONT, ROGER (ed.) *Busing, Taxes, and Desegregation.* Special Monograph No. 4, Management Series. Danville, Ill.: Interstate Printers and Publishers, 1973.

FEATHERSTON, E. GLENN, and D. P. CULP. *Pupil Transportation: State and Local Programs.* New York: Harper & Row Publishers, Inc., 1965.

GENTRY, GARDINER. *Bus Them In.* Grand Rapids, Mich.: Baker Book House, 1976.

GUANIOLO, JOHN. *Transportation Law.* 2nd ed. Dubuque, Iowa: William C. Brown, 1973.

"Here's Cheers for C. B. Ears: They Can Help Your Transportation Program." *American School Board Journal* 165 (November 1978):47.

"Highway Safety Program Standard No. 17." Washington, D.C.: U. S. Department of Transportation, National Highway Traffic Safety Administration. Published in the *Federal Register* 37, No. 89 (May 6, 1972).

HILL, F. W. "Jurisdiction Over School Transportation." *American School and University* 51 (October 1978):12.

HOLDEN, ARMA. *Bus Stops Here: A Study of School Desegregation in Three Cities.* New York: Agathon Press, Inc., 1974.

McCARTY, B. C., et al. "Effect of Contingent Background Music on Inappropriate Bus Behavior." *Journal of Music Therapy* 15 (Fall 1978):150–56.

OZMAN, HOWARD, and SAM CRAVER. *Busing: A Moral Issue.* Fastback Series, No. 7. Bloomington, Ind.: Phi Dalta Kappa, 1972.

PIELE, PHILLIP K. *Computer Applications in Class and Transportation Scheduling.* Educational Management Review Series, No. 1. Washington, D.C.: National Center for Educational Research and Development, 1971.

"Quick! Tell Me How to Buy Transportation." *American School Board Journal* 166 (January 1979):14–15.

RUBIN, LILLIAN B. *Busing and Blacklash.* Berkeley: University of California Press, 1972.

"School Board Neglect of Bus Safety Led to Government's Over-Blown, Under-Researched Regulations." *American School Board Journal* 165 (November 1978):42.

SCHOOL BUS TASK FORCE. *Pupil Transportation Safety Program Plan.* Washington, D.C.: U. S. Department of Transportation, 1973.

SKLOOT, F. "State Funding of Pupil Transportation Programs." *Education Digest* 44 (November 1978):24–27.

STOPHER, PETER R., and ARNIM MEYBERG. *Transportation Systems Evaluation.* Lexington, Mass.: Lexington Books, 1976.

U. S. DEPARTMENT OF TRANSPORTATION. *Selection and Training of School Bus Drivers.* Washington, D.C.: National Highway Traffic Safety Administration, 1971.

WINDER, LESTER C. "Qualifications for Pupil Transportation Personnel." *47th Annual Volume of Proceedings, 1961.* Chicago, Ill.: Association of School Business Officials, International, 1961.

CHAPTER FOURTEEN

School Health, Safety, and Nutrition Programs

The school health program is closely allied to the nutrition program. Although both have profound educational implications, they are commonly considered auxiliary services. In a well-coordinated school district, the school nurse and the cafeteria director work cooperatively in developing menus and childhood eating habits based on accepted nutritional principles. Diet is intimately related to the broader field of general health; it is only logical that it should take an important but subordinate place in the framework of general health. Physical education and safety instruction are other aspects of the school health program.

Responsibility for Health and Nutrition Programs

In the past generation the school has assumed responsibilities for health and nutrition on a larger scale. The reasoning has been as follows:

Major premise. The school exists to assist the students in developing their maximum potentialities.

Minor premise. Students cannot develop to their maximum potential if they are undernourished or if their medical needs are neglected.

Conclusion. Therefore, the school must correct undernourishment and provide for students' medical needs, if necessary.

Goals of Health Education

The immediate justification of the school's interest in student health is educational. From a long-range viewpoint, however, its goal may be said to be the ultimate improvement of the health of society. Its short-range objective is to achieve pupil understanding of the basic facts of health, disease, nutrition, physical fitness, and environment, and to develop a sense of responsibility for improving his or her own health. If students accomplish this, their physical and mental condition should improve so that they may be able to receive the education they need to become contributing members of society. Optimum conduct and the ability to concentrate and think clearly are impossible without good health. If health habits are constantly improved by successive generations, there can be a profound effect upon the evolution of the human race; it is this goal that particularly excites the proponents of health education.

GENERAL GOALS OF HEALTH EDUCATION. In 1934 a joint committee of the National Education Association and the American Medical Association drew up the following aims, still valid today, and recommended them as guides to school health education programs:

1. To instruct children and youth so that they may conserve and improve their own health.
2. To establish in them the habits and principles of living which throughout their school life, and in later years, will assure that abundant vigor and vitality which provide the basis for the greatest possible happiness and service in personal, family, and community life.
3. To influence parents and other adults, through the health education program for children, to better habits and attitudes, so that the school may become an effective agency for the promotion of the social aspects of health education in the family and community as well as in the school itself.
4. To improve the individual and community life of the future; to insure a better second generation, and a still better third generation, and a healthier and fitter nation . . .[1]

The American Association of School Administrators out of concern for health and family life education adopted a resolution at its annual conference in 1970 stating that " the only effective way in which the school can fulfill its responsibility for meeting the health needs of youth is through a comprehensive program of health education in all grades at all levels" so that they are prepared "for their role as future parents and citizens."[2] There

---

[1] National Education Association and American Medical Association, *Health Education*, Report of the Joint Committee on Health Problems in Education, pp. 1–251.

[2] American Association of School Administrators, *Your AASA in Nineteen Sixty-Nine–Seventy*, Official Report of the American Association of School Administrators (Washington, D.C.: AASA, 1970), p. 131.

should be a sound, interrelated, and sequential program which includes sex and family life education as well as the other health topics. The program should be long-range, covering specific areas appropriate to the stage of the student's development.[3]

SPECIFIC GOALS OF HEALTH EDUCATION.   The health program of a school district should strive toward achievement of the following objectives. There should be a health examination and follow-up program for all students which includes counseling for them, their parents, and teachers. Individualized programs of health instruction should be established. The environment of a school can be raised by improving safety and hygiene standards and by serving better food. Students in both elementary and secondary schools should follow a program of health instruction and physical conditioning. Instruction in the avoidance of accidents and communicable diseases should be intensified. Qualified medical advisers and nurses should be employed to make examinations and to help in planning and carrying out the total health program. Handicapped students should be identified as early as possible and optimum facilities provided for their education. Teachers should have inservice training in health and safety. Plans should be developed for extending physical education and recreational activities outward into the community and onward into the years of adult life. Provision must be made to handle emergencies, injuries, and serious illness. Goals should be established to help solve the problems of teenage pregnancy and the use of drugs and alcohol by many young people.

Ecology, a sociological science, is also of concern in health education. Manmade pollution caused by chemicals, garbage, sewage, fumes, noise, and urban overcrowding affects the water we drink, the food we eat, the air we breathe, and the environment we live in. Although man has been contaminating himself for years, our youth are probably the most concerned about it. They will inherit the environment created by past generations—in the name of progress—and will live in this contaminated world after the present generation is gone. Time is running out; something must be done immediately to save our environment and protect the health of everyone. Students must be educated as to what is involved in protecting and purifying our air, our soil, our water, and our food.

Governmental Concern with School Health Programs

Every White House Conference on youth has found cause for alarm in the physical condition of American youth. Their various reports have consistently stressed that between 30 and 40 percent of our children and ado-

---

[3] American Association of School Administrators, *Your AASA*, p. 131.

lescents are operating with limited effectiveness as the result of bad teeth, damaged hearts, impaired hearing, mental retardation, deafness, blindness, or some type of limb disability.

In 1956 the President's Conference on Fitness for American Youth pointed out that fitness of our youth could not be taken for granted in an age of automation. Physical debilitation that results from lack of participation in energetic activities causes erosion of health; and physical fitness goes hand in hand with moral, mental, and emotional fitness.[4] The 1970 White House Conference for Children called for massive expansion of health services and health insurance for children.

In 1961, President Kennedy urged the adoption of the following recommendations made by his Council on Youth Fitness:

1. Identify the physically underdeveloped pupil and work with him to improve his physical capacity.
2. Provide a minimum of fifteen minutes of vigorous activity every day for all pupils.
3. Use valid fitness tests to determine pupils' physical abilities and evaluate their progress.[5]

Government laws relating to nutrition are discussed later in this chapter.

Administration of Health Education

The school health program, like most other matters with which the schools have had to interest themselves, has included several phases that range from simple to complex. The three major stages in the history of school health programs have been:

1. Prophylaxis.
2. Rehabilitation.
3. Preventive hygiene.

THE SCHOOL PLANT IN HEALTH EDUCATION. In the school plant, the following physical conditions should be the subject of constant inspection and improvement wherever needed:

1. Lighting.
2. Heating.
3. Ventilation.

---

[4] President's Conference on Fitness of American Youth, *Fitness of American Youth*, A report to the President of the United States, pp. 3–4.

[5] John F. Kennedy, "A Presidential Message," *CTA Journal* 57, October 1961, p. 5.

4. Water supply.
5. Cleanliness of lavatories.
6. Condition of seating.
7. Food storage.

THE CURRICULUM AND HEALTH EDUCATION.   The core of the health program is the curriculum. Health education, guidance and counseling, the germ theory of disease, the principles of diet and sanitation, the problems of drug abuse, alcoholism, sex education—all should be taught in relation to the overall curriculum. In large districts, curricular blocs may be set up to deal specifically with health problems:

1. Sight-conservation classes.
2. Speech therapy classes.
3. Lip-reading classes.
4. Remedial physical education classes.
5. Special education for the mentally retarded.
6. Classes for the physically handicapped.
7. Classes in which family life and sex education are taught, with parental consent required.
8. Classes in which knowledge of drugs is taught.

ELEMENTARY SCHOOL HEALTH INSTRUCTION.   In the elementary grades, the creation of beneficial health habits is the principal goal of the health program. Principal stress is placed upon the following factors at the elementary level:

1. Personal cleanliness.
2. Posture.
3. Safety.
4. Diet.
5. Sleep and rest habits.
6. Care of teeth and eyes.
7. Prevention of environmental pollution.

TEENAGE PREGNANCY.   Our youth no longer live in a Victorian age. Social change has occurred, as can be seen in changing mores and sexual attitudes. Teenage sexual intercourse has increased and is not always "safe" in spite of the legalization of the pill.

   The Guttmacher Institute Study estimated that 12.5 million thirteen-to-nineteen-year-old youth have had sexual intercourse at least once.[6]

---

[6] Alan Guttmacher Institute, *11 Million Teenagers: What Can Be Done About the Epidemic of Adolescent Pregnancies in the United States* (New York: Alan Guttmacher Institute, 1976), p. 9.

Studies have shown that the total teenage pregnancies each year in the thirteen-to-nineteen-year age range total 1,030,000.[7] As a result of the Guttmacher Institute Study, Congress passed the Adolescent Health Services, Pregnancy Prevention and Care Act of 1978 which authorized $60 million to be spent in 1979 for community-based adolescent pregnancy programs.[8]

The public schools must deal with the teenage pregnancy problem, but they are handicapped by Section 86:40 which was added to Title IX of the Education Amendments of 1972 in 1974 to protect the rights of pregnant school students. Pregnant students may not be expelled, may not be required to attend special schools, may not be barred from any program or course, may not be required to take special courses, may not be required to leave school at a certain time prior to birth nor required to remain out of school for a specified time, and may not be required to have a doctor supply notes regarding school attendance unless it is in relation to a physical condition.[9]

Hendrixson has proposed that state departments of education mandate family life, parenting, and sexuality education for children from kindergarten to grade 12. There should also be improved counseling and guidance programs for teenage girls as well as school- and community-based prenatal education programs.[10]

Some school districts provide medical, hospital, and accident insurance for students. Under Title IX, school districts that provide full-coverage health services must not discriminate because of sex and must include family planning services and gynecological care.

Faced with the fact that the law permits pregnant students to attend school without their class programs being restricted, principals must work with the school staffs, other students, and parents to accept these girls as they are. They should not be ostracized. In any case, many of these students drop out of school.

DRUG USAGE AND ALCOHOLISM IN YOUTH.   Alcoholism and drug usage among teenagers are problems that may carry over into the classroom. Students may have difficulty in concentrating or paying attention. All school work and activities are affected and absenteeism may increase. Teachers have had students come to class "stoned," "spaced-out," and incoherent, especially on Monday mornings.

How should a teacher handle a student who appears to be under the influence of drugs or alcohol? Should the student be reported? Or ignored?

---

[7] Alan Guttmacher Institute, *11 Million Teenagers*, pp. 16–17.
[8] Linda L. Hendrixson, "Pregnant Children: A Socio-Educational Challenge," *Phi Delta Kappan* 60, No. 9, May 1979, pp. 663–66.
[9] Linda L. Hendrixson, "Pregnant Children," pp. 664–65.
[10] Linda L. Hendrixson, "Pregnant Children," p. 665.

Or sent out of class to sleep it off? Should parents be notified? These and other questions must be dealt with and policies developed to handle them. A suggested procedure follows:

Controlled Substance Procedure

Possessing, using, selling, sharing, or being under the influence of a government-controlled substance or alcoholic beverage on school grounds is unlawful and punishable by suspension from school.

I. *Definition of Evidence*

The nature of the evidence against an individual affects the notification, counseling, disciplinary and documentation procedures used.

  A. Hard Evidence

    1. An admission of involvement by the student.

    2. Discovery of the substance and/or alcoholic beverage on the student's person or in possessions, such as lockers or backpacks, under the student's control.

    3. Eyewitness testimony of any school personnel on the actual usage.

    4. Eyewitness testimony of two or more students on the actual usage.

  B. Soft Evidence

  Soft evidence is more subjective; it involves all other forms of evidence and is usually based on observation of student behavior.

II. *Hard Evidence Procedures*

In cases with hard evidence, the following steps shall be taken:

  A. The Police Department or the Sheriff shall be notified.

  B. The student shall be suspended.

  C. The parent shall be informed of the police notification and suspension.

III. *Soft Evidence Procedures*

Soft evidence cases will usually involve situations in which the student is suspected of being under the influence of a government-controlled substance or alcoholic beverage. The following steps shall be taken:

  A. The administrator may consult with the school nurse and may require the completion of a behavioral form.

  B. Referrals to the nurse:

    1. If the nurse feels that the student's behavior is abnormal, the parent and/or guardian shall be called to pick up the student.

    2. If the nurse is uncertain about the student's behavior, the student will be detained for further observation until a determination is made.

    3. If, in the nurse's judgment, the student's behavior is normal, the student shall be returned to class.

  C. A search for hard evidence shall be made.

In all cases, the school principal must be informed. The procedure should be kept low-key, and school personnel must be careful of accusing a student unjustly.

Drug dealers have infiltrated some schools or will meet students outside the campus. Students have hidden drugs in their lockers to use or sell surreptitiously on the grounds. School employees have searched lockers in attempts to locate drugs. Since they are not government employees, search warrants are not necessary. School employees have a right and even an obligation to inspect and search. Several court cases have upheld this right.[11] However, if police are involved, warrants must be obtained or a search would be illegal.[12]

In some school districts, undercover police officers, with the school's permission, have posed as students and arrested drug dealers operating on the campuses.

Bernard Bard[13] has pointed out that secondary school drug education programs have failed. Several states reported that the use of drugs actually increased after short courses were taken to show drug dangers. Criticisms of school drug education programs indicated that teachers are poorly trained, inaccuracies are purveyed, lectures and films are not satisfactory and often full of errors, sensationalism and scare tactics are not related to sound educational practice, and current programs do not prevent drug abuse and may encourage experimentation. Students frequently know more than the instructors. Moralizing does not work.

Many educational drug programs have been used across the country, but there is no consensus as to what is the best program. Some of the schools that have shown good results utilize well-trained teachers who understand, relate to, and can be trusted by students; focus on high-risk drug abusers; develop programs that are ongoing throughout the year; or operate peer-group programs utilizing students who may know more about drugs than teachers.

One of the problems is the difficulty in identifying students who may be high risks as potential drug or alcohol abusers. In any case, students who are having drug or alcohol problems need counseling by the school counselor and nurse and probably a referral to outside agencies if the condition persists.

SCHOOL PERSONNEL AND THE HEALTH PROGRAM.   Key persons involved in the health program would include: the classroom teacher, the school nurse, the school physician, a dental hygienist, the school psychologist, the school counselor, the cafeteria manager, and the health service aide.

---

[11] *Overton* v. *New York*, 299 N.E. 2d 596 (1967); *State* v. *Stein*, 456 P. 2d 1 (Kans. 1969); *People* v. *Jackson*, 319 N.Y.S. 2d 731 (1971).

[12] Chester Nolte, *Duties and Liabilities of School Administrators* (West Nyack, N.Y.: Parker Publishing Co., 1973), pp. 182–83.

[13] Bernard Bard, "The Failure of Our Drug Abuse Programs," *Phi Delta Kappan* 57, No. 4, December 1975, pp. 251–55.

Larger districts may employ nutrition specialists, eye, ear, nose, and throat specialists, dentists, sanitation experts, and environmental experts for lighting and heating. Social workers may be employed to work with parents and schools on a cooperative basis. School health problems are often related to the home environment; the social worker can promote home–school relationships as they affect the child.

In smaller districts, health personnel may be secured on a part-time, a fee, or a contract basis when economics and the pupil population do not warrant full-time employment. It is also possible for adjoining districts to share the cost and services. County health departments sometimes provide health services on a cooperative, jointly financed basis.

These school employees, in addition to the administrators most directly concerned, should be entrusted with the organization and implementation of the health program. Often they will work as a team with the program being cooperatively constructed. Teachers should welcome the services and knowledge of the school nurse in helping them with health education. The school custodian who is responsible for the cleanliness of lavatories and drinking fountains and for keeping dust and dirt from accumulating can be an important asset. An explanation by the custodian to the students could recruit their assistance in helping to maintain the cleanliness of the school plant.

Teachers and counselors who are involved with family life and sex education, alcoholism, and drug usage need special knowledge and training.

The School Nurse

Whenever a school's size and income preclude the employment of a full staff. of health personnel, it is generally conceded that at least a school nurse should be hired. Some states require a registered nurse. There should be one nurse to every 1,000 to 1,500 pupils in elementary schools and a slightly higher ratio in secondary schools. Most elementary schools share nurses, unless the schools are large. Secondary schools are more likely to have a full-time nurse.

Because of budget cutbacks and decreasing enrollments, some districts are reducing or eliminating the number of nurses. This course is unsatisfactory and penalizes the schools and their students. The only answer is to provide a district-wide health team, utilize county services, or contract for health services.

A nurse's functions would include:

1. Inspecting the school and recommending health and safety improvements.
2. Assessing the school's health needs.

3. Informing administrators about the problems, needs, and accomplishments of the health program.
4. Developing and implementing a health care plan.
5. Administering or supervising screening tests: vision, hearing, weight, height, dental, cardiac, and communicable disease.
6. Assuming responsibility for maintaining a system of current health records and data for each student.
7. Identifying and assessing factors that could contribute to learning disorders.
8. Working with students to help them understand emotional problems and to function under emotional stress.
9. Supervising the health service aide.

When accidents happen, the nurse gives first aid. If an accident is serious, the nurse can give whatever medical aid is necessary until an ambulance, hospital, or doctor takes over, or the parent is contacted. Otherwise, the nurse performs no medical services; does not prescribe; does not treat. Medicines, including aspirin, should never be given by a nurse and should not be allowed to be kept in the school. Only a doctor or parent should give a student medicine.

The nurse works closely with classroom teachers in subject fields of science, homemaking, and physical education. Relations with the cafeteria director are necessarily close; the maintenance and operation personnel will be guided by the nurse's recommendations in anything bearing directly upon the health and safety of the students. The nurse is a resource person.

Health service aides are being employed in many school districts to carry out assigned routines and technical tasks related to the school health services program. This frees the school nurse to give more attention to the coordination of the total health program. It also makes it possible to provide team services to several schools without the nurse running back and forth for emergencies or problems.

The aide works as an unlicensed, noncertificated paraprofessional employee with special training skills. He or she should perform duties such as the following: typing, preparing and maintaining records and reports, making appointments and handling communications, arranging health displays and exhibits, helping teachers with duplicating and distributing health materials, and ordering, inventorying, and distributing health and first-aid supplies and equipment.

In addition, the health service aide can carry out the following direct health services:

1. Performing appraisal services through screening of vision, hearing, and other areas.
2. Reporting to the school nurse names of students requiring further physical evaluations.

3. Interpreting first-aid emergency procedures and school health policies to the school staff.
4. Seeing that teachers and others submit necessary reports.
5. Taking care of emergency illness or accidents.
6. Organizing and participating in health activities as directed by the school nurse (testing and immunization programs, preschool orientation, etc.).
7. Checking absentee records and following up on students with frequent absences.

A large school system should have a head nurse or health supervisor at the district level. This officer would be in charge of employing, discharging, and coordinating the activities of all school nurses and other health personnel. The position would involve coordination between the health department and the other departments of the school district and the community.

States may receive assistance to implement Part B of the Education of the Handicapped Act, effective October 1, 1977. The purpose is to insure that all handicapped students receive a free appropriate public education which includes special education and related services to meet their unique needs. (Handicapped students are those who have been identified "as being mentally retarded, hard of hearing, deaf, speech impaired, visually handicapped, seriously emotionally disturbed, orthopedically impaired, other health impaired, deaf-blind, multi-handicapped, or as having specific learning disabilities" (Section 121a.5(a).) Those students who are in need of special education and related services must be identified, located, and evaluated. The school nurse, along with other health personnel, are the key persons in carrying out the provisions of the Act.

IMMUNIZATIONS AND INOCULATIONS. Immunizations and inoculations are necessary to protect the students receiving them as well as those with whom they come in contact. The federal government does not prescribe any immunizations or inoculations. States, however, require them prior to a child's enrollment in school. California, as an example, requires three polio vaccinations, one dose for measles, and four diphtheria–tetanus–pertussis doses.

There have been many court cases regarding the rules for inoculations and immunizations as a prerequisite for public school enrollment or attendance. Some have been based on religious grounds. Courts generally have upheld the school's right to regulate the health of its students for the benefit of society as a whole, regardless of the religious beliefs of the parents.

At the time of enrollment, the parent or guardian should fill out a form such as that shown in Figure 14–1. It not only shows what immunizations the child has taken but the diseases the student has had. The form

HEALTH INFORMATION
(New Pupils Only)

Pupil's Last Name _____ First _____ Birth Date _____ Teacher _____

Please check and date any of the following diseases your child has had:

Chicken pox _____ Year Measles—German _____ Year Scarlet Fever _____ Year

Mumps _____ Year Poliomyelitis _____ Year Diphtheria _____ Year

Whooping cough _____ Year Measles—Red _____ Year Rheumatic fever _____ Year

Other _____ Year

Give the date the child had the following:

Smallpox vaccination _____ Diphtheria–tetanus–pertusis doses _____

Tuberculin test _____ Chest X-ray _____ Results _____

Polio vaccine 1. _____ 2. _____ 3. _____

Are there any other health problems to discuss with the nurse? _____

Person to be notified in case of emergency _____ Phone _____

In case of emergency and if I cannot be located, I give my permission to take my child to an emergency hospital.

_____
Signature of Parent or Guardian

_____ Date _____

FIGURE 14–1. Example of Enrollment Health Information Form.

should also have a signature approving the disposition of the student in case of an emergency. The school nurse should keep this form on file.

Teachers and Classroom Health

The teacher is often the key person in screening health problems in the classroom. Teachers are well qualified to observe pupils' physical conditions, to note personal health habits and attitudes, social health habits, and emotional reactions or problems. Their skill is due to their training, knowledge, and experience in working with students every day. The school nurse seldom sees individual students other than through referrals or by calling in a group to the nurse's office for examinations or consultation. Whenever a teacher observes a condition in need of remediation, the principal or the nurse should be consulted to determine what steps to take.

The Health of Teachers and Administrators

Too often teachers and administrators are only concerned with the health of students and neglect their own health. Teaching and administrating are demanding work which saps physical energy and mental sharpness if not controlled. School workdays do not end at 3:30 P.M. or 5:00 P.M. Teachers and administrators cannot go home and forget their job until tomorrow because there are plans to make, papers to grade, and PTA meetings to attend. Most of them work toward advanced degrees. Others participate actively and assume leadership roles in teacher organizations, service clubs, churches, and the like or work as youth leaders. If these extra activities are not controlled, school personnel become overly tired and run down mentally, physically, and emotionally. For teachers, this is not fair to their students; for administrators, it is not fair to their staffs.

Health Supplies and Equipment

Certain items of health equipment should be distributed throughout every school district so that every school, and preferably every classroom, has them available. Standard items include: a first-aid kit, weight scales, eye-test card, tongue depressors, height and weight charts, thermometer, and height-measuring device.

The school health center should be large enough to accommodate a twenty-foot clear space to test visual acuity and soundproofed for hearing examinations. At least one cot in a screened-off space should be provided to isolate students with communicable diseases. There should be a sink and counter for the nurse's use, a lavatory room, and a shower room if cleanliness is a problem in the community. In schools that use the services of doctors and dentists, it will be necessary to provide an examining room and possibly a dentist's chair. Locked cupboards should be provided for the storage of health supplies.

Health records should be kept in every school so that teachers and guidance personnel have easy and immediate access to the information they contain. Records should be kept up to date as a part of the school nurse's regular duties. Records should contain pertinent data on pupil height, weight, dental care, immunizations, childhood diseases, psychological test results, and any serious physical disorders or conditions that might inhibit the child's success in school. The health card should be cumulative and should follow the student from grade to grade, and from school district to school district if necessary.

All schools should keep daily reports of referrals to the nurse's office stating the name of the pupil, the symptoms, the first aid administered, any contact with parents, the final disposition of the case, and the person handling it. In addition, injuries to the head, back, teeth, bones, or anything that might be construed as of major significance usually call for reports to the district office. Injuries should also be reported to the school's insurance company if accident insurance is carried on pupils. A written report should be made of all accidents, whether they involve students or staff members.

Administration of the School Health Program

The health program should be considered an integral part of the educational program. It is properly described as a special service, but should not be thought of as an auxiliary or subordinate service. Since education deals with all aspects of growth of a child, health education becomes coequal with the academic curriculum. Laws vary from state to state regarding what is required or prohibited in teaching certain aspects of health. To determine a health instruction program for a school, the legal requirements must be ascertained first. Although a vocal minority has opposed sex education and family planning courses in the public schools, students look forward to such courses. They cannot be kept igonrant and will learn about sex whether or not the subject is taught in the schools. Trained teachers who have a good relationship with students can set them right.

PHYSICAL EDUCATION AND HEALTH. Separate periods, usually thirty or forty minutes, are set aside in elementary schools for instruction in physical education. Attention should be given to exercises and group games, with rhythm an important emphasis of the instruction.

Physical education in high school is a much more expensive and technical proposition than it is on the elementary level. Gymnasiums, athletic fields, and trained personnel are necessary. Both interscholastic and intramural sports are customary, with proper balance allotted to each of these important phases of the athletic program. Recreational activities that can carry over into adult life should be emphasized.

SAFETY EDUCATION.   The rising accident rate in the United States points up the growing need for adequate instruction in the principles of safety. Except in the area of driver training and education, safety education is largely the province of the classroom teacher.

In the field of accident prevention, primary emphasis should be placed on freedom from school-related accidents. There is very little to be gained by giving theoretical instruction in safety education on a broad scale unless it is supported by specific training in avoiding accidents in the school area itself. Areas where school-related accidents most commonly occur, in order of their frequency, are as follows: streets and highways adjacent to the school, playgrounds, gymnasiums, laboratories, and shops.

Schools, as well as other agencies, are required by law to be safety- and health-conscious. The Occupational Safety and Health Act of 1970 (OSHA) "develops and promulgates occupational safety and health standards; develops and issues regulations; conducts investigations and inspections to determine the status of compliance with safety and health standards and regulations; and issues citations and proposes penalties for noncompliance."[14] To protect themselves, schools must comply with this act.

Principals have the ultimate responsibility for the safety of students and school personnel even though they may delegate certain responsibilities to the nurse, custodian, playground director, or teachers. Periodic inspections should be made of the grounds and buildings to detect unsafe conditions. A school safety committee can be formed, consisting of a teacher, a student, the school nurse, and perhaps a parent. This committee can help develop safety rules, report hazardous conditions, deter unsafe acts, and help in developing the school's safety consciousness.

School accident prevention usually follows the pattern outlined below:

1. Close supervision of pupils on their way to and from school.
2. Academic instruction in safety and accident prevention.
3. Safety engineering to ensure maximum safeguarding of school sites, buildings, and facilities.

---

[14] *United States Government Manual, 1978–79*, Office of General Services Administration (Washington, D.C.: U.S. Government Printing Office, 1978), p. 393.

4. Cooperation between the school and other agencies for the promotion of accident control.

In spite of everything, accidents do occur. The board of education, administrators, and/or various school personnel may be sued, and the number of suits appears to be increasing. However, the doctrine of *in loco parentis* usually applies to school employees. Courts generally rule that a school employee cannot be everywhere with every student at all times. M. Chester Nolte has explained that there is no liability when there is no negligence.[15] To prove negligence, there must be evidence that someone acted wrongly and did something that should not have been done or failed to do something that should have been done to cause the injury. Also, administrators cannot be held liable for wrongful acts or negligence on the part of subordinates.

In cases where accidents occur in or around a school, a report giving the following information should be filed with the school nurse:

1. Pupil's Name.
2. Pupil's Address.
3. Age.
4. Grade.
5. Date and hour accident occurred.
6. Cause of injury.
7. Place where accident occurred.
8. Names of persons present (witnesses).
9. Name of teacher in attendance.
10. Nature of the injury.
11. What was done for the injured.

Disasters, such as fires, storms, earthquakes, explosions, bomb threats, or falling airplanes or parts, may strike schools without warning at any time. Students may panic. So may teachers or other adults. What should be done? The procedures to be followed and the emergency drills to be practiced should be in conformance with state, county, city, and local requirements as well as with the rules and regulations adopted by the district's board of education. The local boards should adopt policies that prescribe the safety rules to be followed and the evacuation procedures to be used. Although these may vary from district to district, they must conform to governmental regulations. Parents must be informed as to where their children will be taken following an evacuation.

---

[15] M. Chester Nolte, *Duties and Liabilities of School Administrators* (West Nyack, N.Y.: Parker Publishing Co., 1973), pp. 138–40.

To legally protect themselves and not be held negligent, administrators must have knowledge of these regulations and carry out the policies and instructions which the boards of education should have adopted. For example, if fire drills are required monthly, they must be held monthly and a record kept. Teachers must know what to do, when to do it, and how to do it. Students who are well-trained and knowledgeable and under the control of informed teachers will probably not panic. Keeping calm is important.

School districts should carry liability insurance for the protection of all personnel. It is also recommended that administrators carry their own personal liability insurance, not only for protection in case negligence is proven but for any other type of suit that may be filed against them.

SCHOOL SAFETY. In addition to teaching safety, the school buildings themselves must be safe. Fire and unsafe hazards should be eliminated, flammable materials stored safely, playground equipment checked periodically, and fire fighting equipment accessible and in working order. Custodians and the office staff should know the location of main gas and water valves, furnace controls, and electric panels. These should be conspicuously labeled. The principal and custodian should make periodic inspections of buildings, furniture, and equipment and order them repaired as needed.

School Nutrition Programs

Most of our larger school districts, and many smaller ones, now provide cafeteria facilities and services for their pupils. The Department of Agriculture has reported that three billion meals are served annually in the schools. These daily hot lunches result in an improvement in nutritional standards which cannot be underestimated. The same reasoning that justifies the modern school's interest in health and safety underlies its concern with nutrition.

OBJECTIVES OF THE SCHOOL LUNCH PROGRAM. The main objective of the school lunch program is to provide sufficient attractive, nutritious, and palatable food at the lowest possible cost. In a larger sense, however, the goal is that of the entire school health program: the creation and maintenance of a healthy pupil capable of profiting to the optimum degree from the educational instruction offered. Malnourished children are "more likely to be apathetic, irritable, and lack a long attention span."[16] More and more,

---

[16] Rita Bakan, "Malnutrition and Learning," *Phi Delta Kappan* 51, June 1970, p. 529.

food is also being made available to pupils at intervals throughout the school day. Early morning nutrition for students who come to school with little or no breakfast is increasing, as is the custom of offering mid-morning snacks, especially for students in the primary grades. Experimental studies have indicated the positive value of good nutrition on learning ability and high pupil morale.[17]

THE FEDERAL GOVERNMENT AIDS NUTRITION. The federal government entered food service programs for schools with the National School Lunch Act of 1946 and the School Milk Act of 1954. Since that time other acts and amendments have been added in an attempt to improve the nutrition of schoolchildren.

The overall purpose of the National School Lunch Act, which has been amended by numerous public laws, is to make school lunch programs available to all schoolchildren in order to promote their health and well-being. The states are assisted by federal cash grants and donations. Participating public and nonprofit private schools are reimbursed by federally appropriated National School Lunch Program funds. Rates of reimbursements are adjusted semiannually based on the Consumer Price Index.[18]

The Child Nutrition Act of 1966 has been amended by several public laws to assist states in providing nutritious breakfasts for schoolchildren in elementary through high school grades by cash grants and food donations. The purpose is to help schools which draw their attendance from poor economic conditions, where students must travel a long distance, or where there is a special need to improve nutrition and diet. The breakfasts are served free or at a reduced price.[19]

There is also nonfood assistance for school food service programs. Public laws of the Child Nutrition Act provide up to 100 percent of the cost for schools without food service, in low-income areas, so that these schools can buy equipment for storing, preparing, transporting, and serving food to students.[20]

---

[17] The reader is referred to the following publications for further information on the relationship between nutrition and learning: M. Winick, "Malnutrition and Brain Development," *Journal of Pediatrics*, May 1969, p. 667; R. H. Barnes, A. U. Moore, I. M. Read, and W. G. Pond, "Effect of Food Deprivation on Behavioral Patterns," in N. S. Scrimshaw and J. E. Gordon (eds.) *Malnutrition, Learning, and Behavior* (Cambridge, Mass.: MIT Press, 1968), p. 168; H. F. Eichenwald and P. C. Fry, "Nutrition and Learning," *Science*, February 1969, p. 664; and Margaret Mead, "The Changing Significance of Food," *American Scientist*, March–April 1970, p. 176.

[18] U.S. Department of Health, Education, and Welfare, *Federal Education Assistance Programs—1976* (Washington, D.C.: U.S. Government Printing Office, 1976), pp. 14–15.

[19] U.S. Department of Health, Education, and Welfare, *Federal Education Assistance*, pp. 10–11.

[20] U.S. Department of Health, Education, and Welfare, *Federal Education Assistance*, pp. 12–13.

There is also a special milk program for students. Amendments to the Child Nutrition Act of 1966 were enacted to encourage milk consumption by elementary through high school grade students. Eligible schools that inaugurate or expand milk distribution service are reimbursed with the rate being adjusted annually. Eligible children receive a half-pint of milk.[21]

ORGANIZATION OF NUTRITION PROGRAMS. States maintain nutritional offices and expert consultants whose duty it is to improve on existing menus and to advise schools on proper techniques of feeding large numbers of students at different age levels. Some states follow the example of the national government in giving food subsidies and financial aid. Most state departments of education publish minimum requirements for school menus, establishing proper amounts of fats, carbohydrates, proteins, and vitamins to be included in the weekly lunch program.

Counties often give supervisory assistance in the establishment and improvement of nutritional programs. In its commonly assumed function of supervising the accounts and records of school districts, the office of county superintendent of schools often renders valuable service in placing the financial portion of the school lunch program on a sound basis.

Local school districts operate the nutrition programs. They organize the distribution of food, hire and pay the personnel who administer it, and evaluate the success of the system after it has been in operation for a sufficient length of time. The building and equipping of the cafeteria are functions of the local district alone. Often, the meals are subsidized in part from the district's general fund; this subsidy most often is applied to the cafeteria director's salary.

Private community organizations may contribute funds for nutrition. Meals for needy students are often pledged by such groups, and PTA organizations often finance mid-morning snacks for kindergarten and first-grade students. In small schools, parents and other interested persons may volunteer their services to serve and prepare meals, enabling districts to offer pupils lunches that otherwise would have been impossible financially.

ADMINISTRATION OF THE NUTRITION PROGRAM. The nutrition program involves more than the preparation and serving of food. Modern schools consider the lunch period an important part of the educational program and stress instructional aspects such as menu preparation, principles of sound diet, and good table manners. Standard meals are advisable, with the menu being changed each day. Menus can be cooperatively planned by pupils, teachers, and cafeteria personnel within the framework of state standards. In all but very small districts, a food services director should be

---

[21] U.S. Department of Health, Education, and Welfare, *Federal Education Assistance,* pp. 16–17.

placed in charge of the program, and should work under the general supervision of the business manager or superintendent of schools. The cafeteria director should be a person of wide experience in mass feeding, and preferably should be especially acquainted with the nutritional needs and habits of children. Larger districts may employ a dietician to plan the meals.

Usually school district cafeterias attempt to be self-supporting, except for the cafeteria director's salary, which is normally subsidized by the school district. No attempt should be made to show a profit of any kind from serving meals to pupils and teachers. The object of the program should always be to serve the largest possible number of pupils, and to this end the cost of meals should be kept as low as possible.

What should the cafeteria manager do when students turn in trays with food left on them—sometimes with dishes that have hardly been touched? What should be done when half or more of the milk is left in the carton? Smaller amounts can be served to students in lower grades if the district buys its own food. The National School Lunch Program, however, creates another problem.[22] This program provides nutritious meals to families who sign affidavits of eligibility based on income. Surplus foods are provided to participating school districts through state agencies. Reimbursement to the districts is based on a complicated formula. Free lunch recipients cannot be identified. The *entire* Type A lunch prescribed by the Program must be served to all recipients whether they want it or not. No choices are allowed except to senior high school students.

Many students, particularly in the lower grades, cannot eat all the food; others do not like it and refuse to eat it. The uneaten food is wasted and ends up in garbage cans. It has been estimated that 20 percent of the National School Lunch Program food is thrown away. Since the government's subsidy is 2.6 billion dollars, the wasted food would be valued at about half a billion dollars. The best solution is education and suggestion, emphasizing the importance of a balanced diet, a hot lunch, and the value of milk to the body. As an incentive, a point can be made regarding the millions of starving children in the under-developed countries.

A cafeteria clerk may be employed by large districts to keep necessary accounts, order and receive supplies, and conduct the annual inventorying and budgeting necessitated by a sizable operation. The clerk would work under the direction of the cafeteria director, and in close cooperation with the district business office.

There must be communication and coordination between:

1. The superintendent, who has overall responsibility for the cafeteria program—establishing policies and procedures, and organizing central administration.

---

[22] Lewis Lyman, "The National School Lunch Program: Boon or Boondoggle?", *Phi Delta Kappan* 60, No. 6, February 1979, pp. 436–38.

2. The business administrator, who has responsibility for food-service financial management; the purchase, storage, and distribution of food supplies; the purchase and maintenance of kitchen equipment and facilities, and cafeteria personnel.
3. The food services director, who has responsibility for menu planning, food purchasing, distribution and preparation, supervision and training of cafeteria personnel, cafeteria budget preparation, monthly financial reports, and equipment purchases. The director works closely with school principals, school cafeteria managers, and the district business administrator.
4. The school principal, who has responsibility for the management of the cafeteria within his school, the scheduling and supervising of students for lunch and snack hours, the collection and handling of money within the school, adherence to district policies and compliance with health laws, and the working relationships of the school staff with cafeteria personnel and the district office.

School cafeterias must attract from one-third to one-half of the student population in order to be successful. Students prefer simple food that is well prepared. They dislike long lines and slow handling of the trays and cash registers or ticket collection. Although they like "junk foods," schools should not make them available. Students like to socialize while eating, with a minimum of supervision. High school students prefer snack-type lunches with freedom of choice rather than the traditional tray lunch that is served in elementary schools. Schools operating under the federal nutrition programs do not have the flexibility to prepare lunches that students prefer.

Many schools are freeing teachers from lunch-hour supervision and employing teacher aides or lunch-hour supervisors for this duty. This lunch-hour freedom is one of the items that teacher associations negotiate with the board of education. Lunch-hour helpers are usually lay persons, parents, or PTA members paid on an hourly basis.

DESIRABLE STANDARDS FOR FOOD SERVICES.   The following standards will assist a school district in developing an adequate food-service program:[23]

I. Organization.
   A. Every school should provide cafeteria service for pupils.
   B. The district should operate its own food service.
   C. When three or more cafeterias are in operation, the program should be headed by a trained and experienced district cafeteria director.
   D. Cafeteria facilities should serve 50 percent or more of the pupils enrolled.

---

[23] Irving R. Melbo et al. *Report of the Survey of the Bear Valley Unified School District* (Los Angeles: University of Southern California, 1962), pp. 230–33.

    E. The food service should be related to the health program of the school.

    F. The district should take advantage of federal food-surplus commodities to reduce costs for pupils.

    G. The food-service program should be on a nonprofit but self-supporting basis.

    H. Food service for pupils should be the primary aim of the program, rather than primarily service for community groups or employed personnel.

    I. The food-service program should be operated on a school board-approved policy basis, subject to review as conditions change.

II. Personnel.

    A. The employment and termination of food-service personnel should be recommended by the superintendent and approved by the school board.

    B. The district should make provision for an adequate inservice training program and an impartial appraisal of food-service personnel performance.

    C. Prior to service, all those who handle food should be given a general health examination by a district physician at district expense.

    D. Food-service personnel should be provided with equitable benefits, including salary, leaves, vacations, health insurance, etc.

    E. Student help should be shielded from the operation of machines with moving parts or other dangers. Student work in cafeterias should be a learning experience and should not interfere with study programs. Such work should be paid for at an hourly rate, not by provision of free meals.

    F. Cafeteria workers should wear appropriate white uniforms.

    G. Food-service personnel should be given priority to earn overtime pay when the facilities are used by school-related associations.

    H. Food-service personnel play an important role in the nourishment and well-being of pupils and faculty and should receive appropriate recognition by administrators.

III. Operation.

    A. All disbursal of funds and payment of bills should be made through the business office.

    B. Cash registers with tapes and totalizers should be used to collect money at cafeterias and snack bars.

    C. All receipts should be double-checked and deposited in the local bank each day.

    D. A financial report of food-service operations should be submitted to the school board at the close of each month and at the close of each fiscal year.

    E. Charge accounts should not be permitted; free meals should be provided by tax overrides or by welfare agencies.

    F. The cafeteria account should be audited at the close of each fiscal year.

G. Central purchasing and warehousing of staple food and supplies is recommended.

H. A standard replacement policy for equipment should be approved by the school board.

I. Dishes, utensils, and equipment should be kept clean and hygienic by cafeteria workers. Floors, windows, and the like should be cleaned by custodians.

J. Periodic inspections by the county health department and other agencies should be welcomed.

K. Every effort should be made to decrease the length of lines and other delays at the cafeteria and snack bars.

Summary

The goal of health education is the gradual improvement of the health of society. In order to do this, health programs are set up in schools to improve health habits, provide knowledge about health, influence parents and other adults indirectly, and to ensure that each successive generation is healthier than its predecessor.

General and specific goals for health education should be established. School health programs should stress prophylaxis, rehabilitation, and preventive hygiene. Physical conditions of the school plant need constant inspection and improvement.

The health program curriculum should include sight conservation, speech therapy, remedial physical education, special education for the handicapped, sex education, and the dangers of drug abuse. Provisions must be made for pregnant teenagers. Procedures must be adopted for handling the problems of drug abuse and alcoholism in youth.

The school nurse is indispensable in the health program as is the classroom teacher who does most of the screening of health problems. Both teachers and administrators should set an example of health habits. Immunizations and inoculations for school enrollment must conform to the state's legal requirements. Health supplies should be widely available throughout the district, the health program being considered an integral part of the district-wide instructional picture. Health education should occur in both elementary and secondary schools, as well as in physical education classes.

Safety education, in addition to its part in driver education, should be taught in regular classes. Schools must comply with the federal Occupational Safety and Health Act. Principals are responsible for the safety of students and school personnel. Negligence must be avoided to prevent administrators being held liable for unsafe acts or conditions. The school itself should be safe, with fire prevention and safe wiring being first priority. Policies must be developed for the handling of disasters.

School nutritional programs have become an important part of the overall health program. Their objectives include not only the provision of good meals at low cost, but more particularly the creation and maintenance of healthy pupils capable of profiting optimally from the instruction offered. In the last twenty years, all levels of American government—federal, state, county, and local—have been involved in the problem of pupil nutrition. Food waste is a problem that can be handled best by education and counseling.

Most school cafeterias are self-supporting, although the director's salary is paid from school budget sources. Large districts employ an accounting clerk, in addition to cooks and other personnel. Centralized cooking is becoming more common.

The chapter lists desirable standards for organization, personnel, and operation of the nutrition program.

Administrative Problems

> **In Basket**

Problem 1

The principal of the Lakewood Elementary School has asked the school nurse, Mrs. Simpkins, to go into classrooms to give health instruction. The principal believes that this aspect of her services is as important as weighing and measuring pupils and giving first aid. However, several teachers have refused to let her talk to their pupils. They do not like the way she talks to students and have told her that they do not want her interfering with their class schedules, insisting they will teach health courses. Mrs. Simpkins has gone to the principal and explained that she is not permitted to give health talks to some of the classes.

What should the principal do?
How might the principal have arranged the health program to prevent this problem?

Problem 2

Danville High School is having a problem with school cafeteria usage. Fewer and fewer students are eating in the cafeteria, claiming that they do not like the food. The cafeteria is losing money, which loss perturbs the business manager. The district cafeteria director is also upset because the planned menus have been balanced and of good quality. The problem is aggravated because every noon students leave the school grounds in droves and patronize a nearby taco-and-hamburger lunch stand.

What can the principal do to alleviate the situation?
What can the cafeteria director do?
What can the business manager do?
What can the teachers do?

Problem 3

Reports have been circulating that an increasing number of students at Washington High School are using drugs. There have been rumors that marijuana is being smoked in the lavatories and that LSD is also being used. Teachers have reported to the principal that they suspect drugs are being stored in lockers and sold surreptitiously. A number of parents have complained about the rising drug problem; their children have been heard talking about it at home and in the neighborhood. Up to now, the principal had thought that the school had been relatively free of a drug problem.

What steps should the principal take to determine the extent of the drug problem?

When the problem has been analyzed, what steps should the principal take to alleviate it?

What can be done, or not done, legally?

Selected References

ANDERSON, C. L., and WILLIAM H. CRESWELL, JR. *School Health Practice.* 6th ed. St. Louis, Mo.: C. V. Mosby Co., 1976.

ARCO EDITORIAL BOARD. *Food Service Supervisor; School Lunch Manager.* New York: Arco Publishing Co., Inc., 1968.

BAKAN, RITA. "Malnutrition and Learning." *Phi Delta Kappan* 51 (June 1970).

BRION, HELEN H. "School Nurse to the Rescue." *Today's Education* 59 (November 1970).

CAMPBELL, ROALD F., JOHN E. CORBALLY, JR., and JOHN A. RAMSEYER. *Introduction to Educational Administration*, 3rd ed. Boston: Allyn and Bacon, Inc., 1966.

EDDY, REGINA. "Changing Trends in School Health Services." *Thrust for Education Leadership* 2 (February 1973).

DAHL, C. *Food and Menu Dictionary.* 2nd ed. Boston: Cahners Publishing Co., Inc., 1972.

ESHBACK, CHARLES E. *Food Service Trends.* Boston: Cahners Publishing Co., Inc., 1974.

HALE, ARLENE. *School Nurse.* New York: Ace Books, 1976.

KIME, ROBERT E., RICHARD G. SCHLAADT, and LEONARD E. TRITSCH. *Health Instruction, An Action Approach.* Englewood Cliffs, N.J.: Prentice-Hall, Inc., 1977.

LEHMANN, P. E. "Toward Junking Junk Foods." *Education Digest* 44 (January 1979):29–31.

LILLICROP, L. O. *Food and Beverage Service.* Boston: Herman Publishing Co., 1975.

MELBO, IRVING R., et al. *Report of the Survey of the Bear Valley Unified School District.* Los Angeles: University of Southern California, 1962.

NEMIR, ALMA, and WARREN E. SCHALLER. *School Health Program.* 4th ed. Philadephia, Pa.: W. B. Saunders Co., 1975.

President's Conference of American Fitness on Youth. *Fitness of American Youth.* A report to the President of the United States. Washington, D.C.: U. S. Government Printing Office, 1956.

STOOPS, EMERY, and RUSSELL E. JOHNSON. *Elementary School Administration.* New York: McGraw-Hill Books Co., 1967.

TURNER, C. E. *School Health and Health Education.* 7th ed. St. Louis, Mo.: C. V. Mosby Co., 1976.

PART SIX

Administration of the Instructional Program

CHAPTER FIFTEEN

Administering the Instructional Program

The only rationale that justifies the building and administering of schools in the first place is the need for students to have a place in which to acquire learning. The schools may be well-run, sufficiently financed, and efficiently staffed. They may boast enlightened public relations programs. They may even be civic centers in their spare time. But if their pupils learn little and emerge from them only quasi-literate, then the schools—and their administrators—have failed. School administration today is vastly more complicated than ever before, if only because it is asked to do so many more things. It follows that school administrators—and the term is used generically—require much more varied training and experience than in the past.

The Administrator's Role as Instructional Leader

In developing a role for administrators as leaders of the instructional program within a school district, there are three levels to be considered: (1) the superintendency, (2) district-level administrators to whom the superintendent delegates this responsibility (e.g., the assistant superintendent or director), and (3) the building principal. The term "adminis-

In collaboration with the authors, the sections on the administrator's role as instructional leader was prepared by Dr. Sarkis A. Takesian, Assistant Superintendent of Educational Services, Redondo Beach City Schools, Redondo, California; the sections on special education were prepared by Dr. Hugh Pendleton, Palos Verdes School District, California; and the sections on early childhood education were prepared by Dr. Othella Daniels, Administrator, Children's Center and Pre-School Education, Los Angeles Unified School District.

trator" hereafter will apply to any or all of these members of the administrative team.

The superintendent has many responsibilities in connection with the instructional program, all of which are continuously changing. The following list is an example of some of the instructional responsibilities for which the superintendent must furnish leadership:

1. Selecting high-caliber teachers, counselors, and administrators.
2. Providing for inservice training.
3. Budgeting for the instructional program, materials, supplies, and equipment.
4. Providing for supervision.
5. Encouraging continuous curriculum planning and development.
6. Promoting articulation between various school levels.
7. Encouraging vertical and horizontal communication.
8. Improving public relations for the instructional program.
9. Strengthening guidance services.
10. Providing for special instruction for atypical students.
11. Ensuring proper placement and promotion for students.
12. Providing health services, adult education, attendance, student-welfare, and library services to aid the instructional program.
13. Providing for educational research.
14. Providing evaluation of all educational programs and services to ensure that developing programs are moving in proper directions.

The Administrator and Instructional Accountability

The administrator must be alert to the growing demands of accountability. Management theory in the operation of schools allows administrators to justify and account for costs and student achievement. Popham[1] has long been an advocate of measurable instructional objectives.

Throughout the educational scene, numerous attempts have been made to adapt management theory to school district operation. In addition to the notion of general accountability to the taxpayer, federal grants to school districts have forced the development of systems analysis in public schools. School districts are becoming acquainted with terms such as educational goals, measurable objectives, alternative approaches, monitoring systems, and evaluation of results based on prestated objectives.

Administrators must recognize that all teachers have not accepted wholeheartedly the concept of accountability. Some feel that accountabil-

---

[1] W. James Popham et al. *Instructional Objectives*, pp. 32–52.

ity in education is an indictment and a threat since the initial idea came from individuals and groups with little or no experience in teaching: the conservative community, disadvantaged groups, and liberal spokespeople concerned with the value received from their tax money for education.[2] Teachers also feel threatened because accountability is assessed in terms of output, not input. Bernard McKenna states that "performance itself is important, no matter what its relation to learning outcomes," although better teaching "leads to better results with students." He explains further that teaching performance is an end in itself "whether or not it can be demonstrated to result in specific outcomes.[3] Teachers generally believe they should only be held accountable if:

1. They share in the development of goals and objectives.
2. There is adequate funding of the educational program.
3. Salaries are commensurate with other professions.
4. Teachers and the school board share jointly in the negotiation of comprehensive contracts and in the development of policies.
5. Clearly defined goals are developed cooperatively by teachers, school board, administrators, students, parents, and the community.
6. There is appropriate evaluation of all instructional goals.
7. The educational process is as highly valued as learning outcomes.
8. Students participate in decision making.
9. Teachers are assigned only to classes they are qualified to teach.
10. The teacher has time to carry out all teaching tasks and is free from nonteaching duties.
11. There are adequate facilities, resources, and support personnel.
12. The teacher has a voice in the selection, evaluation, and purchase of educational equipment and supplies.
13. There is strong administrative backing for the maintenance of discipline.
14. The teacher shares in evaluation and testing programs.[4]

In assessing needs and developing goals, a district should establish a schedule for the following steps:

1. The board of education commits itself to the program by official action.
2. Through community–school cooperation, the district's educational philosophy is developed.

---

[2] Joseph Stocker, "Accountability and the Classroom Teacher," *Today's Education*, p. 42.

[3] Bernard H. McKenna, "Teacher Evaluation: Some Implications," *Today's Education*, p. 56.

[4] Stocker, "Accountability," pp. 47–49.

3. Needs are assessed with staff and community working together as a team.
4. Decisions are made on goals and goal indicators, based on these needs.
5. The board of education approves and publishes the goals.
6. The goals are translated into workable plans or program objectives.
7. Priorities for action are developed.
8. Goals and objectives are implemented.
9. The degree of attainment of objectives is assessed.
10. Areas requiring change are identified.
11. Changes and alternatives are developed to shorten the distance between "what is" and "what ought to be."
12. Re-evaluation and re-assessment continue.

Instructional programs in the United States are characterized more by process than by purpose. Educational offerings are typically concerned with techniques, methodology, materials, and equipment to a much greater degree than they are with clarifying the direction education should take. Most textbooks, curriculum guides, instructional materials, whether commercially or district prepared, and other instructional support materials reveal almost complete concern with how-to-do-it instructions. Relatively few materials deal with the educational purpose or rationale to support their use. Lack of emphasis on purpose and direction often results in failure of innovative programs.

FORMULATION OF AN EDUCATIONAL PHILOSOPHY LEADING TO GOAL STRUCTURE. Most school districts have a statement of educational philosophy. However, most school district statements on their philosophy are so general that many differing interpretations can be drawn from the same document. As a result, not much attention is given to the existing philosophy. A systems approach model is extremely valuable for administrators as they can create a systematic delineation of philosophical expression. The translation of district philosophy through educational goals to specific instructional objectives reveals a common expression to school personnel and the community, and the expressed philosophy bears meaning at the instructional level.

NEEDS ASSESSMENT. Typically, educators formulate educational policy through elected board members with little community involvement, assuming knowledge of the needs and desires of the community. For this reason, many innovative programs have failed. It should occur to educators at some point in time that the instructional program must be in concert with the needs of the community.

Throughout the nation, legislatures are passing a rash of laws forcing school districts to assess the value structure of their communities in order to plan the best educational program to meet the needs of their particular districts. The relatively new term, "needs assessment," is a management tool that assists "in making more systematic and rational decisions."[5] An educational need is defined as "the situation which occurs when student performance is below that which is specified in a behavioral objective." It can only be identified by assessing "stated performance objectives to determine whether or not objectives are being accomplished."[6] ESEA Title III programs, for example, demand educational needs assessment that identifies local educational deficiencies. The assessment can be carried out by using measurable objectives developed by the district or the community. Community and students rank the objectives to be included in the school's curriculum. When the rankings are averaged, enlightened determinations of the curriculum preferences of the school's constituents can be made. Needs assessments can also be made in any area of the school district's responsibilities: finance, administration, personnel evaluation, transportation services, and so forth.

Needs can be assessed by questionnaires, surveys, discussions, and publications. Parents, businessmen, teachers, administrators, and students should be involved in helping the district identify needs. All economic, ethnic, and geographic segments of the community must be involved directly. James Popham[7] states that "many astute school people will see the use of objectives-based needs assessments as a reasonable vehicle for allowing appropriate groups to express their educational preferences."[8]

In the selection of assessment techniques, the following questions should be asked:

1. Are the objectives to be measured truly the important ones?
2. Is the technique of assessment the most efficient means of determining the achievement of the desired objectives?
3. What is the effect of the assessment technique on its user?
4. What is the effect of accountability practices on the student?[9]

GOAL SETTING. After the district's educational philosophy has been shaped and its special needs assessed, educational goals and sub-goals must

---

[5] Arthur N. Thayer, "Needs Assessment: Component I," *Thrust for Education Leadership*, p. 34.

[6] *Needs Assessment*, Booklet for developing evaluative skills (Tucson, Ariz.: Educational Innovators Press, 1970), p. 8.

[7] W. James Popham, "Objectives '72," *Phi Delta Kappan*, p. 434.

[8] Popham, "Objectives," p. 434.

[9] Arthur W. Combs, *Educational Accountability: Beyond Behavioral Objectives*, pp. 2–3.

be established in a cooperative venture with the community. This reduces the credibility gap that so often exists between community and school. The goal structure is born out of the district philosophy. Goals are broad statements but more definitive than the original philosophical framework. Goals are not usually measurable but are the most specific descriptions of the values expressed in the school's philosophy. Throughout the process of educational goal development, the administrator as instructional leader plays a vital role. The administrator's active participation in all facets of the project is important to subsequent instructional direction. It is this determination of purpose that provides meaning to the process of educating students.

PERFORMANCE OBJECTIVES. Following the agreement on goals, performance or behavioral objectives should be developed which indicate:

1. Who is going to perform the specified behavior.
2. The behavior that is expected to occur.
3. The situation in which the behavior will be observed.
4. The expected proficiency level.
5. The time needed to bring about the behavior.
6. The method by which the behavior is going to be measured.[10]

Performance objectives are difficult to write because of the many variables that must be considered. They must be defined for the level or for the person to which they apply and they should be specific.

EVALUATION. After classroom or performance objectives have been written and implemented, they must be evaluated to determine whether they are being met. In the past, school districts, schools, and educational programs have been evaluated quantitatively. Needs assessment focuses attention on quality. In the evaluation process, information must be collected and analyzed to make valid decisions on attainment levels. This process leads to accountability in education.

Needs assessment is a step-by-step development of an educational accountability model through the implementation of educational goals and objectives involving community, profession, and students. It is one of the major tasks of all school administrators as schools are forced to assess the value structure of their communities in order to plan the best program for the needs of their particular districts.

INSTRUCTIONAL LEADERSHIP. As a leader, the administrator needs all the human characteristics so necessary in person-to-person relationships to

---

[10] *Needs Assessment,* p. 8.

yield the most in educational productivity. Because of existing laws and district policies that empower administrators with authority, they are in a position to be a vital force in instructional leadership.

For too often the administrator's authority is used as a unilateral force that excludes the thinking of subordinates. This is not to say that the administrator has no responsibility for decision making. Rather, the organization of any sector of the school district can be such that decision making by the administrator materializes through the cooperative effort of the entire staff. The basic involvements of the total staff, including administrators, should contain the elements of confidence, trust, and respect.

The basic operation of the school enterprise lies in the classroom environment. All other activities and personnel are in support of this function. The administrators are the change agents who provide the necessary environment for change. Teachers also must be included in all the facets of instructional planning that involve them. Thus, administrative leadership involves perceiving the changing environment, possessing the know-how by which changes can be made, and using the strengths of all staff members in a humane manner for maximum effort. This combination of skills allows the administrator to function effectively as the instructional leader.

Administration of Co-curricular Activities

Co-curricular activities have become an integral part of the total educational program of a school and are considered by many to be as important as the academic curriculum. They require coordination and personnel with specialized interests and skills. They should complement the education of all students, rather than cater to a few. Co-curricular activities have grown rapidly in scope and importance and have been demonstrated to be of major educational value.

Role of Co-curricular Activities

Modern schools, especially secondary schools, devote a great deal of time and effort to the development of student activities outside regular classroom hours. This area of the school program has traditionally been referred to as "extracurricular activities," because it covered areas not included in the academic curriculum. The recent growth of the concept that all school-directed activities should be considered part of the curriculum has brought the term "extracurricular" into disuse, and has popularized an alternate term, "co-curricular." Whatever its name, the importance of this phase of the school program is not to be underestimated.

In terms of totality of experience, student activities are essential. Many times, they are scheduled as regular class periods with credit granted.

In analyzing the value of such experiences, it is important to justify them in terms of their contributions to the overall objectives of the school. Unless they produce a measurable contribution to the program as a whole, they should be eliminated as noneducational. Often certain activities proliferate with little thought given to their basic value. The school calendar often becomes overcrowded. A student demand is not sufficient for allowing an activity; it must also be demonstrated to have positive educational value.

CRITERIA. Within the framework of educational value, the following questions should be used to judge a school activity:

1. Is it conducive to democratic citizenship?
2. Does it meet a recognized need of a sufficient number of students?
3. Has it arisen in response to a permanent rather than a transient need?
4. Has it sprung from a broadly based demand, rather than from a small group?
5. Is the activity allowed to interfere in any way with the classroom program?
6. Are the students who benefit from the activity willing to spend enough time and energy to carry the main burden of its operation?

For the co-curricular program as a whole, the following opportunities should be provided for all students if the program is to be considered a success: opportunities in athletics and physical development; speech and drama; journalistic and creative writing; music; recreation; hobbies; social development; and academic and other interests not covered in a regular curriculum, clubs, and student government.

Broadness and scope characterize a good activity program. Often a tendency exists to sanction certain popular and glamorous activities, such as interscholastic athletics, and to play down areas of the co-curricular program such as language clubs and literary societies. Each is of equal educational importance if it meets a real need for a sufficient number of students.

EDUCATIONAL GOALS. Some educational goals that may be achieved by co-curricular participation are:

1. Leadership development.
2. Improvement of school morale.
3. Practice in democratic processes.

4. Social development.
5. Growth in student responsibility.

Elementary School Activities

The elementary school curriculum, normally less subject-centered than the secondary, provides many opportunities for extra activities. Some of these are: hobby clubs, science clubs, square dancing, chess and checkers, sports, and student government. They can be carried on before school, after school, during the noon hour or recess, and possibly during class time.

Student government can start in the classroom at any elementary grade level. First grade is not too early to explore the democratic process by electing monitors. Class officers can be elected, perhaps monthly, so that many pupils have the opportunity to develop leadership skills. A teacher should sponsor the student government and develop rules with students to determine the officers needed, the term of office, the method of conducting elections, and what official duties will be. The elected officers can meet with class representatives and plan assemblies. Since these pupils are young, they will need a great deal of help from the sponsor, not only in planning but in developing leadership.

At the elementary level, student government should be less structured and less formal than at the secondary level. There are some educators who believe that elementary schools should not have school-wide student government because the pupils do not have the maturity to carry out the program; these educators prefer student government to remain at the classroom level.

Elementary school music (band, orchestra, or chorus) is usually taught by music specialists or a musically talented teacher. It may be scheduled during class time, with pupils excused from their regular class for the special music period. Sometimes music practices are scheduled as an extra class period.

It is possible to organize intramural games, an extension of the physical education program, for out-of-school hours. Some schools schedule games during part of the noon hour, although most believe that free play is more important. Interschool competition takes place in some districts although it is less prevalent today. At the elementary level, participation in athletics should be less structured and less competitive than in secondary schools. The desire to win at all costs, intensive coaching, and the possibility of injury have no place in the elementary co-curricular program.

With the increasing amount of leisure time available in modern society, elementary school is not too early to begin preparation for it. Recognizing this, many elementary schools have organized "Lifetime Sport Activities" in their after-school programs. Examples of these activities are: archery, tennis, table tennis, bowling, badminton, swimming, and chess and checkers. Some do depend on the existence of proper facilities.

In summary, most elementary co-curricular activities usually can be left to individual teachers and conducted in the classroom, with a minimum of organizational regulations. Certain basic rules should be understood by all concerned, but these should relate to safety, conduct, and time schedules.

Secondary School Activities

A well-organized high school co-curricular program provides various types of activities to meet the needs and interests of many students. Typical activities are the following:

> Subject-matter clubs: art, foreign language, literary, and science.
> Assemblies.
> Athletics.
> Cheerleading and drill teams.
> Class organizations.
> Speech-arts groups: debating, dramatic, and oratorical clubs.
> Honor societies.
> Student newspapers and yearbooks.
> Musical organizations: band, orchestra, glee club.
> Dances and other social functions.
> Photography.
> Student government.
> Hobbies.

Extra-class activities often grow unchecked and complicate scheduling and supervision problems.

The principal, in consultation with the school staff and student leadership, must determine what activities should be permitted and how they are to be scheduled. Faculty members must be assigned as coaches, directors, supervisors, or sponsors. These assignments are critical since the success of any activity depends upon its leadership, which should be enthusiastic and supportive. Teachers should encourage each activity group to be self-motivating.[11]

---

[11] Muriel Karlin and Regina Berger, *The Effective Student Activities Program*, p. 189.

Many teachers are needed to furnish leadership for co-curricular activities. In the past, they either volunteered or were assigned to sponsor or supervise a club or activity. Such assignments are now part of the teacher organization's annually negotiated package. The package includes the extent of the extra duties and the amount of extra pay to be received. Written, agreed-upon policies help to minimize personnel problems with extra assignments. Those who do take on co-curricular responsibilities find that it is rewarding to see the closer understanding that develops between students and teachers when they work together in student activities.

A great and continuing effort should be made to spread the benefits of the co-curricular program to as large a percentage of the student body as possible. Otherwise, a relatively small percentage of student leaders find themselves involved in a disproportionate number of activities, and a large minority or a majority of their classmates never participate.

THE INTRAMURAL ATHLETIC PROGRAM. Lifetime, carry-over sports grow out of the intramural program, not from interscholastic games. "Intramural" refers to activities that take place *within* the school. The intramural athletic program provides the best opportunity for any or all students to participate in sports, and at less expense than interscholastic sports. Every type of sport or game can be scheduled. The advantages afforded by the intramural program are:

1. Less expense is involved than in interscholastic sports.
2. Uniforms are not needed, although some type of identification should be worn.
3. Participation is open to everyone, not just those who qualify for the school team.
4. The intramural program is less commercialized.
5. Although rivalry is high, there is less emphasis on winning and more on participation.
6. There is more variety of sports than in interscholastic sports.

Activities are usually scheduled for after-school hours and sometimes on weekends. Sports may be team or individual ones, such as handball, tennis, or squash.

Teams can be organized by classes, homerooms, clubs, or created without regard to organizational identity. The intramural program might prove a good place to initiate coeducational competition.

A faculty director should be responsible for working with student leadership to plan the intramural program. The director should:

1. Draw up schedules.
2. Arrange for the school areas and equipment to be used.
3. Establish agreement on rules.

4. Assign umpires and referees.
5. Arrange for reporting results and determining winners.
6. Arrange for winner recognition.
7. Work with the student council to see that these functions are carried out.

Intramural activities are particularly important in junior high schools. The emphasis should be on a broad scope of activities without the competitiveness of interschool rivalry. Athletic skills and sportsmanship can be developed by more students, helping them to prepare for high school.

REQUIREMENTS FOR CO-CURRICULAR PARTICIPATION.   There is a difference of opinion on the requirements for participating in co-curricular activities. Some believe that students with poor behavior or poor grades should be prevented from taking part in co-curricular activities, particularly student government or athletics. Coaches often exclude from playing those who violate team rules. Students are often not permitted to run for a school office unless they demonstrate "good behavior" or are "good students." There are those who believe a student should "earn" the right to participate; others believe that this deprives students of the right to do something in which they might achieve success. The achievement of success in a co-curricular activity might be the incentive a student needs to become a better student or citizen. Some schools are reducing or removing academic and behavior restrictions on participation in co-curricular activities.

STUDENT GOVERNMENT IN SECONDARY SCHOOLS.   Student government provides an excellent opportunity for secondary school students to develop leadership and to learn how democracy functions. Students, with the guidance of teachers, should cooperatively develop policies that establish and control student government and are approved by the principal. The council should operate under a constitution and bylaws, with committees to carry out the various functions. Students should be given as much responsibility as they can handle for conducting elections, running meetings, and planning activities. The council should be composed of the elected and appointed student body officers, class representatives, and possibly club representatives. Each class should elect its own officers, hold its own meetings, and schedule its own activities.

Some of the activities that the student government can plan are: assemblies, festivals, exhibits, hobby displays, play days, special-event days, event of the year, weekend trips, and interschool exchange of officers. In many of these activities, parents and the community can be invited to help or to participate—a good public relations gesture.

The council can perform many services for the school, such as: planning and conducting assemblies, supervising school areas, serving as visitor guide, preventing vandalism, planning social and recreational activities, and helping with the intramural program. It can be instrumental in promoting school spirit. In some schools, the student council forms a leadership class for credit and meets under the direction of a teacher–sponsor.

Organization and Supervision

The expansion of the services rendered America by its public schools is reflected in the area of co-curricular activities. As the extra-class program grows from year to year in complexity and size, the administrator must of necessity devote more time and attention to its organization and supervision. The administrator's task will be made easier by adhering to principles such as the following:

1. Activities should be developed by the cooperative planning of students, teachers, and building administrators.
2. Sponsors should be selected carefully and should have enough interest and experience to make each activity a successful one.
3. Co-curricular activities should be worthwhile and have administrative approval before commencing. (Some student organizations have challenged administrative authority over their activities.)
4. Counseling and guidance will help students plan a co-curricular program to meet their needs and interests.
5. A master calendar should be kept on which all co-curricular activities are posted in order to avoid conflicts.

Although co-curricular activities should be under the autonomous direction of the school principal, the school district should exercise some control. The activities should be supervised by the assistant superintendent for instruction because of their educational values. All school activities and clubs should have their funds under the direct supervision of the school district business office in order to minimize the dangers of strict student control of finances. Reports on student activity income, expenditures, and balances should be given periodically to the board of education and should be audited annually. The district personnel administrator should also be involved. Because of the multiplicity of co-curricular activities, especially in the secondary schools, this staff person must see that newly employed teachers can fill any co-curricular vacancies.

It is customarily left up to the building principal to handle the coordination and direction of co-curricular assignments at the individual school level. The principal may delegate this task to an assistant principal or a faculty chairman, but larger schools should have a director of co-curricular activities. This arrangement has the advantage of centralizing the responsibility and helping to assure a standardization of organization and control to promote ease of operation. The director of activities should be responsible for:

1. Approving activities.
2. Scheduling and coordination.
3. Assigning faculty sponsors.
4. Supervision.
5. Scheduling transportation as needed.
6. Arranging for credit.
7. Inservice for sponsors.
8. Finances.
9. Adherence to the constitution, bylaws, and policies of the student government.

If athletics is a major program, the director of athletics supervises sports activities in cooperation with the director of activities. Coordination is often difficult and the principal may have to advise.

Schools that collect funds and charge admission for activities should assign a clerk to collect money, prepare financial reports, and bank funds, subject to the approval of the person assigned to supervise all co-curricular activities. The clerk should work directly with the district business office.

Administering Special Education Programs

Students differ from each other in a variety of ways—physically, socially, intellectually, and emotionally. When differences exist to a degree such that the student cannot profit fully from regular school instructional offerings, special education programs should be developed. The term "exceptional children" is used to describe pupils whose educational needs are very different from those of the majority of schoolchildren. Special education programs require specially trained teachers who have an interest in and an empathy for handicapped students. Others on the school staff should have an understanding of the special education programs so that students can be integrated into as many regular school activities as possible.

Administration of Special Education Programs

It is necessary for the administrator to be aware of the needs and means of providing a program for the education and development of the exceptional child. School administrators have a responsibility to provide leadership and apply in practice the following principles:

1. The American promise of equality of opportunity extends to all students within the borders of this country, whatever their gifts, their capacity, or their handicaps.
2. The school is responsible for the "normalization" of the student's school experiences to the greatest possible extent. Thus, placement in a regular, ongoing program is preferable to placement in a special class; and placement in a special class is preferred to leaving the child at home.
3. The school must interpret the exceptional students, their needs, and their abilities to form an attitude favorable to their acceptance and development in the community.
4. Every resource of the community must be utilized to aid in maintaining the exceptional students' family life and in furnishing guidance and encouragement to their parents.
5. The school should strive to educate and train the exceptional student, utilizing strengths of learning rather than concentrating on disabilities.
6. Teachers of exceptional students must possess the personality and develop or acquire the understanding, knowledge, skill, and special preparation that will enable them to inspire, motivate, and teach the arts of living and enjoying life.

Special Education Terminology

The term "special education" is difficult to define because its meaning has changed and is still redefining itself. Currently used, the term identifies a program of education or training provided for children or young adults with exceptional educational needs that cannot be adequately met in regular school programs.

The term "exceptional child" essentially is used for a student who deviates physically, intellectually, socially, or emotionally from what is considered to be normal growth and development and who cannot satisfactorily benefit from a regular school program. Special or supplementary class services and instruction are required by such a student.

Within the field of special education, many terms have rather flexible definitions. The practicing administrator may work with very precise legal definitions required by state funding regulations, and these often vary from state to state. This situation is especially true in relation to the intellectually exceptional child. The most common groups of intellectually exceptional children for whom school administrators are frequently responsible at the building level are the gifted and the mentally retarded child.

The term "gifted child" encompasses students characterized by high mental ability. Defined statistically, these students perform beyond two standard deviations from the mean in the typical normal distribution of intelligence on an IQ test. In order to qualify for gifted programs, many states and school districts require that the student's intellect measure above a 130 IQ on a standardized, individual mental abilities test. Frequently, requirements state that the gifted child be performing within the top 2 percent of the normal pupil population. Some schools use other performance criteria that take into consideration creative abilities and talents for admission to gifted programs.

Organized programs for the gifted have developed slowly and have been limited in support and scope because of the frequent failure on the part of the public to identify these students as exceptional.

At the other end of the spectrum of intellectual exceptionality are the "mentally handicapped" or "mentally retarded" students. Again, working definitions and legal definitions may vary from state to state and from school district to district. Statistically, these students perform below two standard deviations from the mean in the typical normal distribution, with IQs below approximately 70 on individually administered mental abilities tests. Frequently, for class grouping purposes a further division is made; students whose intelligence quotient falls below 55 or 60 are classed as *trainable*. The lower limits of this group may be 30 and occasionally lower, depending on local policy. In contrast, the "educable" student is one with an intelligence quotient between 50 or 60 and 70 plus. Many school systems are recognizing that difficulties exist in accurate and appropriate identification of intellectually exceptional students by a single criterion. This recognition especially applies to the evaluation and placement of children from different cultural or social backgrounds.

A second major grouping consists of "physically handicapped" students. Within this large category are a number of separate and distinct groups of children, each of which requires special educational assistance. Included in this category are children with orthopedic, vision, hearing, speech, and neurological impairments.

The third group of exceptionalities requiring special educational assistance includes those students who are emotionally, educationally, or socially handicapped. Frequently, such youngsters function fairly well in regular class settings as their handicap is not as visible. Educational programs for this group are less available than for students with more visible handicaps.

This term, "educationally handicapped," is a broad one that operationally identifies the students described above. Agreement on a common term to describe these learning handicaps has not yet been reached.

Finally, the individual student who has more than one type of exceptionality is frequently referred to as "multi-handicapped." In some cases, such a student may have more than two conditions, each disabling.

Placement of Students

The determination of the most appropriate placement for the exceptional child requires teamwork. Utilizing the expertise of the student's teacher, a school psychologist, a physician or school nurse, plus the principal and director of special education, an admissions and discharge committee should be formed to consider placement for the special student. The committee will make use of all available information compiled by its members concerning the strengths and handicaps of the student in selecting the most appropriate placement. The committee will need to consider placement alternatives in light of available options. Few exceptional students precisely fit the legal classifications that are used for funding the programs.

Inherent in the placement of a pupil in a special program is the danger of labeling, classifying, and categorizing a handicapped child or youth. Frequently, the label may further handicap the student by becoming a self-fulfilling prophecy that limits the expectations of the student, parents, and teachers.

There appears to be a current developing trend for removing labels from handicapped students in the school system. Dean suggests that there is a movement to stress the student's ability rather than disability.[12] Most handicapped pupils have the same needs, desires, and expectations as do so-called normal children.

The Principal's Role in Special Education

The success of special education programs depends upon many people, especially the school administrator and the administrative staff. The school principal has a vital role in the functioning of any special education program. Because exceptional students differ from their normal peers, special educational programs and services should differ from those for regular pupils. The school administrator responsible for special education programs should be well prepared for the task. A broad knowledge and understanding of the principles of child growth and development are essential, as well as a full knowledge of the laws concerning special

---

[12] Martin J. Dean, "Some Major Issues in Special Education in Large Cities," *Thrust for Education Leadership*, p. 32.

education. The principal should be aware of the services of public and private agencies in assisting the handicapped. Since parents of exceptional children have many concerns and special responsibilities, the principal should be skilled in counseling and assisting them and should be able to utilize information from professional literature and research concerning the instruction of the handicapped.

ORGANIZATION OF SPECIAL EDUCATION PROGRAMS. The building administrator's special responsibilities vary according to the way classes for the handicapped are organized within the school system. In large school systems, classes for the severely handicapped are located in schools designed solely for special education. The more frequent pattern of special education is to locate one or two special classes at an existing elementary or secondary school. In rural areas and in small school districts where there are insufficient numbers of students to warrant specialized programs, classes are frequently maintained cooperatively by several districts or by the intermediate school unit. In such a situation, handicapped pupils are bused to the school maintaining the special class or classes.

For the most severely handicapped youngsters, residential schools are maintained by the state. The current trend is toward phasing out state institutions and returning children to their local communities, although the need will likely continue for such state-maintained residential school programs.

SUPERVISION OF STUDENT MEDICATION. In recent years, there has been increasing use of medication to assist youngsters in learning and behavior problems. Frequently, stimulant medication is prescribed in the treatment of specific behavioral disturbances. In certain situations, these medications have the paradoxical effect of calming and assisting students in controlling their behavioral impulses and in aiding them to gain the ability to attend to a learning task for a long period of time.

The physician prescribing medication is frequently assisted by information on the student's success in school. Once the medication is begun, information on the student's performance in school will be needed by the physician. Teachers can assist by relaying their observations to the parent or directly to the physician.

Each school administrator has the responsibility of identifying students under medication, of establishing safety rules for the administration of such drugs during school time, and of setting school policy on teacher communication with parents regarding observations of pupils under medication.

THE PRINCIPAL'S ROLE IN "INTEGRATION" AND "MAINSTREAMING." A frequently stated objective of special education programs is to assist students to develop, to the greatest potential, their academic, physical, and social abilities, in order to function as satisfactorily as possible as independent adults. Special education classes serving youngsters by legally defined categories are able to concentrate on development and remediation of academic and physical skills. In so doing, the task of developing social skills with normal students is often difficult to accomplish. The building administrator can be the key person in seeing that social developmental experiences are provided for special students.

"Integration" refers to the provision for regular scheduling of special pupils or classes in all-school instructional activities, where success can be achieved. Many opportunities for integration exist when one or several special classes are located at the campus of a regular school. The degree of integration accomplished depends upon the emphasis given to it by the school's principal and the special class teachers.

The term "mainstreaming" is applied to the practice of placing in regular classes special students who are ready to cope with a regular class. Again, the principal is the key person in the success of mainstreaming the special youngster. Through leadership by example, other staff members and the community will treat handicapped youngsters with understanding. The key criterion for mainstreaming is the ability of the handicapped student to achieve success in a regular class.

The benefits of integration and mainstreaming apply both to special students and to their classmates. The development of appreciation of the handicapped as individuals is dependent to a large degree upon the care taken in class placement, the skill of the teachers, and the support of the school's administrators.

The movement toward mainstreaming handicapped students rather than isolating them in special classes is rapid. The fact has been recognized that these students must eventually take their places in the real world and work and socialize with so-called "normal" people. The more they are integrated with regular classes and participate in the school's activities, even for part of the school day, the better they will be able to cope with life when they leave school. Teachers who are assigned these pupils need special assistance in understanding and teaching them as well as being given information regarding the handicap. There may also be a need for special equipment and facilities in the regular classroom and on the playground. As mainstreaming becomes more prevalent, the need for special education classes and teachers will be diminished.

Assisting Special Education Teachers

Teachers of special classes often work more independently than the regular class teacher. Instruction must be individualized according to the special needs of the pupil. Special instructional materials must be located or created by the teacher. Transportation to and from school needs frequent teacher supervision. The readiness of students for integration into regular programs is determined by the special class teacher. Counseling and conferring with children and their parents is an ongoing need.

DIRECTOR OF SPECIAL EDUCATION.   Depending on the size of the school system and the organization of special programs, several individuals will be the major sources of help for the special education teacher. The director or coordinator of special education should be a member of the district office staff, assigned to direct the program of special education. Generally, the person in this position is selected on the basis of experience and knowledge in special education as well as the ability to administrate. The director of special education should be able to see the global picture of all aspects of the school system's special programs and must keep informed of the newest developments in all phases of the system's program for exceptional students. Provision of teaching materials, facilities, staffing, placement of pupils, and inservice training for all special teachers is handled by the director.

SUPERVISORS OF SPECIAL EDUCATION.   The role of the supervisor in special education is primarily that of a consultant, contributing to the improvement of instruction and the growth of teachers. The supervisor is available to give assistance to beginning teachers, particularly to those who have special education assignments without complete training in this field. Most teachers of special education appreciate a frequent visit from someone who is interested, understands their problems, and provides continual reassurance.

In large school systems with sizable special education enrollments, one or several supervisors of special classes and programs are employed. The supervisor also assists school principals in the management of many extra administrative responsibilities which are always present in special education programs.

RESPONSIBILITIES OF THE BUILDING PRINCIPAL.   With few exceptions, the building principal should be the one to render daily assistance to the special teacher. It is the principal's responsibility to see that the special teacher receives materials and services to meet the needs of special pupils. If the special education program is to be a success, the principal should fulfill a dual role as instructional leader and administrator. The principal should plan inservice experiences that will result in the teacher's professional growth, such as expediting the special teacher's observation of teaching demonstrations, attendance at conferences, and visitation to observe other special schools and classrooms.

School systems throughout the nation are recognizing the need of exceptional students for a number of services to compensate for their disabilities, including: extra guidance and counseling, regular psychometric evaluation, physical and speech therapy, and small pupil-to-staff ratios. To give effective assistance to the special education teacher, the principal must be able to organize such services so that they are readily available when the need arises.

Financing Special Education Programs

The education of exceptional students requires added services, smaller classes, specially trained teachers, and often, specially built classrooms. Additional supplies and equipment are needed, some of which are quite different from those required in regular classrooms. For these reasons, school systems find that educating a special youngster is more expensive than educating an average student. This situation has retarded the full development of special education programs.

The concept of support of public education at the state level has been universally accepted in the United States; the expansion of state financing to include the increased costs of educating exceptional students has been much more recent, however. State school systems have attempted to encourage the creation of classes for the exceptional child by what is known as "the excess cost principle." The local district continues its responsibility for educating all children, but the state reimburses expenses incurred for special class pupils.

Several methods are used by states to reimburse school districts for excess costs. Some reimburse according to actual pupil attendance, others by classroom units, and still others by numbers of teachers and special personnel. Extra responsibilities for the school administrator result from receiving such reimbursement. Included are reports of programs, pupils, and teaching activities which must be filed regularly with the state department of education.

To a limited degree both state and federal governments have supported and promoted research in special education by providing funds for (1) local pilot projects, (2) studies leading to the improvement of services, and (3) studies on the prevention and correction of disabling conditions. It is the responsibility of the local school administrator to keep abreast of new research. As effective new methods and programs are found, the administrator should seek the necessary support to make the appropriate ones available.

Costs for special education on a per-pupil basis appear high until the possible benefits to the exceptional child are considered. Often the individual handicapped students, their families, and the community reap benefits far in excess of the costs as individuals become self-sufficient and self-supporting. State legislators have encouraged state support of special education in order to reduce costs to welfare departments. Keeping some handicapped children at home and providing the supplements they need in school is not only best for the child and family, but markedly less expensive to the state.

Administering Early Childhood Education Programs

"Early childhood education" is a term increasingly utilized by schools and parent groups, despite a great deal of confusion concerning its clear definition. James L. Hymes characterizes early childhood as a period of high dependency when children themselves feel young, small, and like a child. Usually, it is described as that period from birth to the onset of preadolescence around age eight or nine.[13]

With the advent of Head Start in 1965 came a new focus on early childhood education programs involving nursery schools, day care centers, and parent participation programs, many of which had been in existence for decades.

Hundreds of early childhood education programs are in existence under the auspices of diverse funding agencies and groups. It is hoped that those that are described in this chapter will provide insight into the profession of early childhood education.

Goals for Early Childhood Education

Early childhood education programs that are more than merely custodial in purpose embrace goals such as the following:

1. Enhancing each child's physical, psychosocial, and cognitive development by:
   a. Facilitating the child's development of communication skills.
   b. Promoting the development of a sense of self-worth and well-being within each child.
   c. Encouraging the child to experience a varied social environment.

2. Involving parents in the education process by:
   a. Enumerating ways parents can help their children.
   b. Suggesting alternative ways of rearing children and coping with problems.
   c. Reassuring parents that they can understand and facilitate the physical, psychosocial, and cognitive development of their children.

---

[13] James L. Hymes, Jr., *Early Childhood Education*, p. 5.

    d. Forming parent advisory committees as vehicles for parent participation in planning, development, operation, and evaluation of programs.

    e. Assisting parents in the continuation of their self-development and education.

    f. Providing opportunities for parents to develop appropriate ways and means of improving existing institutions.

3. Demonstrating methods for developing similar programs by:

    a. Setting up model programs.

    b. Training and utilizing volunteer personnel.

    c. Developing effective articulation of early childhood education programs with other educational and community agencies.[14]

Administration of
Early Childhood Education Programs

A discussion of the administration of early childhood education programs must of necessity be general in nature and broad in scope.

LEGAL REQUIREMENTS. Most states have a licensing law administered by the state health, welfare, or educational agency. The purpose of such a law is to ensure the health and safety of children. Covered in its requirements are standards relating to the type and location of building used, the amount of space required for indoor and outdoor activities, the provision of a safe staff–pupil ratio, training and certification of teachers, nutritious meals, and health and safety regulations.

SITES AND FACILITIES. Local zoning ordinances often have an impact upon the location of facilities. It is advantageous to consider selecting sites and facilities near homes of the children served unless transportation is provided. Locating facilities on streets where public transportation is available is another important consideration. All facilities must be in compliance with applicable state and local laws, regulations, and ordinances, including those pertaining to zoning, fire protection and fire safety, building safety, and health.

FUNDING SOURCES. Sources of financial support for early childhood education programs vary. Some programs operate with one funding source and others have many. It is important to determine which sources of funding are available and how each may be used to assure long-term financing. Some programs are supported totally from tuition or fees.

    Other programs receive some financial support from private donors through United Way, Community Chest, United Givers Fund, or individual

---

[14] California State Department of Education, *Guidelines for Compensatory Pre-school Educational Programs* (Sacramento, Ca.: State Printing Office, 1972), pp. 1–3.

donations. Programs that receive community support serve more families who would otherwise be unable to pay the full cost of the program.

Local, state, and federal funds are sometimes available to finance early childhood education programs. Usually when such funds are granted, low-income families receive priority for enrolling their children.

ORGANIZATIONAL STRUCTURE. Early childhood education programs operating within school districts are directed by the board of education through administrative structure approved by the board. Some programs operate under the supervision of a project director for special programs in cooperation with a parent advisory council whose members participate in the planning, organization, and evaluation of the program. Other programs operated by school districts are part of the elementary school and are under the administrative direction of the elementary school principal. The teacher of the early childhood education class is a member of the school staff as are any assigned paraprofessional aides. The parent advisory council for the school should be involved with the early childhood class as well, but the final authority should reside in the board of education.

A community program is usually directed by a group of citizens interested in early childhood education. The community expects the board to provide early childhood programs for families and children who need them.

STAFFING PRACTICES. Staff selection and development are important elements in a good early childhood education program. The staff creates the environment in which learning takes place and in which each child's needs are identified and, hopefully, fulfilled.

Staff members should have such personal attributes as dedication, sensitivity, warmth, good health, emotional stability and maturity, patience, and the ability to develop trusting relationships with children and adults. In addition, they should have the knowledge, training, and experience to assume the responsibilities of their positions. The teacher, the aide, the nurse, or any other staff member must observe numerous regulations, policies, and procedures.

Employment conditions have a direct relationship to staff morale, stability, and effectiveness. Effective personnel practices such as the following protect the staff from unnecessary pressures.

1. Written personnel policies.
2. Up-to-date job descriptions and staff organizational chart.
3. Objective hiring practices.
4. Fair and equitable wages and salaries.
5. Continuing staff development.
6. Objective supervision.

7. Regular, periodic staff evaluation.
8. Fair resignation and termination procedures.[15]

HEALTH AND MEDICAL SERVICES. Early childhood education programs must provide for the health of the children enrolled. Practices and procedures must be established to detect illness and physical impairment; to protect children from communicable diseases; to assist parents in arranging for the elimination of correctable impairments; to emphasize positive health practices and preventative medicine; and to provide for immediate medical attention when accidents occur.

As a pre-enrollment requirement, good health programs provide for an assessment of the child's health status which includes:

Report by a licensed physician of a medical history and a physical examination of the child certifying the child's freedom from communicable disease.
Description of abnormal conditions.
Instructions for staff and a record of immunization against the common childhood diseases.
Report of a dental examination.
Routine blood studies and a urinalysis.

Desirable components in the health curriculum are:

Screening tests to identify hearing, sight, and motor coordination.
A continual immunization program.
Daily health inspections.
Nutritionally balanced meals and snacks.
Nutrition education as a part of the curriculum.
Isolation of ill children.
Dental treatment.
Procedure for coping with accidents and injuries.
Medical insurance plans.

Each staff member should receive copies of health and safety policies and procedures, be thoroughly familiar with all responsibilities, and also have first-aid training.

PARENT INVOLVEMENT. Parent involvement begins with parent education, usually conducted within the framework of a parents' group affiliated with the early childhood education program. As parents are encouraged, they will increase their participation in the planning, organization, and evaluation of the program.

---

[15] U.S. Department of Health, Education and Welfare, Office of Child Development, *Day Care Administration*, pp. 19–23.

Teachers, supervisors, and administrators should examine every aspect of their work to create opportunities for parent involvement and to incorporate parents' views and recommendations into their plans and practices.

When genuine parent involvement develops, children benefit from the reinforcement at home and school of new, exciting concepts of early childhood education.[16]

Early Childhood Education Research and Evaluation

The evaluation of early childhood education programs appears to be in a state of transition. A prevalent tendency to examine and evaluate the process, rather than the product, is beginning to disappear as advanced management and systems technologies become better understood.

An approach to program evaluation gaining recognition and acceptance is one of assessing and measuring results. This approach looks at the program and attempts to determine its effectiveness and its efficiency. Effectiveness is assessed both quantitatively and qualitatively by determining whether or not the program achieved the results it committed itself to achieve within a given period of time. The evaluation determines whether the program achieved few, many, or all of its objectives for the period.

Hundreds of studies and research projects regarding early childhood and the implications for later instruction and schooling have proliferated in the last decade. Shane comments that research is "beginning to form a mosaic of data suggesting that these years of early childhood are more critical than any other stage of human development."[17]

It is not possible in this chapter to do more than mention some of the research that attempts to evaluate early childhood schooling. The interested reader should make a more thorough review of the many studies before making a definite decision as to the effectiveness of any preschool educational program.

RESEARCH SHOWING POSITIVE EFFECTS OF EARLY SCHOOLING. The following paragraphs reveal some of the positive effects of early schooling which have been reported in the research.

Hodges and Spicker reviewed selected research in an attempt to determine how successful preschool intervention programs were in amelio-

---

[16] U.S. Department of Health, Education and Welfare, *Day Care Administration*, pp. 103–5.

[17] Harold G. Shane, "The Renaissance of Early Childhood Education," in R. H. Anderson and H. G. Shane, *As the Twig Is Bent: Readings in Early Childhood Education*, p. 6.

rating deficits reported for severely disadvantaged preschoolers. They concluded that intellectual functioning can be substantially raised; that language development occurred more readily during preschool years; that fine motor proficiency can be improved; and that "intervention programs especially designed to remedy cognitive deficits during the preschool years and to prevent progressive school failures during the later school years have been relatively effective to date."[18]

Studies by Deutsch[19] and Kirk[20] have shown that preschool experiences raised intelligence test scores and led to gains in social maturity.

Robinson and Robinson draw three tentative conclusions from a study of research which assessed the effects of preschool intervention on culturally deprived children: (1) During the first year, there are relatively large gains on intelligence test scores. (2) The spurt is not maintained in the second year. (3) Control groups tend to gain intelligence points when exposed to stimulating school experiences, reducing the difference between experimental and control subjects.[21]

RESEARCH CLAIMING NEGATIVE ASPECTS OF EARLY SCHOOLING. Moore, Moon, and Moore have made an exhaustive study of research on early schooling. Their findings indicate that schooling initiated as early as the age of four or three may have a negative effect and cause possible damage to young children. They conclude that "research and comparisons of school entry ages clearly point to the need (1) to delay any type of educational program that proposes or permits sustained high cortical effort, or strain on the visual or auditory systems, before the child is seven or eight, and for (2) a warm, continuous mother or mother-surrogate relationship (without a succession of different people) until the child is at least seven or eight."[22] They also note that evidence clearly favors the home rather than the school as an early childhood environment.

Stanley reports that careful research by several people has not shown permanent elevation of IQs of disadvantaged children, even after great expenditures of time and effort.[23] Although large gains were common in

---

[18] Walter L. Hodges and Howard H. Spicker, "The Effects of Preschool Experiences on Culturally Deprived Children" in Willard W. Hartup and Nancy L. Smothergill (eds.) *The Young Child, Reviews of Research*, pp. 275–87.

[19] Martin Deutsch, "The Disadvantaged Child and the Learning Process," in A. H. Passow (ed.) *Education in Depressed Areas*, pp. 163–81.

[20] S. A. Kirk, *Early Education of the Mentally Retarded*, pp. 175–202.

[21] Halbert B. Robinson and Nancy M. Robinson, "The Problem of Timing in Pre-School Education," in Robert D. Hess and Roberta Meyer Bear (eds.) *Early Education: Current Theory, Research, and Practice*, pp. 42–44.

[22] Raymond S. Moore, Robert D. Moon, and Dennis R. Moore, "The California Report: Early Schooling for All?" *Phi Delta Kappan*, pp. 620–21.

[23] Julian C. Stanley, "Introduction and Critique," in Julian C. Stanley (ed.) *Compensatory Education for Children, Ages 2 to 8, Recent Studies of Educational Intervention: Proceedings*, pp. 7–8.

the first year, they did not persist through the primary grades. He believes that there are limits to the effectiveness of current preschool intervention programs.

TENTATIVENESS OF RESEARCH ON EARLY CHILDHOOD EDUCATION. Research is inconclusive on the effectiveness of early childhood education. One must be critical of interpreting the beneficial effects of achievement as a result of preschool intervention until the basic processes underlying achievement are uncovered. Achievement may occur, for example, without any substantive change in the process.

Since most research has focused on specific behavioral areas, assessment of creative adaptability is still needed. It needs to be more coordinated and its efforts and findings shared. Research and evaluation should not overlook or diminish human values. Despite problems, research does provide suggestions for improved programs and raises questions for further research.

Summary

School administration has changed and is more complicated than in the past and requires more varied training and experience. The three administrative levels are: the superintendency, district-level administrators, and building principals. All of these have instructional responsibilities. Attempts have been made to measure student achievement and evaluate the accountability of teachers but teachers have not all accepted this concept.

The district should establish an educational philosophy that translates into attainable educational goals and objectives. "Needs assessment" is a management tool to assist in making systematic and rational decisions. Performance or behavioral objectives should be developed and evaluated. The administrator needs the human characteristics that help to develop confidence, trust, and respect.

Co-curricular activities are an important part of the total educational program of a school and should meet set criteria for appropriateness in a school situation, and ideally should provide opportunities for every student.

Elementary schools, although they need to offer far fewer co-curricular experiences than secondary schools, should provide opportunities such as bands, hobby clubs, and science groups. Lifetime sport activities can be commenced in elementary schools. The typical secondary school, on the other hand, offers everything from football to photography, necessitating a highly structured co-curricular program. The intramural program provides the best arrangement for promoting broad student participation. Requirements for co-curricular participation should not be so stringent that they prevent some students from taking part. Student government provides an outlet for students to develop leadership and to experience the democratic process at work. Co-curricular activities should be organized so that they meet the needs of as many students as possible without interfering with their academic program. The principal should have the final power to approve or veto any activity. Many teachers are needed to furnish leadership.

Successful administration of special education requires skill in providing programs for all types of exceptionality, placing pupils advantageously, using all resources, counseling pupils, parents, and teachers, interpreting the programs, and providing special materials and facilities.

A willingness to take the extra time and make the extra effort for students with special needs is a minimum requisite for the administrator responsible for special education. Increasing knowledge, skills, and interest on the part of citizens and legislators in recent years have resulted in accelerating support for special education.

This chapter defines many terms used in special education programs. Students with special needs are being recognized as possessing the needs of normal youngsters, in addition to a need for special assistance to overcome and to compensate for their handicaps. These students can frequently meet with success if they can be "integrated" into many of the school's instructional activities or "mainstreamed" into regular classes.

The principal has a key role in organizing the school's special education program, supervising student medication, placing exceptional students, assisting teachers, and cooperating with parents and community.

Special education programs are expensive since they require specially trained teachers, special equipment and supplies, and added facilities and services.

Early childhood education applies to that period in a child's life spanning birth to about eight or nine. Goals for early childhood education programs focus upon enhancing total development, facilitating communication skills, promoting the development of self-worth, encouraging social experiences, and involving parents in the education process.

The administration of early childhood education focuses upon the significant areas of: legal requirements, sites and facilities, funding sources, organizational structure, staffing practices, health and medical services, parent involvement, and evaluation. Each area serves to delineate important steps that should be taken in order to administer effectively any early childhood education program. Tentative research is reviewed, showing both positive and negative effects of early childhood education.

Administrative Problems

Problem 1

The Mar Vista Consolidated School District has an average daily attendance of 15,000. It has been a relatively stable, conservative, middle-class area for years with little turnover in school personnel. About five years ago, the community began to change. Minority families have been moving in at an increasing rate each year. They have not adopted the mores of the community. The formerly strong Parent Teacher Associations at various schools are having problems and bickering is common.

Discipline, tardiness, truancy, and vandalism are becoming problems for the district. The highly academic curriculum is no longer relevant and does not meet the needs of a changing student population. Bi-lingualism has also created teaching and learning problems. Personnel turnover of teachers, administrators, and classified personnel is upsetting the stability of the school district. The superintendent and Board of Education seem to spend most of their time "putting out fires." They have been unable to cope with the rapidity of the changes that are taking place.

If you were the superintendent, what management techniques would you use to cope with the changes?

Problem 2

You are the principal of a high school with a full interschool athletic program for boys. Girls have only competed in tennis and volleyball. The parents, encouraged by a local women's group, are demanding that girls have an athletic program equal to that of the boys, and including at least basketball, baseball, and track. Furthermore, some girls are asking to try out for the boys' teams. Your school district has no policy regarding this.

How would you proceed?
What would you tell the parents?
How would you handle the girls' request?

Problem 3

The Saugus Unified School District has identified enough educable mentally retarded students to form another class. These students are in three different elementary schools so the decision has been made to place the class at the Lincoln Elementary School, which is centrally located, and to transport students by school buses.

What should the principal do to prepare the staff and pupils for the addition of this class?
How should the principal integrate them into the school program?
What difficulties might arise and how can they be remedied?

Problem 4

The rural Fort Tejon School District has kindergarten classes in each of its six elementary schools, but no preschool program. Many of the families are Mexican-American who speak little or no English in the home. Children entering school have bi-lingual problems, complicating their education. Because of low incomes, many mothers work in the fields. The Board of Education is concerned and has heard that several kinds of preschool programs are available which could help prepare children for formal schooling. The superintendent has asked the assistant superintendent for educational services to investigate preschool programs and prepare a recommendation for the Board.

How should the assistant superintendent proceed?
What recommendation should the assistant superintendent make?
What control should the school district exercise over the preschool program if it is approved?

Selected References

BISSELL, JOAN. *Implementation of Planned Variation in Head Start.* Washington, D.C.: National Institute of Child Health and Human Development, April 1971.

COMBS, ARTHUR W. *Educational Accountability: Beyond Behavioral Objectives.* Washington, D.C.: Association for Supervision and Curriculum Development, 1972.

CRUICKSHANK, WILLIAM M. *The Teacher of Brain-Injured Children.* Syracuse, N.Y.: Syracuse University Press, 1968.

DEAN, MARTIN J. "Some Major Issues in Special Education in Large Cities." *Thrust for Education Leadership* 2 (May 1973).

DEUTSCH, MARTIN. "The Disadvantaged Child and the Learning Process." In A. H. Passow (ed.) *Education in Depressed Areas.* New York: Teachers College, Columbia University, 1963.

ELLIOT, DONALD L., and THOMAS J. SERGIOVANNI. *Educational and Organizational Leadership in Elementary Schools.* Englewood Cliffs, N.J.: Prentice-Hall, Inc., 1975.

EVANS, ELLIS. *Contemporary Influences in Early Childhood Education.* New York: Holt, Rinehart and Winston, 1971.

GERHARD, MURIEL. *Effective Teaching Strategies with the Behavioral Outcomes Approach.* West Nyack, N.Y.: Parker Publishing Co., 1971.

GLICK, JOSEPH. "Some Problems in the Evaluation of Pre-School Intervention Programs." In Robert D. Hess and Roberta Meyer Bear (eds.) *Early Education: Current Theory, Research, and Practice.* Chicago: Social Science Research Council, 1968.

HACK, WALTER G., and LUVERNE L. CUNNINGHAM. *Educational Administration: The Developing Decades.* Berkeley, Ca.: McCutchan Publishing Corporation, 1977.

HANSON, MARK E. *Educational Administration and Organizational Behavior.* Boston: Allyn and Bacon, Inc., 1978.

HARRIS, BEN M. *Supervisory Behavior in Education.* 2nd ed. Englewood Cliffs, N.J.: Prentice-Hall, Inc., 1975.

HODGES, WALTER L., and HOWARD H. SPICKER. "The Effects of Preschool Experiences on Culturally Deprived Children." In Willard W. Hartup and Nancy I. Smothergill (eds.) *The Young Child, Reviews of Research.* Washington, D.C.: National Association for the Education of Young Children, 1970.

HORN, GUNNAR. "Extracurricular Activities: Right or Privilege?" *Today's Education* 61 (May 1972).

HOY, WAYNE K., and CECIL G. MISKEL. *Educational Administration: Theory, Research and Practice.* New York: Random House, Inc., 1978.

HURN, CHRISTOPHER J. "The Prospects for Liberal Education: A Sociological Perspective." *Phi Delta Kappan* 60 (May 1979):630–33.

HYMES, JAMES L., JR. *Early Childhood Education.* Washington, D.C.: National Association for the Education of Young Children, 1968.

JONES, REGINALD L. (ed.) *New Directions in Special Education.* Boston: Allyn and Bacon, Inc., 1970.

KARLIN, MURIEL, and REGINA BERGER. *The Effective Student Activities Program.* West Nyack, N.Y.: Parker Publishing Co., 1971.

KIRK, S. A. *Early Education of the Mentally Retarded.* Urbana, Ill.: University of Illinois Press, 1958.

MAYER, ROCHELLE S. "A Comparative Analysis of Preschool Curriculum." In R. H. Anderson and H. G. Shane (eds.) *As the Twig Is Bent: Readings in Early Childhood Education.* Boston: Houghton Mifflin Co., 1971.

MAYS, MAXINE. "No Stars Please, for Teaching the Retarded." *Today's Education* 61 (March 1972).

MCKENNA, BERNARD H. "Teacher Evaluation: Some Implications." *Today's Education* 62 (February 1973).

MOORE, RAYMOND S., ROBERT D. MOON, and DENNIS R. MOORE. "The California Report: Early Schooling for All?" *Phi Delta Kappan* 53 (June 1972).

MUNDAY, LEO A. "Changing Test Scores: Basic Skills Development in 1977 Compared with 1970." *Phi Delta Kappan* 60 (May 1979):670–71.

MURPHY, BETTY A. "You Can't Mainstream Them All." *NAESP Convention Reporter.* Detroit: National Association of Elementary School Principals, April 1973.

POPHAM, W. JAMES. *Instructional Objectives.* American Educational Research Monograph. Chicago: Rand McNally, 1969.

————. "Objectives '72." *Phi Delta Kappan* 53 (March 1972).

ROBINSON, HALBERT B., and NANCY M. ROBINSON. "The Problem of Timing in Pre-School Education." In Robert D. Hess and Roberta Meyer Bear (eds.) *Early Education: Current Theory, Research, and Practice.* Chicago: Social Science Research Council, 1968.

SERGIOVANNI, THOMAS, and ROBERT J. STARRATT. *Supervision: Human Perspectives.* 2nd ed. New York: McGraw-Hill Book Co., 1979.

SHANE, HAROLD G. "The Renaissance of Early Childhood Education." In R. H. Anderson and H. G. Shane (eds.) *As the Twig Is Bent: Readings in Early Childhood Education.* Boston: Houghton Mifflin Co., 1971.

STANLEY, JULIAN C. "Introduction and Critique." In Julian C. Stanley (ed.) *Compensatory Education for Children, Ages 2 to 8, Recent Studies of Educational Intervention: Proceedings.* 2nd ed. Hyman Blumberg Symposium on Research in Early Childhood Education. Baltimore, Md.: Johns Hopkins University Press, 1973.

STOCKER, JOSEPH. "Accountability and the Classroom Teacher." *Today's Education* 60 (March 1971).

THAYER, ARTHUR N. "Needs Assessment: Component I." *Thrust for Education Leadership* 1 (December–January 1972).

U.S. DEPARTMENT OF HEALTH, EDUCATION, AND WELFARE. *Minimal Brain Dysfunction in Children.* Washington, D.C.: Monograph No. 3, National Institute of Neurological Diseases and Blindness, 1966.

————. *Day Care Administration.* Washington, D.C.: U.S. Government Printing Office, 1971.

WADSWORTH, BARRY. Piaget's Theory of Cognitive Development. New York: David McKay, 1971.

WOODRING, PAUL. "Vocational Education: How Much, What Kind, and When?" *Phi Delta Kappan* 60 (May 1979): 644–46.

PART SEVEN

School Personnel Administration

CHAPTER SIXTEEN

Administering Pupil Personnel Services

Pupil personnel services encompass noninstructional activities that affect the school lives of students. They supplement regular classroom instruction and assist the teacher in understanding and helping students. Services such as the following should be provided by school districts: guidance and counseling, health, psychological, pupil welfare, testing, social work, exceptional student or special education, clinical, child study or case study, and speech, hearing, and visual therapy. Large districts are able to provide more of these services than small districts.

Organization of Pupil Personnel Services

Most school districts provide pupil personnel services. However, they often have been uncoordinated or distributed among several departments or individual schools. A recent trend toward centralizing these services in a single pupil personnel department, headed by an administrator responsible for their coordination, is recommended organization.

Teachers for too long have been expected to help the atypical student alone. Two or three such students take an inordinate amount of the teacher's time, depriving the rest of the class of needed instruction. If teachers want extra help, they might have to contact several different district departments. But when the district has a centralized pupil personnel division, a single referral can provide the assistance of several specialists working together to solve a problem.

Figure 16–1 shows a type of organization for a pupil personnel department appropriate in a large school district. It is recommended that the

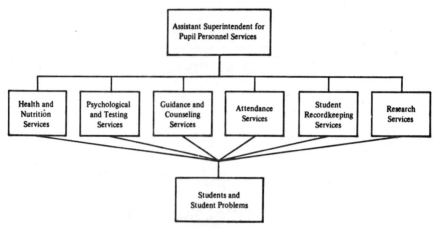

*FIGURE 16–1.   Organization of a Pupil Personnel Department
in a Large District.*

department be administered by an assistant superintendent responsible solely to the superintendent. Various department functions should be considered services and should be headed up by lower level administrators or directors.[1]

Whatever arrangement is developed, it is necessary to have one district administrator, possibly the superintendent in a very small district, responsible for all pupil personnel services. No plan will work unless clearly understood policies and administrative procedures are developed. These should explain lines of communication and levels of responsibility. Counselors and other specialists may be assigned to a specific school, work on a roving basis, or be scheduled from the central office. A principal is considered responsible for all activities that go on in the school.

HEAD OF PUPIL PERSONNEL SERVICES.   If districts are large enough, the administrator in charge of pupil personnel services should be an assistant superintendent. This is both a line and a staff position. It is a line position in organization because it involves making decisions and being responsible for specialists who work out of the office; the administrator is directly responsible to the superintendent. It is also a staff position in that it involves working cooperatively with teachers and school administrators and sharing decision making with others. The head of pupil personnel services also should work closely with the head of the instructional services in a staff relationship.

The pupil personnel administrator has many responsibilities and functions aimed at the well-being of students. Some of these are:

---

[1] Emery Stoops (ed.) *Guidance Services: Organization and Administration.*

1. Maintaining student records: student progress, test data, family histories, psychological studies, educational histories, etc.
2. Dispensing information to colleges and universities, other school districts, welfare agencies, governmental agencies, military services, employment offices, courts, and corrective institutions.
3. Supervising and coordinating the work of specialists.
4. Administering the testing program.
5. Supervising health services.
6. Supervising psychological services.
7. Coordinating guidance and counseling services.
8. Administering procedures for enrolling and transferring students and establishing boundaries for attendance areas.
9. Supervising attendance.
10. Administering assignments to special classes, such as: mentally retarded, physically handicapped, emotionally handicapped, and continuation classes.
11. Conducting research and compiling research reports.
12. Advising school administrators, teachers, and parents.[2]

QUALIFICATIONS OF THE PUPIL PERSONNEL ADMINISTRATOR. The pupil personnel administrator's office is responsible for aiding students in their personal, social, and academic development and for "providing a sound basis on which to build learning skills and to absorb and retain facts and understandings."[3]

Pupil personnel administrators should be, first of all, administrators rather than specialists in psychology, counseling, or guidance. They should be well grounded in classroom procedures and understand the learning obstacles facing many students; possess the personality to relate successfully with teachers, administrators, and parents; have a knowledge of community social, welfare, and health agencies and the ability to work cooperatively with them. Since administrators will often be called upon to speak before community organizations, they should have the ability to speak effectively and to interpret the school's program.

The ability to coordinate is one of the most important qualifications of the pupil personnel administrator. The administrator must have the respect of specialists and skill in human relations. The American Association of School Administrators has stated that "the coordinating function involves not only bringing into appropriate relationships the people who comprise the pupil personnel departments, but also, and more importantly,

---

[2] Edwin A. Fensch and Robert E. Wilson, *The Superintendency Team*, pp. 184–200.

[3] Fensch and Wilson, *The Superintendency Team*, p. 184.

fostering relationships between these pupil service workers and other personnel in the school system."[4]

Another major qualification for the pupil personnel administrator is the ability to evaluate programs, services, and personnel in the pupil personnel department. Administrators should be able to change their course of action, revise programs, or eliminate inefficient personnel. The value of pupil personnel services is determined when the administrator demonstrates that the education of students with problems or handicaps is being improved. The emphasis should be on prevention rather than remediation; this is dependent upon identifying problems before they become acute.

The pupil personnel administrator should study areas such as psychology, methods of evaluating pupil progress, the dynamics of behavior, educational statistics, theory of measurement, research design, education of exceptional students, education of handicapped students, and guidance and counseling techniques. Courses should be taken in school law, school finance, administration, supervision, and public relations. Actual experience in some area of pupil personnel such as teaching the handicapped, guidance, counseling, or testing is desirable. It should be reiterated, however, that the ability to administer, plan, make decisions, and coordinate is the most important qualification.

Enrollment of Students

Prior to actual enrollment, it is necessary for the school district to estimate the number of students it will be educating. This is often difficult to do and there is no method that is completely accurate. The office responsible for attendance accounting should also be responsible for maintaining the census.

SCHOOL CENSUS. The school census developed historically as a basis for pupil accounting and in the early days of public schools was used as a basis for appropriating state monies. An annual census is essential. Long-range estimates are always helpful but are essential in districts with increasing or declining patterns of growth. Age limits for census coverage range from birth to twenty-one years, although the most common ranges are from six to twenty-one years, six to eighteen years, and five to fifteen years.

A commonly used method of analyzing census results is the grade progression method which projects ahead the number of students in each grade. Other types of census techniques are: the periodic, the city directory, and the registration type, which are all maintained on an annual basis

---
[4] American Association of School Administrators, *Profiles of the Administrative Team*, pp. 105–6.

These methods are administratively expensive to operate and inadequate statistically because they use only annually reported information. They are being abandoned in many localities in favor of a more accurate accounting, the continuous census. A continuous census is claimed to be up-to-date throughout the year and from year to year.

The school census has a number of functions:

1. It determines future enrollment by grade level and school attendance areas.
2. It determines the amount of materials and supplies.
3. It provides information for establishing necessary transportation services.
4. It helps to determine educational services, courses, and programs.
5. It determines personnel needs by grade level, subject matter, or school.
6. It analyzes the characteristics of students to determine the need for special classes or programs.
7. It helps in enforcing compulsory attendance laws.
8. It analyzes the mobility of the school population.
9. It helps to determine school plant use and new construction needs.[5]

Unless there is some discussion or cooperation with parents at the time of the census, it may not be possible to determine the number of students with special problems or needs.

ENROLLMENT PROCEDURES. Confusion at the beginning of each school year will be minimized if the district has an effective preregistration program. This can be accomplished before the school year ends and during summer vacation. Presently enrolled elementary pupils can be assigned to their grade and room for the following school year. Secondary students can make out their new programs and consult with their counselors to work out conflicts.

Dates can be set for the pre-enrollment of new students with wide publicity by the local press and radio. Parents should be encouraged to accompany their children when they enroll; this helps establish a good working relationship with school personnel, and parents can help verify required information for younger children.

State or local laws establish entrance age and method of verification for kindergarten or first grade. Health information is often required, such as immunization records for smallpox, poliomyelitis, and measles.

---

[5] Adapted from Roald F. Campbell, John E. Corbally, Jr., and John A. Ramseyer, *Introduction to Educational Administration*, Third Edition, p. 109; Calvin Grieder and William E. Rosenstengel, *Public School Administration*, p. 332; and Edgar L. Morphet, Roe L. Johns, and Theodore L. Reller, *Educational Administration*, pp. 372–73.

Students entering from other schools should present a transfer, report card, or some evidence of grade placement. After enrollment, the school should request the cumulative record from the other school. Students should be assigned to classrooms on a tentative basis until official verification of their status is confirmed. Counselors should help secondary students work out their new class schedules.

ORIENTATION OF NEW STUDENTS.   All new students should be properly oriented to their new surroundings to put them at ease. Orientation should include:

1. A tour of the buildings and grounds, preferably conducted by another student.
2. Explanation of school rules and regulations.
3. Introduction to the office staff, school nurse, school administrators, and counselors.
4. Explanation of the school's class schedules, lunch hour, and bus schedule.
5. What to do if sick or injured at school.
6. How and where to report after an absence.
7. Explanation of the school's co-curricular program such as clubs, student government, and athletic program.
8. Explanation of the academic expectancy and grading system of the school.
9. Whom to see with questions or problems.

WORKING WITH PARENTS.   It is helpful to all parties to invite parents of students enrolling in a public school for the first time to an orientation meeting conducted by the principal. An explanation should be made of what is expected of their children; what the school's rules and regulations are; what parents can do to help their child; and how to verify absences. A Parent Teacher Association officer can explain how their organization functions and invite the new parents to join.

A *Parent's Handbook* provides one of the most successful methods of communicating with parents and in carrying out the administration of pupil personnel. Parents and school personnel should cooperate in developing the handbook. The school has information that it believes parents need to know and parents have questions to which they need answers. Since oral communication is often forgotten, a Parent's Handbook provides a written reference for parents to keep on hand. A few of the topics that should be covered are: the school calendar, including holidays; daily time schedules; cafeteria information; lunch permits; absences; bicycle permits; permission to leave school; playground hours and rules; youth groups; rights accorded by the Family Rights and Privacy Act of August 21, 1974; grading policy; discipline; and student accident insurance.

Administering Attendance and Child Welfare

One of the important functions of the pupil personnel department is that of administering child welfare and attendance. Absences, whatever the reason, must be investigated because they affect the welfare and educational progress of a student. Students who need to work should be granted work permits.

A PHILOSOPHY OF ATTENDANCE. Historically, compulsory education is almost as old as this country. Thirty-five years after the first permanent English settlement was established in Jamestown, Virginia, the Massachusetts Colony in 1642 enacted the first compulsory education law in America.

The first type of attendance officer found in public schools was an officer of the law. The sole job of this person was to obtain reports of pupils who were absent an undue amount of time and then proceed to bring these students back to school.

A major problem of the school is to convince parents and students that the attitudes toward the school attendance "truant officer" have changed; that attendance is not only compliance with the law *per se*, but an opportunity, a privilege, and a responsibility. The main purpose, then, of a child welfare and attendance supervisor should be to *help* the pupil, rather than to *control* the pupil.

The child welfare and attendance supervisor is concerned with the reasons behind pupil nonattendance. An actual count of heads is a mechanical process; discovering why the student is not in school and attempting to remove the causes are the real challenges. "Problem children" should be considered as "children with problems." There must be an attempt to understand students in relation to their home, their community, and the school program. A modern teacher accepts students as they are and attempts to develop a program to fit their needs. The child welfare and attendance person must also attempt to find out where students are with respect to family, environment, peers, school life, and, if possible, themselves. To effect a return to a normal school life for a young person with problems may involve extensive use of resources within the school and community and a considerable cost in effort, time, and money. This cost is justifiable as a means of developing productive members of society.

A philosophy of attendance and child welfare must often be tempered in practice. When confronted with parents who feel that compulsory education is an invasion of parental rights or with recalcitrant teenagers who are immune to any form of guidance, the administrator may find that recourse to laws governing attendance becomes the only alternative.

A BASIC CONCEPT IN CHILD WELFARE AND ATTENDANCE. A child welfare and attendance worker should consider differences in responses by students. Many school problems arise because of the difficulty of recognizing individual pupil needs. Individual differences are many and varied, and because teachers and parents are so close to a situation, they often fail to observe the developing problems. An attendance worker is farther away from the situation, not so involved in the daily care of the child, and in a better position to give the student individual attention. The superintendent should choose an attendance worker who can give valuable help to school officials and parents in solving individual problems.

QUALIFICATIONS FOR CHILD WELFARE AND ATTENDANCE WORKERS. Changing aims in public education require corresponding adjustments in the type of preparation essential to meet new attitudes and new conditions. Few activities in the public school system reflect changed attitudes more clearly than the functions of the school attendance official. This type of service is no longer directed chiefly toward law enforcement; rather, it approaches its responsibility from the standpoint of rendering the greatest assistance for developing children. It is essential, therefore, that a broader and more highly integrated type of professional preparation be provided for those selecting this type of school service.

TRAINING.   Professional training requirements currently stress social service. A bachelor's degree is required and usually one or more years of teaching experience. Typical courses required in professional training for child welfare workers include:

1. Counseling Procedures and Techniques.
2. Mental Hygiene.
3. Psychology of Exceptional Children.
4. Home–School Communication.
5. Use of Community Resources.
6. Abnormal Psychology.
7. Case Study and Case Conference Techniques.
8. Supervised Field Experience.
9. Application of the Laws Relating to Children and Child Welfare.

The credentials for pupil personnel services should cover positions in counseling, child welfare and attendance, psychology, and psychometry.

PERSONAL TRAITS.   The personal traits of a child welfare worker should be the prime consideration in selection since this individual is often the only point of contact between the home and the school. It is necessary that the representative of the school possess a wholesome, well-balanced personality. This person's most effective tools in bringing about cooperation between home and school will be tact, sympathy, and human understanding. The child welfare worker must possess a strength of character that will not allow sympathy for a difficult family situation to interfere with each child's receiving, as a minimum, a basic elementary and secondary school education.

Cooperation between home and school is possible only after mutual confidence is established. With the majority of parents this cooperation and confidence is a natural feeling. But some parents need help and guidance in interpreting what the school and society require of them and their children. When treated with sincerity, a maturity of judgment regarding family problems, and trustworthiness, parents will often respond to help.

Appearance and grooming of the child welfare counselor plays a significant part in home contacts since initial contacts often create lasting impressions. This impression must be favorable in order to put the parent or child in a receptive mood to accept the guidance offered.

HOME CALLS.   Home calls are initiated principally as a result of absence from school. The majority of calls are made in a routine effort to verify absence when the school has been unable to contact the home or parents. Most home calls are received by parents with appreciation for the concern shown by the schools. The art of home–school communication is on trial when the parent is one who questions compulsory education and has probably instilled in his or her children a certain contempt for school. All school personnel as a team want this child to return to school, but to return with a willingness to learn. The principal, teachers, and attendance counselor must impress the parent with a sincere desire to help. They should try to develop some plan of action, acceptable to both the parents and the school, which plan should be recorded and left with the parent and child. Parents often have questions that need to be checked with other sources, giving the attendance worker a chance to return to the home on a positive basis. If time permits, in many cases a second call builds up a good relationship, and can be justified in terms of preventative therapy.

Every home contact should be recorded. If a home call is requested on a specific form in the school district, there should be space for recording the disposition or specific recommendations. These data are especially important if the particular case develops into a case conference or juvenile court problem.

RELATIONSHIPS WITHIN THE DISTRICT.   Most attendance personnel feel the need for coordination and an effective line of communication with all teachers and administrators. When working with individual schools, they should carry an attitude of service. Coordination between several school agencies is essential. The attendance and health services have many mutual problems and need help from each other; they should be familiar with each other's procedures and records. Guidance and attendance have overlapping features. Since the attendance, health, and guidance services share many problems, some districts are combining these services in the same department. This appears to be a logical organization of "co-related" services. Through amalgamation, the superintendent can secure greater efficiency and reduce overlapping or conflicting services.

ATTENDANCE RECORDS.   Attendance records should be kept as simple as possible. They should account for attendance, absences (excused, unexcused, and truancy) and dropouts. All administrators realize that attendance recordkeeping has a definite place in a modern public school. It is the legal record of compulsory attendance as well as the basis in many states for apportionment of funds. It has always been a chore for teachers, seemingly an extra duty to the prime purpose of classroom instruction.

Centralized attendance is a method whereby a systematic office procedure maintains the individual teacher's attendance records in a central school file. There are several advantages credited to the use of a central attendance program. It relieves the teacher of register keeping. It provides a more accurate record system, in that it is under the supervision of the principal and a clerk whose job concerns attendance. Pupils in elementary grades are given an opportunity to become familiar with reporting to a central attendance office, so that when they matriculate to junior and senior high schools they are not confused. Centralized attendance provides a closer correlation with the school nurse in checking all readmittances; and a better method of recording all verification of illness and absence is provided. There is an opportunity for the child welfare and attendance division to determine more quickly cases in which constructive educational help at home could and should be given. Monthly attendance reports are more easily made and permanent records are more efficiently filed for future reference.

Another method is machine accounting, which provides a refinement of centralized attendance by using electronic business machines, not only for attendance, but for pupil records. This development, being used in many parts of the country, is still on a pilot basis; but the resultant saving of clerical and teacher time indicates its potential.

Many schools also use machines for registration, class cards, transcripts, teachers' class lists, monthly attendance, student programs, and pupil report cards. The main advantage of this system is the ability to use basic information in almost any form desired for lists, reports, summaries, totals, and statistical study. An example of a monthly attendance card is shown in Figure 16–2.

While holding to the basic premise that regular attendance benefits the child, society also recognizes that in practice we must occasionally make exceptions. There are those who cannot benefit from school experience and those who refuse to benefit from school. State laws allow employable preference for certain age groups experiencing problems in school. Certain standards have been established governing their attendance at school.

In states that use the average daily attendance system for apportionment of state funds, the determination of the extent or type of absence can

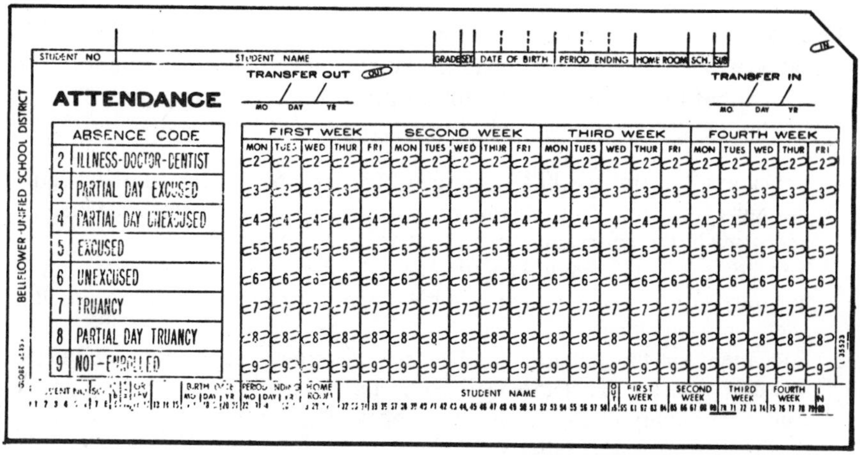

FIGURE 16–2. Example of a Pupil Monthly Attendance Card. Courtesy of the Bellflower Unified School District.

become a major financial problem. Legal and illegal, lawful and unlawful are the usual expressions used by states to determine the type of absence and generally cover similar situations. Illness, medical appointments, and quarantines are the usual legal absences. Illegal absences are those in which the parent and the child do not fully sense the responsibility society has placed on them through compulsory attendance. This includes parental excuses such as entertaining relatives, running errands, attending shows, and refusing to attend school. Some states have a middle ground—an absence which is illegal for appointment purposes, but excused (religious holidays, bereavement, a trip with parents, or a court appearance). All absences should be verified whether they are excused or unexcused. Verifications of absence in the form of notes from parents do not necessarily validate the excuse, but are simply a recognition of absence. The attendance laws of the state decide if the absence is considered excused or unexcused. The administrator is concerned a little more deeply with the reasons for nonattendance than with its legality. If it is possible to identify the reasons for nonattendance and isolate its cause, the administrator is much better prepared to suggest a constructive course. Several types of absenteeism are described in the following paragraphs.

TRUANCY. This term is usually applied to willful or continued unexcused absence. Truancy often leads to other types of delinquent behavior. When it becomes repetitive, the offender is defined as an "habitual truant."

Administrators must accept the challenge of probing for the cause and seeking a solution to the problem of truancy, whether the cause be found in the home, the school, or the young people themselves. Most administrators are aware that the school itself is probably the greatest single cause. Most truancy cases have multiple causes that complicate the solution. The solution can often be effected through a program change, a school change, or possibly even a curriculum change. Home, school, and community resources should be utilized to the fullest prior to a legal complaint. The key to solving truancy is education:

> Education for the teacher, counselor, and school official so they can recognize the truancy problem, react to it swiftly and sympathetically, and provide the counseling to prevent it from happening again.
> Education for the community, to spur individuals and organizations into first recognizing the problem and then sponsoring programs to cure it and its related effects.
> Education for the parents, so they can determine their responsibilities and deal with the problem effectively in the home.
> And most important of all, education for the students, for it is they—now and in later life—who suffer.[6]

Few truancy cases that reach the juvenile courts without a serious attempt for adjustment by the school are justified.

DROPOUTS.   Of general concern to administrators is the increasing number of dropouts from school as students reach the upper limits of the compulsory attendance age. Many reasons have been given for students dropping out. Some of them are school related: lack of reading ability, poor marks, too old for grade, dislike for teachers and subjects, use of drugs, and lack of interest in school activities. Reasons related to the home are: broken homes, working mothers, lack of money, deceased parents, and lack of parental interest and guidance. Many of these problems occur in affluent areas as well as in low socioeconomic areas. In ghetto areas, gangs may put pressure on students to drop out in order to participate in gang activities. The need to work full- or part-time to earn money can cause a student to leave school. In many cases, it is probable that more than one cause contributes to dropping out.

Schools are partially to blame for dropouts because they have not met the needs of all students. Too often the curriculum is geared to something other than actual student needs or abilities, rather than being flexible and relevant. Potential dropouts need sincere and understanding teachers. They may need extra help to improve their reading and writing skills and to improve their study habits. The school counselor can provide the guidance to help these students with their school program and personal problems as well as cooperate with their teachers in getting these students on the right track. Work-study programs can be arranged for to help a student remain in school.

Any request to drop out should receive a holding effort from the school through counseling, and if this is not successful, a considerate exit

---

[6] Gordon T. Morris, "The Truant," *Today's Education* 61, January 1972, p. 42.

interview. The interview should attempt to guide the student to a job location, possible night or continuation classes to further a job possibility, and should be a pleasant departure.

UNEXCUSED ABSENCE. Many unexcused absences are due to a lack of understanding or apathy on the part of parents. In some cases they are not aware of the specific laws that govern attendance. It is a specific duty of the attendance and welfare worker to relay and explain this information to the home. In this process tact is paramount; a firm approach should be presented without alienating the parent. Where the parent continuously treats the problem of unexcused absence lightly, legal recourse should be considered.

EXCUSED ABSENCE. Excused absence usually involves illness or medical appointments. The attendance personnel should assist the school health personnel in an attempt to reduce the extent of these absences. Health education and adequate health habits should receive considerable emphasis, especially with elementary students. A pupil's home environment is revealed by a home call which often provides a chance to reinforce health education.

The overall reduction of absences, both excused and unexcused, demands coordinated and expanded effort from the fields of attendance, counseling and guidance, health, social services, and school administrative personnel. Only through cooperation with these services can school personnel uncover the causes and develop a satisfying program to reduce excessive and unwarranted absences.

WORK PERMITS AND EMPLOYMENT OF MINORS. The control of child labor is the responsibility of the states; the issuance of work permits is usually delegated to the attendance divisions of the public schools. State laws governing the employment of minors tend to be quite specific. Federal laws, specifically the Fair Labor Standards Act and the Walsh–Healy Public Contracts Act, control child labor involved in interstate commerce and government contract work.

Such laws developed from the exploitation of child labor by both employers and parents. This situation existed in rural farming areas as well as in industrialized urban areas, and was a serious social problem until the passage of both state and federal laws. By the year 1909, every state had passed legislation governing child labor in one or more occupations. The scope of this control proved to be so limited in many states as to be almost negligible, especially where the will to enforce it was lacking.

Child labor legislation in the various states established standards for: (1) minimum age, (2) hazardous occupations, (3) maximum daily and weekly hours, and (4) employment or age certificates for minors. The employment certificates are of four types: those furnished to children who desire to work before or after school and on Saturdays; permits to work at specified occupations while school is not in session; permits to work during regular school hours under certain conditions, as age or type of occupation, often with the provision that between certain ages the child attends an extension school; and evidence of age or completion of required minimum education.

Individuals in the school district who are responsible for the issuance and control of work permits must become thoroughly familiar with state and federal laws and regulations of child labor. Before issuing a work permit, they must ascertain that no child will become a source of cheap labor, endanger physical or mental health, or be denied desired educational opportunities. The superintendent usually delegates this function to the director of child welfare and attendance.

Guidance Services

Guidance services include: (1) getting information about the individual, (2) making available infomation about opportunities, (3) counseling as a means of matching interests and abilities with opportunities, (4) making readjustments, and (5) follow-up with needed redirection. These services should be coordinated by the district pupil personnel administrator. Tests must be given, case studies made, conferences held, the help of community agencies enlisted, and school counselors assisted.

COUNSELING AND GUIDANCE FUNCTIONS.   Counseling and guidance functions are school-based but should have coordination and assistance from the district pupil personnel office. They involve much more than merely advising students about their class schedule or rearranging classes. Counselors must be trained in psychology, sociology, test administration, and test interpretation.

Counseling and guidance received great impetus as a result of Dr. James Conant's reports on the American high school and junior high school, in which he emphasized the need for counselors. The federal government recognized the importance of counseling by appropriating millions of dollars under the National Defense Education Act of 1958 for the purpose of improving guidance, counseling, and testing in American secondary schools.

Counseling helps students adjust to their environment, their home and family, and their peers. Vocational and educational interests and possibilities can be investigated. Program planning and class scheduling are guidance functions. Too often, however, this task becomes the major function of counselors.

Although most counseling is handled on an individual basis, most counselors have too many students assigned to do individual counseling effectively. Group counseling, although less common, permits counselors to spread their services and conserve time. In a peer group, students may feel more comfortable as they share their questions, fears, and problems.

Historically, counseling has been mostly evident in high schools. Later, it was extended to junior high schools. Junior high students in their early adolescence have many personal and social adjustments to make. Junior high counselors have a unique opportunity to counsel and guide students as they attempt to understand themselves and their interpersonal relationships. Students can be helped to participate in their educational planning and in looking toward future vocational choices.

Most elementary schools have self-contained classrooms with one teacher responsible for the students all day. These teachers know their children and their problems intimately, and become more familiar with parents and home conditions than can secondary school teachers. They are then in a position to identify problems in the early stages and counsel students frequently and continuously. However, a few students may need so much counseling that they take an inordinate amount of a teacher's time. In such cases, it is wise to call upon the services of an experienced counselor.

Organized counseling programs, using specialized counselors, have not been carried out in elementary schools with the same intensity as in secondary schools. This is unfortunate because the sooner incipient problems are recognized and isolated, the sooner they can be remedied or solved. When students with poor habits and attitudes are allowed to continue uncounseled for a period of time or until they reach secondary schools, they are more difficult to change or improve. Many problems that occur in secondary schools might not exist if counseling services were available in the elementary schools. It is important that counselors at the elementary level understand the maturation process of younger children. Trained counselors can work closely with teachers in understanding problems that arise in their classes, freeing teachers to devote more of their time to actual teaching.

A school's guidance program should be continuous and should complement the instructional program. All students need some guidance whether or not they have problems. Melbo has stated that the school's guidance program should function to help the pupil:

(1) to understand himself, his abilities and interests, and his personal characteristics; (2) to adjust himself satisfactorily to situations, problems and pressures of his environment; (3) to develop the ability to make his own decisions wisely and solve his problems independently; (4) to make the most effective use of his capacities; and (5) to learn about the educational, occupational, and social opportunities available to him, when he

has reached the age or level of maturity at which these knowledges become important in order to make appropriate choices.[7]

THE TESTING PROGRAM.   Testing programs have been praised, criticized, and condemned. Some criticisms of educational tests are:

1. They are constructed poorly or vary in quality.
2. Their use is misunderstood.
3. They do not test what they are purported to test.
4. They are often improperly administered.
5. They stamp students as inferior, mediocre, or superior which, in turn, may affect students' self-esteem and future social status as adults.
6. The tests are used as an infallible record of ability.
7. Their interpretation is subject to error.
8. The scores are kept secret from parents or students.
9. Scores given to parents without complete knowledge of their meaning are incorrectly interpreted.

The proponents of educational testing claim the following purposes:

1. Tests provide the quickest means of determining variability among pupils and identifying the range of achievement.
2. The effectiveness of an educational program can be evaluated, areas of weakness identified, and curriculum revision determined.
3. A testing program provides a screening device to identify atypical students.
4. Tests provide a starting point for the beginning of class instruction.
5. Teachers have a basis upon which to plan remedial work.
6. Counselors are provided with valuable information.
7. Statistical information is available for many uses.

NORM- VERSUS CRITERION-REFERENCED TESTS.   Various types of tests have been used to help determine variabilities among students and to provide information to help teachers and counselors. These include: tests to measure, diagnose, or appraise mental ability, scholastic aptitude, subject matter achievement, personality, interests, physical development, and social traits. The purpose of these tests is to help identify weaknesses and to plot remedial instruction to strengthen them.

Norm-referenced or standardized tests are based on national norms. They are descriptive rather than prescriptive, may be biased, and may have little overlap with teacher objectives. However, these tests are somewhat objective, standardized, inexpensive, readily available, and compara-

---

[7] Irving Melbo, et al. *Report of the Survey, Ventura City Elementary Schools* (Los Angeles: University of Southern California, 1959), p. 271.

ble with other samples of the population.[8] They have little application to individualization of instruction and are not concerned with task or behavioral analysis.[9]

In recent years, criterion-referenced tests have been proposed. They provide an ends-oriented approach rather than a means-oriented approach to instruction.[10] Instructional objectives are developed and the degree of their achievement is measured. Objectives should be developed in terms of the following categories: the cognitive domain, the affective domain, and the psychomotor domain.[11] The means are successful if the objectives have been reached.

Criterion-referenced tests evaluate performance in relation to fixed standards, and are not concerned with grade-level descriptions or national student comparisons. They identify those who have mastered instructional objectives; provide information for planning instruction; are specific as to content; apply directly to individualization of instruction; apply directly to task and behavioral analysis; and are not standardized.[12] This type of evaluation is advantageous because it is adaptable, provides feedback, and is congruent with teacher objectives. However, the length of time it takes to reduce instructional objectives to operational terms and the requirement of writing meaningful objectives introduce problems. It is the responsibility of district administrators to see that teachers are trained and have help in developing objectives, criterion-referenced tests, and in using the results to improve individualized instruction.

To achieve the performance objectives that are able to be evaluated, instruction must be adapted to individuals. Many schools have developed learning activity packages in many subject areas. Some schools have developed student learning contracts. If a student's test shows that the objective has been attained, the student is permitted to go on to another contract.[13]

School Psychologists. Some students have problems or emotional difficulties that require more expert help than most teachers or counselors are prepared to handle. Learning can be impeded unless counseling assistance is provided. The specialized talents of a school psychologist trained in child psychology, child behavior, and learning problems can supply this help. Because of the expense involved, psychologists are more often employed by larger school districts.

---

[8] Thomas E. Neel, "Classroom Performance Standard," *Thrust for Education Leadership*, pp. 17–18.

[9] Jack L. Housden and Lannie LeGear, "An Emerging Model: Criterion-Referenced Evaluation," *Thrust for Education Leadership*, p. 42.

[10] W. James Popham, "The Instructional Objectives Exchange: New Support for Criterion-Referenced Instruction," *Phi Delta Kappan*, p. 174.

[11] John W. Porter, "The Accountability Story in Michigan," *Phi Delta Kappan*, p. 99.

[12] Housden and LeGear, "An Emerging Model," p. 42.

[13] W. James Popham, "Focus on Outcomes: A Guiding Theme of ES '70 Schools," *Phi Delta Kappan*, p. 209.

Some of the functions that school psychologists can perform are:

1. Helping to remedy emotional problems of students.
2. Helping students with educational maladjustments.
3. Performing most of the individual testing (but not group testing).
4. Advising teachers in the interpretation of group testing.
5. Analyzing statistical test results.
6. Assisting in curriculum development and the improvement of the learning environment.
7. Having a concern for the mental health of students.

CASE STUDIES. It is often necessary to make a complete case study in order to plan a course of action for a student's problem. To prepare a case study, the following steps should be taken:

1. Group test records should be compiled.
2. Personality traits should be noted.
3. The pupil's social adjustment should be analyzed.
4. Home conditions should be investigated.
5. The physical and health status should be described.
6. School strengths and weaknesses should be noted and analyzed.
7. The teacher should describe what special steps have been taken in attempting to solve the problem.
8. Anecdotal notes should be made at specified times.
9. Individualized tests should be given.
10. Parent conferences should be scheduled.[14]

The skill of a psychologist is needed to help compile a case study, analyze data, and plan a course of action. The psychologist should involve a team of available educational specialists for case-study staff conferences. Input may be needed from the school nurse, doctor, counselor, teacher, and parent. The student must not be overlooked, as the student alone supplies the key to remedying the problem. The psychologist must plan on continuing a course of action over a period of time. There must be continuous evaluation of progress and revision of remediation as it is deemed necessary.

Control of Behavior

The major purpose of controlling behavior is to provide an environment in which each student is able to receive an education commensurate with the student's ability to learn. Any kind of behavior that interferes with learning

---

[14] Emery Stoops and Russell E. Johnson, *Elementary School Administration* (New York: McGraw-Hill Book Co., 1967), p. 341.

should be considered unacceptable. Control of behavior is a broader term than discipline which connotes only obedience, order, and submission.

Poor behavior previously was dealt with by harsh, immediate, and authoritative means. Students were expected to obey rigid rules and regulations without question. More recently, students themselves have been included in the control process. The modern aim is to have groups and individuals develop social control, self-control, and self-direction.

RIGHTS AND RESPONSIBILITIES OF STUDENTS.   During recent years, students have become more insistent in demanding their rights. They resent it when adults (parents, teachers, or school administrators) tell them what they can or cannot do. They are not willing to accept adult-made rules and regulations. They want the right to help form rules of conduct. Adults must recognize that America's youth are generally more mature and sophisticated than their parents were at the same age.

Administrators and teachers must accept the fact that students have certain rights established by legal precedent in the Bill of Rights. Administrators cannot fight the challenge of youth to influence educational goals and to help formulate school rules. However, they must not permit students to take over the control of schools.

Basic standards should be agreed upon by teachers, administrators, parents, and students. The degree of student participation should be relevant to the students' maturity level. Students who help develop their own standards of behavior have a better understanding of the reasons for establishing them and are more likely to assume personal responsibility for supporting them. Accepting rights without assuming responsibility is a one-way street; there must also be self-discipline and respect for the rights of others. However, students need guidance in evaluating the consequences of their actions. Although students should have a voice in setting standards of behavior, no decision is final until the school board approves and adopts it as policy. All students and staff personnel should be informed of adoptions. Behavior or discipline policies should be reviewed periodically and revised as necessary.

CAUSES OF POOR DISCIPLINE.   Discipline problems are usually symptomatic of other problems. Parents, when asked, almost always list "school discipline" as their number-one concern. Student behavior has become noticeably more violent, and parental control has diminished. Many teachers believe that they are unable to teach effectively because of poor discipline in the classroom. Some factors that may cause poor discipline are:

Emotional and social factors.

Lack of motivation.

Lack of interest in subject matter or the educational program.

Poor presentation of the subject matter by the teacher.

Emotional repression.

Conflict between the student's behavior and social requirements or the teacher's expectations.

Peer conflicts.

Conflicts between parents and children.

Conflicts between home and school.

Conflicts between teacher and child.

Personal problems.

Maltnutrition or physical and health problems.

Thwarted self-expression.

Inferiority complex and feelings of incompetence.

Frustrations in desire to be important.

Lack of sympathy, love, or understanding.

Poor study habits.

Racial, religious, personal, or cultural differences.

Overstimulated life.

Thrill in delinquency that releases tensions.

Overcrowded classrooms.

Causes, such as the above, are related to school, home, or community. The school cannot always solve problems that are not related to it, although it can seek the cooperation of the home and community. It *can* do something about the school environment.

Teachers are usually concerned with dishonesty, disobedience, disorderliness, stealing, cheating, sex, insolence, noisiness, tardiness, and damaging property. Too many are bothered by such trivial behavior as chewing gum, eating candy, or turning around in class. It should be realized that many behaviors are actually normal for an age group, and natural manifestations of growing up. If the solution is punishment, especially for what the student regards as trivial, it causes pressure and rejection, aggravating the problem rather than helping to alleviate it. Nevertheless, the teacher must establish and maintain an orderly classroom climate.

SUGGESTED WAYS OF CONTROLLING BEHAVIOR. Punishment (discussed later in this chapter) is often used to control misbehavior. Except where immediate control is necessary, it is better to diagnose the problem, determine its causes, and then plan a course of action. A positive approach should be used and the cause removed, if possible. A school cannot remove all causes because they do not all originate in the school. The function of the school is to furnish the leadership to gain the cooperation of teachers, parents, pupils, and community service agencies to remedy the causes of misbehavior. The cause should be treated rather than the misbehavior that is the symptom. The ultimate goal is self-discipline for the student. Authoritative force only tends to develop negative attitudes, resistance, and eventually rebellion. If a positive approach is used and cooperation is achieved, misbehavior will have little chance of success. Compromises are necessary since there is little agreement between adults and students on dress codes, hair styles, smoking on school grounds, and so forth. However, workable standards must be worked out and agreed upon.

ROLE OF THE TEACHER IN CONTROLLING BEHAVIOR. Teachers play a major role in controlling behavior. Good classroom organization, sound planning by the teacher, interesting activities, and well-understood procedures promote good behavior. The day should be filled with stimulating, varied activities. Routines should be established so that students know what to expect and what they should do next. Students and the teacher should understand the limits of behavior.

The first priority of the teacher is to set classroom standards. This should be done with the help of the students. Parents should be called upon to review and help enforce these standards. The principal must coordinate the setting of standards among the teaching staff so that rules are applied uniformly. It is disconcerting to a teacher when criticizing a student for breaking a classroom rule to have the student say, "Mrs. Brown doesn't have that rule in *her* English class." A frequent review of classroom standards is a must, since conditions change; new regulations may need to be added and some may be found to be unnecessary. The process of education needs rules as surely as does the National Football League. Lack of rules, and lack of enforcement, lead to anarchy in the classroom just as surely as on the playing field.

The teacher should be firm, sincere, and above all, fair. The teacher should not humiliate or embarrass a student; be consistent in expectations of behavior; and provide the opportunity for every student to experience daily success, if possible. The student should be helped to develop a sense of worth and encouraged to participate creatively in classroom activities. Students should be given responsibilities commensurate with their ability to handle them. Praise should be frequently bestowed to develop pride and a positive attitude.

Teachers should feel free to discuss problems with their principal and to seek the principal's help. In turn, the principal should take the time to help the teachers and to request further help from the district pupil personnel office when it is necessary. Pupil personnel workers and counselors should not administer disciplinary punishment; by doing so, they lose the student trust essential to successful counseling.

PUNISHMENT.   Punishment is a stop-gap, first-aid type of control. It is only a momentary help, not a cure, and does not deal with the source of the problem. If used, it should be appropriate to the offense, be understood by the student, and reasonable. It is a temporary restraint that should only be used until the real cause is ascertained and an effective remedy applied. Punishment should be fair, not harsh or cruel, never administered in the heat of anger, and should cause no embarrassment to the student.

Because punishment is at times necessary for control of a disciplinary problem, the school board should adopt clear, concise policies that define the responsibility of teachers, administrators, students, and counselors. The policies should be broad enough to cover as many situations as possible, but not so detailed that they make policemen out of teachers or administrators. Because schools stand *in loco parentis*, they have the right to enforce reasonable rules and regulations and to punish.

Corporal punishment should only be used as a last resort. States vary in their laws regarding corporal punishment; some do not permit it. If permitted, the school board should spell out when corporal punishment is to be used, who is to administer it, what witnesses are required, whether the parents are to be notified, and what report is to be made and to whom. It should be remembered that corporal punishment rules by fear and never solves a problem.

When all else fails, suspension or expulsion may be the only remedy for the protection of the student and others. Suspension is temporary and expulsion is usually for the duration of the semester. The school board should also adopt policies on suspension and expulsion. The district pupil personnel administrator should be involved before a student is suspended or expelled. The student should be counseled in order to understand the reasons for the action. Time limits should be established and parents notified. It is advisable to hold a conference with the parents before readmission to enlist their help. All suspensions and expulsions should be reported to the school board. In all cases school personnel must follow due process.

Progress Reporting

Schools have an obligation to inform parents of their child's progress in school. Some method of reporting this should be developed. There are two basic methods of grading and reporting to parents as well as informing the student: (1) competitive or norm-referenced and (2) individual progress or criterion-referenced. Parents best understand progress that is related to a norm. They want to know how their child is doing specifically in each subject as well as in relation to other children.[15] Parents often confuse reporting with comparative marking.[16]

The student should understand what the grade means before it is reported. Most schools use number or letter rating scales on report cards; here, the grade represents, in the teacher's judgment, the measure of achievement for a student in relation to other students. This type of grading system is norm-referenced.[17] A typical report card lists subjects with assigned grades. Some of the common grading scales are: A, B, C, D, and E or F; 1, 2, 3, 4, and 5; percentages with 100 (perfect) and 70 (usually the lowest passing grade); "pass" and "fail"; N (needs help) or U (unsatisfactory) and S (satisfactory). Citizenship, work habits, health habits, attitude, effort, and attendance are sometimes added and graded.

Report cards such as these explain very little and leave much to be desired. A "C" grade, for example, can mean that a student is doing "average" work, but can also be a good grade for a slow learner. Without explanation, parents often blame the school or the teacher for a child's poor grade.

A report card based on criterion-referenced testing lists objectives and provides space for indicating those that have been achieved or the proficiency that has been demonstrated. All the objectives that a teacher used cannot be included.[18] This method of reporting does not compare a student with others. The "grade," if a report card is used, shows individual progress toward performance objectives developed by the teacher. The evaluation is based on the individualization of instruction.

No perfect report card has ever been devised. Most school districts, because of complaints or new ideas, revise reporting methods from time to time. There are probably as many types of cards as there are school districts. The trend at the secondary level is toward computerized cards that reduce paper work. Figure 16–3 illustrates an automatically printed type of grade report. Figure 16–4 is an example of an elementary school detailed evaluation of reading. Similar forms are used for other subejcts.

Other methods have been devised to improve the reporting of progress. Letters from the teacher explain progress in narrative form. They may be more personal and explain more fully than report cards, but the method is time-consuming for a teacher, especially at the secondary level where each teacher may be responsible for up to 150 students. Meaningful letters are difficult to compose for large numbers; often the teacher uses a sentence to explain what a single letter or number grade would indicate.

---

[15] Henry J. Otto and David C. Sanders, *Elementary School Organization and Administration*, 4th ed., p. 153.

[16] Otto and Sanders, *Elementary School*, p. 155.

[17] Jason Millman, "Reporting Progress: A Case for a Criterion-Referenced Marking System," *Phi Delta Kappan*, p. 226.

[18] Millman, "Reporting Progress," pp. 226–27.

TO

STUDENT NAME	PERIOD ENDING MO DAY YEAR	SCHOOL	HOME ROOM	QUARTER	LEVEL

JUNIOR HIGH SCHOOL STUDENT GRADE REPORT
Bellflower Unified School District
BELLFLOWER, CALIFORNIA

PERIOD	SUBJECT	TEACHER	GRADE	USE OF ABILITY	CONDUCT

GRADE VALUES

A SUPERIOR
B ABOVE AVERAGE
C AVERAGE FOR ABILITY - SATISFACTORY
D BARELY PASSING
F FAILURE
R RECORDS INSUFFICIENT - NO GRADE

USE OF ABILITY AND CONDUCT

1 OUTSTANDING
2 ABOVE AVERAGE
3 AVERAGE
4 NEEDS TO IMPROVE
5 UNSATISFACTORY

PARENTS ARE ENCOURAGED TO CONTACT THE SCHOOL IF THERE IS ANY QUESTION REGARDING THIS REPORT.

ATTENDANCE CODE

2 ILLNESS / DOCTOR / DENTIST
3 PARTIAL DAY EXCUSED
4 PARTIAL DAY UNEXCUSED
5 EXCUSED
6 UNEXCUSED
7 = TRUANCY
8 = PARTIAL DAY TRUANCY
9 = NOT ENROLLED
H = HOLIDAY

ATTENDANCE FOR PERIOD SHOWN →

1ST WEEK M T W TH F	2ND WEEK M T W TH F	3RD WEEK M T W TH F	4TH WEEK M T W TH F	PERIOD ENDING MO DAY YEAR

Student achievement reports are issued four times during the year, at the close of each quarter. Grades represent achievement for this quarter only.

FIGURE 16–3. Example of a Student Grade Report. Courtesy of the Bellflower Unified School District.

Letters to parents tend to become generalized and stereotyped. Some report cards do provide a space for the teacher to write pertinent comments and a space for the parent to make comments or ask questions.

PARENT–TEACHER CONFERENCES. Many school districts achieve success in reporting to parents with parent–teacher conferences that replace report cards or are scheduled at the time report cards are distributed. An extensive study by Henry Otto showed that parents and teachers were in close agreement about the school's objectives and in full agreement that reports to parents should be in terms of objectives. However, both groups were vague about what to report. Parents and teachers alike agreed that any reporting plan should include arrangements for parent–teacher conferences.[19]

[19] Henry J. Otto et al. *Four Methods of Reporting to Parents* (Austin: The University of Texas Press, 1957).

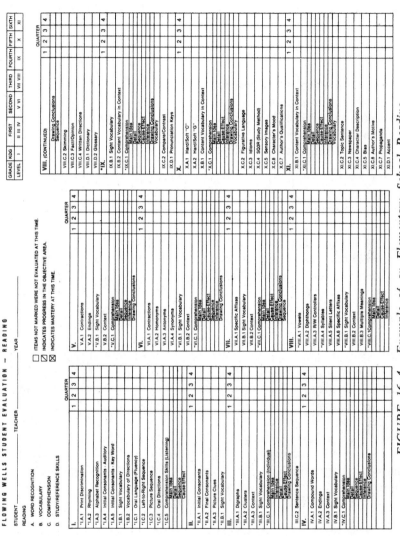

FIGURE 16–4. *Example of an Elementary School Reading Evaluation form.*

Courtesy of Flowing Wells Public Schools, Tucson, Arizona.

355

If rapport is established and the atmosphere is relaxed, teachers and parents understand each other better and can cooperate in planning for the student's educational success. During a conference, feelings are important. The teacher must understand how the parent feels and how the parent may react. A conference should be a two-way communication. Listening is important on the part of the teacher or counselor. The conferees should discuss:

1. Educational philosophy and expectancies.
2. Objectives that have been developed for the individual student.
3. The degree to which the objectives have been achieved.
4. The meaning of the grades if a report card is used.
5. Problems and suggestions for improvement.
6. Successes.

The conference should end on a friendly and positive note.

It is often difficult to arrange a time that is convenient for both parents and teachers. Many districts permit shortened teaching days during the conference period because of the value of this reporting method. Secondary schools find conferences difficult for two reasons: (1) the average secondary teacher needs to schedule approximately 150 conferences and (2) parents of secondary students do not visit the school as frequently as elementary parents do.

William Glasser believes that there should be few meetings with parents on deficiency reports or disciplinary problems because they do more harm than good. Parents should not be called to the school until all the school's efforts to help the student have failed. At the secondary level, students should always be present when they are discussed by the teacher or counselor and the parent. The conference should not start by trying to fix blame. Constructive suggestions should be the objective of the conference, and the student should have an equal voice in attempts to reach a solution. Recommendations should be brief, to the point, and understandable. When "they have been agreed upon, they should be put in writing and the student should commit himself in writing to following them."[20] Conferences at the secondary level can be successful if they are carefully planned and conducted, and involve the student, as well as the parent and teacher or counselor.

METHODS OF REPORTING STUDENT PROGRESS. Most schools use a multiple, rather than a single method of reporting. Some methods in the order of their importance are: (1) teacher–parent conferences, (2) A, B, C, D, F, or numeral marks, (3) descriptive paragraphs and phrases, (4) credit, and (5) miscellaneous methods invented by local districts.

---

[20] William Glasser, *Schools Without Failure*, pp. 225–26.

Whatever reporting method is used, it should not be totally administratively developed. Parents, teachers, administrators, and students should also be involved. Whether or not all agree, the final compromise on grades and method of reporting should be understood by all.

Pupil Personnel Reports and Records

Some administators feel that they spend most of their time compiling, analyzing, and reporting data of all types. Since the actual work is largely clerical, clerks should be trained to compile, record, and file or forward reports and records. Some can be trained to analyze and to summarize statistical information to make it more readily available to administrators. The importance of reporting and recording data cannot be underestimated. Records are used to project enrollment in order to determine needs such as: classrooms, teachers, buses, equipment, materials, and services. Actual enrollment or attendance figures determine the amount of finances the school district will receive.

The following list shows various types of commonly used pupil personnel records:

Grades earned.

Test scores.

Case studies.

Student cumulative records.

Promotion lists.

Ethnic summaries.

Statistical data: dropouts, suspensions, expulsions, arrests, corporal punishment cases, test summaries, etc.

Attendance area charts.

Class loads.

Enrollment.

Attendance.

Psychological studies.

School census.

Population movement.

Student turnover.

The student cumulative record contains a great amount of information to help teachers and administrators as they teach, advise, and counsel students. The folder should contain the life history of each student in the school district. Included should be information regarding the student's family, grades, test scores, health, personality traits, attendance, problems, achievements, co-curricular participation, and leadership. There should be some indication of potential success in college or employment. The cumulative folder should be used as a reference by teachers, counselors, and the pupil personnel office and referred to for college and employment recommendations.

Schools with access to computers have simplified recordkeeping tasks. Data can be recorded on punch cards or tape and run through a computer. Gummed printouts can be used, making it a simple process to stick information on the cumulative folder.

Records and reports have no value unless they are used. An adequate file system is necessary to make information available when needed. There are many types of filing systems; the school district should select the ones that suit its particular needs. Some exemples are: Kardex files, visible files, folder files, needle-sort files, and tape files. Space can be saved if older records and reports are microfilmed and stored in a microfilm file. If properly indexed, they can be retrieved easily. The forward-looking school district will examine the possibility of using a newer type of data retrieval system.

Standardization of records greatly facilitates the keeping of records. Numerous attempts have been made to standardize student records so that they may simply be forwarded as the student matriculates, rather than wasting many clerical hours copying information into a new format. Various state, county, city, or federal agencies periodically request student data. If the reporting forms are standardized, many hours are saved in collecting and tabulating similar data.

At the beginning of the school year, each school should have a supply of all forms it will need. The teacher's handbook should be updated to show examples of all forms and explanations of their use. Typical pupil personnel forms used are:

Enrollment blanks.

Cumulative record folders.

Report cards.

Class schedule cards.

Attendance slips.

Excuse slips.

Office pass slips.

Athletic eligibility forms.

Health forms.

Transfer slips.

Accident report forms.

Nurse referral forms.

Office referral forms.

Attendance registers or cards.

Library cards.

Referral for pupil personnel service.

Transfer permits and transfer report forms.

Readmittance information forms.

Lunch passes.

Bus passes.

Permits for release of child during school hours.

Requests for pupil records.

CONFIDENTIALITY OF STUDENT RECORDS.   It is debatable how much information on students should be made public. What should parents be told? What should prospective employers be told about a student's intelligence, aptitudes, attitudes, or personal qualifications? Perhaps any information that is released should be only for the purpose of helping a student. Parents have a right to know what information about their child is being held on record. Police, governmental agencies, and other schools have a right to expect a school to cooperate in furnishing all necessary, factual information. Employers have a right to information on a student's grades, aptitudes, attendance, and attitudes. Information should be of two types: (1) factual and (2) professional judgments or opinions. Information of a personal nature should not be divulged because the confidentiality of a student must be protected. People or agencies seeking information about a student must prove their (1) need to know and (2) their right to know.

STUDENT PERSONNEL AND DATA PROCESSING.[21]   The many needs for information relative to student personnel have offered a broad field for the application of the new technology. Most schools employing automatic data processing equipment use it for many applications in this field. This relieves teachers of many clerical chores and also aids the clerical staff in accomplishing their tasks expeditiously. If data on pupil personnel are accumulated, processed, stored, and made accessible by a systems approach, it becomes available to counselors, teachers, and administrators when they need it.

---

[21] Written by Dr. Richard H. Strand in: Emery Stoops, Max Rafferty, and Russell E. Johnson, *Handbook of Educational Administration* (Boston: Allyn and Bacon, Inc., 1975), pp. 319–21.

An example of the use of computer technology in the area of counseling is the design, by Systems Development Corporation, of a man–machine counseling system which includes the following major elements: (1) an information retrieval system for information on students; (2) a tracking and monitoring system that will alert the counselor when critical situations occur; (3) an automated report generation for preparing cumulative records, report cards, and other reports or lists; and (4) a prediction system that does not require the counselor to have a technical knowledge of statistics.[22]

The following is an outline illustrative of some applications in the student personnel area.

Data Processing of Student Personnel

I. School census records.
    A. Making population analyses of children ready for school by grades.
    B. Recording background information on parents and guardians with all the data necessary for later communications and reports.
    C. Making the master cumulative record file for each student which will later be expanded and updated.
    D. Reporting school census findings to the state and federal governments as requested or as needed for project and grant requests.
    E. Making the school mailing lists and the address labels for mailing.
    F. Making PTA calling lists.
    G. Listing students with various handicaps or special needs by grade.
    H. Listing nonresident students under inter-district agreements.
    I. Scheduling and routing buses and other means of transportation and issuing bus passes.
    J. Coordinating family vacations in schools operating on a twelve-month school year.

II. Registration and scheduling.
    A. Constructing the master class schedule.
    B. Registering pupils by mark sense cards.
    C. Scheduling pupils into classes.
        1. Balancing class loads and sections and distributing classes and students fairly.
        2. Making class lists, homeroom lists, study hall lists.
        3. Making program schedules for individuals that avoid course conflict in individual programs.

III. Attendance accounting.
    A. Preprinting documents for recording attendance.
    B. Recording and summarizing attendance daily, monthly, annually.
    C. Computing statistics on attendance—ADA, percent of attendance, etc.

---

[22] H. F. Silberman and R. T. Filep, "Information Systems Applications in Education," *Annual Review of Information Science and Technology*, pp. 367–68.

D. Listing new pupils, pupils whose attendance is spotty or shows signs of developing trouble, pupils who drop out and the reasons for leaving school, etc.

IV. Cumulative records.
  A. Collecting pupil personnel data in machine readable form at the time of enrollment (using mark sense cards or forms).
  B. Storing data for machine transmittal later (on punch cards or magnetic tape, etc.).
  C. Updating machine records from new source data collected and transmitted from schools.
  D. Updating cumulative record folders or cards in schools by pasting gummed labels made by the data center from results of test scoring or student report cards.
  E. Printing cumulative record data in part or whole upon request from authorized persons.

V. Testing, scoring, and statistical handling of test data.
  A. Test constructing and evaluating (see Research and Decision-Making Applications outline).
  B. Test preprinting.
  C. Testing by use of mark sense answer sheets or cards.
  D. Scoring tests and recording scores.
  E. Producing gummed labels for scores on standardized tests to update pupil cumulative records.
  F. Computing statistics and reporting test results by preparing rank-in-class lists, reports by subject and school, etc.

VI. Mark reporting and recording.
  A. Preprinting personalized report cards (IBM cards) from pupil file data for each subject on pupil's class list; teachers have only to record a grade on the cards.
  B. Making gummed labels of student grades for pasting on permanent records in the schools.
  C. Computing individual and group statistics on pupil grades.
  D. Preparing lists of student grades.
    1. Rank-in-class lists.
    2. Honor rolls of various kinds.
    3. Scholarship award candidates.
    4. Lists of failures, probable failures, underachievers, and pupils receiving incompletes.

VII. Making district reports of class and school progress.

RESEARCH AND DECISION-MAKING APPLICATIONS OF DATA PROCESSING.[23] Turning machines toward the accomplishment of routine tasks that would

[23] Written by Dr. Richard H. Strand in: Emery Stoops, Max Rafferty, and Russell E. Johnson, *Handbook of Educational Administration* (Boston: Allyn and Bacon, Inc., 1975), pp. 321–23.

require endless repetition of the same operations and procedures by human "slaves" is a liberating operation; but, at a higher level, using machines to help make analyses, predictions, and surveys, all of which may involve massive amounts of data, makes the use of sophisticated equipment most worthwhile. Schools can utilize data processing equipment in much the same manner, as the accompanying list of potentialities will indicate.

Research and Decision-Making Applications of Data Processing

I. Stimulation of research and facilitation of decision making in general.
   A. Freeing teachers and administrators to do research by reducing their routine paper load.
   B. Improving the quality of research through machine-processing capabilities.
   C. Providing operating reports almost on demand to facilitate administrative decision making to control current plans and conditions.
   D. Providing planning reports covering a three-year or longer period from which trends and predictions may be extrapolated.

II. Surveys of community and schools.
   A. Recording and reporting census information related to the school community.
      1. Children's ages.
      2. Mobility patterns.
      3. Housing conditions and patterns.
      4. Economic conditions.
      5. Racial patterns.
      6. Police records.
      7. Parental background factors.
      8. Sibling status.
   B. Polling or surveying students and teachers.
   C. Making class-size and teacher-load studies.
   D. Making plant utilization studies that include simulation studies of proposed plans.
   E. Making college and educational opportunity surveys.

III. Attendance studies.
   A. Studying attendance by school, class, race, and sex.
   B. Discovering attendance patterns of pupils—pinpointing situations that merit attention before they get worse.

IV. Grade (marking) studies.
   A. Making grade distribution studies.
   B. Analyzing course-marking standards and teacher-marking practices.
   C. Computing rank-in-class statistics by different formulas for different purposes.

V. Test development and the use of tests in research.
   A. Perfecting tests by item analysis, correlations, and reliability checks.
   B. Scoring of standardized and teacher-made tests—with any kind of score desired: raw score, percentile, stanine, or standard score.

C. Finding statistical significance of test results wherever tests are used.

D. Making score distribution studies of classes, schools, and district.

E. Producing local norms, expectancy tables, and expected grade curves for a teacher based on pupil ability and achievement tests.

Summary

Pupil personnel services should be centralized under a trained administrator who maintains pupil records and administers testing, psychological, guidance, and other programs. This person should first be an administrator and then a specialist in one or several of the services.

Several kinds of school censuses exist, including the grade-progression method, the periodic, and the registration, all annual. The continuous census is recommended, and is almost a necessity for a successful pupil personnel program. It helps in making preregistration possible and in orienting new students.

Child welfare and attendance are important pupil personnel services. Because school money depends in large part upon average daily attendance, it is important that reasons behind nonattendance be determined. Reasons for absence include varying cultural patterns, inability of the child to cope with school problems, and family pressures. Welfare and attendance workers should be well trained, with a well-balanced personality and an ability to establish good relationships with parents.

Attendance accounting should be kept simple, as centralized as possible, and adapted to business machines. Regularity of attendance should be stressed with special attention to the two main administrative implications of excessive absences: accounting and guidance. Truancy should be combatted by seeking out the cause and treating it appropriately. The problem of the dropout should be handled similarly.

Work permits are usually handled by the pupil personnel director. Students who leave school legally must be followed up with transfers of credits and grades. Suspensions and expulsions are also dealt with by the pupil personnel office.

Guidance and counseling functions are coordinated by the director, with trained counselors used wherever possible. Aptitude and personality tests are often administered by the school psychologist, who may assist also in conducting case studies of individual students.

Discipline is a perennial concern of the schools. Today its achievement is complicated by the concept of student rights. Many causes of poor discipline exist, and are usually dealt with by some combination of rewards and punishments administered mainly by the teacher.

Progress reporting, another pupil personnel service, is mostly for the benefit of the parent. Report cards, letters, and parent–teacher conferences are the devices most frequently used. Conferences can be constructive if planned carefully and conducted in a mutually agreeable manner. At the secondary level, the student should be involved along with the parent, teacher, or counselor.

Pupil personnel records should be kept by clerks and made available to those professionally qualified to use them. Cumulative student records are especially valuable if properly kept; they should be kept as confidential as law and professional ethics permit.

Many of the pupil personnel functions, records and paper work, and research can be handled by computers and data processing equipment, thus freeing personnel from routine and time-wasting duties.

Administrative Problems | In Basket |

Problem 1

Smithsville is a small urban city. In general, its people are middle- or lower-middle-class, and about 15 percent are classified as disadvantaged. It has elected school board members who want academic education stressed. The high school curriculum is oriented to college, despite the fact that only about 20 percent of its graduates go on to college.

Attendance at the high school is poor. Truancy and absences become worse every year as students claim the curriculum is irrelevant and teachers are uninteresting and unsympathetic. Every type of excuse is used and many parents sign notes stating that their children are ill although the school knows it is not true. Many excuses appear to be forged. The district attendance officer spends an inordinate amount of time trying to track down absentees but so far has not been able to improve the attendance.

What can the principal do to improve attendance?
What steps can the attendance officer take?
If you were the superintendent, what would you do?

Problem 2

The superintendent has moved all principals to different schools for the coming school year. Mrs. Goldberg, who is 40 years old, has been assigned as principal to the Clifton Elementary School, which has a reputation for lax discipline. The former principal believed in permissiveness to an extreme. There were fights on the playground or on the way to school, which were excused as youthful exuberance. Students were often tardy, wandered around the halls, and came into the office without excuse. Classes were noisy; rooms were often left messy. Teachers often complained, but the principal thought the "poor discipline" was part of growing up. He explained that the children would learn self-discipline as they matured, if guided properly by the teachers. There were almost no school rules.

Mrs. Goldberg's previous school was noted for its unusually well-mannered students and fine discipline. She was described by others as being strict but fair and understanding. She suspects that the superintendent has assigned her to Clifton to bring order out of chaos.

What procedures can Mrs. Goldberg develop to improve the morale of the school?
What discipline policies should she develop?
How should parents be involved?

Problem 3

The school district described in Problem 1 has twelve elementary schools, two junior high schools, and one senior high school. Many homes are being sold and demolished as the community changes to an apartment and condominium area. The superintendent is concerned about the effect on enrollment and has asked the director of pupil personnel to make a school census, for the purpose of determining the expected school enrollment for the next school year and the projected figures for the next five and ten years.

How should the director of pupil personnel proceed?

Selected References

AMERICAN ASSOCIATION OF SCHOOL ADMINISTRATORS. *Profiles of the Administrative Team.* Washington, D.C.: The Association, 1971.

ATTWELL, ARTHUR A. *School Psychologist's Handbook,* rev. ed. Los Angeles: Western Psychological Services, 1976.

BRADLEY, R. C. *Parent-Teacher Interviews, A Modern Concept of Oral Reporting.* Wolf City, Texas: The University Press, 1971.

CAMPBELL, ROALD F., JOHN E. CORBALLY, JR., and JOHN A. RAMSEYER. *Introduction to Educational Administration.* 3rd ed. Boston: Allyn and Bacon, Inc., 1966.

COMBS, CHARLES R., BENJAMIN COHN, EDWARD J. GIBIAN, and A. MEAD SNIFFIN. "Group Counseling: Applying the Technique." *The School Counselor* 11 (October 1963).

FENSCH, EDWIN A., and ROBERT E. WILSON. *The Superintendency Team.* Columbus, Ohio: Charles E. Merrill Publishing Co., 1964.

GLASSER, WILLIAM. *Schools Without Failure.* New York: Harper & Row Publishers, Inc., 1969.

GRIEDER, CALVIN; TRUMAN M. PIERCE; and WILLIAM E. ROSENSTENGEL. *Public School Administration.* New York: Ronald Press, 1961.

HOUSDEN, JACK L., and LANNIE LeGEAR. "An Emerging Model: Criterion-Referenced Evaluation." *Thrust for Education Leadership* 2 (April 1973).

KNEZEVICH, STEPHEN J. *Administration of Public Education.* Scranton, Pa.: Harper and Row Publishers, Inc., 1975.

MARKS, SIR JAMES R., EMERY STOOPS, and JOYCE KING-STOOPS. *Handbook of Educational Supervision.* 2nd ed. Boston: Allyn and Bacon, Inc., 1978.

MILLMAN, JASON. "Reporting Progress: A Case for a Criterion-Referenced Marking System." *Phi Delta Kappan* 52 (December 1970).

MORPHET, EDGAR L., ROE L. JOHNS, and THEODORE L. RELLER. *Educational Administration: Concepts, Practices and Issues.* Englewood Cliffs, N.J.: Prentice-Hall, 1959.

MORRIS, GORDON T. "The Truant." *Today's Education* 61 (January 1972).

MYRICK, ROBERT D., and JOE WITTMER. *School Counseling: Problems and Methods.* Santa Monica, Ca.: Goodyear Publishing Company, 1974.

National Education Association, Research Division. "Reporting Pupil Progress to Parents." *Research Bulletin* 49 (October 1971).

NEEL, THOMAS E. "Classroom Performance Standards." *Thrust for Education Leadership* 2 (October 1972).

OTTO, HENRY J., and DAVID C. SANDERS. *Elementary School Organization and Administration.* 4th ed. New York: Appleton-Century-Crofts, 1964.

POPHAM, W. JAMES. "Focus on Outcomes: A Guiding Theme of ES '70 Schools." *Phi Delta Kappan* 51 (December 1969).

————. "The Instructional Objectives Exchange: New Support for Criterion-Referenced Instruction." *Phi Delta Kappan* 52 (November 1970).

POPPEN, A. and CHARLES L. THOMPSON. *School Counseling: Theories and Concepts.* Lincoln, Neb.: Professional Educators Publications, Inc., 1974.

PORTER, JOHN W. "The Accountability Story in Michigan." *Phi Delta Kappan* 54 (October 1972).

PROCTOR, WILLIAM M. *Educational and Vocational Guidance.* Darby, Pa.: Arden Library, 1978.

SILBERMAN, H. F., and R. T. FILEP. "Information Systems Applications in Education." *Annual Review of Information Science and Technology* 3, Carlos Cuadra (ed.) Chicago: Encyclopaedia Britannica, Wm. Benton, 1968.

STOOPS, EMERY (ed.) *Guidance Services: Organization and Administration.* New York: McGraw-Hill Book Co., Inc., 1959.

CHAPTER SEVENTEEN

Administration of Certificated Personnel

The administration of certificated personnel is an essential function of the school district. A school is only as good as its teachers and teachers are only as good as their skills and competencies. The recruitment of qualified certificated personnel is one of the most important tasks of a school district. Following employment, teachers need inservice training to increase their teaching skills. Policies must be developed to cover every phase of personnel administration.

Functions of the Personnel Administrator

Because of the importance of personnel functions, the personnel administrator should be one of the top administrators in a school district and a member of the superintendent's staff. The position should be equal in rank with business and educational services.

FUNCTIONS OF THE PERSONNEL ADMINISTRATOR. The personnel administrator has numerous functions. In addition, personnel administrators are often asked to perform other duties such as developing policies, preparing news releases, and serving as the negotiator for the school district. The personnel administrator must be a good communicator, have a knowledge of all the personnel functions in his district, and have good understanding and rapport with certificated personnel.

The preservice and inservice material for this chapter was prepared in collaboration with Dr. Joyce Barlow King-Stoops, University of Southern California, Los Angeles.

The personnel administrator requires an adequate secretarial and clerical staff to handle applications, correspondence, phone calls; to make reports, keep records, and so forth. In larger school districts, this administrator may have one or more assistants.

PROBLEMS OF THE PERSONNEL ADMINISTRATOR. The major areas of concern for the personnel administrator are: "(1) Recruitment and selection of qualified personnel for certain areas; (2) Communications and relationships between board, central office administration, principals, staff, and parents; (3) Effective and equitable evaluation of staff; and (4) Negotiations and transfer of teachers within the district in order to have a racially integrated, balanced staff."[1] The most common daily administrative problems faced by the personnel administrator are: "(1) Termination of employment for incompetents; (2) Obtaining realistic references and uniform credentials concerning teacher applicants; (3) Contracts binding on the school board but not on the staff member (teachers violating contracts); (4) Data processing and/or other recordkeeping concerning personnel; and (5) Teachers' attitude toward services beyond the normal school day."[2] The most difficult of these problems is terminating incompetent employees because of the difficulties in meeting legal requirements, building a tenable case, and meeting community pressures over the issue. Another major problem is the handling of negotiations (often in regard to salary and fringe benefits), especially when the district faces severe financial problems.

SKILLS NEEDED BY THE PERSONNEL ADMINISTRATOR. The personnel administrator needs technical training for "prospect appraisal, the building of salary schedules, formulation of job descriptions, personnel research, administration of the numerous records and fringe benefits, and in the specialized type of adult counseling in this post."[3] Also needed is a knowledge of education, general administration, law, data processing, interviewing techniques, evaluation techniques, and practical psychology.[4] Essential personal attributes that are particularly useful are: "sensitivity and empathy, patience and forbearance, integrity and dependability, imagination and ingenuity, fairness and consistency."[5] An ability is needed to work with the teacher association, since policies and many aspects of personnel functions are arrived at by negotiation.

---

[1] American Association of School Personnel Administrators, "Problems of Practicing School Personnel Administrators," 9, 10 *AASPA Bulletin* (June 13, 1969), p. 1.

[2] American Association of School Personnel Administrators, "Problems," p. 1.

[3] Robert E. Wilson, *Educational Administration* (Columbus, Ohio: Charles E. Merrill Books, 1966), p. 434.

[4] Wilson, *Educational Administration*, p. 434.

[5] American Association of School Administrators, *Profiles of the Administrative Team* (Washington, D.C.: AASA), p. 95.

LINE-AND-STAFF RELATIONSHIPS. There is considerable disagreement as to whether the personnel administrator is a line or a staff officer or a combination of both. In practice, both functions are probably performed. It is imperative that the personnel administrator be responsible to and report directly to the superintendent. Other important functions are to serve as a consultant to the building principal and as a link between other administrators, teachers, teacher organizations, and the superintendent. The personnel administrator is also involved with classified personnel (see chapter 18). The personnel administrator who visits schools and offices to observe firsthand and to be available to answer questions personally improves relationships with personnel.

Personnel Policy Formulation

Policies are the working agreements that clarify relationships, procedures, and ways of reaching goals and objectives. Without adequate personnel policies, sometimes called rules and regulations, the personnel administrator will be unable to function. Some school districts confuse policies with administrative procedures and legal interpretations. Policies are general, broad guidelines for action. Administrative procedures explain the details for making the policy effective. State laws, however, may require procedures to be made a part of the policy document.

Personnel policies cover every phase of personnel administration, including:

Recruiting procedures	Grievance and appeal procedures
Assignment	Probation and tenure
Promotion	Substitute service
Evaluation	Job descriptions
Dismissal	Personnel records
Salaries	Duties and responsibilities
Fringe benefits	Extracurricular duties
Retirement	Vacations and holidays
Leaves of absence	Guidelines for postgraduate study
Work schedules	Inservice education
Negotiation	

The personnel administrator oversees the formulation of personnel policies. Policies are developed by negotiation and collective bargaining with the teacher association (see chapter 19). The board of education and the superintendent should be consulted or informed throughout the procedure. In some districts, they may actively participate in the negotiation process.

The policy that is finally agreed upon should be sent to the district's legal adviser for interpretation and suggestions. The final policy must be presented to the board of education for adoption, policy being effective only when officially adopted and recorded in the board's minutes. After adoption, the personnel administrator is responsible for implementing and enforcing the policies. Few policies are permanent; they must be studied and revised continuously as conditions and social forces change.

Procurement of Certificated Personnel

The superintendent has responsibility for recommending new employees to the board of education (which has the employing authority). The personnel administrator should have the delegated authority to procure all certificated personnel and to recommend their employment to the superintendent. The success of the educational program is dependent upon the selection of qualified teachers and administrators.

The personnel office should advertise openings, recruit and interview applicants, request references, verify certification, and select qualified prospects to recommend to the superintendent. Job descriptions that accurately define the position; its required competencies, experience, and training should be provided.

When schools recruit, they must make an effort to obtain qualifiable employees from ethnic minority groups and women to demonstrate their intention to approach the whole population of the area from which they are recruiting. However, giving preferential treatment to these applicants has caused uneasiness, controversy, and the filing of reverse discrimination complaints by white males.[6]

According to court rulings, Title IX of the Education Amendments of 1972 does not legally regulate employment practices, since employment is not an educational program or activity.

In the past it was possible to find out quite a lot about the background of an applicant. Now it is more difficult because, in hiring, federal law does not permit inquiries regarding an applicant's birthplace, relatives, age, citizenship, arrests, military service, family, marital status, or membership in organizations. A photograph cannot be required.

TEACHER SHORTAGE. A shortage of teachers has been predicted that will make it more difficult to recruit teachers in the coming years. In 1977 there

---

[6] Allan C. Ornstein, "What Does Affirmative Action Affirm? A Viewpoint," *Phi Delta Kappan* 57, No. 4, December 1975, pp. 242–45.

was a major shortage of over 1,000 positions for which qualified teachers were sought in teaching mathematics, bilingual education, and the learning disabled. It has been estimated that up to 1982, there will be increased demands for teachers in the fields of the learning disabled, mathematics, the gifted and talented, and industrial arts.[7] By 1986, it is projected that there will be a need for 231,000 additional teachers, but there will be only 162,000 newly qualified teachers, based on an 8 percent turnover rate.[8]

Several reasons have been proposed for the teacher shortage. The Bureau of the Census has predicted an estimated birth rate increase from 3,165,000 live births in 1976 to 4,007,000 in 1985. Those born in 1976 will enter school in 1982 and those born in 1985, in 1991.[9]

There is also a need for more teachers because the pupil/teacher ratio is dropping. In 1975, it was 22.6 in elementary schools and 18.7 in secondary schools, but in 1986, it is projected to be 19.0 in elementary schools and 17.6 in secondary schools.[10]

There is also a decline in teachers entering the profession due partly to: failure to find jobs, affirmative action programs opening up new job opportunities, lower salaries paid to teachers, and more women deciding to have families. The RAND Corporation predicts "a substantial and lengthy teacher shortage."[11] Mandatory busing is also causing white flight, which is helping to cause lower public school enrollment.

INTERVIEWING APPLICANTS. The interview, an important aspect of selection, largely determines whether the applicant has the personality and qualifications to be desirable for the district. Interviewing is an art that should be structured so that it is not a waste of time. Direct questions elicit factual information, but nondirective questions determine attitudes and personality. The interviewer should be friendly, avoid debate, and concentrate on listening.

Some districts use tests, district developed or furnished by the Educational Testing Service, prior to the interview. Only those who receive a qualifying score are interviewed. Many doubt the value of tests for selection. The Teacher Perceiver Interview (TPI) is being used in many

---

[7] U.S. Department of Health, Education, and Welfare, National Center for Education Statistics, LEA (Local Education Agency) Survey of Teacher and Administrator Shortage, unpublished tabulations.

[8] U.S. Department of Health, Education, and Welfare, National Center for Education Statistics, unpublished data.

[9] U.S. Bureau of the Census, *Projections of the Population of the United States: 1977–2050* (Series II Projections), p. 23.

[10] U.S. Department of Health, Education, and Welfare, National Center for Education Statistics, unpublished data.

[11] Stephen J. Carroll, "The Market for Teachers," *Analysis of the Educational Personnel System*, No. VIII (Santa Monica, Ca.: The RAND Corporation, 1974), p. 25.

districts across the country. TPI is a competency test purported to discriminate good from poor teachers. However, Donald Haefele does not believe that it meets the minimal requirements for instrument validity as a selection instrument.[12] In 1977, a federal district court in South Carolina ruled that the National Teacher Examination scores could be used in the certification and salary determination of public school teachers. This ruling handicaps blacks who historically do less well than whites on this test. The implications of this decision must be considered by those school districts that use the test.[13] Performance tests have been given. Test questions can ask: "How would you teach the following?" "What would you do first?" Personality and professional tests have also been used. However, there is no one answer to the use of tests in the selection of school personnel.

A limited survey of central office administrators that was made in Ohio showed that high interview rankings were given to applicants for: physical appearance, a strong desire to work, good verbal skills, enthusiasm, emotional balance, clearness about professional goals, provision for individual differences, and a sound educational philosophy.[14]

Interviews cannot measure ability or personality. They only measure the ability to talk. Applicants may have different personalities during the interview and in the classroom. It is a myth to think that interviews can predict a good teacher.

A team approach can be used in interviewing applicants, involving the personnel administrator, principals, supervisors, department heads, and teachers. The team should not be so large as to overwhelm an applicant. For interviewing and screening of administrators, most districts use teachers. There are those who think this is inappropriate because they do not believe that teachers should see the personal references of a potential administrator. In the selection of new teachers, the team and the principal should agree on the selection. They usually recommend two candidates for the final decision, usually made by the personnel administrator with the approval of the superintendent. If consideration of applicants has been discounted, they should be told immediately. Too often applicants are kept dangling, thinking they are being considered for a position when they are not. Those who cannot be told immediately should be given a date when they will be informed as to whether they have been accepted, are still being considered, or cannot be used. The placement office that sent the

---

[12] Donald L. Haefele, "The Teacher Interview: How Valid," *Phi Delta Kappan* 59, No. 10, June 1978, pp. 683–84.

[13] Thomas R. McDaniel, "The NTE and Teacher Certification," *Phi Delta Kappan* 59, No. 3, November 1977, pp. 186–88.

[14] Bobby R. Johnson, "What Administrators Look for in Teacher Interviews," *Phi Delta Kappan* 58, No. 3, November 1976, pp. 283–84.

candidate's file should also be kept informed as to the status of applicants. If they are not employed, their file should be returned immediately.

SELECTION OF TEACHERS. After the personnel administrator has completed interviews and reviewed the college placement files, those applicants who are deemed to be unqualified for the needed positions should be eliminated. They should be notified of the decision and their files returned. Further information needs to be sought regarding those who appear to be qualified. Since 1975, the Buckley Amendment to the Educational Rights and Privacy Act of 1974 has required that all information in a personnel file be accessible to individuals. This handicaps employers who have traditionally used closed files in the hiring process. Therefore, phone calls or personal contacts become important to gain information that may not be stated in letters of recommendation. The college placement office, the student teaching supervisor, or the superintendent of a district where an applicant may have taught previously are good sources of information.

A selection problem may be the employment of minority teachers. In the *United States* v. *Hazlewood School District* case, which was decided in June 1977, the majority decision stated that the percentage of minority teachers to be employed should be determined by the relevant labor market. Since there was no clarification as to what the relevant labor market was, the decision leaves questions that the courts will have to decide in future employment discrimination cases. Numerous court cases are pending.[15]

When school openings are known, principals should have a strong voice in selecting their teachers. Large school districts, such as New York City, Los Angeles, Detroit, and Chicago, must involve many people in teacher selection since they employ over a thousand teachers each year. They cannot employ for specific positions that are unknown at the time of the interview. Selected applicants must understand that they are employed by the *district* and will be assigned to a new teacher pool until openings occur. Large districts must also use the services of many people to handle the numerous interviews.

NOTIFICATION AND ASSIGNMENT OF ACCEPTABLE TEACHERS. When applicants have been found acceptable, they should be notified in writing and an offer of employment sent. It should contain a deadline for answering so that the district knows whether to hold the position open or look for other applicants.

Although the superintendent is responsible for assignment, this is usually delegated to the personnel administrator. As soon as it is known

---

[15] Thomas J. Flygare, "The Hazlewood Case: How to Use Statistics to Prove (and Disprove) Hiring Discrimination," *Phi Delta Kappan 59*, No. 3, November 1977, pp. 210–11.

where new teachers are to be assigned, they should be notified and advised to visit the school and meet the principal. There may be a problem in assigning teachers, since the necessity to integrate the staffs can cause problems.

Data-processing techniques can be used for keeping track of applicants, scheduling, notifying, and assigning. It is a complex task to match vacancies with applicants whose training, qualifications, and certification qualify them for assignment.

The Local School's Role in Preservice Teacher Education

Schools must take part in shaping their most important tool, the teacher. Schools of education cannot do it all. Regardless of the excellence of course work, teacher candidates need to relate to students in actual situations and master sequential teaching, learning, organization, management, and other skills in order to become competent.

THE ROLE OF THE PARTICIPATING SCHOOL.   The school's most significant contribution to the teacher education process is the enriching clinical experience it provides for the student teacher. Close cooperation between the school and the training institution is essential for the success of the student teaching (or directed teaching) experience. Because the key person in this process is the supervising teacher, the selection of this teacher should be given priority, and usually is accomplished best by the school in consultation with the college or university.

THE PRINCIPAL'S ROLE.   The principal as the building's educational leader sets the stage for successful directed teaching. He or she introduces the new student teacher to the school and to its teachers and other personnel and sees that rules, regulations, and policies are explained and understood. Terminology that is consistent with that of the training institution should be used. Most colleges avoid the terms "practice teacher" and "practice teaching;" many refer to the student teacher as "associate teacher." The school principal interprets the directed teaching program to the school and community and outlines suggested procedures for all involved. The new student teacher is made to feel welcome in a situation that too frequently is filled with apprehension and anxiety. The principal confers with the professor or coordinator from the training institution and maintains open lines of communication for each individual on the teacher education team.

The principal should be aware of the progress of the student teacher and may be requested to complete a rating form for placement purposes. The student teacher's supervising teacher also should make an evaluation.

An additional advantage to the school, and one that is frequently overlooked, relates to recruitment and selection.[16] The principal and other administrators are able to observe closely and to select early the highly competent prospective teacher. Once selected, the candidate may be groomed specifically for future assignment.

Inservice Improvement in the Local School

No matter how excellent the preservice preparation and how well qualified teachers are at the time of employment, principals must not assign them to a classroom and forget them. Inservice education is an imperative for both teachers and administrators in a rapidly changing, complex environment of systems technology, accountability, needs assessment, and other developments.

It is the responsibility of each individual to seek self-improvement and the responsibility of the school to provide ample opportunities for such improvement. Inservice programs should be based upon competent needs assessment by all individuals involved in the school, including parents, community, and, to a varying degree, students.

Marks, Stoops, and King-Stoops define inservice education as including "all activities of school personnel which contribute to their continued professional growth and competence" and give nine basic principles of inservice education:

1. The inservice program emerges from recognized needs of the school and community.
2. All school personnel need inservice education.
3. Proper supervision is an effective means of accelerating the inservice professional growth of personnel.
4. Improving the quality of instruction is the immediate and long-range objective of inservice education.
5. Inservice education leads to a continuous process of reexamination and revision of the educational program. Additionally, it encourages participants to attain self-realization through competence, accomplishment, and security.
6. Inservice education has become an increasing concern of state agencies, colleges and universities, school boards, school administrators, and teachers.
7. Supervisors should create an atmosphere that will stimulate a desire on the part of teachers for inservice growth.

---

[16] Joyce B. King, "Analysis of the Southern California Elementary Teacher Assistant Program" (unpublished doctoral dissertation, University of Southern California, 1966), pp. 148–50.

8. The inservice program should provide for keeping abreast with research and advances in education.
9. An inservice program is most effective when cooperatively initiated and planned.[17]

An inservice program, using the school as a laboratory, might be organized in the following manner:

1. Through group action and discussion, arrive at a basic agreement upon the educational philosophy, goals, and objectives of the school system, with the emphasis upon greater accountability.
2. Compare collectively the current practices of the school district with the announced objectives.
3. List the conflicts uncovered in order of priority.
4. Set up a schedule for attacking problems, and assign staff members most interested in certain areas to attempt solutions.
5. Invite outside experts and consultants to contribute to the final solutions.
6. Facilitate outside study in related areas so that needed data may be gathered.
7. Experiment under controlled conditions after tentatively adopting a hypothesis indicated by the majority.
8. Evaluate results of the experiment; if a solution to the original problem is found, implement the solution as soon as possible.

The inservice program should be negotiated regarding: the number of days, the time of the meetings, shortened or released days for attendance, the topics to be considered, and what professional or college credit will be allowed by the district.

An important part of inservice education is the development of objectives. What should the students be able to achieve, create, and produce? Under what conditions? And how will teachers get students to that point? Figure 17–1 shows relationships between curriculum variables and teaching in the development of objectives.

Goals and objectives should be defined at the outset by teachers and administrators and should be agreed upon as a basis for competency, direction, growth, improvement of instruction, and evaluation. This procedure precludes either the teacher's or the administrator's planning alone and fosters cooperation and teamwork. The community should be invited to take part in defining the goals whenever possible, thus broadening involvement. Identification of the more specific objectives usually is the professionals' concern and responsibility.

---

[17] James R. Marks, Emery Stoops, and Joyce King-Stoops, *Handbook of Educational Supervision*, 2nd ed., p. 169.

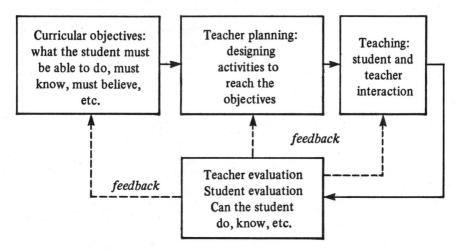

FIGURE 17–1. Relationships Between Curriculum Variables and Teaching.
From S. C. T. Clarke, "General Teaching Theory," The Journal of Teacher Education *2, 3 (Fall 1970), p. 407. Reprinted with permission.*

Measurable, precise, succinct objectives that offer built-in criteria for evaluation of performance are essential for implementation and evaluation of the curriculum and instruction.

Inservice programs should be flexible in order to adapt to the changing needs of the community, curriculum, and staff. By identifying student needs, teachers best identify their own needs. The principal is a key person in observing, consulting with, and advising teachers and helping them select the inservice programs that will make them more proficient.

If a district uses a merit pay plan, it should develop a preparation–experience type of salary schedule which is generous in its financial provisions and is designed to encourage graduate study and participation in extended inservice programs.

Multifaceted Inservice Programs

Within the framework of local school situations, there are a number of methods whereby problem solving can be implemented and inservice improvement rendered more meaningful.

INSTITUTES AND WORKSHOPS. Special presentations and programs arranged either by the school district or by a state or intermediate educational office should be a continuing part of inservice education.

UNIVERSITY WORK. Summer sessions, correspondence courses, and year-long extension course work are valuable inservice education devices.

TRAVEL. Travel is broadening. For example, a teacher of American government can learn from a trip to Washington, D.C.; and a science instructor may conceivably pick up significant teaching data from a tour of the Smithsonian Institute or the Hayden Planetarium. The indiscriminate use of travel as an inservice educational method is not justified.

TEACHERS' MEETINGS. Perhaps the most widely neglected inservice training method is the faculty meeting. The teachers' meeting in inservice training should be used for serious investigation of current problems of real importance. A faculty meeting designed to be part of inservice education may receive reports from committees of teachers and staff members, hear presentations from visiting authorities on instructional matters, and arrive at specific recommendations on current educational practice within the district.

Building administrators have the responsibility for planning teachers' meetings and should do this by working with a committee of teachers in their schools. The plans should include an assessment of needs, time and length of the meeting, topics to be discussed, and resources to be procured. Too often faculty meetings become a waste of time by taking up trivial matters that could have been handled by a bulletin.

TEACHER VISITATIONS. Several times during the school year, individual instructors should be encouraged to turn their pupils over to a capable substitute and visit other teachers within or outside the district from whom they may learn new techniques and a variety of methods.

PROFESSIONAL PUBLICATIONS. All educators should be exposed regularly to professional thinking outside their own immediate surroundings. Books, journals, and bulletins should be provided in a school district's inservice training program.

LECTURES AND FORUMS. In rural and relatively isolated school districts, much can be accomplished in inservice development by bringing in ideas, rather than sending teachers to cities to absorb such information.

TEACHER CENTERS. In 1976, Congress enacted Public Law 94–482 which provided an initial funding of $75 million annually to establish Teacher Centers. The purpose was to provide locally operated inservice programs to break through the traditional methods used to improve classroom skills and techniques. Teacher Centers would provide available research, alternative approaches, and bring in experienced teachers from other districts to provide expertise. Teachers themselves would conduct Teacher Center programs rather than outside "experts" who may not know local problems and needs. Many teachers are bored to exhaustion by most inservice programs run by so-called experts to tell them what should be done.[18]

Constructive Supervision

The most effective way of improving performance is to inform teachers of their strengths and weaknesses. A whole field has grown up around the problem of teacher supervision. Basically, the problem is twofold: first, the supervisory officer and the teacher should reach an agreement on the objectives and how best to attain them; second, the teacher must welcome and be able to profit from suggestions and criticisms that inevitably arise out of supervision.

MODERN SUPERVISION. Instead of a system of routine visitations, notations, and formal conferences, modern supervision stresses cooperative planning and evaluation. It attempts to free teachers from routine directives and regulations, and to encourage them to grow in competency according to their own particular abilities. The goal is actually self-supervision. The supervisor operates within the framework of this philosophy as a consulting expert.

Coordination is arrived at through group planning and mutual understanding. Instead of regarding supervision as an end in itself, modern theory correctly regards it as an important field of inservice teacher training.

AUTONOMOUS SUPERVISION. Flexibility is an essential quality of supervision. It is vital, therefore, that its administration and programming be left in the hands of individual school principals to develop their own supervisory program tailored to their own needs with district supervisors acting as visiting resource persons.

GROUP SUPERVISION. Group supervision ideally should be applied to the needs of both the individual and the faculty as a whole. Cooperative consideration of existing needs and group discussion of research findings in the field of instruction should serve as the basis of any school's supervisory program. The program, once determined by all concerned, should be applied through suitable channels to individual teachers in their daily contacts with pupils.

SUPERVISORY PERSONNEL. Two traditional classifications exist: general and special. The general supervisor is concerned with broad aspects of

---

[18] NEA Government Relations and NEA Instruction and Professional Development, "Congress Enacts NEA Teacher Center Bill," *Tdoay's Education* 66, No. 2, March–April 1977, pp. 74–75.

curriculum and teaching competence. The special supervisor is a specialist in single subject fields, as music and art, but increasingly in the more general subjects such as mathematics and science. The general supervisor is enjoying greater popularity and is assuming an increasing role as an internal district employee rather than as an expert from outside. In many cases the principal is the chief supervisory person in a school, and often may be the only one.

School districts are tending to employ coordinators of instruction as regular staff members and, in larger districts, to use the services of an overall supervisory officer with the title of Assistant Superintendent in Charge of Instruction. Special supervisors are commonly attached today to either state or intermediate educational departments. Their function is to assist several school districts within a given area in problems of specialized subject instruction.

AREAS OF SUPERVISION. The scope of supervision oriented toward the total learning process is broader than it is under a philosophy of supervision as mere improvement of specific techniques. The supervisor, whether general or special, must be concerned at one time or another with the following areas of major importance:

1. Philosophy, goals, and objectives.
2. Curriculum.
3. Community life.
4. Discipline and behavior.
5. Equipment and supplies.
6. Inservice training.
7. Retention and promotion.
8. Professional relations.
9. Extracurricular activities.
10. Personal problems of teachers.

APPRAISAL OF SUPERVISION. The superintendent of schools supervises not instruction, but supervision. Machinery must be set up to facilitate regular evaluation of the supervisory program. The primary duty of the superintendent of schools is the constant improvement of the instructional program. Supervisory personnel are the main contact with that program.

Evaluating Personnel Efficiency

No area of school administration is more fraught with perils than personnel appraisal. School administrators retain their positions over a period of years largely because of their ability to attract and retain effective personnel; yet the techniques and devices upon which this ability depends are in a regrettably primitive stage. To compound the problem, teachers seem at times to oppose actively any scientific attempt to evaluate their competence, rendering still more difficult the efforts of the administration to identify employees who deserve most fully to be retained and promoted. If above-average employees are to be obtained and kept by the district, then the district must evaluate its personnel in some way.

All teachers are rated. They are rated by their students and by the parents of the community, regardless of whether there is a formal rating system used by the school district employing them. Their relative status in the community and in the school depends upon this highly informal and sometimes grossly unfair evaluation, based upon second-hand information and subjective impressions. It is apparent that, since teachers are inevitably rated in one way or another, it would be best to accomplish this through some agreed-upon and logically defensible method of evaluation.

Marks, Stoops, and King-Stoops, in their *Handbook of Educational Supervision,* set forth basic principles for teacher evaluation and suggest ways in which evaluation can be used for inservice training. This approach is valuable because it focuses the whole evaluative process on the improvement of instruction for students.[19]

Teacher evaluation has two main functions: managerial and the professional development of the teacher. The managerial function helps the administrator make the decision concerning retention or release. The professional development function facilitates, guides, and directs the teacher in realistic self-assessment, establishing educational goals, and developing a practical plan to work toward those goals.[20] Some of the purposes of teacher evaluation are:

1. To secure the best possible education for young people through quality instruction.
2. To provide continued opportunities for each teacher to grow in competence and, through proper recognition of the individual's success, to stimulate that person to even greater accomplishments.
3. To assist professional personnel in improving their service to the district.
4. To provide evidence for the selection and retention of new and permanent teachers.
5. To provide a record of professional service.

---

[19] James R. Marks, Emery Stoops, and Joyce King-Stoops, *Handbook of Educational Supervision: A Guide for the Practitioner,* 2nd ed., pp. 289–336.

[20] M. Dale Lambert, "Refocussing Teacher Evaluation: A Process of Guided Self-Analysis," *Thrust for Education Leadership,* p. 41.

6. To provide assurance to the public that the utmost care is being taken to obtain and retain the best teachers for the young people of the community.

PRINCIPLES FOR EVALUATING PERSONNEL.   Professional evaluation involves the formulation of value judgments. The procedures should be based on established principles. The following principles are suggested for adaptation and use by superintendents:

1. Genuinely democratic procedures should be applied.
    a. The evaluator should demonstrate fairness to the employee.
    b. Employees should know what is expected of them, and should be made fully acquainted with the appraisal techniques.
    c. Employees should know the exact nature and degree of any dissatisfaction with their services, and be given time and aid for correction of these deficiencies.
    d. Employees desiring a review of their evaluations should feel free to contact the principal or superintendent.
    e. Age, sex, marital status, religion and other personal matters that do not affect employees' performance of their duties should not be considered in the evaluation.
    f. Ratings, though necessarily subjective, should be based on as much positive, objective evidence as possible.
2. The first step in setting up an evaluation program should be development of a set of performance standards.
3. The community and the school system should be informed about the evaluation program and given a chance to improve it.
4. An evaluation program should be studied critically, and always be subject to revision.
5. Evaluation should be a professional improvement and guidance device.
6. Evaluation is of little value without an attempt to correct weaknesses discovered.
7. Appraisal should be a continuous process.
8. Each employee should be given a copy of evaluation policies when first hired; evaluation policies should be set forth in detail in the district handbook, school handbook, or similar publication.
9. The evaluator should demonstrate impartiality to all employees.
10. Self-appraisal by teachers and others should be encouraged.
11. The primary factor in the success of an evaluation program is the quality of human relations governing use of the evaluation instruments, not the quality of the instruments themselves.
12. Evaluators should rate only those aspects with which they are most familiar, omitting comment on other items.
13. Evaluation programs should discourage comparison of one employee with another.
14. The latest rating of an employee should be the major one considered, rather than an average of all ratings.
15. The evaluator should be alert for symptoms of incipient mental, social, and physical maladjustments, and prescribe preventive activities.

16. Follow-up conferences should accompany the written evaluation.

17. Purposes of the evaluation program should be both administrative and supervisory in nature, the emphasis being on improvement of instruction.

FUNCTIONS OF THE DISTRICT PERSONNEL OFFICE IN THE EVALUATION PROGRAM. The personnel office, although it is not usually responsible for evaluating personnel, has functions such as: coordinating the evaluation program, preparing evaluation forms, orientation of new personnel, in-service training in evaluation procedures, recordkeeping, counseling evaluators and evaluees, and working with the committee responsible for the evaluation process.[21] The personnel office has an intrinsic interest in teacher evaluation because it has the major responsibility for recruiting, employing, and assigning teachers. Personnel administrators, whether or not they help evaluate, should assume a responsibility for visiting new teachers in their classrooms. What they observe will help in future selections, and the teacher will also appreciate their continued interest.

The personnel office should see that teachers are evaluated according to the policies of the district; that time schedules for reports are met; that eligibility for tenure is established; and that earned tenure is granted. In cases involving dismissal, the personnel office notifies the school board and the teacher; notifies teachers of their rights; sees that legal requirements are followed; and prepares the case for possible hearings or court action.

VARIOUS EVALUATION METHODS. Completely objective evaluation is an ideal but unattainable goal. However, it is necessary for the administrator to adopt one or more of the available rating methods.

Traditionally, principals have rated teachers on a checklist type of sheet or card which included such items as: skill as an instructor, attitude toward young people, supervision, judgment and tact, emotional stability, ability to control a class, initiative, daily preparation, knowledge of subject field, classroom environment, accuracy in keeping records, promptness, physical and emotional health, personal appearance, and relationships with staff and parents. Research does not clearly indicate that any of these factors affect pupil progress. Formerly the rating sheet or card was composed by the administration and used exclusively by the supervising officer. Often teachers were never informed of their rating score, and were downgraded or discharged with no actual reasons given. The rating was usually based on one or two short classroom visitations that might or might not have been followed by a conference. Tenured teachers were usually evaluated only once every year or two, often without classroom observations. "Such perfunctory procedures have obvious weaknesses—they are one-sided and subjective; they have little value as documentation in dismissal hearings; they do not provide for any participation by the teacher;

---

[21] American Association of School Administrators, *Profiles*, pp. 81–82.

they provide no real help for the teacher needing improvement; and they assess the teacher rather than the teaching act."[22] One of the problems associated with evaluation is the variability of students.

The trend is toward the use of rating devices as an aid to improvement of instruction rather than solely as a basis for rehiring or dismissal. Regardless of how it is used, the written instrument itself should be developed cooperatively by teachers working on a committee with administrators and supervisors. In this way, the product of the thinking of the group will tend to be acceptable to all, and thus will achieve its maximum utility.

NEW APPROACHES TO TEACHER EVALUATION. Teacher competence is multi-dimensional and difficult to determine. The usual rating sheet does not provide a satisfactory method of evaluating competence. Some of the new experimental methods that presently are used by only a few school systems are discussed in the following paragraphs.[23]

USE OF MULTIPLE EVALUATIONS. To overcome the one-sided (by only the principal) evaluation, assessments are made by a committee of superiors, peers, subordinates, students, and parents. The final evaluation can be made by individuals or by a consensus.

USE OF PERFORMANCE OBJECTIVES. The management-by-objectives program is the most revolutionary evaluation procedure. Long- and short-range goals are determined by the superintendent, district administrators, and the board of education for the district. Sometimes parents, and even students, help to develop the goals. The principal, assistant principal, and teachers determine the goals for a school, for a department, and for a classroom. The teacher may determine goals for each student. The objectives should be attainable, measurable, and as precisely written as possible. Once the objectives for a classroom and the students have been agreed upon, standards of performance should be developed to determine whether the accomplishment can be considered successful. The results should be predetermined as accurately as possible. Acceptable evaluation means that the agreed-upon goals have been met. Since goals may change, evaluation must also change. (It should be pointed out that the one who worries the most is the insecure teacher.)

The evaluation of the goal achievement of the individual teacher should be based on objective judgment and may be made by a single evaluator, the evaluator and the evaluee, or may include opinions from peers, parents, or students.

---

[22] National Education Association, Research Division, "New Approaches in the Evaluation of School Personnel," *Research Bulletin* 50, May 1972, p. 41.

[23] National Education Association, Research Division, "New Approaches," pp. 41–44.

Teachers and teacher associations have been reluctant to accept evaluation based on performance objectives because they have not been able to control the variables necessary for satisfactory achievement of their objectives. These variables include such factors as: the learning environment, classroom load, materials, supplies, equipment, and support services. This reluctance will continue until:

1. Teachers have a strong voice in helping to develop policies.
2. Job descriptions for teachers spell out what is expected of a teacher and what services will be available to help.
3. Teachers are involved in developing performance objectives, expected standards of performance, and the evaluation program.
4. Teachers help determine their classroom load, supplies, materials, and equipment.
5. Administrators are evaluated as to their performance standards in reaching their performance objectives.

It is obvious that the objectives for teachers in one school or other schools in the same district will be different. The achievement of a class in a culturally disadvantaged neighborhood will usually be less than that in an upper-class community. The percentage of gain in achievement in relation to other similar groups can be measured if the data can be made available. For example, a 10 percent gain in reading in a bi-lingual area in relation to other similar areas may be just as great as the same gain in an upper-class community in relation to its similar areas. Yet the actual reading level of the two classes may be totally different. These things must be considered when performance objectives are developed and the teacher is evaluated on achievement in reaching the objectives.

CLIENT-CENTERED EVALUATION. Client-centered evaluation applies to the evaluation of administrators at all levels. It allows clients to be more involved in controlling matters that affect their lives. Teachers, parents, and students can furnish a general evaluation of a principal's overall performance in areas where they have direct contact with the principal. There is an obligation to be objective and constructive. The performance objectives on which the evaluation is based should be cooperatively developed with input from those being guided as well as from their leader. Client-centered evaluation seeks to assess the degree to which the objectives are achieved.[24]

---

[24] George B. Redfern, "Client-Centered Evaluation," *The School Administrator*, pp. 7–10. The Educational Research Service, sponsored jointly by the NEA Research Division and the American Association of School Administrators, has published the following booklets: *Evaluating Administrative/Supervisory Performance*, ERS Circular No. 6, 1971, Stock No. 219–21504, and *Evaluating Teacher Performance*, ERS Circular No. 2, 1972, Stock No. 219–21510.

USE OF MULTIPLE EVALUATION BASES. This combines an evaluation of effective teaching techniques and performance objectives. These two types of evaluation may be made at different times and by different evaluators.

USE OF IN-BASKET DATA. In this evaluation procedure, all good and bad data regarding incidents and facts are placed in the teacher's file. They could include classroom observation reports, transcripts of courses taken, letters of complaint or commendation, reports of participation in school or community activities, achievements earned, leadership positions, inservice participation, and statements regarding suggestions for improvement. Specific documentary data, such as this, is valuable when evidence is needed to justify retention, advancement, or dismissal.

USE OF STUDENT PERFORMANCE. This controversial evaluation procedure is based solely on the achievement of a teacher's students. Achievement goals are established for the class and the evaluation is based on the percentage of students who reach the goals.

When merit pay is based on teachers' accountability, standardized achievement tests may be used. These should be correlated by the guidance department of the district so that the improvement of students may be measured objectively each year.

SELF-EVALUATION. One of the best methods for teachers to determine how they are teaching and progressing is to evaluate themselves. The Purdue Teachers Examination is one of a number of instruments that lend themselves to self-criticism and appraisal.[25] Another valuable device is the National Teacher Examination, which enables teachers to test themselves on their proficiency in areas such as child development, methods of teaching, and major subject fields.[26]

CO-EVALUATION. The method is sometimes called multiple evaluation. As many supervisory officers as possible should participate in the evaluation. Further, the ratings conducted by these several supervisory persons should be made as many different times as possible.

Co-evaluation also includes participation in the rating process by the teacher. A common practice is for the supervisor to invite teachers to fill out their own rating card during the same period of time that the administrator is filling one out. On a specified date, the two then meet to go over the items covered by the rating instrument. A genuine attempt is made to achieve a meeting of minds.

---

[25] I. B. Kelly and J. K. Perkins, *Purdue Teachers Examinations: How I Teach* (Minneapolis: Educational Test Bureau, Educational Publishers, Inc.).

[26] *National Teacher Examinations*, Bulletin of Information (Princeton, N.J.: Educational Testing Service).

MERIT PAY AND EVALUATION. Merit pay is a method of rewarding superior teachers. It has taken many forms:

1. Super-maximums.
2. Accelerated increments.
3. Bonus plans.
4. Multiple track.
5. Periodic merit evaluation.
6. Annual outstanding teacher awards.

The district's teacher association should be involved in formulating a merit-pay salary schedule. The procedures to be used and method of evaluation should be negotiated and agreed upon.

Proponents claim that a merit-pay plan helps retain superior teachers and avoids losing them to supervisory or administrative positions or to other professions. It recognizes differences in ability and rewards competence. Those who oppose merit pay have made statements such as:

1. Evaluation is too subjective to determine a salary.
2. There is a lack of agreement as to what constitutes good teaching.
3. Many of the aims of education are intangible and difficult or impossible to measure.
4. Dissension may be created and resentment between teachers fostered.
5. Teachers generally resent merit-rating salary schedules.

If merit pay is based on evaluation, there should be sufficient supervisory personnel with competence in subject matter, knowledge of learning processes, skill in evaluation, and the ability to work with others. In order to identify superior teachers in each school, an evaluating committee composed of the principal, a supervisor, and three veteran teachers could be used. Teachers and observers must recognize that subjectivity in observing methods is an inherent element in the merit-pay program and cannot be completely avoided. However, there must be a high degree of trust, sincerity, and fairness by all concerned.

EVALUATION OF PRINCIPALS AND ADMINISTRATORS. If the chief purpose in appraisal is the diagnosis of strengths and weaknesses in an effort to bring about professional improvement, the principal as leader of the school requires appraisal even more than teachers. Several methods have been proposed for evaluating principals:

1. By the superintendent.
2. By the superintendent and other superiors.
3. By the parents.

4. By teachers.
5. By other personnel.
6. By a team approach.

Whatever method is used, it should be cooperatively planned and agreements should be reached as to the criteria to be used, the evaluation schedule to be established, and the follow-up procedures to be followed.

Principals and district administrators must be rated for purposes of retention; usually they are assessed in terms of doing a satisfactory or unsatisfactory job. Too often, administrators are not evaluated formally for constructive purposes, aside from retention.

Principals have many responsibilities—more than ever before: developing the curriculum; establishing goals and objectives and the instructional strategies to implement them; supervising and evaluating all personnel; developing community relationships; developing and administering the school's budget; supervising the business management of the school, transportation, and school maintenance and operation. Principals should be evaluated in regard to how well they planned to carry out the above responsibilities and the results. In other words, they should be held accountable for the outcomes in relation to expected performance as shown by their leadership skills.[27]

The only evaluation superintendents usually receive is when the board of education either re-employs them or dismisses them, sometimes without warning.

Rating of administrators as a means of helping them grow professionally is extremely complicated because of the complexity of their responsibilities and functions. A diagnostic rating blank defining and measuring their functions runs into considerable length.

Whether or not administrators are evaluated formally, they should develop their own objectives and the procedures they expect to use to attain them. They can list all their functions and responsibilities and develop a checklist to analyze their strengths and weaknesses. Self-evaluation is as important for the administrator as for the teacher. Evaluation should lead to improved performance.

PUPIL ACHIEVEMENT FOR TEACHER EVALUATION. This pragmatic approach denies the importance of teachers' characteristics and stresses the predominant significance of teachers' results. The only results that can be satisfactorily measured within a reasonable length of time are in the areas of pupil subject achievement and behavior.

---

[27] Michael Brick and Robert Sanchis, "Evaluating the Principal," *Thrust for Education Leadership* 2, No. 1, October 1972, pp. 32–34.

CONSTRUCTIVE USE OF EVALUATION.   Although it is inevitable that rating will always be used to justify the retention or termination of employees, *the principal constructive use of evaluation should be the improvement of individuals in their chosen field.* Rating can and should be the most effective instrument to diagnose strengths and weaknesses. In this connection, the evaluation program should be put to practical use in the following specific ways:

1. Teachers should use rating sheets to compare their opinions of their own teaching ability with those of the evaluators. All discrepancies should be noted, and an honest effort made to ascertain whether or not indicated weaknesses have any basis in actuality. When teachers become aware of areas of their teaching where improvement is shown to be needed, they then will be in a position to undertake the necessary steps toward self-improvement.
2. Teachers can engage in cooperative analysis of teaching weaknesses and strengths. Often certain patterns of general strengths and failings can be discerned within a school system and profitably studied.
3. Administrators also should use the evaluation program to map out a long-range plan for continuing betterment in the implementation of the program itself. Any district-wide rating plan is capable of improvement. The danger lies in complacency.
4. The board of education in any district should use the rating system as an important facet in its appraisal of the success or failure of the entire program of supervision. While it is probably unsuitable and impractical for a school board to engage in examinations of individual ratings, it is certainly appropriate for board members to be constantly informed of the results of the evaluation program.

All evaluative methods described in this chapter have their proper place in the operation of teacher evaluation. The danger lies in relying too exclusively on any one technique. The ideal rating procedure would be a continuous process, going on throughout the school year.

DISMISSAL OR NON-REEMPLOYMENT.   Dismissal refers to removal during the term of a contract. Non-reemployment is failure to recommend employment at the end of the contract period. The term dismissal is commonly used for both situations. Teachers should be retained or dismissed in general accordance with their effectiveness or incompetence, not as a result of personal prejudices or purely subjective impressions.

Typical causes for dismissal are:

1. Immoral or unprofessional conduct.
2. Incompetency.

3. Evident unfitness for service.
4. Physical or mental condition unfitting a teacher to instruct or associate with children.
5. Persistent violations of or refusal to obey school laws or reasonable regulations of the board or the state board.
6. Conviction of a felony or of any crime involving moral turpitude.

More and more teachers are appealing to the courts over dismissal decisions. If the court is to uphold the dismissal action, evidence to support the cause must prove the persistent nature of the difficulties, show that repeated warnings have been given, and frequent assistance has been provided. Dismissal evidence must be specific in nature, extensive in scope, recorded, dated, and timed. Written evidence must consist of the original drafts made at the time or immediately after the observation or conference. State laws must be followed regarding reasons for dismissal, notification dates, legal deadlines that must be met, and notifications given to the teacher. The burden of proof is on the school district. There must be just cause. The procedure to be followed must be fair and meet the requirements of "due process."

Dismissal should usually be regarded as a confession of failure on the part of the administration. Logic leads inexorably to one of two conclusions in the case of the discharged teacher: (1) Improper or inadequate screening led to the original employment of an unfit person. (2) Lack of proper supervisory assistance resulted in either deterioration or failure to improve while in service.

Because of declining enrollments, many schools find it necessary to reduce their staffs. Policies should be developed through the negotiation process to determine the layoff procedures to be used. The best plan is that teachers will be given layoff notices on the basis of the kind of credentials they hold, the types of services and programs the board of education has slated for elimination, the seniority of the teachers, recommendations by administrators, and any additional pertinent information that it available. Since attrition usually occurs, teachers should be re-employed in reverse order to the order of layoff. Teachers who are laid off can also be used as long-term substitutes.

Teacher Tenure

Tenure guarantees maximum security to teachers. The principle behind tenure is that of freedom from arbitrary dismissal. Its strength lies in its assurance to teachers of years of security in which to grow professionally and teach constructively, as long as they do not violate established rules and regulations of the state and school district in which they are employed.

Its weakness lies in the perpetuation of the occasional poor teacher who survives preliminary screening and probationary scrutiny to achieve permanence.

Tenure usually is acquired either by statutory provision or by act of the governing body of the school district. Many states provide that teachers shall be classified as *probationary* until they have completed a prescribed number of years of service in a given district, at which time they achieve permanency. This probationary period should be longer than one year but less than five; three years is probably the optimum period. Most tenure laws provide for dismissal for cause only after the teacher has achieved permanent status.

Since there has been considerable misunderstanding about the function of employee tenure in school systems, the following basic concepts or principles will serve as guidelines for administering the tenure program:

1. The principal reason for tenure should be student benefit; sound and properly administered tenure programs must promote student welfare.
2. Tenure should be considered a privilege, not an inherent right.
3. Tenure policies should be established on a statewide basis.
4. Tenure should be restricted to certificated personnel.
5. Careful initial selection and a successful probationary period (which may actually be considered part of the selection process) should precede the granting of tenure.
6. Tenure provisions should not prevent prompt dismissal of ineffective employees.
7. Tenure legislation should define dismissal procedures in detail.
8. Tenure should recognize the principle of seniority in the event of unavoidable reduction of staff.

STATE REGULATIONS OF TENURE. More than half the states have laws sanctioning some form of tenure for teachers. Most of these laws provide for a teacher to automatically qualify for permanency after completion of a prescribed number of years of service.

Tenure laws of one type or another have been enacted in forty-six states. Kansas, Nebraska, Oregon, and Wisconsin provide for continuing contracts. Georgia, Mississippi, South Carolina, Utah, and Vermont have no tenure provisions but provide annual or long-term contracts. Most tenure laws provide for qualified teachers to qualify automatically for permanent employment after usually two to five years of service. The laws vary from state to state as to who is covered. Some states include certain administrators, supervisors, and other staff members as well as teachers, while others include only teachers. In order to dismiss tenured teachers, all forty-six states provide for due process and most provide for appellate or review processes.[28] There must be just cause for termination of tenure, although it is legal to dismiss teachers for shortages of funds or lack of work. Procedures for dismissal from tenure are subject to bargaining and negotiation, the same as for nontenured teachers.

Many administrators are dissatisfied with permanent tenure laws and would like to have them reformed by extending the probationary period or replacing them with renewable two-to-five-year contracts.

Teacher Workload and Working Conditions

The crux of the excessive work load problem seems to lie with the individual teacher. If teaching is regarded as a chore rather than as a rewarding experience, as a job rather than as a form of creative expression, then almost any minute transgression will constitute an excessive load.

The problem of overloading can be prevented or lessened if elementary classes have twenty-five or fewer pupils and secondary classes twenty or fewer students. The provision of qualified substitute teachers, adequate clerical services, adequate classrooms, facilities, supplies, and equipment help teachers with large classes. Teachers also do a better job if they are assigned to duties closely related to their interests, preparation, and experience. They are more receptive to changes in their assignments or programs when they are consulted beforehand. Excessive teacher load can be significantly ameliorated by inspirational and meaningful leadership and the application of basic principles of good personnel management.

WORKING CONDITIONS.   In addition to a well-ventilated, well-lighted, and well-heated classroom, teacher satisfaction is affected by factors such as: convenient parking facilities, storage cupboards for personal belongings, quiet eating area, adequate restroom facilities, and restful lounge rooms.

Leaves of Absence

A teacher who has provided faithful and competent service, and whom the district wishes to retain, should apply for and receive some type of leave of absence. There are several varieties of leave of absence: sabbatical, maternity, political, military, bereavement, sick, and personal.

The principal has the responsibility for verifying the legitimacy of the request for a leave of absence, and making a recommendation for approval to the board of education.

---

[28] William R. Hazard, "Tenure Laws in Theory and Practice," *Phi Delta Kappan* 56, No. 7, March 1975, pp. 451–54.

SABBATICAL LEAVE. School districts customarily pay a teacher for time spent on professional duties outside the classroom. Such duties may include conventions, conferences, visitations, programs, and professional organization duties. In addition to these short-term absences, teachers properly should be granted long-term leaves at stated intervals in order to pursue advanced degrees, formal or independent study, travel, or a combination of these.

Sabbatical leaves are granted by the board of education on recommendation of the superintendent. Districts vary on the requirements for length of the sabbatical and on payment of full or partial salary. Leaves are usually granted after six to seven years of service in the district, seven years being the most common term. The number of those on leave is limited usually to a percentage, commonly 2 percent of the certificated personnel.

Those requesting sabbatical leaves should make a formal request, stating their purpose. At the expiration of the leave, teachers usually are required to return to the district for a year or two or rescind their salary. Upon return, they should be reinstated in their previous position or, if that is not possible, assigned to work in an area appropriate to their training.

MATERNITY LEAVE. Maternity leave policies generally require the discontinuance of teaching at a specific time, usually about the fourth or fifth month of pregnancy. The National Education Association claims that policies requiring pregnant teachers to take a leave at a designated time are discriminatory and that individual cases should be decided upon individual characteristics.[29]

Subpart E of Title IX prohibits sex discrimination against employees and requires school districts to treat pregnancy as any other temporary disability. This law is controversial, as shown in the *Romeo* case where the judge ruled that Subpart E is unauthorized by the statute and is unenforceable.[30] The ruling is being appealed to the circuit court.

Court rulings leave a state of uncertainty regarding payment for pregnancy leaves of absence. Title VII of the Civil Rights Act of 1964 did not make clear a position regarding pregnancy leave. There is confusion as to whether it is a temporary disability which should be paid for as are other reasons for sick leave.[31]

While court decisions increasingly rule in favor of maternity leaves, the district is not prevented from setting up reasonable regulations for

---

[29] National Education Association, "Discriminating Against the Pregnant Teacher," *Today's Education*, pp. 33–35.

[30] *Romeo Community Schools* v. *HEW*, 438 F. Supp. 1021 (DC Mich. 1977).

[31] Thomas J. Flygare, "A Legal Embarrassment: Paid Sick Leave for Pregnant Teachers," *Phi Delta Kappan* 59, No. 8, April 1978, pp. 558–59.

maternity leaves of absence, based on agreed-upon factors of health and safety.

Districts vary as to the time of return to service, but often the leave is for one year, renewable for a second year. Whatever policy is adopted for maternity leaves, it should be realistic and reasonable, and conform to the statutes.

POLITICAL OR CIVIC LEAVE.   As employees, not as officers of the school district, teachers have a legal right to hold public office. If elected, they should be granted a leave of absence without pay for the duration of their term.

MILITARY LEAVE.   Military leaves must be granted when the employee is called into the armed services for training or extended duty.

BEREAVEMENT LEAVE.   Bereavement leave should be granted with pay when employees lose a member of their immediate family. The term "immediate family" must be defined. Most school districts specify the allowable number of bereavement days, the most common being five days (three days is the next most frequent provision). Some districts combine bereavement leave with sick leave provisions. District policy should spell out the definitions, provisions, and the method of requesting, verifying, and reporting bereavement leave.

SICK LEAVE.   State laws, district policies, or teacher contracts generally specify provisions for sick leave. It is common procedure, especially in larger school districts, to grant five to ten days of sick leave each year with full pay. Some states grant one day of sick leave yearly for each month worked, with the stipulation that the employee work at least 75 percent of the working days in the month. Cumulative sick leave allows those who maintain good health to accrue thirty, fifty, or an unlimited number of sick leave days to use when emergencies arise. The limit of accumulation depends upon state and district regulations. In contrast to this cumulative principle is the bonus method, whereby teachers are rewarded financially at the end of the year by a pay overage based on their approach to perfect attendance, or penalized by subtraction of a portion of their regular salary for each day's absence. Teacher organizations advocate payment of accumulated sick leave days upon retirement.

Various laws pertain to payment for sick leave after the earned days are used up. Provisions include full pay for up to three months if no substitute teacher is employed, or the difference in pay between the employee's salary and the substitute's for up to five months. Under extenuating circumstances, the school board may decide on the amount of pay and the length of the leave.

District policy should state how sick leave is earned, how it is compensated for, how it is to be verified, and what physical examinations, if any, are required.

PERSONAL LEAVE. Personal leave has generally been granted without compensation. Some states and many forward-looking districts provide leaves with pay for emergencies or personal necessity. There have been difficulties in defining carefully which causes are to be considered acceptable for nonillness absences. Teacher organizations propose a plan of granting several days of personal leave each year with pay and without stating the reason. Whatever is decided upon, the regulations regarding personal leave and the method of verification should be clearly stated in the district policy.

OTHER TYPES OF LEAVES OF ABSENCE. There is a trend toward broadening the types of leave that may be granted, either with or without pay. Some school districts, for example, grant leaves for:

1. Jury duty as provided by law.
2. Court appearances as a witness, a litigant, or on behalf of the district.
3. Religious leave for faiths other than Christian.
4. Paternity leave.

Transfer of Certificated Personnel

Certificated personnel are transferred from one assignment to another for various reasons. Although most transfers involve teachers, principals may also be transferred. Some superintendents believe that a principal may become too entrenched or that a move every few years is good for the community and is a challenge to the principal. Moves may also be made to give principals an opportunity to use their abilities more successfully in a new situation.

Teachers may request changes because of unhappy teacher–principal relationships, heavy classroom loads, excessive pupil turnover, desire to work under another principal, desire to work in a new school, desire to work closer to home, or desire to work in a lower or higher socioeconomic area. Principals may request transfers for teachers whom they find incompatible or in order to give a weak teacher an opportunity to achieve in another situation. Teachers who do not do well at one school, or who are misassigned, may do very well in another school or at another level, improving both the satisfaction of the teacher and the educational program. Care in original assignment will help to lessen the need to make changes such as these.

Transfer complications can be lessened if pre-established policies and guidelines are followed. Too often the teacher is not aware of an impending transfer and principals are not consulted by the personnel administrator prior to the final transfer decision.

Teachers who wish to transfer should fill out a transfer request form stating their reasons, hold a conference with their principal (who should indicate approval or disapproval of the request), and forward the form to the personnel office. Figure 17–2 is an example of a form that can be used by a teacher who requests, not only a transfer, but any type of change in assignment. The principal who wishes to have a teacher transferred should follow a similar procedure.

Separation from Service

There are only four ways that a certificated employee can be separated from service: decease, resignation, dismissal, or retirement. When an employee dies, the state department of education must be notified. The personnel administrator can assist in a significant way by helping the members of the family with the paper work involved in collecting state death benefits.

When teachers resign, they should discuss this step with their principal and notify the personnel office or superintendent in writing, setting the effective date of the resignation and the reason. Notice should be given at an early date so that a satisfactory replacement can be employed. The personnel administrator should hold a conference with resigning teachers to determine the reasons for leaving and to give advice regarding their rights, particularly re-employment at a later date.

The dismissal of teachers is discussed in the section on evaluation in this chapter.

Retirement preparations should be started at least one year prior to the retirement date. Planned retirement should be discussed with the principal, the superintendent, or the personnel administrator. The personnel office should assist teachers in preparing the necessary forms for submission to the state, and advise them about retirement benefits and available options. Membership in the American Association of Retired Persons (AARP) or the National Retired Teachers Association (NRTA) provides many advantages and benefits.

The minimum age for retirement can be 55 years but is usually 60 years. In October 1977, Congress passed an amendment to the Age Discrimination in Employment Act that raised the age for involuntary retirement from 65 to 70 years.

Some school districts provide for part- or half-time employment for teachers at the age of 55 years if they request it. Salaries, duties, and

FLOWING WELLS PUBLIC SCHOOLS

PERSONNEL ACTION REQUEST

Employee's name _____   Date __ . __ __ _____

                    LAST   FIRST   M)   Social Security number ___ __ _____
1. Use for all requests for personnel action.
2. Please give complete information and details. (Incomplete   3. For additional comments, attach separate pages.
   forms will be returned.)   4. SEND ALL COPIES TO THE PERSONNEL OFFICE.

REQUEST FOR (CHECK ONE)

☐ Placement in vacant authorized position   ☐ Establishment of new position
☐ Employee transfer   ☐ Resignation approval
☐ Position change (duties, salary, etc.)   ☐ Salary reclassification
☐ Leave of absence authorization   ☐ Other: _ __ __ _____
☐ Job termination

DETAILS OF REQUEST   ☐ Certificated Employee   ☐ Classified Employee

Position title _____ __ __ __ . ___   School _____

Salary step/category _____ __ ___ __ Department _____

Term of contract: _____   ☐ months ☐ weeks ☐ days ☐ other _____

Degree: ☐ BA   ☐ BA+24 ☐ BA+48 ☐ MA   ☐ MA+24 ☐ MA+48   _____ |_____
        ☐ BA+12 ☐ BA+36 ☐ BA+60 ☐ MA+12 ☐ MA+36 ☐ MA+60   Annual Salary   Hourly Pay   Extra Pay

REMARKS:

To become effective _____ _____ Signature _____
                            DATE   PERSON MAKING REQUEST

☐ Approved   ☐ Not Approved   _____
                                                   PRINCIPAL OR ADMINISTRATIVE HEAD

BUDGET CODE
                                              Funds
☐ EL ☐ HS ☐ Other _____ Available _____
                        (Please do not write below this line)   BUSINESS SERVICES

Date received by personnel office _____ ☐ Recommend Approval ☐ Recommend Reconsideration ☐ Recommend Disapproval _____ 　　　　　　　　　　PERSONNEL OFFICE　　INITIAL	REMARKS: (For Admin. use only)

ROUTE TO:

☐ Approved
☐ Not Approved

☐ Approved
☐ Not Approved

SUPERINTENDENT   ☐ Approved
                        ☐ Not Approved

This area for Personnel Office use only

Controller: Copy sent _____
                                          DATE
☐ New personnel _____
                                          SALARY
☐ Salary change: From _____
                  To _____

                  ☐ Permanent
Change is ☐ Temporary until _____
                                          DATE
Copy returned to sender _____
                                          DATE

☐ Approved for Board Agenda by: _____ ☐ Approval
Date of Board Action: _____   ☐ Disapproval
Date Received: _____ Date Effective: _____
       PERSONNEL OFFICE   PERSONNEL OFFICE

ORIGINAL: Controller • 1st COPY: Personnel File • 2nd COPY: Individual

FWS 8-76

FIGURE 17–2. Example of a Personnel Action Request.
Courtesy of Flowing Wells Public Schools, Tucson, Arizona.

benefits are pro-rated. Policies must be developed regarding these items as well as the method of application, deadline dates, number of allowed participants, assignment, and termination or retirement.

Retirement benefits vary from state to state and are determined by a set formula that involves age and length of service. Most teachers belong to state retirement systems, although there are also seventeen city retirement systems. Except in Florida, Michigan, and New York, money is deducted from the salary of public school employees and transmitted to the retirement system. Teachers in thirty-seven states have elected to be covered by Social Security. Educators who are planning to retire need to become informed about their benefits and the way they will be paid.[32]

Substitute Service

Supplying substitutes is one of the important functions of the personnel office. The quality of substitute teachers helps to determine the quality of the school district's educational program. Substitutes can be former teachers, new teachers who do not want to work full-time, or teachers who have been laid off because of lowered enrollment or budget cutbacks. It is sometimes necessary to advertise for substitutes.

The personnel office has the responsibility for recruiting qualified substitutes and orienting them to district procedures. A district *Substitute's Handbook* should explain some of the district's policies and procedures on the proper time to report and leave, renewal of assignment, pay, reports, discipline, attendance reporting, release of students prior to dismissal, fire drills, lunch periods, illness and accidents, and so forth. A workshop for the substitute staff at the beginning of each school year is helpful. A substitute's job is always difficult and often thankless. Administrators and other teachers should make substitutes feel welcome, offer assistance, and give recognition to them as contributing members of the school system. Substitutes should carry on regular classroom instruction and not babysit or carry on solely recreational activities.

There are two types of substitutes: long-term and day-by-day. Long-term substitutes carry on as the regular teacher would. Short-term substitutes do not have this total responsibility but should be prepared with lessons in case the regular teacher has not left any plans.

Procedures should be developed that explain what to do when substitutes are not available. In secondary schools, the principal may require teachers to give up a free or preparation period to cover a class, sometimes for extra pay. In elementary schools, classes might be divided among

---

[32] Byron Spice, "Looking Forward to Retirement?" *Today's Education* 68, No. 1, February–March 1979, pp. 65–66.

several teachers or the principal may teach the class until a substitute can be found.

It is good policy for principals to meet substitutes upon arrival at a school, make them feel welcome, give them the school handbook, answer any questions, and if time permits, take them to the class and introduce them to the students.

The following is a typical list of procedures for handling substitutes that can be adapted to fit the special needs of any school district.

Procedures for Handling Substitutes

Regular Teacher's Responsibility

1. The following materials should be prepared and updated:
   a. Seating chart.
   b. Roll of class.
   c. Weekly program.
   d. Daily lesson plan.
   e. Next day's schedule and assignments.
   f. Room committees.
   g. Location of general supplies and equipment and names of two responsible students who can help.

2. Items *a* to *g* should be in the large drawer of the desk and the desk should be unlocked.

3. Request for substitute services should be made before 2:00 P.M. on the day preceding absence or immediately after 6:30 A.M. if the need for absence is not known until the day of absence. Call to report your absence and give the following information:
   a. Your name.
   b. Your school.
   c. Your grade or subject.
   d. Your parking assignment (if necessary).
   e. Reason for your absence.
   f. Date of your expected return.

4. All absentees must call their principal by 2:00 P.M. *each day* of continued absence in order to report a return or continued absence.

5. Make clear to students that they are as responsible to the substitute teacher as to the regular teacher.

Substitute's Responsibility

1. Report to the school's office one-half hour prior to the beginning of the first class.

2. Read all notices on the bulletin board and take all messages and any other items from the teacher's box.

3. Pick up keys and yard- or cafeteria-duty schedule.

4. Check class attendance carefully and accurately at the beginning of the day. Send this report to the office.

5. Take roll after each recess and lunch.

6. Carry out the teacher's plans and assignments as outlined.

7. Hold students accountable for work, citizenship, and attendance.

8. Leave a written report for the teacher giving:
   a. Work covered.
   b. Plans and assignments for the next day.
   c. Any other pertinent information covering students, bulletins and the like.

9. Adhere to the same school hours as the regular teacher.

10. Check with the school office before leaving to see whether you are released or are to return the next day.

School Office Responsibility

1. Call Personnel Office for a substitute as soon as an impending absence is known.

2. Schedule relief teachers from the faculty when no substitute is available.

3. Keep an accurate record of each teacher's absence for payroll purposes.

4. Notify the Personnel Office each day as to the status of substitute teachers assigned.

There are different methods of handling calls from teachers who are unexpectedly absent. The call can be made to the school or the district office. This method has the advantage of clarifying information on a personal basis, but involves extra clerical help. Large districts may use an automatic recording machine with 60 seconds allowed for the message. This sometimes results in garbled or incomplete information because the caller could not give the required information in the time allowed by the automatic machine. Some districts use an answering service to handle calls from absent teachers because they find it cheaper and more efficient. Each school district must determine what method is best for its own situation.

EVALUATION OF SUBSTITUTES.   As far as it is practical, substitutes should be evaluated by the principal. Personal observation is the best way to gain information on teaching effectiveness. Follow-up conferences can be held if time permits. The regular teacher can report on the substitute's performance. Brief substitute evaluations channeled to the personnel office from the principal's office can serve as a reference for future regular employment.

Personnel Records and Reports

Numerous records that are important for the employee as well as for the district must be kept in the personnel office. A partial listing includes:

Employment applications.

Contracts.

Assignment sheets.

Lists of employees by school, department, or office.

Payroll listings.

Individual Kardex-type card for each employee.

Cumulative folders for each employee containing references, health information, credentials, application, training and experience information, evaluation reports, letters of commendation, recommendations for improvement, contracts, information on leadership roles and community activities, and service credits.

Credentials: active and due to be renewed.

Staff ethnic surveys.

Probationary and tenure lists.

Leaves of absence of all types.

Folders of employees who have left the district or a microfilm file with the same information.

Special teaching categories.

Lists of openings and expected openings.

Substitute teachers.

Statistical records of many types.

The personnel office also must make many reports to the superintendent, the school board, the teacher association, various governmental agencies, and the county and state boards of education.

PERSONNEL APPLICATIONS OF EDUCATIONAL DATA PROCESSING (EDP). School districts should consider the use of EDP to keep up with the increasing quantity of required reports and records and to give assistance in many of the personnel office functions. Some of the personnel applications of EDP follow.[33]

I. Employee records.
   A. Keeping the master personnel file up to date.
   B. Informing employees of needed X-rays, credential renewals, leave expirations, next evaluation, unexpired sick leave days, units needed by a certain date to attain next salary hurdle, etc.
   C. Reporting reasons for termination of employment as determined by exit interviews or questionnaires.

II. Staff selection and assignment.
   A. Aiding in screening applications and interview records according to established job needs and criteria.
   B. Assigning teachers on the basis of known background, skills, and abilities in relation to specified classroom and school needs.
   C. Writing teacher contract documents including salary, method of payment, contract dates, and conditions of employment.
   D. Assigning day-to-day substitute teachers by (1) matching first requests with first available substitutes or (2) matching skills possessed by substitutes with skills requested by regular teachers.

Summary

There should be a specially trained personnel administrator to handle all problems of recruitment, termination, and negotiations; this staff person should operate under cooperatively developed, written policies. Procurement of personnel should follow a set pattern, with the building principal actively involved in selection.

Teacher education represents a partnership venture in which the school should maintain extensive involvement. This requires close cooperation in directed teaching between the local school and the training institution, with the principal playing the main role in interpreting the school and the community to the student teacher, and vice-versa. The principal may also be asked to help evaluate trainees. Constructive supervision is the most important means of implementing inservice improvement. Modern supervision stresses cooperative planning and evaluation and operates autonomously within individual schools. Its organization will depend largely upon the philosophy and goals of the school district. A good inservice program is multifaceted, consisting of institutes and workshops,

---

[33] Written by Dr. Richard H. Strand in: Emery Stoops, Max Rafferty, and Russell E. Johnson, *Handbook of Educational Administration* (Boston: Allyn and Bacon, Inc., 1975), pp. 323–24.

university work, faculty meetings, teacher visitations, professional publications, lectures, and forums.

One of the most difficult areas of school administration is personnel evaluation, which should be based upon established principles that stress democratic procedures and professional improvement. Evaluation should be coordinated by the personnel office and should include the use of multiple evaluators, performance objectives, in-basket data, and student performance. Other types of evaluation include self-evaluation and co-evaluation, in which attention is also given to evaluation of administrators and principals. Dismissal should be based on the most extensive evaluation procedures possible. The evaluations should be written and detailed and should employ many techniques; above all, constructive evaluation should occur *before* dismissal.

Teacher tenure is dependent upon state law, which is currently too rigid. Periodic evaluation and renewal of certification would bestow more flexibility to tenure.

Teacher work load is a highly subjective topic. Meaningful leadership and good personnel management will alleviate unfair work loads.

Leaves of absence are essential under certain conditions. Typical leaves are sabbatical, maternity, political or civic, military, bereavement, sick, and personal.

Teachers are often transferred from one assignment to another. Pre-established policies and guidelines lessen complications. The same principle applies to separation from service. Here, the personnel office can be of vital help (whether the separation is caused by decrease, resignation, dismissal, or retirement), by assisting with advice, preparation of forms, and explanation of options and alternatives.

Many of the personnel functions described in this chapter are finalized during the process of negotiation and collective bargaining.

Another important function of the personnel office is supplying substitute teachers, either long-term or day by day. A *Substitute's Handbook* should be prepared and made available by the office.

Finally, the chapter identifies the necessary components of record-keeping and report making.

Administrative Problems   In Basket

Problem 1

A city school district finds that its teaching staff is maturing and staying in the profession, promising little teacher turnover. Teachers are well-entrenched and confident; they feel that their older methods will work well with the new children soon to be bused in. They expect that the newcomers with their different backgrounds and abilities will adjust, and they see no need to make any special effort to prepare for their admission. The principal has great misgivings about this problem and sees it as part of a larger problem of growing inflexibility on the part of the staff.

What should this principal do to prepare the school for the changes to come?
What are the implications for inservice education?

Problem 2

The evaluation program in the Coldwood Unified School District requires the principal to evaluate probationary teachers twice a year and permanent teachers once a year. The evaluation form is a checklist covering such items as: teaching ability, classroom control, personal characteristics, and professional growth. Under each topic, there are several sub-items and a small space for comments. Principals are required to fill out the checklist and schedule a teacher conference. At the end of the conference, the teacher is asked to sign the checklist, indicating that it has been discussed with the teacher. One copy of the evaluation is given to the teacher and one is sent to the personnel office. A record of classroom visitations is also required.

The teachers have raised many objections to the evalution system. They say that some principals do not visit their classes and others stay only a few minutes. (Secondary principals retort that with over 80 teachers, it is impossible to visit all of them.) Teachers feel that the checklist is an outdated evaluation procedure; that evaluations by a single person—the principal—are not satisfactory and often show personal bias; that evaluation conferences are not always a two-way exchange of ideas and are more often dominated by the principal.

Permanent teachers feel that they should be exempted from yearly evaluation.

The teacher's association, as a result of the complaints, has asked the superintendent to appoint a committee to revise the evaluation procedure. The superintendent has delegated this responsibility to the personnel director.

Whom should the personnel director select for the committee?
What schedule should be established for committee meetings?
What procedure should the committee follow as it works at developing a new evalution policy?
If you were a member of the committee and were asked for your ideas about an evalution policy, what would you recommend?

Problem 3

The transfer of teachers between schools has been a problem in the Gettysburg Consolidated School District for a long time. The district policy is vague and no procedure has been established for effecting transfers.

Teachers have complained that they are sometimes reassigned to other schools without reason. Principals believe that weak teachers are sometimes forced on them because other principals are afraid to evaluate them for dismissal. During the summer, the personnel director sometimes reassigns teachers to fill openings created by resignation if the director cannot find a new teacher to fill the spot. Teachers and principals often do not know about the changes until September when they return from vacation. Although the district office thinks that a transfer is made to strengthen a school or a subject area, teachers often fear that something is wrong with them.

The teacher's association resents the way transfers are handled and is demanding that a comprehensive policy be developed. Principals have joined the teachers in desiring a strong voice in personnel assignment and reassignment.

The superintendent has asked the personnel director to develop a transfer policy to meet the district's needs.

What procedure should the personnel administrator use in developing the policy? What items should the policy cover?

Problem 4

Teachers in the Jefferson Elementary School are rather traditional, most of them having taught five or more years. Elaine Robertson is a new third-grade teacher who has recently graduated from college. She has enthusiastically introduced innovative concepts into her teaching. For example, instead of the usual three-group reading program, Ms. Robertson has developed an individualized reading program. Some of her advanced pupils are reading fourth- and fifth-grade books. Her pupils are excited and are eager to go to school each day.

Several teachers have been vocal in their resentment of Ms. Robertson, who has sensed their attitude. One day she enters the teachr's lounge as Ms. Green, a veteran fourth-grade teacher, is complaining about how her reading program will be ruined when Ms. Robertson's pupils, who have read most of the books she is planning to use, enter her class. Ms. Robertson is very upset over what she hears and goes to her principal and tells the principal what has been happening.

How should the principal counsel Ms. Robertson?
How should the principal proceed with the other teachers?
What should Ms. Robertson do?

Selected References

AMERICAN ASSOCIATION OF SCHOOL ADMINISTRATORS. *Profiles of the Administrative Team.* Washington, D.C.: The Association, 1971.

AMERICAN ASSOCIATION OF SCHOOL PERSONNEL ADMINISTRATORS. "Problems of Practicing School Personnel Administrators." *AASPA Bulletin* 9 (June 13, 1969).

BEECHER, RUSSELL S. "Staff Evaluation: The Essential Administrative Task." *Phi Delta Kappan* 60 (March 1979):515–7.

CASTETTER, W. A. *Administering the School Personnel Program.* New York: The Macmillan Company, 1969.

CHERNOW, FRED B., and CAROL CHERNOW. *School Administrator's Guide to Handling People.* Englewood Cliffs, N.J.: Prentice-Hall, 1976.

CUMMINGS, L. L., and DONALD P. SCHWAB. *Performance in Organizations: Determinants and Appraisal.* Glenview, Ill.: Scott, Foresman and Co., 1973.

HACK, WALTER G., and LUVERNE L. CUNNINGHAM (eds.) *Educational Administration: The Developing Decades.* Berkeley, Ca.: McCutchan Publishing Corporation, 1977.

HAMACHEK, DON. "Characteristics of Good Teachers and Implications for Teacher Education." *Phi Delta Kappan* 50 (February 1969).

HANSON, MARK E. *Educational Administration and Organizational Behavior.* Boston: Allyn and Bacon, Inc., 1978.

HARRIS, BEN M. *Supervisory Behavior in Education.* 2nd ed. Englewood Cliffs, N.J.: Prentice-Hall, 1975.

HOUSTON, W. ROBERT, and ROBERT B. HOWSAM (eds.) *Competency-Based Teacher Education: Progress, Problems, and Prospects.* Chicago: Science Research Associates, 1972.

KING-STOOPS, JOYCE B. "An Analysis of the Southern California Elementary Teacher Assistant Programs." Unpublished doctoral dissertation, University of Southern California, 1966.

LINDSEY, MARGARET. *Teacher Education: Future Directions.* Washington, D.C.: Association of Teacher Educators, National Education Association, 1970.

MARKS, JAMES R., EMERY STOOPS, and JOYCE KING-STOOPS. *Handbook of Educational Supervision.* 2nd ed. Boston: Allyn and Bacon, Inc., 1978.

LAMBERT, M. DALE. "Refocussing Teacher Evaluation: A Process of Guided Self-Analysis." *Thrust for Education Leadership* 1 (February 1972).

National Education Association. "Discriminating Against the Pregnant Teacher." *Today's Education* 60 (December 1971).

———, Research Division. "Merit Pay: Teacher Opinion and Public Opinion." *NEA Research Bulletin* 49 (December 1971).

———, Research Division. "New Approaches in the Evaluation of School Personnel." *NEA Research Bulletin* 50 (May 1972).

———, Research Divison. "Sabbatical Leave for Teachers in State Statutes." *NEA Research Bulletin* 50 (March 1972).

REDFERN, GEORGE B. "Client-Centered Evaluation." *The School Administrator* (March 1972).

ROSNER, BENJAMIN. *The Power of Competency-Based Teacher Education: A Report of the Committee on National Program Priorities in Teacher Education.* Boston: Allyn and Bacon, Inc., 1972.

SPARKS, RICHARD K. "Are We Ready for National Certification of Professional Educators?" *Journal of Teacher Education* 21 (Fall 1970).

SERGIOVANNI, THOMAS, and ROBERT J. STARRATT. *Supervision: Human Perspectives.* 2nd ed. New York: McGraw-Hill Book Co., 1979.

STALLER, NATHAN. *Supervision and the Improvement of Instruction.* New York: Technical Publications, 1978.

UNGER, R. A. "School Principal and the Management of Conflict." *American Secondary Education* 8 (December 1978) :43–48.

WILES, KIMBALL, and JOHN T. LOVELL. *Supervision for Better Schools.* 4th ed. Englewood Cliffs, N.J.: Prentice-Hall, 1975.

WILSON, ROBERT E. *Educational Administration.* Columbus, Ohio: Charles E. Merrill Publishing Co., 1966.

CHAPTER EIGHTEEN

Administration of Classified Personnel

The administration of classified personnel within school districts is assuming a steadily increasing degree of importance. Factors contributing to this trend are the continual increase in the number of noncertificated employees serving within a school district, particularly paraprofessionals or aides to the certificated staff, and the general increase in the caliber of persons seeking types of civil service positions. A trend toward codification of rules and regulations governing the operation of the classified system has resulted from pressures by civil service employee associations and other organizations that are rapidly developing to serve and advance the cause of the classified employee.

Administrative Areas of Classified Service

The scope of responsibility for the operation of the classified service may be categorized into three broad but interlocking areas: (1) the classification and description of the various jobs within an organization into a definable interrelationship that is hierarchical in nature for the purpose of salary assignment, promotion, examination, and evaluation; (2) procurement, selection, training, and advancement procedures; and (3) the employment of positive management practices to attain high employee morale.

Modern management principles are being applied to the previously

Material for this chapter was prepared in collaboration with Dr. Danforth White, Director of Personnel, Lynwood Unified School District, Lynwood, California.

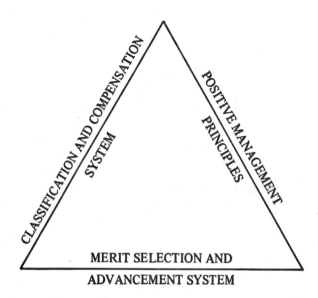

*FIGURE 18–1. Administrative Functions Involving Classified
Personnel.*

neglected area of support, or classified, personnel. These principles include
(1) the emergence of a much more systematized and equitable manner in
which employees are initially recruited and subsequently compensated,
including provisions for merit recognition and security benefits, in addition
to an equitable basic wage; (2) provision for additional training and impartial advancement to higher positions of responsibility; and (3) the use of
supervisory techniques that not only provide employees with knowledge of
how well they are performing on the job, but enable them to feel like vital
and contributing members of the educational system.

A sound organizational definition can fulfill its stated purpose if it is
adhered to. Failure on the part of administration to follow an adopted
definition can easily contribute to poor morale among employees. A figura-
tive triangle can be formed in which a strong system of classification and
compensation form one leg; merit selection and advancement another; and
positive employee management the third (*see* Figure 18–1). Only upon
these three elements can a sound system of classified personnel administration be built.

The System of Job Classification

Establishing a relationship between each job in the school district is the
first step toward developing a sound classified service. In order to establish

this relationship, the scope, duties, and skills required for each position within an organization must be accurately defined. To accomplish this, job descriptions for each function are written. For purposes of exactness as well as building employee morale, many personnel administrators request the employee (or a representative of a group) to initiate written descriptions about the exact nature of the employee's duties. It is essential that the content of the job description include the degree of education required for the position, the minimum amount of experience necessary, the number of people to be supervised (if any), and the extent of reponsibility. Although information may be presented in a variety of ways, the typical job description should contain the following headings:

   I. Definition of Position.
  II. Example of Duties.
 III. Qualifications:
      A. Knowledge.
      B. Ability.
      C. Experience.

As an example, a typical job description for a clerk–typist might be written in this manner:

CLERK–TYPIST

Definition

Under supervision, performs a variety of clerical jobs of average difficulty; operates office machines, a mainly repetitive activity; and performs other work as required.

Job Characteristics

Positions in this class perform general clerical work, such as typing, maintaining files, acting as a receptionist and operating various office machines and appliances. Positions in this class require typing skill, though this requirement varies in degree from position to position. The clerical duties assigned to positions in this class require a working knowledge of subject matter and clerical functions, and good clerical ability. Incumbents exercise initiative and independent judgment within a limited number of standardized procedures. Supervision of other clerical employees normally is not assigned to positions in this class, although assistance in training new or seasonal employees is sometimes required.

Examples of Duties

Types, proofreads, files, checks, and enters information on records; answers telephones and waits on a public counter, giving information on routine, procedural, or directional questions; types a wide variety of materials, including records, tests, reports, memoranda, tables, lists, and requisitions, from oral, rough-draft copy, or notes; cuts stencils; posts information, including attendance and scholarship records; operates office appliances and machines; sorts and files documents and records according to predetermined classifications, maintaining alphabetical, index, and cross-reference files; makes arithmetical calculations; checks records and papers for clerical and arithmetical accuracy and completeness, and for compliance with established standards or procedures; mails out letters, forms, and applications; receives, sorts, and distributes incoming and outgoing mail; acts as receptionist; assists in making out forms; inspects incoming shipments or materials for conformance with orders.

Qualifications

KNOWLEDGE OF: Modern office methods, appliances, and practices; proper English usage, grammar, spelling, and punctuation.

ABILITY TO: Compose routine correspondence independently; make simple arithmetical calculations with speed and accuracy; meet the public tactfully and courteously and answer questions in person or over the telephone; understand and follow oral and written directions.

EXPERIENCE: One year of responsible clerical experience.

EDUCATION: Equivalent to graduation from high school.

SKILLS: Typing speed of at least forty words per minute.

RANKING JOBS. Following the development, or revision, of descriptions for each job within the organization, each individual position is then ranked in relation to similar jobs within its group.

Next an organizational chart is developed to show graphically the hierarchical relationship each job bears to another. A number of jobs of similar nature becomes a "group," while two or more groups performing similar, but not identical, duties become a "class." In turn, classes are clustered together into a hierarchy and ultimately into a total "service." An example of a service might be the segment of classified personnel charged with the maintenance and operation of a district's vehicles. They would be known as "the transportation service," encompassing all employees required to repair, maintain, operate, and supervise the trucks, buses, and mobile mechanical equipment of the district.

The advantage of defining position requirements and representing each graphically becomes apparent when using the information for recruitment, selection, training, and evaluation of employees. These guidelines, established by the personnel administrator, serve as a basis for composing advertisements for job openings circulated among employment agencies, posted on public bulletin boards, and advertised in other media. They also provide a basis for measuring employees for purposes of inservice training, pay recognition, and promotion, demotion, or dismissal.

Wage and Salary Administration

Wage and salary administration relies on accurate job classification and description that provides for the development of wages, salaries, and other benefits for the employee.

Rules and policies for salary administration should be developed prior to entry into actual salary negotiations. Factors to be taken into account in developing a classified salary system are the relationships between each position class, comparison data, and the internal structure of the schedule itself. Most salary systems employ a grid system in which a range of salaries is represented on a percentage increase from a base figure. Table 18–1 represents a typical arrangement in which each range represents a typical arrangement in which each range represents 2½ percent increase over the previous one. Each position is assigned a range. Hourly equivalents are used for temporary or part-time employees in each position range.

A typical salary hierarchy for a secretarial group showing position titles, salary ranges, and the relationship of each position to other positions within the group is illustrated in Table 18–2.

There are two systems for developing salary schedules. The bench mark system chooses one position within a group as a comparison position, or bench mark. It is compared with salary rates in other school districts, industries and businesses. If the selected position is low, the bench mark is up-graded and all other positions related to it are adjusted. The job comparison system determines salaries by comparing them through a job-by-job salary comparison. This method is more time-consuming and does not provide for the continuation of internal salary consistency.

FRINGE BENEFITS. In addition to considering actual wages, increasing attention has been focused on the use of ancillary or fringe benefits for

TABLE 18–1.   A Typical Classified Salary Schedule.

RANGE NUMBER	ANNUAL SALARY INCREMENTS					HOURLY EQUIV-ALENT
	1	2	3	4	5	
1	$ 558	$ 586	$ 615	$ 647	$ 679	$3.22
2	571	600	631	663	696	3.29
3	586	615	647	679	714	3.38
4	600	631	663	696	732	3.46
5	615	647	679	714	750	3.55
6	631	663	696	732	769	3.64
7	647	679	714	750	788	3.73
8	663	696	732	769	808	3.83
9	679	714	750	788	828	3.92
10	696	732	769	808	848	4.02
11	714	750	788	828	870	4.12
12	732	769	808	848	891	4.22
13	750	788	828	870	914	4.33
14	769	808	848	891	936	4.44
15	788	828	870	914	960	4.55
16	808	848	891	936	984	4.66
17	828	870	914	960	1008	4.78
18	848	891	936	984	1034	4.89
19	870	914	960	1008	1060	5.02
20	891	936	984	1034	1086	5.14
21	914	960	1008	1060	1113	5.27
22	936	984	1034	1086	1141	5.40
23	960	1008	1060	1113	1170	5.54
24	984	1034	1086	1141	1199	5.68
25	1008	1060	1113	1170	1229	5.82
26	1034	1086	1141	1199	1259	5.97
27	1060	1113	1170	1229	1291	6.12
28	1086	1141	1199	1259	1323	6.27
29	1113	1170	1229	1291	1356	6.42
30	1141	1199	1259	1323	1390	6.58
31	1170	1229	1291	1356	1425	6.74
32	1199	1259	1323	1390	1461	6.90
33	1229	1291	1356	1425	1497	7.06
34	1259	1323	1390	1461	1535	7.23
35	1291	1356	1425	1497	1573	7.40

employees. This trend in public education has been prompted by the example of business and industry; by employees' demand for ever-increasing job security and protection both for themselves and their families; and by the fact that in some states, monies derived for the payment of fringe benefits come from separate tax sources and do not constitute a drain on the general funds of the school district. Thus, in a time of increasingly tight school budgets, fringe benefits provide a means for the employee who

TABLE 18–2. An Example of a Salary Hierarchy for a Secretarial Group.

POSITION	SALARY RANGE NUMBER	POSITION (BENCH MARK) RELATIONSHIP
Clerk–Typist	19	Bench Mark
PBX Operator	19	Direct alignment with Clerk–Typist
Senior Clerk–Typist	23	Four (4) schedules above Clerk–Typist
Library Clerk	23	Four (4) schedules above Clerk–Typist
Elementary School Clerk	24	Five (5) schedules above Clerk–Typist
Secretary	24	Five (5) schedules above Clerk–Typist
Adult School Clerk	24	Five (5) schedules above Clerk–Typist
Continuation School Clerk	24	Five (5) schedules above Clerk–Typist
Senior Secretary	29	Five (5) schedules above Elementary School Clerk
Secondary School Secretary	29	Direct alignment with Senior Secretary
Administrative Secretary	31	Two (2) schedules above Senior Secretary

otherwise might not be awarded cash salary increases to be compensated. Fringe benefits for classified employees should be comparable to those for certificated employees. Common fringe benefits are:

1. Major medical health insurance for the employee and the employee's family.
2. Dental coverage.
3. Income protection in case of severe illness.
4. Life insurance.
5. Tax sheltered annuities.

GUIDING PRINCIPLES. Three principles of wage and salary benefits should govern their administration: (1) The administration of wages and benefits should be executed according to a predetermined plan, adopted long before employee–employer salary negotiations are undertaken. (2) The system used should ensure that the internal relationships developed between classifications are maintained when salaries are revised. At the same time, salaries adopted for a particular group should be equal to those paid for similar work in other businesses or industries. (3) Fringe benefits should reflect the needs and desires of each individual employee, rather than of a particular group of employees.

Classified employee associations are exerting more and more pressure on school districts to negotiate salaries, fringe benefits, and working conditions. Because of the increasing problems facing the personnel administrator who is involved in bargaining with both classified and certified personnel, many school districts are separating the positions and are employing a classified personnel administrator to administer classified personnel.

Procurement, Selection, Training, Evaluation, and Advancement

The second area of responsibility in the administration of classified personnel pertains to the establishment of procurement procedures; the selection of qualified employees; orientation and training; evaluation; and providing opportunities for advancement. This area is referred to as the merit system in the triangle decribed earlier in the chapter.

JOB ANNOUNCEMENT. A job announcement seeking applicants is designed to accomplish three main purposes: to attract qualified persons to investigate the merits of the position through its salary and advancement potential; to outline the duties and requirements of the position; and to explain various mechanics of application, testing, and selection procedures. It should promise advancement opportunities and outline how the individual is identified with the growth and success of the organization as a whole.

Civil rights interpretations by the Equal Employment Opportunities Commission and the U.S. Supreme Court have held that job qualifications should not contain "artificial barriers to employment." Specifically, these include stipulations that bar individuals from applying for a position because they do not possess qualifications or requirements not directly related to the skills necessary for the position.

EXAMINATION PROCESS. The system of job classification enables the employing organization to construct an examination process that directly relates to the requirements of the position and to determine the individual's potential success in the position. The federal government has decreed that examination procedures must be directly related to the requirements of the position and must fairly measure the individual's potential for success in the position.

A personal interview should also be a part of the examination process for classified employees. It helps to determine the personalities of applicants and how they will fit into the school system and also offers an opportunity to delve in depth into their qualifications to perform the job. The interviewer should have training in interview techniques.

ORIENTATION, SUPERVISION, AND EVALUATION. The job description enables individuals who are hired to know what is expected of them. Prudent supervisory practice should provide for a review of job requirements for the new employee by the immediate superior. Employees should confirm their understanding of the position. If employees are later terminated for poor performance, their signature will not allow them to claim that they did not know the requirements of the position.

The system of classification also serves to measure the performance of the individual against a job specification. It is upon the job description criteria that ratings are made and the inservice training needs of the employee are met. Ratings developed from established job criteria also provide valuable data to determine potential for future promotion into higher classifications. Success within one classification often predicts an individual's ability to handle positions demanding a higher degree of skill and responsibility.

TRAINING PROGRAM.   Once the individual has been selected as an employee of the school district, the responsibility of the organization shifts to a program of continuous training that will enable the individual to carry out the responsibilities of the job classification and to learn new skills.

Although most training is of the "how-to" type, some school districts provide leadership training for those looking for advancement. Training programs should have the endorsement, acceptance, and participation of top school administrators. Although training can be costly, it is essential.

Most large school districts have specialists to conduct inservice training. They can also serve as consultants to smaller school districts. Specialists outside the field of education can also be employed to conduct training programs, although the cost may be prohibitive in smaller districts. In general, there are four varieties of employee training that are discussed in the following paragraphs.

PRE-ENTRY.   This is a program conducted on an apprenticeship basis. Individuals are given some training for the position they are to occupy prior to actual performance on the job. This program may involve classroom work dealing with practices of the trade or work with the actual tools of the trade.

INDUCTION.   This type of inservice program is aimed at specifically orienting the employee to the tasks of the job classification. Since it is assumed the employee has the general knowledge required for the position, this program is not as extensive as that of the apprentice program. Training is usually conducted in the actual working situation.

ON-THE-JOB TRAINING.   One of the most frequently used programs, on-the-job training takes the employee's present level and extends the employee's knowledge and skills. For example, in training a new custodian, the supervisor remains cognizant of the individual's potential to assume a more responsible role.

SUPPLEMENTARY.   This type of inservice activity parallels on-the-job training, but is carried out away from the specific job location. The most common type of supplementary training is received through educational courses at local trade schools or colleges. The school organization itself can set up courses, conducted either by district employees or outside consultants. Supplementary work should deal with either the technical aspects of the job or the techniques of supervision.

The purpose of any inservice program is to meet the needs of the individual and through training to carry out the job adequately, as well as to gain new skills for advancement.

EVALUATION. As important an aspect of the employee's growth as inservice training is the evaluation of the employee's performance by the employee and the supervisor. As indicated previously, evaluation is closely related to the basic job description because the employee is initially made aware of the expectations of the supervisor through this medium.

The evaluation form in and of itself is an important part of the process as it serves as a guideline upon which judgment of the employee's performance is based. The document should be simple in its construction and content. It should be specific in indicating performance levels associated with evaluative terms such as good, poor, superior, and so forth. At the same time, it should be flexible enough to measure the individuality of the person being rated.

In order to avoid rating inconsistencies, school districts provide training in rating procedures that specifically focus on what is being rated, what to look for, and what behaviors are being observed. The evaluation form should indicate what behaviors are associated with various levels of performance.

The primary purpose of evaluation is to enable the employee to improve work performance. Management practices now stress a method of evaluation whereby employees set their own performance goals and then at some future date determine their degree of accomplishment. Through the identification of their own desired areas of improvement, employees feel more committed to professional growth.

ADVANCEMENT. Employees in a school district should be given every opportunity to advance. If the district has an effective inservice training program, employees interested in advancement will be prepared to apply for higher positions. A school district spends unnecessary funds if it goes outside the district to select personnel for higher positions when it may have qualified people within the district.

The Administration of Equitable Rules and Regulations

The employment, classification, and compensation of employees imply a need for developing and adhering to specific administrative rules and regulations to govern the operation of the classified personnel service. The development and administration of sound personnel practices constitutes the third portion of the triangle in Figure 18–1 (p. 411).

While the mechanics of recruiting, selecting, and rewarding the employee are important in developing and maintaining positive morale within the organization, increasingly sophisticated management trends emphasize the importance of developing positive, overall working relationships as well. The development of specific procedures contributes to positive morale.

DEVELOPMENT OF POLICIES, RULES AND REGULATIONS. Many classified employees have organized into or are members of associations and are using negotiation or collective bargaining to arrive at policies, rules, and regulations that govern their conditions of employment. Policies are the broad guidelines upon which the rules and regulations are based. When agreement has been reached, they should be adopted by the board of education. Negotiation generally concerns the following:

Employment.

Classification and assignment: job descriptions, vacancies, changes in assignment, and transfer.

Compensation: salary schedules for full-time, part-time, temporary, and substitute employment, and overtime pay.

Work periods: school calendar, hours of work.

Insurance: accident, health, workmen's compensation.

Tax-sheltered annuities.

Probation and permanency: probationary period, promotion, and reinstatement.

Suspensions, demotions, and termination: grounds for demotion, suspension or dismissal, disciplinary action, hearings, resignations, layoffs, and retirement.

Leaves of absence: sick, industrial, accident, personal, bereavement, maternity, military, emergency, and jury duty.

Vacations.

Performance and evaluation: periodic evaluations, inservice training, and complaints.

Rules and regulations should be compiled in a policy or regulations handbook which explains, in simple language, the policies under which various programs are administered. Handbooks should be printed in a compact, handy form and distributed to all employees. As policies and regulations are changed or superseded, revisions should be distributed to all employees. Periodically, the handbook should be reviewed by the administration and a representative employee group, and, if need be, completely revised and reprinted.

GROUNDS FOR DEMOTION, SUSPENSION, OR DISMISSAL. The continued employment of personnel should be contingent upon proper performance of assigned duties and personal fitness. Typical causes for demotions, suspension, or dismissal are the following:

1. Incompetency or inefficiency in the performance of duties.
2. Insubordination.
3. Carelessness or negligence in the care or use of district property.
4. Dishonesty.
5. Narcotic addiction or alcoholism affecting job performance.
6. Engaging in political activity during assigned hours of employment.
7. Conviction of any crime involving moral turpitude.
8. Repeated and/or unexcused absence or tardiness.
9. Falsifying any information supplied to the school district.
10. Persistent violation or refusal to obey rules or regulations.
11. Abandonment of position.

GRIEVANCE PROCEDURES. A grievance is an allegation by a grievant that there has been a misinterpretation, a misapplication, or a violation of the Agreement that has been agreed upon by the classified employees association and adopted by the board of education. A grievant is an individual employee in the bargaining unit or the association who alleges a grievance.

The initial step in any grievance procedure generally includes an informal conference between the grievant and the superior (assumed to be the individual against whom the grievance has been lodged) which attempts to resolve the problem on a low-level, informal basis. If the grievance cannot be resolved at this point, mechanics should be developed to formally register the grievant's complaint in written form and to forward it to higher authority. The grievant's employee organization should step in at this point in an effort to solve the problem or to assist in the processing of the grievance. Additional mechanics provided for the processing of the grievance should include: the steps through which it is to be channeled; time intervals or limitations for administrative reply to the grievance, as well as a time limitation in which the grievant must act in order to continue the case; and the individual or group by whom the final resolution of the grievance will be made.

In many states, the resolution of a grievance within an educational organization lies with the board of education and/or a type of civil service commission. There is also an increasing trend toward resolution of grievances through the use of a third party or outside mediator. In the latter case, however, many state laws still rest ultimate decision-making power in the board of education, rendering the third party an advisory body. In other states, arbitration is binding on both parties regardless of the mechanics of the grievance procedure or the means by which the problem is settled.

Proper management of employees necessitates a procedure by which problems can be brought forth and attempts at resolutions made. Employees should be encouraged to register a grievance if they feel it is of genuine concern to them. In addition, they should be assured that the registration of such a greivance will in no way be held against them or jeopardize their position in the future.

Summary

The administration of classified personnel should emphasize the importance of systematic development of rules and procedures to guide classified employee and administrator in providing the vital auxiliary services of the school district. As more and more noncertificated employees enter the educational ranks as paraprofessionals charged with assisting teaching personnel, it is vital that the rules and regulations under which they work be clearly developed and understood by all. The federal government's emphasis on improving employee selection, promotion, and working conditions tends to reinforce the importance of such a system.

While the administration of classified personnel can be divided into several broad areas, this chapter attempts to show that the key aspect of any system of administration lies in the proper definition and description of each of the jobs within the classified service. Job description should be clearly expressed in written form and made thoroughly familiar to the employee.

The development of a basic job description leads to the identification of a complete hierarchy of classified positions. Such a system, once identified and reproduced in graphic or organizational form, enables administrators to grasp the overall functioning of the organization. In addition, an organizational scheme lends itself to the identification of salary determination, promotional opportunities, and inservice training needs. The identification of specific job requirements enables the individal to know what skills are required to obtain a given position, the type of examination procedures likely to be encountered to prove the applicant possesses these skills, and the responsibility and duties connected with the position. Performance as measured against this job definition enables the employee and the supervisor to assess the employee's success in the position, and to identify further training and the structure of inservice programs. This assessment of the employee and the job also enables the worker to identify skills required for promotion.

The process by which job descriptions and procedures are developed is as important an administrative task as the procedures themselves. Increasing emphasis of this aspect of personnel administration comes from the field of industrial psychology.

Emphasis is now placed on employee participation in determining job conditions and in assisting in the development of organizational rules, regulations, or procedures. Commitment to these principles leads the employee toward increased participation and commitment to the overall aims of the organization.

Administrative Problems

> **In Basket**

Problem 1

The new director of classified personnel finds that there are few job descriptions for classified personnel. This situation has caused problems with relationships between various groups of personnel, particularly in regard to duties and salaries. Morale is low.

How should the director proceed in the development of job descriptions?
When developed, how can discrepancies be remedied?
What can be done to raise morale?

Problem 2

Bill Gray, the head custodian at Mayfair Elementary School, has been performing poorly, althought in the past he has done outstanding work. Specifically, he has not followed district custodial regulations in certain instances, such as poor cleaning, leaving early, taking long coffee breaks, not training his helpers, and occasionally failing to secure the buildings. There have been numerous teacher complaints.

The principal, Mr. Redfern, has held numerous conferences with Mr. Gray. Although he has given him written suggestions about what he must do to improve, there has been little improvement. His last two evaluations have been below district standards. Mr. Redfern has decided that Mr. Gray should be dismissed.

How should Mr. Redfern proceed to effect Mr. Gray's dismissal?
What evidence will he need?

Problem 3

Assume the same situation as in Problem 2. Bill Gray has been given due notice that he is being terminated. He believes that the principal is unfair in his evaluation, that the complaints are not valid, and that he should be given another chance to improve. He appeals to his Grievance Committee which accepts his case. The district personnel director has become involved.

What should the principal do?
How should the personnel director proceed?

Selected References

CASTETTER, W. A. *Administering the School Personnel Program.* New York: The Macmillan Company, 1969.

DAVIS, KEITH. *Human Relations at Work.* New York: McGraw-Hill Book Co., 1967.

CHERNOW, FRED B., and CAROL CHERNOW. *School Administrator's Guide to Handling People.* Englewood Cliffs, N.J.: Prentice-Hall, 1976.

FIEDLER, FRED E., and MARTIN M. CHEMERS. *Leadership and Effective Management.* Glenview, Ill.: Scott, Foresman and Co., 1974.

GELLERMAN, SAUL W. *Management by Motivation.* New York: American Management Association, 1968.

HANSON, MARK E. *Educational Administration and Organizational Behavior.* Boston: Allyn and Bacon, Inc., 1978.

HOLDEN, ARMA. *Bus Stops Here: A Study of School Desegration in Three Cities.* New York: Agathon Press, Inc., 1974.

KOCH, HARRY W. *Janitorial and Maintenance Examinations.* San Francisco: Ken-Books, 1975.

MINTZBERG, HENRY. *The Nature of Managerial Work.* New York: Harper and Row Publishers, Inc., 1973.

MORGAN, JAMES E. *Supervision of Employees.* Englewood Cliffs, N.J.: Prentice-Hall, 1973.

Oregon State Department of Education. *Oregon Custodial Training Program.* Salem, Oregon: State Department of Education, 1978.

PIGORS, PAUL, et al. *Management of Human Resources.* New York: Mc-Graw-Hill Book Co., 1969.

———, and CHARLES A. MYERS. *Personnel Administration.* New York: McGraw-Hill Book Co., 1965.

POSTER, CYRIL. *School Decision-Making.* Exeter, N.H.: Heinemann Educational Books, Inc., 1976.

ROBBINS, JERRY H., and STIRLING B. WILLIAMS, JR. *School Custodian's Handbook.* Danville, Ill.: Interstate, 1970.

RUDMAN, JACK. *District Supervision of School Custodians.* Syosset, N.Y.: National Learning Corporation, 1979.

SAINT, AVICE MARION. *Supervision of Employees—Study and Teaching.* Chicago, Ill.: Nelson-Hall Co., 1974.

SERGIOVANNI, THOMAS, and ROBERT J. STARRATT. *Supervision: Human Perspectives.* 2nd ed. New York: McGraw-Hill Book Co., 1979.

SWEENEY, CAROL, and EMERY STOOPS. *Handbook for School Secretaries.* Boston: Allyn and Bacon, Inc. (in press).

WEHRMEYER, LILLIAN B. *School Librarian as Educator.* Littleton, Colo.: Libraries Unlimited, Inc., 1976.

CHAPTER NINETEEN

Employee Organizations and Professional Negotiation

Change has occurred in all aspects of employee representation in the education field, but the extent of this change has been most substantial in the last two decades. A national, unified, and multifaceted teachers' organization in this century would surely not have been predicted a generation ago; nor would the movement toward collective bargaining have been foreseen.

This chapter deals with teacher, administrator, and noncertificated employee organizations and the role they play in the negotiation process and in collective bargaining. The real and periphery objectives of such groups may or may not be similar; but they have all undergone drastic and traumatic revisions. They are equally deserving of consideration in the context of their respective or cumulative effects on the educational structure. Teachers and noncertificated coworkers are not merely extending the industrial union concept. Nor do administrators and their organizations represent the antithesis of this concept. All of these groups, individually and collectively, represent industry counterparts to some degree; but a deeper analysis is required before too many inferences are drawn.

Employee Organizations

Teacher, administrator, and noncertificated (or classified) organizations have developed at different rates and for somewhat different reasons. One

In collaboration with the authors, the section on employee organizations was prepared by Dr. Paul E. Dundon, Superintendent of Schools, Garden Grove Unified School District, Garden Grove, California, and the section on professional negotiation was prepared by Dr. James E. Black, District Superintendent, Burlingame Elementary School District, Burlingame, California.

of the first and primary interests was to increase salaries, followed by attempts to improve working conditions. All of these groups, individually and collectively, represent industry and union counterparts to some degree. Teachers' organizations have been the strongest and most aggressive, although noncertificated groups, depending upon their leadership, have been forceful. In most cases, administrator organizations have been slower to develop strength and have tended to be more professional and less militant in demanding recognition. Middle-management personnel are also moving into the negotiation arena.

TEACHER ORGANIZATIONS.   Until the 1950s, teacher organizations consisted generally of local chapters of educators, state organizations, and only one national teacher-representative structure, the National Education Association (NEA). At the present time the NEA requires unified membership in the local, state, and national associations, although no one is forced to join. Another major teacher organization is the American Federation of Teachers (AFT). There is rivalry between the two organizations as they compete for membership. In the many elections that have been held to determine which organization shall represent the majority of teachers, the NEA usually wins.

Beginning in the sixties and continuing into the seventies, many teachers believed that the only real and lasting control over their destinies lay in political power. The theme of teacher organizations, as we move into the eighties, is "teacher power." The NEA, with a membership of approximately two million, is a powerful political force. It claims to have been instrumental in electing NEA-backed candidates to political office in local, state, and national elections. It claims also to have influenced the passage of NEA-sponsored legislation. Some of these claims have been discounted by others. Members spend innumerable hours in campaigning, serving as party volunteers, and in sending delegates to national conventions. Lobbying is extensive at both state and national levels. Political action committees are exerting their influence at all levels. The NEA has proposed to defeat every politician who opposes its goals. Teachers throughout the country have been elected to city councils and state legislatures. Some have been elected to boards of education, either in their own or in other districts.

The power of teachers has polarized many citizens who either strongly support or oppose teacher organizations and their politics over the question of whether the public or the teacher organizations will control education.

ADMINISTRATOR ORGANIZATIONS.   Traditionally, administators have organized themselves in a more effective manner than teachers. The local educational power structure generally was assumed to lie with the school principal or district superintendent. State and national organizational structure was efficient enough to reinforce these individuals from a professional standpoint. Membership dues were ample to provide staff services on a rather sophisticated level. Common areas of concern and methods of successful problem solving were shared with the membership. Many administrators, especially those in district office positions, belong to the American Association of School Administrators (AASA) or their state professional associations. There are also professional associations for every administrative and supervisory level.

A factor in the development of administrator groups was the cooperative and supportive attitude of school board members. State and national school board associations generally set up organizations to parallel administrators.

Administrators who belong to a teacher organization are being forced to take a back seat. Certainly, they are outnumbered and have such a minority vote that they are ineffective. Bargaining has placed then in an adversary position within the teacher organization. The middle-management ranks of administrators and supervisory personnel are forced either to join ranks with teachers or form their own bargaining units. So far, job functions have determined the eligibility of administrators for collective bargaining.

Administrator bargaining units are increasing at a rapid pace. In 1977, there were 1,275 administrator bargaining units and 300 of these had negotiated written agreements with the board of education. An American Federation of School Administrators was organized and granted full-fledged status in the AFL–CIO in July 1976. By 1977, seventeen states had passed enabling legislation for administrator bargaining. There are more striking differences than similarities between the negotiated contracts for teachers and administrators.[1]

The eighties should see an increase in the number of administrators who organize. Supervisors' and elementary and secondary administrator organizations will join forces as they bargain for what they see as their rights, in much the same way that teacher organizations do.

NONCERTIFICATED ORGANIZATIONS. There is no effective way in which school districts can function without the cooperative efforts of non-certificated personnel.

The development of organizational patterns of growth for classified personnel is not especially clear. As school districts grew in size and number, the work force in secretarial, clerical, maintenance and the like groups expanded proportionately. In some instances, local organizations were started and affiliated with state associations. Groups attempting to

---

[1] Edwin M. Bridges and Bruce S. Cooper, "Collective Bargaining for School Administrators: A Significant Development in the Field of Labor Relations," *Thrust for Educational Leadership* 6, No. 4, May 1977, pp. 25–29.

organize the noncertificated personnel range from local employee organizations to the AFL–CIO. Although generally about one-half the size of the teacher group, the importance of this group of school personnel cannot be overemphasized.

Many states have an agency specifically for noncertificated personnel. Titles for this agency vary; some are called personnel commissions or merit commissions. The function of such a commission generally is to ensure the fairness of testing and hiring procedures, job classifications, evaluations, and grievance procedures. This agency could be compared to the federal government's civil service operation. Such administrative structures are set up by election of the employees themselves or by legislative mandate, depending upon the state. In some cases, the employees or the public may also vote the agency out of existence.

State personnel commissions have been criticized because they operate as bargaining agents jealously guarding their position. An agency established to safeguard employee rights should not function as a bargaining agent or solicit membership. The agency originally set up to ensure equity and fairness is now the target of employee organizations that believe they should be the guardians of employee rights.

As we move into the 1980s, noncertificated organizations are becoming increasingly stronger and more forceful and are demanding the same bargaining rights and procedures that teachers are.

Professional Negotiation and Collective Bargaining

Collective action by teachers emerged as a new factor in personnel administration in the 1960s, became an increasing concern to teachers, administrators, and school board members in the 1970s, and is becoming even a stronger force in the 1980s. Teacher associations now focus primarily upon issues for negotiation and school personnel administrators devote considerable time to dealing with issues and procedures involved in the negotiation process. Noncertificated groups, as well as certificated associations, are demanding the right to negotiate.

Collective bargaining by teachers began in 1961 when a local chapter of the American Federation of Teachers won the right to bargain for the teachers of New York City. In 1972, twenty-nine states had public education collective bargaining laws. In the beginning of the 1980s, most states had enacted legislation providing for some type of collective bargaining. Courts in some states have upheld the constitutionality of collective bargaining. The National Education Association is intense in its concern for federal collective bargaining legislation for teachers. If such legislation is passed, it would intrude upon representative government at the state and local level, particularly district board/teacher relationships. Local boards of education are elected to represent the public's desires at the community level. Too much power over local concerns would be placed in distant hands at the federal level.

Legislatures, the courts, and judges have a major impact on education. Laws affecting personnel are made by legislatures. The courts interpret these laws. Suits are filed; legal actions taken; due process, grievance procedures and hearings, and appeals take place. All of these take so much time that some administrators feel they have little time for the educational programs.

School personnel are in a changing social and political setting. Teachers view collective bargaining as the democratic means to participate in the decisions that affect them and view their rights in the formulation of policy as being productive rather than destructive. They believe that it is professional to share responsibility. Whether liked or not, the era of negotiation and collective bargaining is here and must be dealt with. The power of school boards is shrinking, not only due to bargaining, but also due to increased legislation and authority by state legislatures.

Teachers have said that they feel more secure and have improved staff morale under collective bargaining and have less fear of arbitrary action by administrators. Part of the problem of militant teachers is the lack of communication between themselves and administrators, particularly the superintendent and the school board members, except when there is a problem or conflict. Too often, communication has been by written memoranda and bulletins handed down from above. Employee relations are neglected when an adversary relationship is permitted to exist. Collective bargaining does not have to be a win–lose relationship. There do not have to be negative attitudes. Positive attitudes, trust, and mutual understanding that are established between the two parties involved will determine the tenor of the negotiation process and the quality of the final contract or agreement. Everyone can contribute and problems can be solved.

Collective bargaining should not diminish the leadership role of the principal. There can still be frank discussion, the exchange of ideas, and the sharing of information. Dissent does not mean that the diessenter is unprofessional. Mature relationships can still be arrived at after initial strife, conflict, and grievances. Principals must work with, not against teachers to achieve common goals.[2]

There are some problems connected with negotiation and collective bargaining. Districts that are new to the negotiation process may lack skill

---

[2] Richard C. Williams, "The Principal and Collective Bargaining," *Thrust for Educational Leadership* 7, No. 1, October 1977, pp. 11–14, 29.

and experience in negotiation techniques and should seek expert assistance early. Teachers backed by their local and state associations have a reservoir of expertise to call upon. Another problem is that the cost of bargaining can be enormous. For example, if it is negotiated that class size be lowered by one student, it can cost the district thousands of dollars, the amount determined by the size of the district. Still another problem is that the elected school board that represents the public must share its decisions with the bargaining unit. The public then has no way of holding the representatives of the employee organization responsible for its actions or results.

REGIONAL COLLECTIVE BARGAINING.   The trend is for states to provide more money to local school districts, and where the money goes there is usually some control. As states move toward establishing minimum educational standards; student assessment programs, especially for graduating high school seniors; rules for desegregation; and legislation covering every aspect of personnel, including collective bargaining; local boards of education will have less to say about how their districts can function. District administrators will spend an increasing amount of time implementing state regulations at the local level.

Regional service centers are proposed to provide all types of service for school districts, including available computerized data processing. These regional centers can become the blanket under which local collective bargaining takes place, although it is too early to determine how rapidly this will take place.

Goals for Negotiation

If it is professionally accomplished, negotiation can lead to a strengthened partnership between teachers, administration, and the school board. Negotiation is based on the democratic concept that those who are governed should have a voice in their government. Intelligent, professionally trained teachers have skills and knowledge to contribute.

Four goals that should be considered in the negotiation process are:

1.   To develop better two-way channels of communication.
2.   To develop a problem-solving basis for action.
3.   To seek common values.
4.   To develop effective continuing relationships.

To be most effective and professional, teachers should be more concerned with the improvement of education than with their own economic welfare or free lunch periods, important as these items are. Responsibilities should receive as much attention as rights; i.e., the economic welfare of teachers should not take precedence over the improvement of education. The ultimate goal is to serve the educational welfare of children, which can only be accomplished by the full cooperation of all employees.

Principles of Negotiation

There are a number of principles that will help to make the negotiation process easier.

1. Proceed carefully. Agree on general principles before discussing specific proposals.
2. Show that all parties have a mutual interest, although there is seldom identity of interest.
3. Demonstrate a sincere attitude and purpose.
4. Know and admit the impact of budget demands on educational programs.
5. Use persuasion to help people make up their own minds.
6. Try to win agreements rather than arguments; hostility and argumentation waste time and divert energies.
7. Try to reach an agreement, even on one item, as it tends to spawn other agreements.
8. Never confuse opposition with hostility.
9. Negotiate in good faith and assume that others are doing likewise.
10. Separate facts from opinion and be able to interpret facts correctly.[3]
11. Respect the intelligence, skill, and resource of the adversary.
12. Keep a sense of humor.
13. Listen attentively and without interruption.
14. Concede to win a concession.
15. Submit a proposal but be prepared to accept amendments.
16. Use the caucus.
17. Present proposals early, preferably at the first meeting.
18. Dispel myth of noneconomic demands.
19. Raise questions on precise application of each proposal.
20. Anticipate questions from adversary.
21. Find out why proposal is rejected; a simple change in phrasing might make it acceptable.
22. Agreement on parts of a proposal should be tentative until agreement is reached on the entire proposal.

---

[3] *Ten Principles of Negotiations*, Professional Services Bulletin.

23. Be prepared to make counter-proposals.
24. Keep careful, accurate, and complete notes.
25. Begin session on positive note; review areas of tentative agreement reached at last meeting.

What Should be Negotiated?

Almost every issue related to education and teacher employment has been put forth for negotiation. The following list illustrates some of the items that are commonly negotiated by teachers:

Grievance procedures.

Salaries.

Teaching hours and work loads.

Class size.

Use of specialists.

Nonteaching duties.

Teacher employment and assignment.

Transfers.

Vacancies and promotions.

Summer school and night school.

Teacher evaluation.

Discipline of teachers.

Individual teacher contracts.

Teacher facilities.

Use of school facilities.

Leaves of absence: sick, temporary, extended, sabbatical.

Student control and discipline.

Protection of teachers.

Insurance: health, life, family, or dependent coverage.

Retirement.

Professional development and educational improvement.

Textbooks.

Dues deduction.

Inservice.

Who Negotiates?

If there is only one teacher organization and all teachers are members, teachers should be represented by a duly elected negotiation committee. But in many districts, there may be two or more teacher organizations; and some teachers may not belong to any of them or may belong to more than one. There is no universally accepted way to handle this situation, and state laws and local procedures vary. However, each district should develop a policy that explains how representation is to be attained.

Another complex problem relates to administrator representation. If adminisators have dual membership in the teacher organization and the administrator organization, what is their status in the negotiation process? These problems should be clarified if negotiation is to be fair and equal.

Under collective bargaining, the employee organization selected by a majority of the employees in a secret ballot election is required to represent all employees as their exclusive bargaining agent in employment relations with the public school employer. Minority organizations have no official voice. Employees may either join the selected organization or pay a "service fee." Free riders are those employees who do not pay dues to the recognized organization but receive the benefits of collective bargaining. Under an agency shop plan, all must pay something as a condition of employment. There are conflicts, sometimes bitter, between the NEA and the AFT regarding collective bagaining elections for exclusive representation. The NEA with its larger membership has usually won out.

Opinions differ over who should represent the school board and the administration. Traditionally, the superintendent represented teachers to the school board and the school board to the teachers. In representing the board and administration, the superintendent may serve as a negotiator with full authority; negotiator with limited authority; adviser to negotiators for the board; adviser to negotiators for both board and teachers; neutral resource person; or nonparticipant.[4] Opinions also differ as to whether the superintendent or the school board should be actively involved in negotiation. If the people responsible for making final recommendations and decisions participate in the negotiation process, it complicates the issues and the autonomy of the superintendent may be eroded. The superintendent, as a leader of people, must retain the ultimate authority to communicate recommendations to the board of education.

Some superintendents delegate responsibility to the personnel administrator to negotiate for the district and the school board. This creates a problem for personnel administrators because they must uphold and enforce the policies they have helped negotiate. However, since employee

---

[4] National Education Association, Research Division, "State Patterns in Negotiation," *NEA Research Bulletin*, pp. 15–17.

relations are an important personnel function, "the personnel administrator must not be left out of negotiation dialogue between top-level administrators and leaders of teacher organizations when matters of great significance to good personnel administration are being considered."[5]

Teacher associations are employing professional negotiators to advise and represent them, intensifying the negotiation process. Many school boards now employ paid negotiators who have the expertise to negotiate effectively. They must have full authority as representatives of the board to negotiate.

The Negotiation Process

The negotiation process should be conducted in a business-like manner following agreed-upon rules. Arrangements should be made to release negotiators from their duties and substitutes employed to fill their vacancies. There is disagreement as to whether negotiation meetings should take place during or after school hours. Both sides should submit agenda items. Although some states do not permit closed-door sessions for public employees, the news media should not be permitted to observe negotiation meetings. Some items may take weeks of discussion, and tentative agreements may be arrived at for review before any final agreement is accepted, so a tight schedule should be avoided. In some cases, a great deal of research is necessary and data needs to be collected. Each side will probably have compromise or back-up positions that are never made public until there appears to be no hope of reaching a settlement or agreement. Each side should record its own minutes and news releases should be made jointly by both sides. Final agreements should be specific and written. It is advisable to have an attorney look them over to determine whether they are legally sound.

Figure 19–1 is a negotiations process model for assessing needs, setting goals, presenting proposals, defining the negotiation process, solving impasses, and reaching agreement.

After decisions have been agreed upon, they should be presented to the board of education for approval. Further study and revision may be suggested, since the board has the final authority over adoption of the negotiated decision. After board adoption, the final agreement or master contract should be communicated to all personnel and implemented according to the dates in the agreement. Since most negotiation involves personnel problems or policies, the personnel administrator must carry out most of the decisions.

---

[5] American Association of School Administrators, *Profiles of the Administrative Team* (Washington, D.C.: AASA, 1971), p. 81.

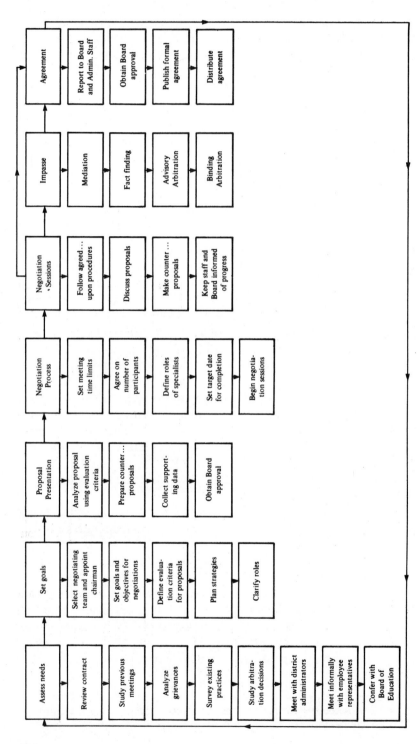

FIGURE 19–1. Negotiations Process Model.

If logical, planned procedures are followed, negotiation can be a worthwhile process. The following checklist has been developed to help administrators check off important points during the negotiation process.

Negotiation Process Checklist

I. Select negotiating team.
   —— **A.** Determine membership.
   —— **B.** Clarify roles.
   —— **C.** Set goals.

II. Prior to submission of association demands:
   A. Review:
      —— **1.** Last negotiation meeting and board rules.
      —— **2.** Management's proposals.
         —— **a.** List suggestions for change.
         —— **b.** Review board policies in other districts for beneficial language.
         —— **c.** Identify what provisions adversely affect efficiency.
         —— **d.** Describe what provisions result in excessive grievances.
         —— **e.** Avoid vague and ambiguous provisions.
         —— **f.** Identify provisions restricting management's right to act.
         —— **g.** Anticipate unforeseen costs.
         —— **h.** Draft new proposals.
      —— **3.** Anticipate association demands.
         —— **a.** Study demands by associations in other districts.
         —— **b.** Research resolutions passed at association convention.
         —— **c.** Analyze speeches by association officials.
         —— **d.** List of grievances filed.
      —— **4.** Inservice training of administrative personnel.
         —— **a.** Identify roles of administrators in the negotiation process.
         —— **b.** Explain the negotiation process.
      —— **5.** Appraisal of the rights of management.
         —— **a.** Clarify right to maintain efficiency of operations.
         —— **b.** Describe right to hire, dismiss for cause, and other personnel management rights.
         —— **c.** Identify right to take all necessary action in emergency situations.
         —— **d.** State right to administer, innovate, and change the educational program.
      —— **6.** Advise of any rules or regulations that affect employees.
         —— **a.** Ensure uniform application.
         —— **b.** Read sections and keep them current.

—— 7. Set forth permissive conduct with respect to association activities.
    —— **a.** Use of bulletin boards.
    —— **b.** Role of building representatives.
    —— **c.** Furnishing of nonconfidential information.

III. Analyze association demands.
    A. Each demand should initially be analyzed as to:
        —— **1.** Affect on legal responsibility.
        —— **2.** Cost.
        —— **3.** Tax rate.
        —— **4.** Impact on instructional program.
    B. Questions to be asked on every proposal:
        —— **1.** Is there a real problem?
        —— **2.** Is it a continuing problem?
        —— **3.** Is it general in nature or specific and limited?
        —— **4.** Will the proposal change the problem?
        —— **5.** Does the proposal address the problem?
        —— **6.** Is the proposal free from adverse operating effects or unanticipated costs, now or in the future, and does it infringe on management's rights?
        —— **7.** Is the cost reasonable in relation to the problem?
        —— **8.** Is the cost reasonable in relation to the total cost impact of the settlement?
    C. Administrative personnel should always be involved with the implication of the demands and their effect on the operations of a department. This involvement also allows for uniform application of adopted proposals.
    D. Analyzing cost factors:
        1. Internal data.
            —— **a.** Current wage and fringe-benefit levels and their cost.
            —— **b.** Number of employees in each job classification.
            —— **c.** Breakdown of the number of employees by sex, marital status, number of dependents, and age.
            —— **d.** Total fringe benefits including days off.
            —— **e.** Actual dollar amount per employee.
            —— **f.** What a one-cent increase and multiples thereof will mean in total cost.
            —— **g.** Effect on tax rate.
            —— **h.** Budget and review projections for year to be covered.
            —— **i.** Analysis of effect of changes on employees not covered in the unit.
        2. External data.
            —— **a.** Information on recent settlements in other cities.
            —— **b.** Comparative data surveys.
            —— **c.** Cost of living and base period.
            —— **d.** Surveys of fringe benefits in surrounding areas.

——— e. Salary surveys in both public and private sector.
——— f. Other pertinent surveys.

IV. Analyze the association negotiator and:
——— A. Learn as much as possible about the negotiator and the negotiating committee.
——— B. Does the negotiator live up to commitments?
——— C. What approach is taken in the negotiating process?
——— D. Will the negotiator control the committee or will it control the negotiator?
——— E. Will the negotiator wait until there is no other alternative to a quick settlement?
——— F. Will the negotiator make a deal outside the negotiating room?
——— G. Is any member of the committee emotional, unreasonable, or involved in a particular crusade?
——— H. Identify each member of the committee as to job, militancy, capabilities, or other pertinent information.

V. Administration's goals and objectives:
——— A. Set guidelines for management's negotiator.
——— 1. Long-term goals.
——— 2. Short-term goals.
——— 3. Salary objectives.
——— 4. Supplemental benefit objectives.
——— 5. Alternative objectives.
——— 6. Negotiating plan.
——— B. Communicate status of negotiations with all administrative personnel and the school board.
——— 1. Minutes.
——— 2. Negotiation bulletins.
——— 3. Review meetings.
——— C. Constant communications with governing agency on status of negotiations.
——— D. Make determination as to whether you want to communicate with employees on progress of negotiations.

John Ralph Pisapia has explored the idea of trilateral practices in public sector bargaining, because citizens are asking for access to the collective bargaining process.[6] Trilateral bargaining is not mandated by any state. Some, however, require proposals to be published, access to bargaining by observers, and contracts reviewed by citizens prior to ratification. Some states are more liberal than others in granting a voice in the bargaining process. Thirty-four states have "sunshine laws" which provide for

---

[6] John Ralph Pisapia, "Trilateral Practices and the Public Sector Bargaining Model," *Phi Delta Kappan* 60, No. 6, February 1979, pp. 424–27.

public access to meetings, actions, minutes, and records during negotiation. Courts generally have ruled that these laws do not apply in the public sector.

Three trilateral practices have been used by school districts. (1) Pre-bargaining practices involve citizens or community advisory groups during the formulation of policies to propose issues, give advice, or react to the position taken. Proposals can be made public to test the reaction before a position is taken. (2) In bargaining practices, citizens may observe or have an actual voice in discussions. Bargaining practices may use closed sessions, open sessions, or sessions allowing voice input during discussions. (3) Postbargaining practices give citizens the opportunity to scrutinize the agreements or add their influence before the agreements are signed.

Pisapia has stated that in the future, trilateral practices will be adopted by school boards whether or not they are required by law. Although there is no evidence yet that they influence the bargaining process, they gain citizen support, make leaders more sensitive to public opinion, and perhaps persuade the teacher associations to temper their demands. There is as yet little information on how to handle trilateral practices during bargaining.

IMPASSES.   An impasse may result if negotiation fails to solve an issue or if negotiation is refused. Policies should be included in the master contract for the resolution of an impasse. However, skillful negotiations avoid most impasses.

There are four ways to resolve an impasse: mediation, fact finding, conciliation, and arbitration. If there is persistent disagreement and an impasse is reached, the problem should be mediated. Mediation uses a neutral person, approved by both sides, who attempts to open channels of communication and coax the parties into agreement. The mediator does not judge or rule but merely helps. This is the most satisfactory procedure for settling persistent disagreements.

If mediation is not successful, the next step is fact finding without recommendation. This is essentially an attempt to establish the real facts underlying a dispute and to re-establish the meet-and-confer process. If no solution is reached, it may be necessary to initiate fact finding with recommendation, using the services of a third person who tells the school board and the employee organization what the terms of the agreement should be. The board and the organization may either accept or reject the recommendation.

Conciliation is a third way to solve an impasse. It can be successful if neither party makes initial unreasonable demands. Facts should be found and presented honestly. An approach that builds on the positive is necessary. Both sides should keep an open mind. If there is friendliness and mutual understanding, conciliation is an effective way to resolve an impasse.

If an impasse persists, the final step is binding arbitration. The third party tells the board and the employee organization what the settlement will be and the decision must be accepted whatever it is.

Grievance Procedures

Problems often arise over the interpretation of or adherence to a policy. Nothing should prevent an employee from resolving a complaint informally outside the grievance procedure, as long as the adjustment of the complaint is consistent with the statutes, board policies and regulations, or administratice rules and procedures. For these reasons, the school district must have clearly defined grievance procedures. The purpose of a grievance procedure is to assure certificated employees that they have direct communication with the person responsible for the alleged grievance and that they have channels open for redress of a grievance if not settled at a lower level. It will also eliminate fear of reprisal and raise morale. Grievance procedures should be included in the district's master contract.

DEFINITIONS.   A "grievant" is usually an employee or group of employees or the recognized teacher association filing a grievance. A "grievance" is a written statement by a grievant stating that a controversy, dispute, violation, or misapplication of the terms of an agreement's policies, statutes, or board policies exists. "Employer" refers to the board of education or school administration. In order to avoid conflicts, "days" should be designated as "teacher work days," "custodian work days," "calendar days," and so forth.

A "grievance procedure" has been defined as "a method by which an individual employee can express a complaint, problem, or dispute without fear of reprisal and obtain a fair hearing at progressively higher administrative levels."[7]

TYPES OF GRIEVANCES.   The most common types of grievance problems are:

1. Legal problems: professionally connected, personal, or both.
2. Professionally related personal problems: disagreement with evaluation, assignment practices, personality conflicts, physical or mental health problems, and failure to follow procedures.
3. Teacher organization problems: administrator–teacher relationships, teacher–board relationships, teacher–teacher organization relationships, and ethics.

---

[7] National Education Association, Research Division, "Hearing Teachers' Grievances," *NEA Research Bulletin*, October 1967, p. 81.

PROCEDURE AND STEPS. Grievance procedures provide equitable interpretation and application of personnel policies and practices and should be
negotiated and made a part of the negotiation agreement. Grievance procedures vary from district to district due to local needs and conditions but
in general should:

1. Define a grievance.
2. Explain the procedure for filing a grievance.
3. Specify the time schedule for filing a grievance, holding discussions,
   reporting decisions, appealing decisions, and holding hearings.
4. Designate eligible participants.
5. Provide for investigation of the problem.
6. Explain appeal procedures.
7. Explain how impasses shall be handled.
8. Establish rules for mediation.
9. Explain how communications are to be handled.

The following steps show the procedures that can be followed in
solving a grievance:

Step 1:   Informal Complaint

Within sixty days from the event upon which the grievance is based, or
within sixty days of knowledge of the act or condition that is the basis of
the complaint, the grievant may file a grievance with the school principal or
his immediate supervisor.

Within five days following the filing of the grievance, the aggrieved
shall discuss the problem at a prearranged meeting with the principal or
the immediate supervisor. At the informal conference a conscientious
attempt should be made to resolve the complaint. Step 2 of the grievance
policy should be initiated only when this informal effort fails to accomplish
a satisfactory and equitable resolution of the problem.

The school principal or designated representative, or the immediate
supervisor or designated representative, shall have five days following the
informal conference to render a written decision to the grievant.

Step 2:   The Personnel Office Level

If the principal or immediate supervisor does not comply with the terms
of Step 1, or the grievant is dissatisfied with the decision, the grievant may,
within five days, file the grievance with the office of personnel services.
Within five days after receipt of the grievance, the assistant superintendent
of personnel services shall have met with the grievant and issued a decision
in writing.

Step 3:   The Superintendent's Level

If the grievance is not settled in Step 2, the grievant may move to Step 3 through written notice to the superintendent of schools within ten days. The superintendent of schools or designated representative has ten days to give a written decision after receipt of the grievance.

Step 4:   The Board of Education Level

If the grievance is not settled in Step 3, the grievant may move it to Step 4 by written notice to the board of education within ten days after receiving the superintendent's reply. The board shall meet with the aggrieved employee within ten days after receipt of the appeal; seventy-two hours notice of the meeting shall be given the aggrieved employee. The board shall notify the aggrieved employee in writing of its decision within five school days after the hearing.

Step 5:   Arbitration

If the grievance is not settled in Step 4, the grievant may within ten days move the matter to arbitration under the voluntary labor arbitration rules of the American Arbitration Association. Neither party to the grievance shall refuse to proceed to arbitration upon the grounds that the matter in question is not arbitrable. If a question of the right to arbitrate an issue is raised by either party, such questions shall be determined in the first instance by the arbitrator. The parties further agree to accept the arbitrator's award as final and binding upon them.

Many districts do not accept the idea of binding arbitration but prefer fact finding with recommendation or "nonbinding arbitration." Binding arbitration may be required in all school districts before long. The word "days" in the above steps should be stated as previously explained.

TEACHER ASSOCIATION REPRESENTATION.   All employees should have the right of teacher association representation at each step of the grievance procedure and should not be required to be present themselves at any step. Copies of employer decisions given at any step of the grievance procedure should be speedily delivered to the teacher association. A grievant should not be represented by any person who might be required to take action, or against whom action might be taken, in order to adjust the grievance.

RELEASED TIME.   Grievances ordinarily should be processed during the regular work day, and released time provided for all participants in the investigation and processing of representatives and witnesses.

GENERAL STATEMENTS ON THE GRIEVANCE PROCEDURE.   The time limits specified in any level of the procedure may be modified by mutual agreement. Failure by an employee to process the grievance from one level to the next within the time limits provided for should result in a disposition of the grievance unfavorable to the grievant; conversely, a failure of an administrator, superintendent, or school board to reply or act within the specified time limits should result in a disposition of the grievance favorable to the grievant.

Once a grievance is submitted, the subject matter should be treated as confidential personnel information. Nothing in the bringing of a grievance, favorably or unfavorably resolved, should operate to impair the professional rights and privileges of an employee (specifically, personnel file entries or information communicated to others by board members or employees).

At any level of the grievance procedure, the aggrieved should have the right to be represented by a person or persons of their choosing.

Work Stoppages

The term "work stoppage" has a better connotation than "strike," although the literature uses the word "strike" most of the time. The word "sickout" is also used.

Work stoppages have been prevalent during the past decade and appear to be increasing in number as well as length. They occur because teacher organizations are unwilling to accept the decisions of the administration and the board of education, and negotiation breaks down. A teacher vote will decide whether or not to stop work. If a work stoppage is voted, the district can seek a court injunction to stop it.

Although some states have outlawed strikes in the public sector, the problems have not been solved and strikes have not been prevented even where illegal. The Supreme Court, in 1970, declined to review such cases. Teacher association leaders believe that public sector labor policies should be based on the private sector system. On the other hand, legislation cannot prohibit or limit conflict. Instead, it should legislate a process that will help solve conflict. Agreement in conflict management is difficult to reach in most states where laws limit the scope of negotiation.[8]

PROBLEMS THAT CAN OCCUR. It is difficult to anticipate everything that might happen during a work stoppage. Custodians, secretaries, and others may join the stoppage or refuse to cross picket lines. Supply deliveries may be hindered because vendors will not cross picket lines. A new era is here

---

[8] Terry Herndon, "The Case for Collective Bargaining Statistics," *Phi Delta Kappan* 60, No. 9, May 1979, pp. 651–52.

and teachers on picket lines are no longer a novelty. Students may not attend school during a work stoppage.

Everything in a school may be tampered with—locks, supplies, equipment, and books. Teachers' desks may be locked or emptied and lesson plans taken. There may be parades and rallies. Substitutes may be threatened, called scabs, and may choose not to cross picket lines. False information may be given out to the press and the public in an attempt to discredit the schools and criticize the administration.

PLANS THAT SHOULD BE MADE. A contingency plan and organizational strategies should be drawn up if a work stoppage seems inevitable. Administrators should be given assignments. Arrangements should be made for personal and building security. It may seem advisable to arrange for police protection, usually as a last resort as it may cause controversies.

Districts where problems are anticipated have made long-range plans with nearby districts to develop a shared substitute pool as it may be necessary to employ many substitutes. Substitutes from the district can be notified to be on call when a work stoppage appears to be imminent. In case the district's substitutes refuse to cross a picket line, substitutes must be borrowed from another district.

School principals play an important role. They must be able to anticipate problems and act quickly and resourcefully. They should collect teachers' roll books and keys on the day prior to the work stoppage— which is usually announced ahead of time. Principals should be visible, stay calm, be tolerant, and not threaten. Many times, principals are sympathetic with the teachers, even though principals must represent administration during a work stoppage.

Relationships after returning to work are often strained, especially if some teachers did not participate in the work stoppage. The principal must assume the leadership role in smoothing out tensions and getting things back to normal. There should be no retaliation but the district policies must be followed. Students are often affected, especially if they have seen their teachers on the picket line. Secondary students may wonder about their grades. There may be a need for increased counseling. Parents may have many questions which the principal must answer. Parents also need assurance that their child's educational program will not be affected. It should never be forgotten that work stoppages always end.

Negotiating Salaries and Fringe Benefits

Salaries are extremely important to all school personnel. They provide systematized remuneration and encouragement to improve. Simplicity is a goal to keep in mind when constructing salary schedules because it makes them easier to understand and administer. Constant salary increases concern administrators and school boards because they are the largest expenditures in a school district's budget and, as salaries rise, more money is needed. The annual rate of increase in the average annual salary of instructional staffs from 1968–69 to 1978–79 was 6.6 percent.[9] But due to inflation, salary raises may actually result in a loss in real income. This is of concern to school personnel, particularly teachers, who in many districts, are bargaining for raises of 12 to 15 percent to make up for losses in the purchasing power of the dollar. But when there is not enough income, something must give. Many districts end up by cutting services and supplies, and eliminating positions.

Although the estimated average annual salary of instructional staffs in the United States was $15,615 in 1978–79, it ranged from a low of $11,448 in Arkansas to a high of $25,185 in Alaska.[10] It should also be noted that salaries vary markedly from district to district within a state.

Some states have considered laws establishing state-wide salary schedules for teachers. One purpose would be to equalize salary schedules among districts. Disadvantages would be the loss of local control, the difficulty to provide for variation in living costs in different areas, and the possibility that states could regulate class size, fringe benefits, and working conditions once they start taking control. These are items that teacher associations want to negotiate at the local level.

Salaries and fringe benefits are two of the most important items that are negotiated by teacher associations. Teachers will have their proposed salary schedule but usually have an unannounced alternative proposal. So will the administration. The adoption of a salary schedule is no longer accomplished simply and in a short time. Neither is it developed solely by administration. Negotiations may take months and are often a year-round proposition. It is interesting to note that the Bureau of National Affairs has stated that teachers' salaries have risen faster in states that do not have a public bargaining law than in states with such a law.[11]

PRINCIPLES FOR DEVELOPING TEACHER SALARY SCHEDULES. All schedules should be based on sound principles and policies that have been agreed

---

[9] National Education Association, NEA Research, *Estimates of School Statistics, 1978–79,* Research Memo (Washington, D.C.: The Association, 1979). Copyright © 1979 by the National Education Association, p. 17.

[10] National Education Association, NEA Research, *Estimates of School Statistics, 1978–79,* Research Memo (Washington, D.C.: The Association, 1979). Copyright © 1979 by the National Education Association, p. 32.

[11] Bureau of National Affairs, *Special Report: Teachers and Labor Relations, 1977–78* (Washington, D.C.: BNA Research and Special Projects Division, November 27, 1978).

to, regardless of the exact amounts being negotiated. The following principles are recommended for consideration:

1. The welfare of the student should be the first consideration in determining teachers' salaries.
2. A salary schedule is one part of a district's total program of personnel administration.
3. A salary schedule should be developed in terms of the basic concept of an annual salary sufficient to attract and hold capable personnel.
4. The salary schedule should be based primarily on training and experience.
5. The salary schedule should provide incentives for satisfactory performance and continued professional growth.
6. Changes in placement from one class to another, or from one step to another within a class, should be accomplished on an annual basis at a fixed point in the fiscal year.
7. The use of the merit concept for the placement of teachers on a salary schedule should not be attempted without adequate study by teachers, administrators, and the governing board.
8. Previous experience outside the district should be recognized.
9. In adopting a new salary schedule, no employee should be penalized by readjustment of placement.
10. The salary schedule should be supplemented with statements relating to the district's policy on frequency of payment, deductions, and retirement.[12]
11. The maximum should be two times the minimum.

TYPES OF SALARY SCHEDULES.   The following list outlines some common salary schedules:

1. Position schedules pay according to the position the teacher holds: elementary, junior high, high school. This method is practically extinct.
2. Preparation schedules pay according to the degree held.
3. Experience schedules pay according to the years of teaching experience.
4. Cost-of-living schedules base increments upon the Consumer Price Index or some other means of determining the rise in the cost of living.
5. Merit-pay salary schedules are based on the teaching efficiency of the teacher.
6. Differentiated salary schedules are based on the level of responsibility.
7. Extra pay for extra duty plans are frequently used to supplement the regular salary schedule.

---

[12] Irving R. Melbo, et al. *Report of the Survey, Laguna Beach Unified School District* (Los Angeles: University of Southern California, 1961), pp. 260–61.

8. Fringe benefits supplement the regular salary schedule by providing money for insurance of all types and for retirement benefits.

Longevity increments also have been added to some salary schedules. An added bonus, for example, may be added every three to five years after a maximum has been reached. Some school districts require factors such as "superior" evaluation reports or completion of extra, approved college courses before a teacher can qualify for a salary increase. Most school districts use various combinations of the above in their schedule development. The typical salary schedule has several training classifications, such as the bachelor's degree, the bachelor's degree plus required units, the master's degree, and the master's degree plus required units, and in some districts, the doctoral degree. Step increments are added for each year of experience in each of the classifications. New teachers are "rated in" according to their academic degree and years of experience. It is possible to advance on the schedule in two ways: "across," or from one preparation classification to another, and "down," or from one experience step to the next. Placement upon the salary schedule becomes an automatic procedure, facilitating the routine work of the administrator and enabling teachers to forecast their own salary future. It has the further advantage of encouraging teachers to pursue advanced study and degrees.

Table 19–1 shows a sample preparation and experience salary schedule; naturally, the amounts will not remain current.

SALARY SCHEDULE POLICIES. The following policies are typical of those pertaining to a negotiated salary schedule:

1. All teachers must hold a valid state teaching credential.
2. All teachers will be placed on a salary schedule commensurate with their units, degrees, and years of credited service.
3. A maximum of five years credit shall be granted for out-of-district teaching service. Credit for such experience shall be on a year-by-year basis. Credit will be given for full years of experience only.
4. Private school experience while holding a valid teaching credential may be given full credit on the salary schedule.
5. One year (twelve months) of verified military service may be counted in lieu of teaching experience.
6. Teachers employed to teach industrial education subjects may be granted up to four years of credit for work experience, including work as a journeyman, in lieu of teaching experience, whether or not they hold a B.A. degree.
7. New teachers will be given a tentative placement on the salary schedule by the personnel administrator according to the evidence of experience and training submitted. Final placement on the salary

TABLE 19–1.   Teacher Salary Schedule, 1980–81.

STEPS	GROUP I B.A.	GROUP II B.A.+ 15	GROUP III B.A.+ 30	GROUP IV B.A.+ 45	GROUP V B.A.+ 60
1	11,274	11,979	12,683	13,388	14,093
2	11,979	12,683	13,388	14,093	14,797
3	12,683	13,388	14,093	14,797	15,502
4	13,388	14,093	14,797	15,502	16,206
5	14,093	14,797	15,502	16,206	16,911
6	14,797	15,502	16,206	16,911	17,616
7	15,502	16,206	16,911	17,616	18,320
8		16,911	17,616	18,320	19,025
9			18,320	19,025	19,730
10			19,025	19,730	20,434
11				20,434	21,139
12				21,139	21,843
13					22,548
16	Anniversary Increment (Groups IV & V Only)			21,843	23,253
20	Anniversary Increment (Group V Only)				23,957

schedule will be made when complete college transcripts and verification of experience have been received. All verifications must be received by September 1 of the school year.

8. Units earned in an accredited training institution will qualify the teacher for column or classification status provided such units are in accordance with district policy.

9. Each teacher shall advance one step per year on the salary schedule. Service must be for at least 75 percent of the teaching days of the district's school year.

10. Regulations that are related to the salary schedule, such as leaves of absence, deductions, frequency of payment, institute attendance, and the like, shall be set forth in the negotiated bargaining contract.

11. Horizontal movement on the salary schedule shall be made on September 1 of the fiscal year upon verification of the required academic units or inservice education units.

12. The school year for certificated employees who are paid on the teachers' salary schedule shall be on a calendar-month basis from September 1 through June 30. The active days of service shall be approximately 183 working days.

EXTRA COMPENSATION AND FRINGE BENEFITS.   The base salary is not all that teachers can earn. They can receive extra compensation for special assignments:

Director of student activities.

Music.

Drama.

Speech.

Journalism.

Drill team.

Department chairpersons.

Athletic director.

Coaching.

Adult education.

Home teaching.

The compensation may be a flat fee based on the time taken to handle the activity and/or responsibility level or it may be based on a percentage of a step on the salary schedule. Employees whose responsibilities require travel to more than one site may receive mileage reimbursement, such as fifteen cents a mile.

Fringe benefits are usually: health insurance, dental insurance, life insurance, a supplemental pension plan, or a tax-sheltered annuity plan. Insurance may cover the employee alone or the employee and his/her eligible dependents. The district may pay all or part of the premiums. It may also set a maximum amount, such as $1690 per employee, for fringe benefits. In lieu of increasing salaries, some districts grant larger fringe benefits. All final decisions regarding fringe benefits are arrived at during negotiation or collective bargaining with the teacher association. Agreements (or contracts) should also include specific policies covering such items as the effective dates of the benefits, the duration of the benefits, extended illness absences, teachers who are on leave with or without pay, and teachers who have resigned or been terminated.

MERIT PAY.   Merit pay as a method of rewarding superior teachers has been discussed in the literature for over fifty years and is still a controversial subject. Research on merit pay has been meager. Merit pay plans have taken many forms:

1. Super-maximums.
2. Accelerated increments.
3. Bonus plans.
4. Multiple track.
5. Periodic merit evaluation.
6. Annual outstanding teacher awards.
7. Summer merit teacher projects programs.

Many programs combine two or more of these basic plans.

Proponents claim that a merit-pay plan helps retain superior teachers an avoids losing them to supervisory or administrative positions or to other professions. It recognizes differences in ability, and rewards competence. Improvement in teaching performance is encouraged and teacher complacency is reduced.

Opponents of merit pay have said that evaluation is too subjective to determine salary and there is a lack of agreement as to what constitutes good teaching. Many of the aims of education are intangible, and difficult or impossible to measure. Basing evaluation or compensation on the test results of students raises a furor among most teachers. Dissension may be created and resentment among teachers fostered when some find out (as they seem to do) that others are paid more than they are. Comments such as the following have been heard: "Who does she think she is, getting more than I do?" "I'm just as good a teacher as he is." "Who decides these things anyway?" Teachers generally resent merit-rating salary schedules. The problem of merit pay is a difficult one and if proposed is a subject for negotiation.

DIFFERENTIATED STAFFING. One of the newer and most controversial salary innovations is that of differentiated staffing. Unlike merit pay, which pays only according to the quality of performance, it pays according to the level of responsibility.[13] Although comparatively few districts use this plan, a great many are showing an interest in it. It is generally considered to be an outgrowth and refinement of team teaching based on a diversity of teaching tasks and the use of auxiliary personnel to relieve teachers of noninstructional duties. Differentiated teaching goes even further and differentiates a teacher's role and responsibilities according to interest, ability, and ambition. It assumes that all teachers are not alike in skills; that all cannot participate competently in the decision-making process, nor set their own standards.

No two school systems with differentiated staffing appear to follow the same plan for designating salary differentials, although all permit teachers to earn more than the regular salary schedule. Various titles have been used to differentiate levels of responsibilty, such as: associate instructor, instructor, senior instructor, or apprentice teacher, junior resident, and senior resident.

Because of the controversial nature of the program and its lack of wide acceptance, administrators should investigate existing programs before embarking on one of their own.

ADMINISTRATORS' SALARIES. Administrators generally receive higher salaries than teachers within the same school system. It is false, however, to

---

[13] *Differentiated Staffing in Schools,* Bulletin No. 411–12754 (Washington, D.C.: National School Public Relations Association).

assume that they earn considerably more than teachers for a working month. The contracts of most administrators are for twelve months; although they may receive a month's vacation, they usually work through school vacations. There is even less difference on an hourly basis since most administrators attend many meetings after school hours (such as school board and community meetings). Their work day does not end when school is dismissed. Because of the necessity to become involved in community activities, many administrators join community organizations such as service and civic clubs. This involves expense that is not reimbursed but is valuable in the establishment of cooperative, friendly, school–community relationships.

Many principals now earn over $25,000; superintendents' salaries range from $30,000 to over $50,000. The amount depends upon the size of the school district and its ability to finance high salary schedules; larger school districts or those in affluent areas pay the highest salaries.

Administrators usually develop their salary schedules and supplemental benefits through their own organizations. Some states require this procedure. Because administrators have been excluded from negotiations with teacher organizations, they have developed their own bargaining techniques and are moving into administrative collective bargaining—more or less being forced into it. The procedures are similar to those used by teachers, although there appears to be no consensus on the best method for establishing administrative salaries.

Administrative salaries are arrived at in many ways but often are based on the level of responsibilty, such as assistant superintendent, director, supervisor, coordinator, principal, assistant principal, and so forth. Some are based on a ratio to the teachers' salary schedule and rise in proportion to the raises granted teachers. Others include a responsibility factor that may depend upon the size of the school or the level of administration.

NONCERTIFICATED SALARY SCHEDULES.   Noncertificated (or classified) salary schedules are negotiated in much the same manner as the teachers' salary schedule. A further explanation is made in chapter 18.

The Role of Administration in Negotiation

Negotiation and collective bargaining have created a changing role for administration. They have polarized the feelings between administrators and the teaching staff. Administrators, particularly principals, no longer represent teachers, acting as go-betweens between teachers and the board of education. Teacher association agreements exclude superintendents, associate or assistant superintendents, administrative assistants, directors, coordinators, supervisors, and other district office administrators, as well as principals and assistant principals or deans. Legally, the superintendent represents the board of education and is directly responsible to it. Most states exclude the superintendent from participating in the teacher-organization bargaining process.

Within the framework of permissive legislation, superintendents must see that cooperatively written and mutually agreed-upon policies and procedures are adopted for negotiation and collective bargaining. This should be done *before* problems arise. The superintendent who is alert to the demands that exist will involve teachers in decision-making as soon as possible. If decisions are made on a partnership basis, there should be fewer problems to be negotiated.

The superintendent's responsibilities in the negotiation process need to be defined more clearly. Up to this time, the superintendent has served as:

1. Negotiator with full authority.
2. Negotiator with limited authority.
3. Advisor to negotiators for school board only.
4. Advisor to negotiators for school board and teachers.
5. Neutral resource person.
6. Nonparticipant.

The principalship has taken on new dimensions in recent years. Building administrators should be involved in helping to formulate the board of education's bargaining position. Principals should be represented on the administration's negotiation team during the bargaining process and should be given an opportunity to evaluate the implications of the items considered during collective bargaining. After a collective bargaining agreement has been reached, it is the principal who must administer the master contract at the school level. The principal must communicate with the school's staff and work with teachers in interpreting and enforcing the terms of the contract that has been reached with the teacher organization and the board of education. Tensions can be reduced and problems avoided if the principal meets regularly with the school's elected teacher-association representative.[14]

Collective bargaining adds conflict resolution to a principal's management skills, since the agreement that is reached may have an impact on teaching assignments, faculty meetings, co-curricular and other extra duties, rights and privileges, and the role of the teacher organization during school hours.[15]

---

[14] Richard A. Gorton, *School Administration, Challenge and Opportunity for Leadership* (Dubuque, Iowa: Wm. C. Brown Co., 1976), pp. 172–82.

[15] Lowell McGinnis, "The Principal and the Collective Agreement," *Thrust for Educational Leadership* 6, No. 3, January 1977, pp. 23–24.

Since principals are considered part of the management team, they are often bypassed by teachers as the teachers work with their organizations and deal directly with the superintendent and the board of education. Although the principal is no longer the sole authority in the school and has lost autonomy, the principal has been given added responsibilities for the school's budget, personnel, finances, and needs.[16] How effective the principal is will depend upon the management skills that are possessed.

Summary

The changing patterns of employee organizations over the past twenty years are related to social patterns that have changed at an even more rapid rate. Because education is charged with passing on to new generations the knowledge and values of past and present society, it is forced to focus on social realities.

Professional negotiation or collective bargaining has been established in education. Teacher associations have furnished the impetus and leadership. Negotiations have also created a rift between teachers and administrators as more and more districts are moving toward collective bargaining.

If negotiation is professionally accomplished, it can lead to a stronger partnership among teachers, administrators, and school boards. The goals of negotiation include the development of better two-way channels of communication and the seeking of common values. The ultimate goal should be the improvement of education for the benefit of students.

The principles of negotiation stress human relationships, sincerity, use of persuasion, and compromise. Good faith and respect by both parties is essential. Recommendations for conducting productive negotiations are presented.

Teachers believe that almost everything that pertains to their professional life is negotiable. Since negotiation should not be one-sided, administrators should also present policies for negotiation.

Teachers usually negotiate through their representative committee or council. Their association may employ a professional negotiator; school boards and/or administrators should do likewise. The superintendents' role is not clear; they may negotiate, delegate this function, advise, or remain neutral.

The negotiation process should be planned, negotiated, and adopted. It should be business-like and follow agreed-upon rules. When an item has been finalized, it should be written, published, and put into effect. A

---

[16] Marianne Michels, "The Changing Role of the Principal as a Response to Teacher Unionism in Educational Organization," *Thrust for Educational Leadership* 5, No. 5, May 1976, pp. 23–25.

negotiation process checklist is presented for administrators to suggest a logical plan to follow in reaching negotiated solutions.

Impasses are sometimes reached when negotiation fails. They can be solved by mediation, fact finding, conciliation, or arbitration.

Grievances occur when there are problems over the interpretation of or adherence to a policy. They may be related to legal, personal, or teacher-organization problems. Grievances must be defined, filed, investigated, and solved. The procedural steps for solving grievances are: (1) informal complaint; (2) the superintendent's level; (3) the board of education level; and (4) arbitration.

More work stoppages are occurring because teacher organizations are increasingly unwilling to accept final decisions.

Salaries are rising but not enough to keep up with inflation, causing teacher associations to put increasing pressure on school boards, who may need to reduce services and eliminate positions in order to meet demands. Salaries based on merit systems or differentiated staffing are controversial and not widely used.

Master contracts containing the conditions under which a teacher will work, salary, and fringe benefits are negotiated in many districts. Master contracts limit the freedom of personnel administrators in applying policies, rules, and regulations to individual cases.

Noncertificated personnel, supported by their associations, are also demanding the right to negotiate.

Every school district should have clearly defined, agreed-upon policies for negotiating, handling impasses, solving grievances, and dealing with work stoppages.

Administrative Problems

> In Basket

Problem 1

Although the small Mountain Empire School District has had few personnel problems and no negotiation process, the superintendent realizes that teachers are becoming increasingly militant and thinks it would be wise to develop a negotiation process before problems arise.

How should the superintendent proceed?
Who should be involved?

Problem 2

The Amherst Unified School District has had an established negotiation policy for several years that has worked well. This year the local teacher association has elected several dynamic and forceful officers whose program includes smaller class loads, a 12 percent salary raise, more fringe benefits, and a broader leave-of-absence policy. In particular they threaten to strike if their salary and fringe benefit demands are not met.

In the past, the personnel administrator has been delegated to be the negotiator for the board of education. Now, the teacher's association has hired a professional negotiator to work with their committee and to speak for them. Administration has no professional negotiator. Furthermore, the teachers' negotiation committee is refusing to meet with the personnel administrator and says that it will meet only with the superintendent.

What action should the superintendent take?
What can the board of education do?

Problem 3

The local executive director of the teacher organization has asked to meet with the district administrator in charge of personnel services to discuss a matter that has come to the executive director's attention involving one of the teacher members and the teacher's principal. The executive director has suggested a luncheon meeting.

If you were the district personnel administrator, how would you handle this request?

Problem 4

A local noncertificated group representing the majority of employees has asked for a meeting with the Board of Education's representative to establish jurisdiction in a maintenance department. A job classification study requested by this group indicates that two of five painters should be downgraded in salary by 5 percent; this compromising situation has been complicated by the demands of another noncertificated organization to represent the painters because of the outcome of the survey.

What are the criteria for determining jurisdiction, assuming there is no state-wide or national contractual arrangement?
What obligation is there for the district to follow the job classification survey? Can it accept some portions and ignore others?
Would it be proper and/or more logical from an administrative standpoint to encourage the noncertificated employees to select a single bargaining unit (assuming no formal contractual arrangements now exist with any organization)? Explain the reason for your answer.

Selected References

AMERICAN ASSOCIATION OF SCHOOL ADMINISTRATORS. *Profiles of the Administrative Team.* Washington, D.C.: The Association, 1971.

―――. *School Administrators View Professional Negotiation.* Washington, D.C.: The Association, 1966.

AMERICAN FEDERATION OF TEACHERS. "Bakke: Amicus Curiae Brief." *Phi Delta Kappan* 59, No. 7 (March 1978):447–50.

ANGELL, GEORGE W. "Grievance Procedures under Collective Bargaining: Boon or Burden?" *Phi Delta Kappan* 52 (April 1972).

ASSOCIATION OF CALIFORNIA SCHOOL ADMINISTRATORS. "Persistent Disagreement." *Management Action Paper* 1, n.d.

BEAUBIER, EDWARD W., and ARTHUR N. THAYER. (eds.) *Participative Management: Decentralized Decision Making.* Burlingame, Ca.: Association of California School Administrators, 1973.

BRIDGES, EDWIN M., and BRUCE S. COOPER. "Collective Bargaining for School Administrators: A Significant Development in the Field of Labor Relations." *Thrust for Educational Leadership* 6 (May 1977).

BUREAU OF NATIONAL AFFAIRS. *Special Report: Teachers and Labor Relations, 1977–78.* Washington, D.C.: BNA Research and Special Projects Division, November 27, 1978.

CRESSWELL, ANTHONY M., and MICHAEL J. MURPHY. *Education and Collective Bargaining: Readings in Policy and Research.* Bloomington, Ind.: Phi Delta Kappa, 1976.

DUNLAP, JOHN F. "California's Chicken-or-Egg Question: Statewide Union or Statewide Bargaining First?" *Phi Delta Kappan* 59 (March 1978):459–61.

GORTON, RICHARD A. *School Administration, Challenge and Opportunity for Leadership.* Dubuque, Iowa: Wm. C. Brown Co., 1976.

HERNDON, TERRY. "The Case for Collective Bargaining Statutes." *Phi Delta Kappan* 60 (May 1979):651–52.

KNOESTER, WILLIAM P. "Administrative Unionization: What Kind of Solution?" *Phi Delta Kappan* 59 (February 1978):419–22.

LIEBERMAN, MYRON. "The Future of Collective Bargaining." *Phi Delta Kappan* 53 (December 1971).

NATIONAL EDUCATION ASSOCIATION, Research Division. "Hearing Teachers' Grievances." *NEA Research Bulletin* 45 (October 1967).

———, Research Division. "State Patterns in Negotiation." *NEA Research Bulletin* 46 (March 1968).

———, Research Division. "The Superintendent's Role in Negotiation." *NEA Research Bulletin* 45 (October 1967).

———, "Bakke: Amicus Curiae Brief." *Phi Delta Kappan* 59, No. 7 (March 1978):451–55.

STINNETT, T. M. "Teachers in Politics: The Larger Roles." *Today's Education* 57 (October 1968).

STINNETT, TIMOTHY M., et al. *Professional Negotiations in Public Education.* New York: The Macmillan Company, 1966.

SVENNING, LYNNE L. *Collective Decision-Making in Organizations.* San Mateo County, Ca.: Board of Education, 1970.

ZIEGLER, WARREN L. *An Approach to the Future: Perspectives in American Education.* Syracuse, N.Y.: University Research Corporation, 1970.

PART EIGHT

Public Relations
and a Look
at the Future

CHAPTER TWENTY

Public Relations

No other area of school administration betrays the dilemma of the average educator more vividly than the difficult but essential art of public relations. The scholarly mind is the antithesis of the public relations mind; it tends to be introverted, while public relations requires a gregariousness and extroversion more typical of the salesman or advertising man than of the educator. It is significant that efforts have been made for many years to supplant the term "public relations" with something less negative, such as the term "school–community relations."

First, there must be something good to publicize. Public relations begin by making the school program better, and better, and better. When maximum improvements have been made, the public will want to listen.

Remember, tell the public what it wants to hear—not what *you* want them to hear. It must have been Will Rogers who suggested that if you want to catch fish, use bait that the fish (not the fisherman) like. The people who pay the taxes want a good reading program. Build them one. Then tell them how good it is. Ask them to help you build the program. If they participate, they will be telling *you* how good the program is. This is the ultimate strategy in making friendly supporters for your school.

Take a look at business and industry. They improve their products and services. Then they spend millions telling you about it. They get you, the public, to make testimonials, and help them sell their products back to you. You can do the same with your instructional program. Involve the students, school employees, parents, and the general public. Make it good and make it known.

We live in an era of publicity and publicity is a one-way process. The public schools, which mirror and stem from the body politic, cannot retreat and plead professional immunity from the same desire to inform the public that is expressed by other occupations and businesses. Unless school administrators accurately inform the people of what the schools are doing, someone else will tell them, and probably inaccurately. Public relations, then, has become a necessity; whether or not the necessity becomes an unpleasant one depends almost entirely on how well the administrator organizes and administers the program of public information. Public relations is communication and communication is human relations. Its effectiveness is largely dependent upon the personal relationships that exist between the communicating parties. It should be a two-way process.

Interpretive Public Relations Programs

Many schools equate public relations with press agentry. They assume the desirability of defending the status quo or justifying any or all of the ramifying activities of the schools.

The so-called "preventive" school of public relations designs its public information program to meet possible future criticism in certain specific or general fields. It piles up ammunition for contingencies, and maintains a constant attack on the critics of the schools, hoping that a continuous offensive will help prevent attacks on the schools by diverting attention. This is not good public relations either, and often amounts to manipulation of public relations for personal reasons.

The administrator who interprets public relations for school districts as equivalent to public relations for private business is also wrong. Industrial public relations programs are set up to sell products. Any superintendent who organizes a public relations program primarily to "sell" the school system ignores its weak points, whitewashes acknowledged flaws, and overemphasizes desirable features. Business, highly competitive and operating within a framework of public tolerance for "pardonable" exaggerations, manages to escape potent criticism. Public education clearly cannot.

The sole purpose of school public relations should be to explain the school district's educational program, activities, and general operation. Everything that the district does is a matter of public interest and concern. Public relations should not attempt to justify, to palliate, or to cover up. It should not be used to aggrandize the status or reputation of the superintendent. The goal should and must be to tell the truth. If the pursuit of this goal requires the admission of errors or shortcomings in certain departments, such confession should be made, along with details of what is being done to correct the situation. The people of a community will be far more apt to respect and support a school system that candidly admits its own failings than one that pretends to uphold an impossible standard of perfection.

Basic Criteria for a School District Public Relations Program

A public relations program should not operate as a reflex response to a specific stimulus. A district that spontaneously invents some method of informing the public about a forthcoming bond election often establishes a system permanently oriented toward a financial interpretation of school affairs. Similarly, a superintendent may hurriedly create machinery designed to sway community opinion as a reaction to an actual or threatened attack upon the superintendent's tenure, with the resulting system becoming a lasting personal bulwark to an individual employee of the district. Any such origin for a public relations program is at once inadequate and one-sided. To avoid this, it is necessary to erect a school information program on certain well-grounded principles.

CRITERIA FOR AN EFFECTIVE PUBLIC RELATIONS PROGRAM. The school district should develop certain criteria for an effective public relations program. The following criteria developed by Bloom might be used as a guide:

Philosophy

The board of education should adopt a general statement of philosophy of education as a foundation for policies which would give direction to the public information program of the school district.

Policy

The public information program should be based upon written policies adopted by the board of education.

Dynamics

The public information aspects of successful school public relations must be founded upon an outstanding educational program.

Form

The public information program should be vigorous but dignified.

Scope

All operations of the school district should be included in a comprehensive public information program.

Completeness

The community should be afforded access to all the facets of school operations through the public information program.

Sensitivity

School public relations should be a two-way process. The public information program should establish channels of communication through which the school can be kept sensitive to the attitudes and desires of the community.

Agents

The public information program should be organized to make effective use of all officials and employed personnel of the school district.

Agencies

All possible agencies, written, oral and social, should be utilized in the public information program by selecting the best media for the specific purpose to be achieved.

Integrity

The information given to the community should accurately reflect the practices within the schools of the district.

Continuity

The public information program should provide a continous flow of interpretive information to the community.

Review

There should be an annual review of the public information program by the superintendent and board of education and revisions made according to the findings of the review.[1]

POLICY BASIS FOR A SCHOOL DISTRICT PUBLIC RELATIONS PROGRAM.   Few school districts have policies relating to a sound public relations program. Public information is a function of administration and particularly of the superintendent, even if it is delegated to another administrator. Administration is responsible to the board of education which establishes policy. A public relations policy should:

1. Be based on the district's educational philosophy.
2. Define objectives.
3. Develop an organizational chart with clear and understandable lines of communication.
4. Specify the methods to be used for internal communication (pupils, teachers, staff, central office) and for external communication (parents, public, organizations, local government, news media).

---

[1] Clarence H. Bloom, "Appraisal of Schools by Certain Community Groups: A Study of Public Information Programs" (unpublished doctoral dissertation, University of Southern California, 1965), pp. 212–15.

5. Designate who is to be responsible for public relations and provide a position description.
6. Establish the means for periodically evaluating the effectiveness of the public relations program.

Many superintendents have little experience in the field of public relations and may waste valuable time handling the program. If the school system has 4,000 or more students, it would be wise to employ a full-time public relations professional, and one on a part-time basis in smaller districts. Such a person can do a better job and allow other administrators to pursue their educational responsibilities.

PUBLIC RELATIONS AS A FACET OF THE EDUCATIONAL PROGRAM. Once it is realized that public relations fits comfortably into the overall function of education, the dissemination of information in an organized manner becomes a recognized function of public education. This realization is essential to the construction of a good information program because it leads inevitably to publicizing, on an equal basis, all phases of the school program. Curriculum and guidance as well as sports and social activities should be stressed in releases to the various media of public information. In addition, the activities and accomplishments of the board of education, teachers, administrators, and nonteaching personnel should be publicized. The varied activities of a school district should present a well-rounded picture, not a distorted caricature. All public relations should be student-centered and educationally oriented.[2]

An advantage of integrating public relations into the school program is its ability to assume an inconspicuous role in the existing scheme of things. It does not present a glaring target for unthinking criticism by either district employees or taxpayers. When public information is handled by working educators, as distinguished from professional press agents faintly disguised as administrative assistants, it becomes more sensitive and legitimate. It is only as an extension of education that school public relations can achieve its optimum possibilities.

PUBLIC RELATIONS AND THE COMMUNITY. It is a mistake to glorify the schools. They exist as servants of society and creatures of the state. Any public relations design must take this fundamental truth into direct cognizance. Public relations programs attempt to reconcile the apparently conflicting stereotypes of the school as the servant versus the school as the leader.

Schools cannot diverge too greatly from the community way of life. If they do, they find themselves increasingly out of touch with the society

---

[2] American Association of School Administrators, *Profiles*, p. 133.

they seek to serve. On the other hand, it is the duty of the schools to stress aspects of culture and learning, and to constantly press for the acceptance of higher standards of citizenship and morality. In so doing, a school acts as a leader instead of a servant. It is not only possible but essential that leadership be equated with service. Good public relations places these two functions in proper focus.

PUBLIC RELATIONS IS A TWO-WAY STREET.   Good public relations involves receiving information as well as giving it. Educators must understand what is going on around them. District employees directly concerned with public relations should develop appropriate devices to collect, tabulate, and measure community opinion and reactions on a continuing basis. Polls, surveys, and questionnaires are useful, as well as contacts with chambers of commerce, church groups, and fraternal organizations.

A citizens' committee interested in working with the schools to communicate lay opinions and criticisms to school personnel is very effective. Each school person affiliated with Rotary or Kiwanis also serves to detect and transmit community opinion about the schools. Most important and difficult to measure is the role of friendly individuals scattered among the homes and businesses of the school district. When on personal terms with representatives of the schools, these people can be invaluable carriers of community comment and thought. Face-to-face communication is one of the most effective means of communicating because public relations is really the practice of human relations. A good public relations program evaluates the importance of all these information sources and provides for fostering them. Too often, the system becomes a one-way transmitter—sending, not receiving, information.

USE OF ALL AVAILABLE CHANNELS FOR PUBLIC RELATIONS.   A school system may establish excellent contacts with the press, but fail to exploit the possibilities of radio and television. Another may work effectively with civic and fraternal groups, but lose sight of the importance of pupil and teacher contacts with the public. Specialized abilities of the public relations director often are the cause of this imbalance. Occasionally, one-sidedness stems from some combination of local circumstances, such as the presence of the newspaper editor or radio station owner on the board of education.

No school system can afford to rely exclusively upon a limited use of public relations media. The best way to achieve a balanced use of media is to adopt a carefully organized plan, using the several instruments of news dissemination, with ample materials and time allotted to each one.

PUBLIC RELATIONS AND PUBLIC UNDERSTANDING.   There is more to public relations than a constant pitch for community support. An uninformed support for school activities is the antithesis of good public relations. Public relations should furnish a constant stream of suggestions and constructive criticisms to the school. If a philosophy is adopted that strives solely or largely for indiscriminate applause, this stream of ideas is dammed up. If the school authorities hear only what they wish to hear, they lose all awareness of the reality of public opinion that may oppose the policies and practices which they had fondly believed to be universally accepted.

If mutual understanding rather than support is established as the goal, the problem tends to solve itself. The administration is then constantly engaged in an evaluative process, questioning practices that outside sources of information have criticized. One of two results occur: either a practice is abandoned or modified, or a release of accurate information convinces the citizenry of its desirability. In either case, the outcome redounds to the ultimate advantage of the schools.

CONTINUOUS PUBLIC RELATIONS. Public relations as a continuing process involves a positive approach to the community. Continuing public relations programs are preventive programs. In contrast to public relations programs that react only to specific crises, continuous programs avoid creating the impression of immediate urgency or an avoidance of criticism. By building a clear and easily understood picture of community education in the public's mind over a period of years, the long-range program will ensure an accurate representation of the school's activities.

Intermittent public relations, on the other hand, only operate to confront temporary crises, such as the need for a tax or bond referendum, or to meet criticism of the schools. Otherwise, they are not active on a continuing basis.

PUBLIC RELATIONS: INFORMAL, INTERESTING, AND VARIED. To be effective, public relations programs should be honest, inclusive, understandable, dignified, comprehensive, and sensitive to the public. Statistical data from school offices used are insufficient as public relations. The vast majority of people in any community are only mildly interested in the problems of the schools. They are not apt to wade through budget material. The reservoir of public goodwill runs dry rather quickly if it is frequently subjected to long and dreary proclamations from the superintendent's office.

Public relations programs must face reality. Because people are understandably unwilling to be bored by figures, they should be eliminated as much as possible. Verbosity in bulletins and messages home should be replaced with short, humorous notes designed to catch the eye and hold attention. In both written and spoken communications, short sentences, concrete terminology, and specific examples should be used. The central idea should be clearly explained and all other material should be related to the central theme. The last paragraph should summarize the contents briefly and clearly.

Statistics should be presented to the public with charts and diagrams. The information should be carefully packaged with an eye to the particular audience for whom it is intended. A technician or professional person reacts quite differently than a day laborer. A rural population's response differs from that of an urban citizenry. It follows that the school representative charged with a public relations responsibility must develop a profound knowledge of the makeup of the community which should be used in preparing news releases.

Agents of Good School Public Relations

School public relations is not exclusively the job of the professional expert. The most valuable and lasting contacts that the school has with the general public are oral, not written. Although the public relations professional can help a school district communicate with the public, pupils and school personnel are usually more effective.

PUPILS AND THE PUBLIC RELATIONS PROGRAM. A dissatisfied student body can negate all administrative efforts in public relations. On the other hand, pupils who are satisfied with their school and who admire and respect their teachers are worth dozens of highly paid press agents.

Natural public relations by sudents occurs if:

1. The pupils are taught with a well-balanced curriculum stressing content that the parents understand and appreciate.
2. The pupils are reminded shortly before the closing bell of the various accomplishments of the school day. The most satisfactory way to bring this about is to schedule a five-minute period at the end of each high school class period, or at the end of each elementary school day, for a brief but intensive review of the day's work.
3. The pupils are taught a unit on education. *About Our Schools,* a 1955 unit-text designed to teach high school pupils about public education, should be adapted and used by local administrators for students.[3]

SCHOOL PERSONNEL. The administrator has a considerable public relations impact upon the people of the district. The better trained the administrator is to present the facts to the public, the greater the impact; this principle also applies to principals, supervisors, and board members. Never-

---

[3] See Emery Stoops and M. L. Rafferty, Jr., *About Our Schools, A Unit on Public Education.*

theless, it is the rank and file of school employees who contact the public most regularly and frequently, and who consequently achieve the greatest effect upon public opinion. Whether or not a public relations administrator is employed, public relations is the responsibility of every employee.

Teachers who complain openly about their jobs and their superiors harm the morale of the entire school district. Custodians who joke publicly about the relative ease of their work and the slipshod manner in which they perform their duties raise doubts in the minds of the taxpayers that public relations programs have difficulty allaying. Most school people also have families who, in turn, have friends; these many contacts with the community are of tremendous importance to any plan of public information.

The school bus driver who brags about the fine new equipment and the good behavior of the students who ride the bus is a walking, talking advertisement for the school district. So is the school secretary who tells friends about the well-organized accounting procedures used in the school office, and the polite behavior of the pupils who bring absence notes to the secretary's desk.

School personnel are often uninformed about their school district. Bacon found that:

1. Fewer than 25 percent of the teachers had correct information about the school district.
2. At least 50 percent of the teachers were incorrectly informed about the government, service organizations, and fraternal groups of the area in which they taught.
3. Teachers were not well-informed about employment in the community.
4. Teachers who were residents of the district were better informed.
5. Many statements about school–community relationships given high priority by writers were rejected by teachers.[4]

Bacon recommends that:

1. Representatives of community organizations should have more opportunities to work with teacher groups on school projects.
2. Teachers should examine the many community avenues open to them to enrich both their instructional programs and their social interaction in the school community.
3. There should be better communication between teachers and administrators in defining mutual roles and in sharing information.

---

[4] Leonard Bacon, "Teacher–Community Interaction Viewpoints Regarding Teacher Public Relations" (unpublished doctoral dissertation, University of Southern California, 1965), pp. 279–80, 297.

4. A teacher's most effective role in public relations is that of creating a favorable image of the institution the teacher represents.
5. Educators should seek to build channels of school–community interaction.
6. Teachers' associations should re-emphasize to the profession and public that their chief aim is to further functions that contribute to the optimum educational opportunities for youth.[5]

One of the first duties of the person charged with the proper functioning of school public relations should be the thorough introduction of district philosophy to school personnel. They should be the target of an active campaign of information designed to acquaint them with what is going on in departments other than their own; what is being taught in the classrooms; and how the administration is working to overcome existing problems and difficulties.

In addition, school employees should be appealed to directly and frequently to remember that they are representatives of the school system, whether on duty or off. Staff complaints should initially be discussed with administrators. This tends to minimize publicized complaints by channeling problems properly. If such cooperation is secured, it reduces greatly the amount of grumbling and gossiping that otherwise would be brought to the ears of citizens and improperly magnified. A school system with happy, informed employees seldom worries about poor public relations.

LAY COMMITTEES.   A citizens' committee or lay advisory group composed of prominent and representative members of the local citizenry, most of whom presumably are in close touch with crosscurrents of community thought, is a helpful adjunct to public relations. Committees may be specialized, such as recreation commissions, school band supporters, athletic team booster clubs, and similar groups. Organizations of this type are admirable points of contact with representative segments of special community interests, and as such should be cultivated by the school administration. Decisions pending in their particular areas of interest should be discussed fully with them before being translated into action. Soliciting the advice of their members and weighing it carefully before taking action will usually enhance public relations for the district, and also promote an efficiency of operation.

Another increasingly common type of lay committee is one set up to advise the board of education on policy. A committee of this nature may be short-term (e.g., to consult on a bond issue or building program) or long-term (e.g., intended to meet at regular intervals over an extended period of time for consultation on a wide range of school problems). The

---

[5] Bacon, "Teacher–Community Interaction," pp. 287–301.

long-term committee customarily concerns itself with problems of long-range building needs, curriculum questions, and school–community relations and should represent the community widely. Many superintendents, however, believe that lay committees should not be permanent but should have an assigned task that, once completed, ends the life of the committee. Lay committees with no specifically assigned task possibly may interfere with normal district operation. Some citizens' groups become self-appointed and unwanted "boards of education," taking it upon themselves to issue decisions and statements about matters that are properly beyond their domain. Good leadership that stresses subordination to the legal authority of the school board and unwaveringly emphasizes the strictly advisory function of the lay committee avoids this pitfall and exploits the proper public relations value of such a group.

SCHOOL–COMMUNITY COUNCILS. Sometimes called citizen advisory committees or advisory boards, they are a type of lay committee organized at the school, rather than the district, level. They are the answer to many criticisms of school administration. Minority groups have felt that their desires about curriculum and school administration have not been represented at the district level. There has been criticism of overcentralization of authority in a few people too far removed from the local school community. Boards of education, especially in large cities, have been accused of not understanding the educational desires of the community. There has been an increasing emphasis on decentralizing authority and increasing the autonomy of the local schools. In order for the school to satisfy the educational desires of its attendance area, it must involve the parents in the decision-making process. The principal should consult the school–community council on all substantive matters.

Controversies have arisen about the method of selecting these councils. In some cases, they have been appointed by the principal, often creating a bias in their composition. Minority groups resent this method because they do not believe such a council is truly representative of the whole school community. Some states and school districts require the election of council members. However, the method of nominating or electing members is not always spelled out. Decisions are not always made about what to do with an on-going, appointed council once elections have been mandated. Some of these problems will be clarified and solved in the future. It is generally agreed that these councils should be democratically elected so that all people and segments of the community have a voice in selecting members. Council members, whether elected or appointed, should be willing to serve, represent varying points of view, reflect the ethnic composition of the school, be reasonable, have imagination, and be concerned about the welfare of the school. Teachers should also be members of the council.

Once it has been decided to create a school–community council, certain decisions must be made:

1. The purposes of the council must be defined.

2. The method of selecting the council members must be determined.
   a. If elected: How are prospective members nominated? How is the election conducted?
   b. If appointed: Who appoints? Who should be appointed?

3. The size of the council must be established.

4. Determination must be made regarding meetings:
   a. Time of meetings.
   b. Place of meetings.
   c. Frequency and dates of meetings.

5. Officers must be selected.
   a. There must be a presiding chairperson who should be appointed by the council rather than by the principal.
   b. A secretary should be appointed to keep the minutes.

6. The order of business should be agreed upon. A decision should be made as to what should be discussed in the council meeting.

7. There should be agreement as to what action should be taken after the council has made a decision or recommendation.

Whether a lay council is established at the school or the district level, it should be *advisory* only. If it does make decisions, they should not be binding on the school administrator; the administrator is the ultimate authority on what is best for the administration of the school. A community council should never expect or be permitted to dictate a school or district program. Statesmanship is necessary if administrators are to keep the council's role and their administrative leadership in proper perspective.

PARENT–TEACHER ASSOCIATIONS.   A school–home association should be intended primarily as a device to bring about better understanding between the parent and the instructor for the benefit of the child. As such, it is only indirectly an instrument for improving school public relations. However, such an organization may be of tremendous value in building a better understanding between groups and individuals. In the final analysis, this is the principal goal of public relations. Particularly important is the stress placed by parent–teacher associations on cooperative leadership by lay people and professional personnel. It is always highly advisable to associate as many lay persons as possible in any process that involves interpreting school policy to the citizenry. The cooperative aspect of parent–teacher organizations should be especially useful in this respect.

Parent–teacher groups have been accused in recent years of alleged domination by school administrators. In view of such criticism, it behooves educators to encourage lay leadership in these associations and to accept constructive suggestions from the nonprofessional membership. Administrators must develop a genuine partnership with responsible lay members of parent–school organizations if they wish such groups to be of maximum service in relaying information about school policy to the community and in reporting community attitudes and criticisms to the schools.

ADULT EDUCATION. The best way to gain support for a good school program is to expose a maximum number of people to its effects. Because most public relations programs are aimed at adults, an extensive system of adult education is one of the best investments a school district can make. This program may include night classes, lectures, forums, organized recreation, discussion groups, or a combination of all of these. Courses are now offered in hundreds of schools in subjects ranging from agriculture to typing; the variety of offerings seems certain to multiply during the next few years.

The administrator who is conscious of public relations will strengthen the adult curriculum and make every reasonable effort to increase the number of participants. Each person who can be persuaded to visit the school and become familiar with what is being done there is an almost certain future supporter. These people tend to identify themselves with the school, to take a personal interest in its problems, and to react strongly against capricious and unfounded criticism of the local school.

An adult program that has been designed to meet specific community needs and that has been worked out cooperatively by educators and civic leaders is of greater value from a public relations standpoint than one that is purely the product of school planning.

Types of Media in a Good Public Relations Program

In addition to the various individuals and groups that may be drawn into a good school public relations program as effective agents for news dissemination, certain institutions and organizations should also be relied upon for rapid spreading of news and general information. Most of them are commercial in nature, so they tend to be susceptible to a business-like approach, and to handle information with brevity and color.

NEWSPAPERS. Despite the billions spent on other froms of advertising, the daily newspaper is still the most effective means of communicating an idea to the public. The school public relations director should give a great deal of thought to the preparation of copy especially designed to meet the standards set by the press of the community. What the editor may see as important school news may not necessarily coincide with what the administrator feels is significant. In fact, there is almost certain to be a strong divergence of opinion here.

Newspapers usually indicate that they are interested in receiving announcements of activities at individual schools; materials about district administration; curriculum changes and offerings, including class schedules; special achievements of individuals or groups; special feature or human interest material; adult education services; and provision for scholarships and awards for students. Most school news reported in newspapers covers co-curricular activities, especially athletic events and personalities. Other topics that are focused upon by the news media are: school vandalism, test scores and student achievement, school taxes and finance, board of education meetings, administrative problems, and new educational programs, particularly if they are controversial. Administrators, on the other hand, usually consider desirable topics to be: the value of education, student progress and achievement, student health, school building programs, courses of instruction, and methods of instruction. A file of feature articles about school district activities can be developed and released during quiet news periods.

The school administrator and the newspaper editor have a long way to go before they can achieve basic agreement as to what constitutes important school news. The worst mistake the school representative can make, however, is to assume that the editor is deliberately downgrading the important items to glorify the less important. Actually, the editor probably does not care one way or another, but is headlining the categories of school news which the editor believes to be of primary interest to the casual reader. It is up to the school to demonstrate that the editor is wrong in this emphasis or, if the editor is proved right, to tackle the much harder task of re-educating the reading public.

Curricular and related news that is cleverly written, informal, and condensed increases newspaper coverage. Especially in smaller communities, busy editors are usually eager to print such material verbatim. Basic principles of good journalistic style should be followed.

Community people are interested in the daily affairs of a school, particuarly human interest items—if they are related in an interesting style. Some examples are:

A teacher who has had a class develop an unusual science experiment.

The custodian who works hard to keep the classrooms and building clean and sparkling.

A day in the life of a school secretary, especially the method used for dealing with an angry parent.

The many tasks of a principal, many of which are not known by the general public.

How the cafeteria manager prepares tasty food to help maintain the health of children.

How supplies are ordered and delivered so that they are always available when needed.

How the bus driver maintains sanity in transporting seventy students safely to and from school.

SCHOOL PUBLICATIONS AND BULLETINS.   The school newspaper is a potentially potent medium of news dissemination. However, most high school papers are put out simply as a function of the journalism classes, reporting campus news sporadically, but with little organized attempt to interpret the school to the public.

Other school publications such as handbooks for students, teachers, and other district employees are often widely distributed throughout the community, and may be read by persons other than school employees. Folders and brochures designed to attract prospective teachers to the district can become important media for public relations. Even the report card can fill a useful niche if it is constructed to express the purposes of the school. It is often the main written contact between school and parent, and as such should carefully explain the school's intent and the objectives of the reporting system. Leaflets, prepared by the superintendent's office, can be designed to interpret proposed or existing departures from previous practice, to explain school finances and the budget, personnel changes, testing programs, and reports of various kinds.

RADIO AND TELEVISION.   Most schools using the highly specialized media of radio and television to disseminate information place themselves at the mercy of studio programmers and script writers. The production of radio and television programs is complex and technical, and few school districts employ people with the necessary skill and experience to perform creditably in this medium. Although there are many apparent similarities between radio and the newspaper, the former has not attained the importance of the latter in the school public relations picture. Radio and television are more commercialized than newspapers, and desirable evening time is seldom available for school programs. These media are more interested in sensational reporting events such as teacher or student strikes, school board arguments, unsatisfactory test reports, minority dissatisfactions, and transportation problems. Many school activities do not lend themselves readily to audio-visual presentation. Radio and television audiences are accustomed to evaluating all programs in terms of their entertainment value; most school programs are informative rather than entertaining.

The increasing use of filmed programs in television and transcriptions in radio should result eventually in better use by the schools of these media. Tape recordings allow for program editing, making possible a more polished product. Unless a community boasts an extraordinarily public-spirited station owner, however, commercialism and scheduling will continue to minimize use of television and radio for school public relations. Where a cooperative station management exists, the schools should make every effort to present programs free from excessive lecturing, unimaginativeness, and sloppy workmanship.

PUBLIC SCHOOL WEEK. The public has been conditioned for many years to think seriously about its schools only once or twice a year, during such special events as Public School Week and American Education Week. While this may be undesirable to an educator who wants to make the public relations program a continuing operation, it should not preclude making use of the limited opportunities presented by these special occurrences.

A large percentage of the general public rarely enters the door of the school except to attend programs of this sort. The administrator should seize the opportunity to get as broad a message across as possible during the brief time involved in such events. "Open house" should be made a part of the evening's program. "Back-to-school" nights, with parents visiting classes and teachers, can also be used to good advantage. The printed announcements and schedules of events should contain meaningful material about the educational picture. Both the needs and accomplishments of the schools should be tastefully stressed, and an effort made to encourage those who attend to visit their schools more regularly and purposefully.

ADULT FORUMS. Adult forums are particularly valuable if the school district funds can accommodate visiting speakers monthly. Especially in rural or semi-isolated communities, the cultural opportunities offered by a series of such forums tends to inhibit their provincialism. Larger groups of lay people are attracted into the school by this method than by any other. Furthermore, members of forum audiences are apt to be among the more thoughtful and serious-minded citizenry of the community, i.e., the people that the typical public relations program attempts to inform. A public relations program has a far greater chance of success if the persons at whom it is aimed are already convinced that the schools are places dedicated to vital and cultural activities and the exchange of topical information.

TEACHERS AND PUBLIC RELATIONS TECHNIQUES. Teachers are the key agents of a school's public relations program. To most parents, the school centers around the child's teacher. Most teachers' understanding of good public relations procedures exceeds their actual practice. Although teachers generally consider newsletters, parent–teacher conferences, and room-parent organization as effective means of communication, most communication is through the parent–teacher association.

Inservice training conducted by a dynamic person from the business field can help teachers gain public relations confidence, give them technical know-how, help them become more effective, and enlarge their field of communication. Two-way school and community contacts that enhance the knowledge of both parties about each other can be made with all the various community political, social, business, industrial, youth, and fraternal agencies. Communication is unlimited when creative talents are called into play.

Organized Public Relations Programs

Even a one-room school should consider its public relations. In a school district employing only a few teachers, a definite proportion of their time and effort should be allocated and directed to informing the community about the school and its work. When several schools and a substantial number of personnel are involved, it often becomes both prudent and effective to assign the organization and conduct of the public relations program to certain district employees. Whether the emphasis should be placed on public relations at the local school level or at the district level depends upon the underlying philosophy of the district, which should be clarified by the school board's policy statements. District administration should implement the adopted policy by clear-cut administrative procedures.

LOCAL SCHOOL PROGRAM.   In a district that places stress on the autonomous operation of public relations at a local school level, the principal is the key individual and should work out with school personnel a program that seems best suited to the school and its needs. An appropriate percentage of the principal's time and of the faculty's time should be devoted to the production of regular and significant news releases to press, television, and radio outlets located in the area served by the school. The principal should arrange for teachers and staff members to make themselves available for talks before civic and fraternal organizations on topics within their spheres of competence and should work with PTA groups and citizens' committees, telling the school's story and listening acutely for the community's reactions.

In a situation placing emphasis on local orientation, the best organizational plan is a three- or five-member committee of certificated and noncertificated school employees interested in public relations. All school publicity should be planned by this body, and the principal should act as chairperson of it. The principal should require all written handouts to be channeled through the office so that school publicity is coordinated and duplications are avoided. One or two key lay citizens attached to this committee in an advisory capacity enhance its legitimacy. The local newspaper editor or radio station owner also can serve as an expert in their respective media.

The program that results from the deliberations of this group should be a continuing one, tailored to the idiosyncracies of the community supporting the school. Factors such as economic levels, cultural backgrounds, and political bias should be taken into consideration in planning the program. Every effort should be made to achieve simplicity and to avoid pomposity, educational terminology, and excessive verbiage. Ideally, the result should be a well-rounded process of news dissemination, well received by the citizenry and characterized by reciprocity.

CENTRALIZED DISTRICT PROGRAM.   The heart of a systemwide program is the superintendent's office. In districts of moderate size, superintendents themselves may handle most of the details involved in editing and releasing school news. Superintendents consider school–community relations to be one of their three most important functions. A study by Robert Filbin showed that seventy-six superintendents representing school districts in twenty-six states with school populations ranging from 1,055 to 95,263 spent an average of 15.1 percent of their time in some function of community relations (see Figure 20–1).[6]

Many school districts distribute monthly or weekly publications designed to acquaint the average lay citizen with what the schools are doing. These bulletins should be issued from a central administrative point and individual school bulletins with conflicting viewpoints should be avoided. District bulletins can be made more attractive and readable when they are illustrated with charts, diagrams, or pictures. To be effective, their distribution should be on a regularly scheduled basis. It is better to mail them than to depend upon student delivery. Mailing also makes it possible to include citizens and community organizations as well as parents.

Where districts are more sizable, superintendents may select one of their assistants or employ a part-time administrator to perform public relations functions. The centralized method, however, necessitates the employment of a full-time public relations director. This person should be a specialist in public relations with training in educational methods and administration, and the office should be solely concerned with public rela-

---

[6] See Robert Filbin, Ed.D., "Do Superintendents Spend Enough Time on PR?" *Phi Delta Kappan* 53, 3, November 1971, p. 193.

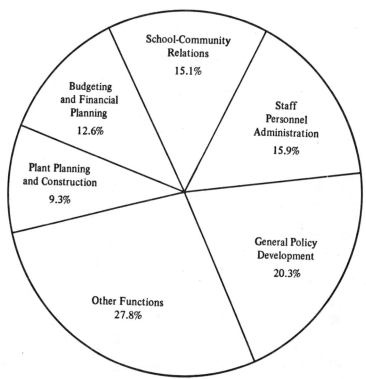

FIGURE 20–1. *Percentage of Time Spent by Superintendents on Various Functions.*
Source: *Robert Filbin,* Ed. D., *"Do Superintendents Spend Enough Time on PR?" Phi Delta Kappan 53 (November 1971), p. 193.*

tions. All public communications should be cleared through the public relations office, although this does not mean that it should monopolize functions of public relations. Public relations is peculiarly and inescapably a function of the board and the superintendent. The expert is employed to advise them, not to govern their affairs. Perhaps the best way to avoid the appearance of press agentry is to work through a coordinating council composed of representatives of youth groups, the PTA, civic and fraternal organizations, and various school facilities. In establishing such a council, a policy of limited goals is advisable at first.

The major duties and responsibilities of the public relations administrator should be:

1. Press, radio, and TV contacts.
2. Writing press releases.
3. Staff newsletter and publications.

4. Community newsletter and publications.
5. Election and bond referendum campaigns.
6. Superintendent's annual report.
7. Working with community, civic, and service groups.
8. Special projects (American Education Week, B.I.E., Day, etc.).
9. Publicity on federal projects.
10. Editorial services for central office staff.
11. Writing speeches, reports, or papers for central office staff and board of education.
12. Speakers' bureau.
13. Inservice public relations training for school staffs.
14. Assessment of public attitudes.
15. Development of teacher recruitment materials.
16. Photographic services.[7]

Because all problems in which the public is involved eventually reach the superintendent, the community relations administrator must work closely with the superintendent. The superintendent, in turn, must have complete confidence in the public relations administrator. The superintendent, as in all other educational activities, is the ultimate authority for the direction of any public relations program.

Coordination is the most difficult achievement for the centralized system; the larger the district, the greater the difficulty. Public relations minded principals should not be allowed to furnish the majority of the publicity or to dominate the entire program. The best way to avoid this is to assign percentage quotas to the several schools and to apply these quotas to the sum of all releases. Each school should have a contributor selected cooperatively by the public relations director and the building principal. This person's duty should be to serve largely as a liaison between school personnel and the central office, regularly submitting news in previously selected priority areas. Where a flow of news has been properly encouraged and organized, the job of the public relations director then becomes one of editing, writing, and supervising, rather than ferreting out news on the director's own initiative.

The centralized program is outlined as follows:

1. A director of public relations is hired by the district and given whatever assistance may be needed.
2. The director should work closely with a coordinating council composed of school and lay people.
3. The council should map out areas of needed publicity, and re-evaluate the program at regular intervals.

---

[7] NEA Research Division, "The School Public Relations Administrator," 46, *National Education Association Research Bulletin*, March 1968, p. 30.

4. The director should assign to each school in the district an appropriate role in gathering and promulgating school information.
5. The director should constantly strive to keep the balance of publicity even, insofar as the individual schools are concerned.
6. The director should be the final judge of the form, style, and choice of material to be released to the various news media.

Internal communication is as important as external communication. Procedures must be established for easy two-way communication among schools, departments, central office, individuals, administration, and the school board. Teacher–administrator communication is as important, if not more so, than administrator–teacher communication. The public relations administrator should be responsible for internal communication.

Evaluating the Public Relations Program

There are many ways to evaluate a school district's public relations program: listing public relations activities; checking upon results; polling the various publics; studying the qualifications of public relations personnel; calling upon outside consultants; and using checklists. A valuable checklist for superintendents has been developed by the American Association of School Administrators.[8] Superintendents should look upon evaluation as a continuous process and use varied techniques. They can ask themselves questions such as:

1. Am I aware of the needs of the community?
2. Are all the available news media such as newspapers, the radio, and television used?
3. Are we using all community resources?
4. Do we have a representative public relations committee that meets regularly to consider ways in which the school and the community can communicate with each other?
5. Are newsletters or bulletins sent regularly to parents and others in the community?
6. Are people reading or paying attention to our public relations efforts? Do they understand them?
7. If failures are found in our public relations program, what efforts are being made to remedy the problem?
8. How many of our employees participate actively in community organizations?
9. Do we have staff members who are able and available to speak before local civic and club groups?

---

[8] American Association of School Administrators, "ABC's of School Public Relations: A Check List."

10. Do we have clearly defined policies and procedures for our public relations program? Are they revised periodically?
11. Is our educational program good enough? Are we doing all that we can to let people know about the "good" things?[9]

Summary

School public relations programs, increasingly becoming an absolute necessity for successful administration, should be interpretive rather than offensive or defensive. School public relations differs from industrial public relations, which is designed only to sell products. School public relations exists only to explain the school district's program, activities, and operation.

A public relations program should be erected on these basic concepts: (1) development of district criteria; (2) its establishment on a policy basis; (3) recognition that the public relations program is one facet of the entire educational picture; (4) portrayal of the schools in their proper relation to the community; (5) acknowledgment that public relations is a two-way street; (6) use of all available media; (7) attempts to achieve public unlerstanding rather than support; (8) recognition that the program should be continuous, not spasmodic; and (9) constant attempts to render public relations releases informal, interesting, and varied.

Good school public relations should use many agents: pupils, school personnel, lay committees, parent–teacher associations, and adult education. Similarly, one test of a good public relations program is the number and variety of media it uses, including newspapers, school publications and bulletins, radio and television, Public Schools Week, adult classes and forums, and teacher appraisal.

All districts require organized public relations programs. In a district with considerable autonomy, the principal is the key individual, preferably acting as chairperson of a committee of district employees that generates the program. In a centralized district, the superintendent handles most of the public relations, in conjunction with a director of public relations. Coordination of duties and responsibilities is essential and can best be accomplished by using a coordinating council of school and lay people.

Administrative Problems

> In Basket

Problem 1

The people in the city of Sanger claim that they know little about their school system. Although school board meetings are open, few people attend. The local

---

[9] Emery Stoops and Russell E. Johnson, *Elementary School Administration*, p. 275.

newspaper publishes short summaries of Board of Education decisions and sporadic news items, although many people do not subscribe to the paper. Some schools send bulletins home from time to time. Businessmen, in particular, resent that the only time the district really communicates is during a tax or bond election.

Young, dynamic Dr. Conger has been employed as the school district's new superintendent. The Board selected him because of his outgoing personality and interest in good school–community relations as well as his successful administrative experience.

How can Dr. Conger proceed in improving communication between the school district and the community?
What channels can be used?

Problem 2

Assume the same situation as in Problem 1. The superintendent has decided that one of the first things he will do to help communication is to send a monthly district bulletin to every home.

Whom should Dr. Conger involve to write articles for the bulletin?
What topics should be covered?
What format should be developed for the bulletin?

Problem 3

Assume the same situation as in Problem 1. Dr. Conger, believing that each school can be a major factor in improving school–community relations in its attendance area, has asked all principals to develop a plan for improving communication with the public in their school communities. He has also explained that communication should not entirely be from school to community but should be also from community to school.

If you were one of the principals, what would you propose?
On what basis would you make your decision?
Whom would you involve? In what way?

Selected References

AMERICAN ASSOCIATION OF SCHOOL ADMINISTRATORS. "ABC's of School Public Relations: A Check List." Washington, D.C.: The Association, 1959.

———. *Profiles of the Administrative Team.* Washington, D.C.: The Association, 1971.

CAMPBELL, ROALD F., et al. *Organization and Control of American Schools.* 3rd ed. Columbus, Ohio: Charles E. Merrill Publishing Co., 1975.

DOSS, CALVIN L. *School and Community Relations: A Book of Readings.* Washington, D.C.: University Press of America, 1976.

DUBIA, DOROTHY E. "Developing Goals, Planning, and Implementing a Positive PR Program." *Thrust for Education Leadership* 3 (October 1973).

FILBIN, ROBERT. "Do Superintendents Spend Enough Time on PR?" *Phi Delta Kappan* 53 (November 1971).

FREY, GEORGE T. "Improving School-Community Relations." *Today's Education* 60 (January 1971).

GELMS, KENNETH J. "To Be or Not to Be Read." *Thrust for Education Leadership* 3 (October 1973).

JONES, MAXWELL, and GENE STANFORD. "Transforming Schools into Learning Communities." *Phi Delta Kappan* 60 (November 1973).

KINDRED, L. W., et al. *School and Community Relations.* 2nd ed. Englewood Cliffs, N.J.: Prentice-Hall, 1976.

KNEZEVICH, STEPHEN J. *Administration of Public Education.* Scranton, Pa.: Harper and Row Publishers, Inc., 1975.

MARKS, SIR JAMES R., EMERY STOOPS, and JOYCE KING-STOOPS. *Handbook of Educational Supervision,* 2d ed. Boston: Allyn and Bacon, Inc., 1978.

NANCE, EVERETTE. *Community Council: Its Organization and Function.* Midland, Mich.: Pendell Publishing Co., 1975.

NATIONAL EDUCATION ASSOCIATION, Research Division. "The School Public Relations Administrator." *Research Bulletin* 46 (March 1968).

NORTON, MICHAEL M. "PR Program Runs Farther, Faster with Volunteer 'People Power'." *Thrust for Education Leadership* 3 (October 1973).

"Public Relations and the Press." *Independent School Bulletin* 34, No. 2, 1974.

SAXE, RICHARD. *School Community Interaction.* Berkeley, Ca.: McCutchan Publishing Corporation, 1975.

STOOPS, EMERY, and RUSSELL E. JOHNSON. *Elementary School Administration.* New York: McGraw-Hill Book Co., 1967.

STOOPS, EMERY, and M. L. RAFFERTY, JR. *About Our Schools, A Unit on Public Education.* Los Angeles: California Education Press, 1955.

WILLIAMS, CATHARINE. *Community as Textbook.* Bloomington, Ind.: Phi Delta Kappa, Fastback Series 64, 1975.

CHAPTER TWENTY-ONE

Some Significant Trends in School Administration

Admiral "Bull" Halsey rode backward on his flagship knowing full well that he could tell where he was going by knowing where he had been. School administrators are being backed into an uncertain future that can best be predicted with a thorough understanding of historical and current trends in education. By understanding how this situation has come about, they are less apt to repeat the mistakes of the past.

The authors lay no claim to being soothsayers, clairvoyants, or inspired prophets. They do, however, see cloud formations on the educational horizon that portend trouble, as well as life-giving showers that make for a world of growth and renewal.

It is true that school administrators face trends that are both frightening and satisfying. The trends now shaping, or soon to take shape, will fashion school systems and schools that superintendents and principals will administer tomorrow.

A few of the major trends that affect public school (and to a degree private school) administration will be described. Many more trends could be named. Local administrators should prepare their own lists.

Toward Greater Financial Support of Public Education from State and Federal Sources

When Stoops and Rafferty wrote *Practices and Trends in School Administration* in 1961, they observed that state support of public education was near the 39.5 percent level and recommended that state support be increased to at least 50 percent. For the first time in the history of American public education, state support did rise, in 1978–79, above the local level. This new development was reported by the National Education Association as: state support, 47.4 percent; local, 43.8 percent; and federal, 8.8 percent.[1]

Federal support has been escalating since the landmark passage of Public Law 89–10, the Elementary and Secondary Education Act of 1965. Public education is indeed a federal concern. Federal financing will continue to increase, but not entirely in the way that educators would like. Most school executives as represented by the American Association of School Administrators prefer *general* rather than *categorical* aid.

The system of categorical aid violates the fundamental principle of local control. It places decision making in Washington rather than at the closest point to operation. It is wasteful. Washington never sends back as much money as it receives. Furthermore, large percentages of monies get skimmed off in commissions and consultancies before they reach the classroom-learning line.

School administrators for years have advocated "federal support with local control." These hopeful administrators overlooked one political verity—prerogative is chained to financial power. Dollars flow from Washington and so do the decisions. Categorical versus general aid will continue as an issue.

The trend toward both federal and state financing of public education must continue, because local property owners have been over-taxed. They rebelled. The voters have defeated tax overrides and bond issues in wholesale fashion. The trend will not reverse itself and will place heavier burdens upon local property owners.

This trend toward central financing of public education has become the cause of the following trend.

Toward Decreasing Local Control and Increasing Centralization

Local control of education has always been the pride and joy of the American people. Boards of trustees and administrators have enjoyed the privilege of decision making as in no other country. Little by little, this privilege has been washed away. What began as an eroding rivulet is now a raging torrent sweeping local control of education along with other institutional prerogatives toward state and national capitals.

There was a time when local boards of education performed legislative, administrative, and semijudicial functions. But now boards of edu-

---

[1] "A First: States Spend Most for School Support," *Phi Delta Kappan* 60, April 1979, p. 555.

cation serve more as enforcement agencies for countless state statutes and federal regulations. State and federal judges have imposed themselves upon school systems, not only as arbiters, but as policy determiners. In Boston and Los Angeles, for example, policy formation had to await judicial opinion.

As school systems in America have grown larger, the governing boards have relied more and more upon well-trained school administrators. Bit by bit, local control has been swept away, leaving a highly paid administrator to perform the secretarial function of studying regulations, directives, and codes. School boards govern "by the book" instead of relying upon their professionally trained administrator to recommend creative programs to enrich the lives of youth and adults. Some states go so far as to bind their local boards and administrators by permissive legislation, meaning that it cannot be done unless it is already in law. Every time the legislature meets, more laws are passed and more clamps are placed on local control.

The process of rawhiding local boards and administrators with new legislation has assumed frightening proportions, except in one area— greater financial support in time for inclusion in yearly budgets. Politicians are smart. They know that legislation for schools is a good way to gain publicity, and to get votes. As to type of legislation, a large percentage of new statutes during the last decade have veered toward collective bargaining and students' rights. These laws intensify the administrative load.

Just as great icebergs fall into the Antarctic stream, blocks of local initiatives keep falling into the swelling torrent that flows toward state and federal reservoirs. This tide upon which we are now afloat will not turn back. Judges and politicians have tasted the sweet sauce of educational control. They will remain at the banquet.

Toward "Fundamental Schools"

Parental pressure exerted on elected school boards produced one of the most significant educational trends in the 1970s: the phenomenal growth of the so-called "fundamental schools." Starting in Pasadena, California with the John Marshall School, the movement spread from coast to coast, until by the end of the decade more than a hundred such schools existed in such districts as Cincinnati, Miami, Philadelphia and St. Louis. Most of these are elementary schools, but a number of junior and senior high schools also have been converted to "fundamental schools."

As the name implies, these institutions stress the basics and tighten up on discipline. Attendance is purely voluntary, but almost always the demand has far exceeded the available space. Where enrollment has been on a "first come, first served" basis, long lines of parents have stood for many hours to ensure acceptance of their children.

Results are necessarily fragmentary to date, but surprising gains in reading, English, and mathematics have been reported from many of these schools, sometimes as much as a two-years' gain in nine months according to nationally printed and normed achievement tests.

Toward Falling Achievement Levels

In the early 1970s, the College Board Exams were the first to call attention to the nationwide decline in pupil test scores in such areas as reading, English grammar, and mathematics. Since then, the scores on such national tests as the Scholastic Aptitude Test and the American College Testing Program have been analyzed and show a steady dropoff ever since the late 1960s. In 1979, the decline slowed somewhat, but insufficient data were available to show whether this was the beginning of a reversal or merely a temporary slackening of the slide.

Many reasons are adduced for this occurrence, but the most significant factor seems to be the lessening importance attached by the nation's teacher-training institutions to basic literacy. At this writing, there are some indications that this trend may be reversed in the eighties.

Toward Replacement of Mere Student Disruption with Felonious Violence and Vandalism

Prior to World War II, teachers were concerned when students whispered without permission, blew bubble gum, threw erasers across the room and marked on desks or walls. This was "no-no" behavior calling for discipline. That was child's play compared to the hard-core behavior seen on today's campuses.

Violence, crimes against persons, and *vandalism*, crimes against property, have displaced the annoyances of whispering and gum-chewing. Teachers and administrators are baffled—and endangered!

Just to indicate briefly the trend toward student criminality, the authors have referred to items from recent literature. *Phi Delta Kappan* has reported offenses, committed on 8,000 campuses and reported to police, as: rape, robbery, assault, personal theft, burglary, disorderly conduct, drug abuse, arson, bombings, alcohol abuse, and carrying weapons. In these criminal categories, 280,703 offenses were reported to police during a five-month period.[2] Richard W. Green, chief of security in Los Angeles,

---

[2] Shirley Boes Neill, "Violence and Vandalism: Dimensions and Correctiveness," *Phi Delta Kappan* 59, January 1978, pp. 302–7.

has estimated an average of one student or gang member killing per week in that district.[3] *The U.S. News and World Report* has stated that, "Every month, more than 5,000 teachers are attacked in schools." The article indicated that one school in four was vandalized each month.[4] *The National Inquirer* surveyed 1,000 teachers and got 472 responses. Of those it was found that 22 percent had been assaulted by students with 5 percent of the assaults being severe enough to require medical attention.[5] The *TWA Ambassador* reported that American school children (1977–78) committed 100 murders, 204,000 aggravated assaults, 270,000 school burglaries, and 9,000 rapes.[6] These sordid statistics support a trend that dedicated educators felt would never happen.

The cost of vandalism in America has reached shocking proportions. Instead of disfigurement by writing on walls, students and community thugs destroy and burn down school property. Arson is the costliest crime, ranging from minor damage to a cost that runs into the millions. The American taxpayers' cost for vandalism is uncertain, but most authorities estimate somewhere between $500,000,000 and $1,000,000,000. Into this figure may go the cost of security systems, police dogs, night watchmen, expensive lighting, and the like. The best conservative and justifiable statistic for school property destruction is $600,000,000 annually. This figure is more than all American schools spend for textbooks!

This trend of student misbehavior signals more and more felonious acts by younger and younger youths. Increasingly larger numbers of students have been booked for such hard-core crimes as armed assault, arson, and burglary.

The only hopeful sign in this mounting trend of juvenile crime is that the upward curve seems to be leveling out. Even though some signs point to a less rapid increase in juvenile crime, students, teachers, administrators, parents, and all lay persons should make maximum effort to further slow this vicious trend, and hopefully someday reverse its direction.

Toward Due Process for Children

During the 1970s, a series of court decisions set guidelines for "children's rights," many of which affected the public schools. Some of these decisions struck down total segregation of mentally retarded or "special" pupils, mandating a reasonable amount of mainstreaming in regular classrooms

---

[3] Neill, "Violence and Vandalism," pp. 302–7.

[4] *U.S. News and World Report*, April 3, 1978.

[5] *The National Inquirer*, September 26, 1978.

[6] Connie Cronley, "Blackboard Jungle Updated," *TWA Ambassador* 11, September 1978, pp. 25–28.

with normal students. Other rulings have ordered administrators to give at least minimum "due process" hearings to pupils before suspending or expelling them.

On the other hand, attempts by illiterate or quasi-illiterate high school graduates to sue school districts and officials for failing to educate them properly have been uniformly thrown out of court. Attempts to deny teachers and administrators the right to administer corporal punishment to pupils for various forms of misconduct in school have likewise been rebuffed by most of the nation's judges who have tried such cases.

The upshot of all this has been a somewhat more formalized and legalized school approach to children's rights, but no insurmountable roadblocks in the way of effective school and classroom administration.

Toward More Integration Problems

The problem of integration for racial balance in the schools will continue to be in a state of flux. There have been many suits and court decisions; many appeals have been made; and many are waiting decisions. It takes time for appeals to work their way up to the Supreme Court, and it may take months to years before final decisions are made. At the lower level, decisions in several states sometimes are in conflict and laws are interpreted differently. Judges make decisions and tell the school districts what they can or cannot do regarding busing and student exchange for integration purposes. School administrators must make decisions that are based on what the courts tell them to do.

Busing has created many problems when it is required for integration purposes. School districts have been forced to buy extra buses, employ more drivers, reschedule classes, and change time schedules. Nationwide, the cost runs into millions of dollars which could have been better spent on educational programs.

Buses going to predominantly black School A with white students from School B pass buses going from white School B with white students going to black School A. Many people think this situation is ridiculous. Because of forced busing in some school districts to meet court-ordered integration, "white flight" has taken place and will increase unless the situation is reversed. Citizen groups are up in arms and have formed anti-busing committees in some areas.

There will be no end to problems such as students riding buses up to an hour each way; disruption of athletic teams; changes in class schedules; integration of bused students into student bodies; and conflicts in scheduling youth activities such as Cub, Boy, and Girl Scouts, and the YMCA in after-school hours. Numerous schools have reported increased violence and vandalism because students from other schools do not have the same feeling for their temporary school as do the regular students from the school neighborhood. The future looks bleak until courts and legislation, nationally, come to some sort of agreement on what best can be done.

Toward Increased Emphasis on Collective Bargaining

There is no backing-up from an era of increasing emphasis on collective bargaining, since the old idea of "meet and confer" is gone. Teacher power is here and will not diminish. It is predicted that there will be federal legislation requiring collective bargaining for all public employees, including teachers. In the meantime, states without collective bargaining statutes will pass such laws in one degree or another. Administrative groups, including middle-management personnel, will also have permissive legislation to bargain.

Practically all matters relating to personnel—salaries, fringe benefits, working conditions, hours of work, inservice meetings and programs, extra duties and assignments, meetings, and even the curriculum and instructional program—will be decided by the collective action of teachers. Teacher organizations will become increasingly more powerful in controlling district policies, especially those policies that pertain to their individual members. Those teachers who do not choose to join will be caught up in the power struggle and will either have to join, lose their minority vote and rights, or follow the dictates of the majority.

Toward a Reassessment of the Role of School Administrators

School administration is growing more complex, and administrators must learn how to plan for and manage change. They can no longer rely on traditional knowledge and experience. A new era awaits administrators as line-staff or heirarchical decision making is replaced by participative decision making.

Administrators need to develop new management competencies in areas such as:

1. Instructional leadership.
2. Managerial skills.
3. Leadership skills.
4. Political awareness.
5. Ability to resolve conflicts.
6. Staff development.

7. Interpersonal relationships.
8. Ability to manage stress.
9. Identification and solution of problems.
10. Needs assessment.
11. Problem solving.
12. Establishment of priorities.
13. Community involvement; working with citizen committees and advisory groups.
14. Participation in management decisions.

Superintendents will not be able to function individually or with a select small group of district administrators, as in the past, but must develop a strong management *team* utilizing the knowledge and experience of middle-management personnel. The team should consist of associate and assistant superintendents, principals, supervisors, directors, and coordinators, as well as the directors of noncertificated personnel. Bringing middle-management personnel into district administration may stall their organizing separate bargaining groups within the district.

The prestige and authority of the superintendency is being eroded, causing an increase in the turnover of superintendents as pressures increase. Regional centers will proably become numerous and take over some of the responsibilities formerly handled by district administration. Collective bargaining by teachers is also taking over some of the administrative aspects of the superintendency.

Superintendents need continuing inservice training to keep up with change, to learn how to handle it, and to develop the skills needed to develop a strong management team. The transformation in the role of administrators is ongoing and is not yet complete.

Administrative Problems | In Basket |

Problem 1

You are the newly selected superintendent of a school district with 11,000 students, K–12, in a middle-class community. The governing board has furnished you with all available reports and historical documents.

The board has asked you to study practices in curriculum, business management, financing, political procedures, personnel management, transportation, food service, school–parent relations, physical facilities, protection of persons and property, operation and maintenance, lay-public relationships, student rights, extracurricular activities, secretarial services, and the like. As a result of this study, the board wants you to prepare a list of trends in the several areas so that the board's deliberations will fit developing needs.

Prepare your list of trends with some justification for each one.

Problem 2

You are a principal in the school system described in Problem 1. The superintendent has called upon you to prepare a list of trends that apply to your own school. Special consideration is to be given to such areas as: student discipline, falling achievement scores, special education, cost of athletics and other extracurricular activities, reporting to parents, teaching of moral values, supervision of militant and "senior" teachers, evaluation of teachers and classified workers, racial integration, and the like.

Prepare a list of trends that will help the superintendent understand where your school is headed.

Index

e Due